COMPARATIVE PERSPECTIVES ON
Race Relations

MELVIN M. TUMIN

COMPARATIVE PERSPECTIVES ON

RACE RELATIONS

COMPARATIVE PERSPECTIVES ON

RACE RELATIONS

Edited and with Introduction by

MELVIN M. TUMIN

Princeton University

LITTLE, BROWN AND COMPANY   Boston

FIRST PRINTING

Published simultaneously in Canada
by Little, Brown & Company (Canada) Limited

PRINTED IN THE UNITED STATES OF AMERICA

PREFACE

Among the most problematic of all group relationships are those which take place between people who see each other as inherently and importantly different. The "inherent" feature of the differences is believed to arise from genetic sources and refers to both physical and cultural traits, that is, to appearance and to behavior. Indeed, the most common belief is that the same genes that give people their distinctive appearance also cause them to have the customs that set them apart.

For such relations, the term "race relations" is fitting insofar as "race" refers to a set of distinctive gene-based traits. Since there is no scientifically respectable evidence to support the notion that group customs are in any way genetically based, there is ground for serious apprehension about employing a term that would lend credibility to such a notion. But it is incontestable that many of the most problematic features of group relationships do in fact arise from the *belief* that customs are inherited in much the same way that anatomical and physical features are inherited. It is in recognition of the centrality of this belief to the nature of the relationships that I have reluctantly decided to include the term "race relations" in the title of this book. I trust that it will be remembered throughout that I am referring to relations in which a common belief that the groups are separated by racial distinctions is a crucial ingredient.

In selecting the materials for inclusion in this volume, I have been guided mainly by the desire to present a range of cases from major geographical areas throughout the world that would at the same time reveal the very diverse forms and functions of "race relations." Undoubtedly, quite different selections might have been made that would have served the same purposes. But restrictions of space have made it impossible to present even the cases included in anything approximating

v

their full complexity, and omission of many other variations on the theme of race relations was unavoidable. It is my hope that the student may be sufficiently stimulated to extend his reading to other studies.

I have expectedly been perplexed by the problem of the order in which the selections in this book should be presented. For example, if one chooses as a criterion of organization the rigidity of the structure of opportunity, an order emerges that is substantially different from that which would result if another feature, such as degree of visible physical differences between the groups involved, were to guide the arrangement. Since no principle of organization seemed more fitting than any other, I have chosen to compromise the issue by following an alphabetical order, so that a selection on Africa comes first and one on the West Indies comes last.

The primary debt that any editor of a collection of readings owes is to the authors whose contributions he includes. The substantive worth of the book derives from the quality of the works presented. I have tried to highlight the collective contributions of these selections to our understanding of race relations with an introduction which raises some major theoretical and empirical issues to which the various readings are relevant.

In all of this work I have been helped greatly by James McGregor, Marguerite Pellerin, and Margaret Waldron, to whom I here extend my deep appreciation.

Melvin M. Tumin
Princeton University

TABLE OF CONTENTS

vii

Introduction

MELVIN M. TUMIN

Throughout the world today, intense conflicts are taking place between organized groups of men. In some instances, groups are divided by different political ideologies and national loyalties as in the war in Vietnam; in others, religious differences are at stake as in the Moslem-Hindu case; language barriers apparently are the key issue in instances such as the Flemish-Walloon dispute; intranational political ideologies are in conflict, as in the United States, Mexico, and China, to mention only some; and in an increasingly large number of cases, "racial" differences, with all their implications and complications, separate the opposing parties, as, for instance, in the United States, South Africa, and Rhodesia.

It is usually the case that the greater the number of differences among conflicting parties, the more intense, prolonged, and bitter is the conflict likely to be. It follows that where the parties have much in common, the greater is the chance that, by appeal to common interests, the conflict will be relatively short-lived and less costly. Sometimes, however, intense encounters occur among people who are very similar to each other but who raise the one or only few differences between them to a level of furious irreconcilability. Feuds between members of the same families are the typical examples here, as are the prolonged wars between rival sultans or rulers in Middle-Eastern kingdoms. Taking into account these exceptional instances, it still remains generally true that the greater the spread of differences among conflicting parties, the greater is the time that conflict is likely to endure and the more intense will it be throughout.

In view of the ubiquity of social conflict over almost any and every possible source of difference, one is likely to draw the conclusion that these differences are natural and inevitable sources of conflict. In one sense, of course, this is true. When people fight, they fight because they differ: in their ideas about right and wrong, about the true God, about the rights of nations, or about which language ought to be taught in the schools. Where there are no such differences, conflict is not likely to ensue.

But it is one thing to say that people fight over differences and it is another to say that they *must* always fight over differences. For every example of conflict among differing groups, there are ten instances where the same differences among other groups of men *do not* result in conflict. Thus, most nations are not at war with each other; most different linguistic stocks are not in conflict over which language ought to be used where; most differing religious groups live in relative peace with each other, even in the same country; most countries are made up of people of very different political preferences and ideologies, who argue and struggle with each other for dominance, but who do not normally bring their differences into an arena of fierce conflict or warfare; and, of course, throughout the world, people of different physical appearances live and work side by side, often to some degree of mutual dissatisfaction, but nevertheless relatively peacefully. Hawaii, Brazil, England, Puerto Rico, and Israel are but some examples of multi-racial regions in which relative peace, marred only occasionally by outbreaks of conflict, prevails.

Note, too, that people of the same nationality often fight about other things, just as people of the same language often are in conflict over other than language matters; and people of the same racial origins can and do engage in the most intense and destructive conflicts. The last two European wars among people identified primarily as white Europeans and the present day bitterly destructive conflict between the Nigerian Federal forces and those of the people of Biafra are examples of intense conflict among people of the same race.

In light of these variations in the possible ways in which people with differing characteristics can relate to each other, it is important to recognize that the presence of differences per se is not sufficient ground on which to predict that conflict will ensue or to explain conflict when and if it does occur. We must always ask what other circumstances are present that might help explain why, in the given instance, the difference has become a focus of conflict, while in similar instances relative peace and harmony, or at least something far short of open conflict, exists.

That question — What are the conditions under which people who differ in some significant identity, nation, language, religion, or race, live at peace or compete or conflict with each other? — is the central question around which this reader is organized. Our special focus in on the matter of so-called "race" differences. The book is devoted to revealing the wide range of possible relationships among differing racial groups that prevail in the societies of the world today.

That there is such a wide range can be easily seen, even by casual glance at the materials contained herein. Contrast, for instance, just the barest outlines of the relationships among differing groups in Hawaii, Brazil, and Puerto Rico with those among racial groups in South Africa, the United States, and India. Why should there be such enduring social accommodations to each other in some instances of these group contacts while in others the different groups appear ready to destroy each other as soon as possible? What in the histories of how these people came to live side by side might help account for the differences? What ideas do they hold about each other that might be important? What is in the general political framework or economic structure within which they coexist that might cause conflict? Do they have different visions of the good life? Are there common ideologies to which they both give allegiance, while continuing to oppose each other over lesser matters? The selections chosen for inclusion in this book are meant to provide some answers, albeit incomplete, to these most important questions.

Before further introducing the selections, it is important to spend some time considering our basic term, namely, "race relations." On the surface, it would appear we are talking of relations among persons of different racial characteristics or origins. To put it that way immediately implies something substantial and fundamental about race as a human characteristic. Since this implication coincides with the very widespread belief that mankind is made up of different races, the members of which differ from each other in certain fundamental traits of appearance, character, personality, temperament, and capacity, it is important to examine what evidence there is if any to support this notion.

It stands to reason that if, in fact, people of the various racial groups do differ from each other substantially in such matters as character, temperament, and capacity, and not just in appearance, then it is likely to be much more difficult to work out a pattern of mutually satisfactory and acceptable life conditions for the various racial groups who coexist within the same territory or political jurisdiction and who must interact for their daily livelihoods. If it is true, as many claim, that some groups are by nature inherently inferior or superior to others (in such areas as their capacity to conform to existing laws or their abilities to learn and become skilled at various occupations), then however goodwilled and peaceful the intentions of all the parties concerned may be, however democratic-minded they are and committed to the idea of equality for all, the pattern of satisfactory coexistence is likely to be very different than that which could be worked out if the so-called different races really were not fundamentally dissimilar in their abilities and capacities. In the same vein, if there are basic differences among racial groups in culturally-relevant capacities and *no* democratic ideology of equality, the dominant group is likely to feel far more justified in maintaining a basically unequal kind of society than if it could not appeal to the differences as a rationale for inequality. The United States is an example of a society in which, according to the best public opinion polls we have (see the article by Herbert Hyman and Paul Sheatsley in this reader), the majority of the people say that Negroes and Whites are not different in their natural intelligence, and in which also there is a dominant ideology, though not a matching practice, of the equal rights of all, regardless of race, to a fair share of the good things in life. Its present interracial struggle thus shows very different dimensions and qualities than do the relationships between Blacks and Whites in South Africa or between the castes in India. In both of the latter instances, there is a fundamental belief, widely held by most members of the dominant populations and perhaps even shared by the dominated populations, that the politically weaker people are also inferior, polluted, or characterized by basic faults that they inherit along with their physical appearance.

The question of natural differences in socially relevant characteristics, then, is important, even for people who are committed to equality of opportunity for all people. One would not, for instance, try to insure that there will be proportionally equal numbers of doctors and professors and lawyers from both Black and White in America if it were unquestionably true that the Blacks were basically inferior in their mental capacities, or, as an alternative, that the Whites were basically inferior to the Blacks. To insist on equal quotas of professionals in the face of unequal natural handicaps in one or the other group would simply be to push equality to an unmanageable point. And if, out of political conviction, such an effort were made, it could be achieved only by having very different standards and criteria of professional acceptability for the two groups. Neither would be well served by such a situation.

So — are there race differences that matter? To answer this, we have first to ask what we mean by a race. And here we have to introduce a basic distinction between the idea of race that is held by some laymen and that sponsored and supported by most members of the scientific community.

The scientific community views a race as a group of humans who possess a distinctive gene frequency, that is, who are distinguished from other humans by the possession of one or more traits that are biologically inherited and that endure as they are passed from generation to generation in the reproduction process. Since there is no agreement as to how many such distinctive traits any group must possess to qualify for the term race, the assumption must be that one or more of such traits suffice. By the terms of this definition, there are literally thousands of races of human beings because every possible biologically-inherited characteristic can be used to define a racial community.

When, therefore, we hear mention of the three major races of mankind, we are immediately asked to think in terms that are far different from those implied by the scientific definition of race. For these three major groupings are artificial: they do not correspond, even roughly, to any natural lines of distinction among humans. The fact that the three major races tend to be distinguished first by color of skin does not improve the matter, for skin color is a continuous characteristic, that is, it runs throughout the species from the near absence of color on one extreme to very dark hued, or "black," on the other, and the division of this continuum into three segments, black, yellow, and white, or some variation on those colors, is purely arbitrary. One could, with equal justification, divide the human species into six, eight, fourteen, four hundred different skin color groups. Three just happens to be convenient. Similarly, if one tried to divide mankind on any other single or combination of hereditary traits, such as head shape, eye color, the thickness of shin bone, or whatever, the same problems of arbitrary selection of the traits in question and arbitrary division of all of mankind into number of segments would still be present.

Further complications ensue when we ask by what principle we ought to choose traits and numbers of divisions. The classifications we make ought to serve some purpose: the groups classified by our criteria ought to constitute meaningful groups that make some sense out of either human appearance or human behavior or both that we could not make without such a classification.

By this criterion of the utility of the classification, the term race, as scientifically defined, has little utility other than for those who are interested in studying the inheritance patterns of various physical traits. None of these physical traits, by any available evidence today, has anything to do with the social and cultural capacities or personalities of the people in question. The scientific literature is almost unanimous about this point: none of the genetic traits by which groups of mankind are distinguished from each other in terms of their appearance or their organic makeup have anything discernible to do, in any direct or significant way, with the capacities of these groups to conduct the business of life. The races of mankind, in short, do not have distinctive sets of abilities, temperaments, or capacities, or disabilities, inferiorities, or inadequacies. A group of newborn children chosen at random from any racial group in the world would have about the same range of capacities as another group of newborns chosen at random from any other racial group in the world.

We stress this scientific version of race and the scientific findings about racial differences because much popular treatment of the term and the range of attitudes throughout the world toward racial characteristics are substantially different from it. In the first place, popular usage applies the term race to all kinds of groups other than those that are genetically homogeneous: nations, linguistic stocks, religions, cultural groups, and the like. The terms Aryan, Jew, and Italian — the first a language stock, the second a culture or religion, and the third a nationality — are all used as prefatory adjectives to the word race. But these are strictly misnomers from the scientific point of view, and that must be kept in mind when examining the relations of these groups with others so that it shall not be thought that any part of their relationship derives from racial traits in the scientific sense. Contrary to much popular belief, Aryan-speaking people, Jews, and Italians include numerous and diverse physical types.

The second reason why it is important to keep the scientific findings in mind is that popular usage very often assumes that racial groups are not only physically homogeneous, but also naturally alike in certain behavior propensities or capacities. Everywhere in situations of race relations we find firm ideas about what the "others" are like by nature, and these firm ideas are often among the most important causes of disturbed and conflicting relations among the different groups.

From the point of view of the student of social relations, the application of the term race to different cultural, religious, and national groups is useless, even when these groups are also marked by different physical appearances. In the United States, many of the people called Negro or Black are different in certain physical traits from people called White (though many resemble each other closely, too); but their cultural habits and social relations are due not to the physical differences between them, but to what the culture of American society has made of these differences. The different skin color, where it exists, doesn't command or direct any particular set of relations. Rather, the determinants are the sets of beliefs about skin color held by White Americans, historically and contemporaneously; the Negroes' origins in America as slaves; the hundreds of years of White denial of equal opportunities for Blacks; and the continuous exploitation of Blacks by Whites even after emancipation in the middle of the 19th Century.

The student must also take seriously into account the way in which certain superficial physical differences such as skin color are used as hooks on which to hang cultural distinctions and differentiations. That is where and how skin color becomes relevant: as a trait to which other traits are ascribed, or from which it is assumed other traits may be inferred. The belief is that knowledge of a man's skin color implies something as well about his native intelligence, musical capacity, capacity for passionate love, or some such thing. These beliefs are either indisputably false or undemonstrable by any evidence. But they are believed in — and that is what gives them their power. For men act on what they believe to be real, often regardless of any scientific evidence to the contrary.

An important feature of such beliefs is that physical distinctiveness is not necessary to get negative and derogatory beliefs developing around a group. Consider for instance, as Wagatsuma shows us in his article on the Japanese Eta, the lower caste group in Japan, how the knowledge that people are Eta evokes the same kinds of attitudes toward them as one finds on the part of Whites in America and South Africa toward the Blacks in their countries, even though the Eta are physically indistinguishable from many of their non-Eta neighbors. The Japanese believe that the Eta are by nature different, and undesirably so.

CHARACTERISTICS OF RACIAL THINKING
1. *Appearance and Behavior Both Hereditary*

We can now explore in some detail the basic mode of thought and behavior that might well be called racial insofar as it is thinking about, believing about, and acting toward groups which are said to be races. In its most general form, it represents the tendency to see and explain similarities and differences among human beings as due to certain qualities which are as inborn and inherent as skin color, height, eye shape, or hair form. In its most widely practiced form, this mode of thought combines the appearance of a group of people with its customs — religious, political, familial, or whatever — and makes the assumption that the same genes or units of inheritance that give the people their distinctive, or presumably distinctive, physical appearance also cause them to behave the way they do.

In pre-scientific days, this form of thinking about humans and explaining their conduct was altogether expectable. As people wandered or traveled throughout the world, they encountered groups who both looked and behaved quite differently from the groups to which the travelers belonged. What more natural, simple conclusion was there than to associate the different looks and different behavior? And who could then criticize such theories for failing to understand how different ways of life are *learned*, rather than biologically inherited? The sciences of anthropology, sociology, and psychology had not yet emerged and hence no scientific corrective on this mode of thought was available. Such thinking about human differences, then, became standard to the mentality of people throughout the world. And still today, this type of racial thinking — of thinking in terms of inherent characteristics most often associated more or less with differences in physical appearance of people — occurs all over the world. It is perhaps the single most dominant mode of thought about human similarities and differences. It is assumed that where people are alike, they are alike by nature; and where different, they differ by nature. Explanations that rely upon culture patterns, learning, beliefs, and attitudes do not have much currency in the thinking of many men throughout the world — even today's so-called enlightened world.

2. Hierarchical Patterns

Racial thinking is also characteristically hierarchical, that is, the differences among people are said to be not only inherent but they are also almost always evaluated as good or bad — never just different. It is not that differences *command* this kind of evaluation — many differences among people are not even noticed, much less evaluated. Rather, once differences *are* noted, and once they are believed to be inherent, they are almost always evaluated in a hierarchy of social and moral worth and, correlatively, of social and moral danger. Even where the group in question is considered superior in one regard or another, its superiority is considered dangerous — as in the case of the stereotypes regarding the superior intelligence of Jews in the United States, Swedes in Finland, and Chinese and Indians throughout the West Indies and East Asia.

3. Categorical and Stereotypical

It is clear, too, that racial thinking is categorical and stereotypical in character: all the members of a group identified as belonging to a given racial category tend to be assigned the same traits, whatever they may be. Variations from the generalizations embodied in the stereotypes are accounted for as exceptions, not as instances that challenge the generalization.

4. Self-Confirming

As with most categorical and stereotypical thinking, assumptions about the characteristics of racial groups tend to be self-confirming; that is, given the premises which are taken as true, people then tend to respond to the members of the racial group in terms of these assumed characteristics, and they thereby help to make these characteristics come into being. Or, if they do not actually produce the expected behavior or traits in the majority of the members of the group, they selectively notice only the minority of instances in which the behavior appears, and then point to this minority of instances as proof of the correctness of the stereotype. The American treatment of Negroes is an example of both of these processes. In the first instance, acting upon the belief that Negroes are by nature intellectually inferior — as was the widespread belief until recently — Whites withheld schooling from, or provided only inferior schooling to Negroes on the grounds that they could not take advantage of equal schooling. As a result, Negroes were proportionately less well educated than Whites (and still are), and their poorer outcome in the schools was pointed to by the Whites as proof of the correctness of the original assumption of natural inferiority. In the second instance, Whites frequently act in terms of rather widespread beliefs that Negroes are more lawless or disregarding of law than they, to create life situations for Negroes, such as poverty, which are sure to produce a higher rate of crime. Whites then point to the incidence of criminality among Negroes for confirmation of their original contention, even though only a small minority of Negroes is ever involved in crime. We see here the operations of *selective perception*, that is, choosing the cases that fit one's biases and ignoring the evidence to the contrary. In this way, the original biases are falsely confirmed.

5. Norms of Racial Thinking Taught to Children

Another important feature of racial categorizations and stereotypes is that the prevailing beliefs and attitudes toward the different group or groups are taught early in life to children so that racial awareness and consciousness becomes a firm part of their *general* outlook in life. Just as loyalties and pride in one's own group are everywhere early instilled, so are the negative attitudes toward members of other groups instilled early and with equal force. One's racial identity, and with it one's sense of difference from members of other races, thus tend to become important parts of one's total identity.

6. Norms of Social Distance Taught

Not only are beliefs and attitudes taught, but behavior toward members of other groups is also taught. This behavior often includes an insistence on total distance and separation, especially in regard to any intimacy among members of the diverse groups. Genuine interracial mixing, especially among members of opposite sexes in both races, occurs under the conditions that those involved have never acquired their notions of the undesirability of the members of the other group, have deliberately suspended them in the interest of other values, or have broken with their earlier instruction. But when distance between groups is maintained, and especially when any intimacy is prohibited, the initial stereotypes tend to be confirmed by the absence of any opportunity to have experiences that would challenge them.

7. The Mutuality of Stereotypes

Another interesting feature of racial thinking and acting is the mutuality of stereotypes. The range of mutual stereotypes depends on the situation, of course, but in general where one group is considered superior and the other inferior, the inferior group will tend to have stereotypes which burlesque and parody the traits of the superior group in their conduct with the inferiors. They will mock and mimic and make grotesqueries out of the ways in which the members of the superior group evince their superiority when they are interacting with members of the inferior group.

8. The Victims Absorb the Stereotypes about Themselves

One of the most difficult problems in race relations arises from the fact that very often the members of the inferior group will accept, albeit grudgingly and often unwittingly, the criteria that their "superiors" employ to demean and denigrate them as bases of evaluating members of their own group. Thus, for a very long time light skin color and straight hair have been important marks of prestige in the American Black community, as though in direct response to the extent to which these same features have been used by the Whites as marks of *their* own superiority over the Blacks. The rise of Black African consciousness in America today, with its deliberate effot to create a belief that "Black is Beautiful," must be seen as a reaction to the extent to which American White society has managed to make many Blacks ashamed of being Black and of having the other physical traits that identify them, even if only stereotypically.

In the same way, other inferior groups all over the world, in their search for escape from their own demeaned identities, adopt and absorb the superior group's criteria of beauty, speech, conduct, and dress, and seek to imitate or duplicate them.

There are other characteristics of racial thinking but these will suffice to characterize it as a distinctive and ubiquitous mode of thought.

SOURCES OF VARIABILITY IN RACIAL THINKING

Variations in intensity of racial thinking are attributable to a number of circumstances. One important circumstance is the availability of scientific knowledge in the community. By and large, it seems true that those most exposed to instruction in the modern social and psychological sciences are least susceptible to this racist mode of thought.

Another circumstance, correlated with the first, is the degree of commitment in the political ideology of the group to the basic canons of democratic society and democratic social relations. This commitment to democracy entails a renunciation of racial thinking; or, at least, it requires a renunciation of acting in terms of racial categories, whatever the actual beliefs and feelings may be.

A third circumstance that causes variability is the extent to which the people involved see each other as threats, economically, socially, or psychologically. When people who appear different are not in fact in competition with each other for scarce and desired goods and services, they are less likely to need to hold on to racial stereotypes.

Variation also occurs when the members of the different groups interact and mix with each other frequently and thus get a chance to come to know each other as individuals. Such contacts are especially effective in breaking down racial stereotypes when they occur among persons in equal status situations that are relatively devoid of conflict and competition — as in the instances of professional associations or integrated housing units occupied by people on common socioeconomic class levels. But frequency of contact does not have any inherent power if those contacts are regulated at all times by the code of racial etiquette which prescribes rigid observation of superior-inferior norms.

Finally, variation occurs whenever obstacles are set up that prevent the translation of prejudicial beliefs into discriminatory behavior. We are here making a crucial distinction between prejudice and discrimination. Prejudice refers to thinking, believing, and feeling. Discrimination refers to acting. These two aspects of behavior are separable. There are prejudiced people who discriminate and others who do not; in turn, only some of those who discriminate are prejudiced and others are not. How much prejudice will be translated into discrimination depends importantly on the structure of custom and law in the community, including the restraints or sanctions that may exist to discourage, prevent, or even punish discriminatory actions.

There is much value to this distinction between prejudice and discrimination for it implies the possibility of driving wedges between them by interposing countervailing forces that require the prejudiced individual to keep his prejudices to himself. In so doing, forces are introduced that reduce the likelihood of self-confirmation of the initial racial premises. When there is a diminution in such self-proving behavior, then there are fewer instances observable in the community of people who confirm the truth of the original premises. When, for example, beliefs about Negro intellectual inferiority are prevented by custom and law from being translated into inferior schools, then more equal chances for decent education result in fewer badly-educated Negroes. As the standard of education of Negroes rises, the original assumption of Negro inferiority loses proof. The separation of prejudice from discrimination also means that there can be change over generations. Parents who are prejudiced, but who believe it wrong to behave discriminatively, are able to teach their children to be neither prejudiced nor discriminatory, and are able to refrain more than they otherwise would be from engaging in discriminatory actions that strengthen prejudices. These are outstanding instances of changing the actions of men without necessarily changing what is in their minds and hearts; or of men acting in accordance with one set of beliefs they hold about fair play, rather than in terms of other sets of prejudicial beliefs they had been taught earlier.

If one wishes to understand the mixed character of race relations in the United States, South Africa, India, and other places typically thought of as being overwhelmingly racist, one must take into account this separability of prejudice from discrimination and realize that in every one of these communities there are segments of the population, sometimes majorities indeed, who have become committed to justice among people, whatever the prevailing norms may be.

RACE IS WHAT IT IS BELIEVED TO BE

We can now say that the relations between two groups of people may be called race relations insofar as one or both of the groups define the other as belonging to a race and treat it in accordance with their views of its characteristics and qualities. By this definition, then, an American Negro is one who is defined by others as a Negro, or calls himself Negro, and who is treated in accordance with the beliefs associated with that identity.

It is clear that the implications of race relations for the lives of people involved in them can and usually do go way beyond anything the objective differences between them could possibly justify or account for. Here we see that what men define as real is real in its consequences; or, alternatively, that men will act in terms of what they believe to be true, whether it is actually so or not.

There would be no significant cause for concern in this regard if it were not for the fact that usually one group has the power to impose its definition of the situation upon the other and to shape its life accordingly. In short, race relations are usually consequential and to the detriment of one of the parties in the relationship.

As noted before, the extent to which a given group manifests the characteristics ascribed to it by another is most often a result of having had its life shaped by the other dominant group in accordance with the prejudicial stereotypes by which it was originally defined and viewed. The dominant group has largely created the characteristics of the subordinate group; and so long as the dominant group believes that those characteristics are in the nature of the other, that long will they continue to treat them in ways that will produce the characteristics. People treated as though they were inherently stupid, animal-like, or excessively shrewd or clannish will have little chance to avoid acquiring the characteristics ascribed to them. Either they will be forced into the characteristic by being deprived of opportunities to the contrary, or they will resort to the trait in question in defense against maltreatment by the dominant group. Either way, the victims often come to manifest the traits ascribed to them by the vicitimizing group.

RACE RELATIONS: CASTE AND CLASS STRUCTURES

It has been customary in social science to sum up distinctions among varying types of race relations in terms of "class" and "caste." The definition of a caste situation includes the following: the groups in question are separated by what are believed to be fundamental differences in their genetic or hereditary makeup; the groups are arranged in a hierarchy of inferior and superior value and entitlement; one is born into his group and in principle can never leave it; intermarriage between the caste groups is prohibited; certain persisting features of identification such as a traditional occupation, a religious ritual, or a physical appearance are taken as outward marks of caste membership; in the more extreme cases, any contact with a member of another caste is considered degrading or contaminating; and, finally, no matter how equal members of different castes may be in their wealth or other such marks of success, they can neither change their caste membership nor claim equality with members of higher castes.

So defined, caste and race relations may appear to be identical on the surface or different terms for the same situation. In fact, however, though there are many similarities, there are some important distinctions as well, so that people defined as members of different races can be related as castes or as classes. The most important factor is the extent to which the differences between the people are considered to be native, inherited, and ineradicable, requiring that the groups refrain from sharing any real intimacies. In the archtypical caste situation there is a fundamental belief in a religious-ritual inferiority and impurity of the lower caste, such that any intimate contact with these people is likely to result in a degrading contamination of body and soul. According to sociological scholars, this belief is the keystone of a caste relationship. It and the others cited above are the defining terms of a full caste situation. In fact, all instances of race relations exhibit only some of these features. No total caste situation is to be found anywhere in the world, though some cases, such as traditional India, come close to exemplifying the full picture.

The class-structured situation of race relations can be described as differing from the caste situation primarily in terms of the absence of any beliefs in fixed, hereditary, and ritually contaminating characteristics of members of other classes. By definition, then, class implies mobility, or at least the possibility of moving out of one's class of origin into another, through achievement. Intermarriage occurs between members of different classes. One gets his *caste* membership by *ascription* — he is assigned; but he gets his *class* membership by *achievement*, by manifesting the criteria of membership, such as education, wealth, or a type of occupation. In actual practice, there is no totally open class system, anymore than there is a totally closed caste system. In the actual world of class situations, it is always a matter of "more or less." Some mobility is possible, but often there are caste-like restraints on such mobility; the sons of the poorer and less-educated people have less chance to improve their situations than do the sons of the richer and better-educated. Some intermarriages occur, but, by and large, there is class homogeneity in marriages, and in patterns of friendship, association, and intimacy.

Given the fact that all actual situations are a mixture of some elements of caste and class, we see that these terms are thus useful concepts, indicating the opposite ends of a continuum of possibilities, from the rigid, closed, self-perpetuating caste at the one end to the open, fluid, mobile, ever-changing class situation at the other. When the continuum of possibilities is described in these terms, it is clear that some inequality among groups is always present. At the caste end are fixed and permanent inequalities that affect the whole pattern of life. At the class end are temporary and volatile inequalities that are in theory much less consequential.

Properly, this continuum ought to be extended at the class end to include a range of cases of diminishing and less consequential inequalities, reaching finally to the imaginary polar society in which there is total equality in the sense that no group is believed inferior or superior to another, entitled to more of the good things of life than another, or more socially valuable than another. At this point is the egalitarian society which has been the focal point of interest and striving of those who believe in a socialist society.

RACE RELATIONS TEND TOWARD CASTE

Any situation of group relationships in which the differences between the groups are assumed to include some hereditary features that make one of them naturally superior to the other tends more to the caste than the class end of the continuum of possibilities. The cases presented in this volume show a good deal of variation in this particular regard. The strict caste-like situations in South Africa and India contrast with the less racial and more class-like characteristics of Hawaii, Puerto Rico, and Brazil. The same range of variation is found within countries as well, and perhaps the United States is the best example of where from region to region, state to state, and person to person the meaning of Negro or White is variable in its implications for hereditary superiority and inferiority.

In every case reported here, however, there is significance to race; that is, in none of the cases is there a total absence of racial thinking such that the physical differences between the people, as perceived, are seen only as physical differences without any implications of superiority and inferiority. All of the cases include some aspect of such thinking and are to that extent caste-like in character, however much there is relatively equal opportunity for people of all identities. Here, again, the United States is a good example of a mixture of points of view, insofar as while racial thinking about Negroes and Whites still is characteristic, there are many who insist on the full equality of opportunities for all people, regardless of color or racial origin.

It is possible, then, to have mixtures of both caste and class in any situation of race relations. In all but the most rigid caste-like situations here described, one will find caste-like restraints, if not legal prohibitions, against intermarriage side-by-side with at least an ideology, if not an actual practice, of equal economic and political opportunities for peoples of all races. One must be careful therefore to distinguish the mixed elements of caste and class in all these cases. For instance, it would be just as untrue to say that the relations between Negroes and Whites in the United States are uniformly caste-like as to insist that they are uniformly class-like and devoid of any caste-like elements.

The mixture found in such cases closely follows the lines suggested in what Gunnar Myrdal called the "rank order of discrimination," that is, a hierarchy of situations in which there is more and less resistance to equality between the races. Equality of opportunity is more easily worked toward and partly achieved in such situations as jobs, voting, and schools that do not demand intimacy; and it is most fiercely resisted in such situations as clubs, neighborhoods, dating, and marriage, that do call for intimacy.

One must not ignore these distinctions because in practice the more class-like the relations become in certain crucial areas, such as occupation and education, the more challenged and threatened are the existing ideologies of differential entitlement that give strength to caste or racial thinking. Class equality, with attendant power through education, votes, money, and organization, tends to undermine caste inequality. This is a basic principle found in all the situations of race relations reported here or elsewhere — even in the most rigid caste situations.

IDEOLOGY AND POWER IN RACE RELATIONS

Two connecting links between racial classification and life chances have just been specified: one is the ideology of entitlement, that is, what members of one category are believed to be entitled to; and the other is the capacity of a dominant group to enforce this ideology in concrete terms. Ideology plus power thus become important ingredients in shaping the life chances of members of racial categories. It stands to reason, then, that disadvantaged racial groups can pursue an improvement in their welfare, either by changing the ideology that defines them and their entitlements or by somehow securing the power they need to prevent the disadvantageous ideology from being imposed on them.

The cases reported in this volume reveal a range from the one extreme to another. First, there are Hawaii, Brazil, and Puerto Rico, where discriminatory ideologies of entitlement for people of different colors are not publicly maintained, however much they may be privately believed; and where the structures of power are used neither to sharpen the distinctions among skin color groups nor to insist on their differential entitlements and their separation from each other.

At the other extreme is South Africa where the ideology of differential entitlement is clear and strong; where power resides almost totally in the hands of the dominant white minority; and, moreover, where there is formal law, and not simply custom, that reinforces the ideology and gives a structural and durable dimension to the political power. India's caste system is like this to a lesser degree; and parts of the United States exemplify these characteristics, with some substantial legal disabilities still on the local levels, even though the national law forbids discrimination.

RACE RELATIONS AND
THE CLASS STRUCTURE

Some of the most enduring cases of discrimination against various racial groups occur not so much because of constant legal enforcement of these disadvantages but rather more through the operations of the economic and social class system of the society. The sequence of steps here is clear. Starting with differential power and privilege, the advantaged group, for various reasons, refuses members of the disadvantaged group access to education. The disadvantaged are hence confined to categories of unskilled and semi-skilled labor; and, by the same token, they do not have equal chances to compete for positions of power in the formal governmental hierarchy. Once this has happened, once these discriminating lines of opportunities have been drawn, a process of impersonal but effective discrimination has been put into motion that endures often without much formal enforcement at all. For one generation of disadvantaged parents breeds a second generation of disadvantaged children, bereft of education, choices, and the capacity to raise *their* children in ways that might make it possible for *them* to move up the socioeconomic class ladder into positions of privilege and power. When several generations have undergone this kind of discrimination, it becomes possible for the members of any generation to assume that this condition of unequal position and privilege in the society reflects natural differences between the different groups. In short, the premises of the first generation regarding the inferiority and unequal entitlement of the disadvantaged group have been made to come true by the actions taken in the name of these premises.

In even some of the most open societies, these impersonal disadvantages for people of the "wrong" color or race still persist so that one gets disproportionate representations of the skin colors in the various social and economic class layers. This is precisely the case in Puerto Rico where, though there is little effective ideology regarding race differences and neither formal law nor serious community norms that insist on differential advantage, it is nevertheless true that a disproportionate percentage of people of dark skin color are at the bottom of the social class ladder.

CLASS PREFERENCE AND LIFE STYLE

Matters are compounded and made more difficult for disadvantaged groups by the fact that social class differences not only entail differences in opportunities but in life styles as well — that is, in the subcultural patterns of language, dress, food, and family relationships that are practiced. These differences are then used as visible symbols of difference on the basis of which rationales for the maintenance of distance between the groups are developed and solidified. Thus, color or race becomes a symbol of disadvantage, and disadvantage becomes a symbol of color or race. Class and race become mixed and reinforce each other. The advantaged group informs the disadvantaged that there would be no discrimination against them if only they "measured up to standards"; but their lessened capacity to live up to these standards and their lack of awareness of or interest in achieving them are themselves directly due to the imposition of disadvantages at the outset.

COLOR AND CLASS

There is, of course, a great deal of argument today, in such areas as the United States, parts of Latin America, the West Indies, Brazil, and Japan, on the question of whether the disadvantages suffered by people of different races are really due to their color or race, on the one hand, or to their class position, on the other. As posed, the question is like that of whether a person's behavior is due more to his heredity or to his environment. We cannot easily sift out the relative contribution of either. In every case, we know that in any given generation class position is in part dependent on color category; and that, in turn, disadvantages suffered by groups arise in large part from their unequal opportunities in the social and economic class arena. We are left to wonder whether if class differences were eliminated, would there be no residue of distinction based on color alone?

We have some tests of this question in virtually every society reported on here. There are some class equivalences among people of various racial categories; and in each case we see that even when the members of different groups are equal in their educational, occupational, and income characteristics they nevertheless do not mix as easily, share as much intimacy, or feel as much at ease with members of another color group as they do with members of their own. Even in the best of cases reported, this residue of non-class discrimination is found. In that sense, we have an answer to our question of whether the distinctions among groups are purely a matter of class. They are not. But we also see that this is variable, for the statement that green money turns black people white is differently applicable from one country to another. In Brazil this holds true more than in the United States, and in the United States more than in South Africa. In Latin America and the West Indies it is about equally applicable. Malaysia, East Asia, and the continent of Africa also share in these variations.

If we know, then, that it is never class alone that separates people of different color in these instances, we still do not know, except as we look into each case separately, how much either color or class contribute to the distinctions in opportunities and life styles among the people who belong to the differing groups. Much depends on how long members of a given color group have been forced into or have retreated into a society and culture of their own, developing distinctive ways of looking and thinking about themselves and others, distinctive ways of behaving among themselves, and distinctive forms of art, music, and dance.

The arguments one hears so forcefully today in the United States about Black culture are very relevant here. The question is being raised of whether the Black community, by virtue of its isolation from the White, and by reason of its ancient African genesis, has developed a special and identifiable culture pattern of its own that may be defined as its heritage, and, by force of the doctrine of cultural relativism, whether it may be deemed as worthy of preservation and continuity as the White culture, whatever that may be said to be. Putting the issue this way again confounds the case with class distinctions. The culture pattern of the college-educated, professionally employed, prestigious White is probably more different from that of the unskilled, uneducated, low-prestige White than it is from that of the college-educated, professional, prestigious Negro. In short, cultural similarities tend to conform often to class boundaries. But there still remains the question of whether there isn't something exclusive and unique to the acquired cultural patterns of Blacks as such, by virtue of their previous places in American society, that transcends all class differences among themselves and that sets them aside from their class peers in the White group. This is a matter for serious study and for factual determination.

The contrast between the effects of color and those of class reminds us once again that both factors seem to be important in race relations situations, and that to that extent it is wrong or misleading to use the term race relations. Most students of relationship systems are agreed that however much ethnocentrism may be involved, that is, however much there may be rejection by one group of another on the basis of differences in customs, language, or religion, socioeconomic class considerations are always present. Sometimes, as with Chinese and Indian minorities in some parts of the world, the outsider group tends to be better off, on the average, than the host group within whose society it lives. Most of the time, however, the outsider or rejected group is considerably worse off. These matters vary, too, with the size of the outsider group — there are outsiders who are majorities of the population, as in South Africa, Latin America, or the Caribbean area. And the outsider, of course, can be the native group, in the sense that it was present in the territory before the dominant group came in, usually by conquest, again as in South Africa, the Caribbean, and Latin America.

In any of these cases, there is always a discernibly dominant group, whether minority or majority, native or immigrant, and it is the group that has the control over the available physical force embodied in government and armies; that usually controls the economy and the educational system; and that determines what opportunities will be allowed to the weaker group. The fact that in allocating these opportunities or quotas to the weaker group there may be important elements of ethnocentric sentiment, including beliefs in the inferiority, evil, or undesirability of contact with the weaker group, does not alter the importance of class considerations and elements in the structure of the relationship. Class, defined by differences in power, property, prestige, and general social evaluation, is always present — though, as we have seen, in mixed ways.

The relationships between the dominant and the subordinate groups in these situations of race relations will obviously be considerably different depending in part on what the class situation happens to be. Where the outsider or weaker group is a minority, wealthier and better educated than the dominant group, and defined by stereotypes as fearsome for its shrewdness, clannishness, and general intelligence, the group is always in a precarious situation. It is subject to quotas of admission to various facilities, such as universities, to restriction to certain occupations, or, more drastically, to expropriation, disenfranchisement, and ultimately expulsion from the territory of the dominant group. The well-to-do, educated minorities throughout the world today — the Chinese and Indians in the West Indies, East Asia, and Africa, the Jews in the United States and other European countries, and the Swedes in Finland, among others — are relatively well-to-do compared to their host populations, but their security and safety depend on the good will of the host majorities among whom they live.

These situations of well-off minorities contrast strongly with those of the Negro in the United States and the Caribbean, the Indians in some Latin American countries, the darker-skinned peoples in Brazil, and the Coloured in Britain. It is not alone that in the latter areas there is a skin color or racial component; the visible stigmata or differences matter, but they don't matter that much in the last analysis. What matters more is power, property, and access to education and jobs. These define the essential differences between the fortunate minorities throughout the world and the less fortunate or seriously underprivileged and deprived groups, majorities though they may be.

RACE, CLASS, AND SOCIAL DISTANCE

In discussing ethnocentrism in race relations, the most important concept is that of social distance, by which is meant separation of groups, usually enforced by one against the other, and most pointedly expressed in the rejection of intimacy in social relationships, most particularly inter-marriage.

The measure of whether two groups of people consider each other equal is to be found, in the last analysis, in the freedom and ease with which the children of these groups can meet, court, and marry. Admission into each other's kinship structures is the mark of the disappearance of the distinction between insider and outsider, dominant and subordinate, and superior and inferior. There are other marks of partial acceptance, short of the final intimacy of marriage and kinship, and groups lose their distinctiveness and distance from each other as formerly separate echelons of people come to share social situations with each other. It is clear, too, that intimacies have a tendency to escalate: each new separation eliminated or bridged makes the next level of intimacy easier and more likely.

The dynamics of the relationship between class and ethnocentrism can be made clear here. While ethnocentrism is an important factor in determining the initial beliefs and discriminatory practices of the dominant against the subordinate group, it is social and economic equality that in the long run eliminates those ethnocentric sentiments and reduces the social distance between previously separated groups.

One must not assume, however, that class equality automatically means social equality in terms of social acceptance as equals. The groups who remain outside the pale, even though at a superior socioeconomic position to that of the dominant group, are evidence in point. But what is true is that the chances of acceptance as equals in intimate situations is much greater when the rejected outsiders have achieved strong and prestigious positions on the ladders of social and economic well-being. This is the meaning of the statement that green money turns black people white.

PATTERNS OF MOBILITY

We can make explicit now the implicit model of mobility that we have been describing in these past pages — the movement of the outsider "in." The greatest distance between outsiders and insiders occurs when both race and class separate the people involved. We are speaking here of race metaphorically, using it to refer to that large number of possible ethnocentric sentiments of difference, whether these be religious, linguistic, or whatever. And we are using class to refer to those possible differences in power, property, prestige, and general social evaluation.

The usual pattern of mobility or change occurs first in the reduction in class differences between groups. Full economic equality — in the sense of equal wealth and even equality of representation in key economic institutions — is capable of being reached between the insiders and the outsiders without any *matching* reduction in the ethnocentric distance between the groups. The next stage of equality is reached when, through a variety of possible ways, the beliefs about differences between people begin to disappear and they begin to admit each other to various degrees of intimacy. Usually, in the rare cases in which this happens, the outsider group in effect surrenders its separate identity or renders it so nominal as to require its members only to testify to their membership in the group, since they are not visibly distinct in looks, bearing, names, language, clothes, or customs from the dominant group into which they assimilate.

Needless to say, the achievement of economic parity, and with it, educational equality, and of the graces, deportment, language, and culture that go with education, do much to render meaningless the ethnocentric prejudices and stereotypes that the inside group may have entertained toward the outsiders in the past. Nevertheless, it is a rare occurrence in race relations when people who have been defined as distinct and separate and arranged in a hierarchial order of inferiority and superiority, or desirability and undesirability for intimate relationships, achieve any such full social parity. Assimilation of the outsider into the dominant group sometimes occurs, and with it the blurring of former distinctions; but full acceptance of the outsider with his distinctiveness almost never occurs.

VISIBILITY

The chances for mobility and for assimilation and disappearance of distinctive identity depend to a significant degree on the visibility of one's membership in a demeaned group. One can lose identifiability based on language, food, clothing, or religious worship; but one cannot lose visible distinctions based on skin color or other genetically determined physical features — at least not until there is a substantial amount of intermar-

riage. Almost all the cases reported in this volume involve such permanently visible groups whose chances for assimilation through loss of
visibility are small or nil. Only under conditions of thorough mixture, as
in Hawaii or, to a lesser degree, in Brazil and other parts of Latin
America, does it become possible for some degree of invisibility to
emerge and thereby to confound and confuse the former stereotypes
about color and its implications. Otherwise, in the absence of intermarriage or intermating, and in the presence of distinctive physical traits,
the subordinate racial group has available to it only the alternative of
requesting, demanding, or wresting from the dominant group social and
economic equality and, with it, the possible reduction of the significance
attributed to the color that separates the people. The upward mobility of
a subordinate group depends either on this reduction in the importance
ascribed to physical differences or on the creation of a pluralist society
in which visibly different people work out a pattern of peaceful coexistence.

PLURALISM

In a fully pluralistic society the differences between peoples, in such
things as language, customs, religion, and physical appearance, would
have all the significance that the people wanted them to have, but
would have no relevance to their fates and careers as citizens in the
common society. For instance, there would be full religious pluralism in
the United States if each religious denomination could develop to the
fullest extent that it wished without religious affiliation ever influencing
opportunities in education, politics, occupation, and so forth.

Can such a situation be fully achieved? On the basis of available evidence, the answer must be no. There are no such societies reported in
this volume and none are known of anywhere in the world. Everywhere,
differences in culture, language, religion, or race seem to matter, at least
somewhat. They enter into the rating systems of societies; into their
systems of privilege and power; into their determinations of open and
closed doors in facilities; and into the shaping of their circles of intimacies.

But it must also be reported that there is great variability in the degree of significance given to differences between people within the same
society. Some societies have structures that permit differing groups to
coexist without frequent and destructive conflict. Most important here
are those societies that have political structures in which people from
different groups share formal power and thus act as restraints on each
other, providing some bridges across cultural differences. The West Indies
are perhaps as good an example as any of this kind of power-sharing between Black and White people. These arrangements are not necessarily

stable or durable, but they are at least more egalitarian in their consequences than those in societies where one of the racial groups tends to
have a monopoly of power over the other, as in India, South Africa, and
to some extent the United States. An alternative pattern is found in some
Latin American countries, in the Middle East, and in those African
countries where parallel tribal or intra-group structures rival central governments in their powers, even if only informally.

How long-lived such pluralistic society arrangements are likely to be is
hard to estimate. They show marked signs of instability and strain, and it
may very well be that the formerly subject peoples will come to organize
themselves sufficiently powerfully to take over the reins not only of the
governments but of the economies as well.

If it now sounds as if a diversity of cultures is too difficult to sustain
within the framework of one society, this must be immediately qualified
by pointing to the great diversity of cultures found within societies everywhere, even indeed in the United States and western European nations
such as England, Italy, West Germany, and Switzerland. These exhibit
various degrees of relatively peaceful coexistence of diverse nationalities
and ethnic groups. In each case, the basic facilitation is a commitment
to democratic politics and a central government in which membership
does not depend on cultural or racial group membership. Additional support is given by a coordinated educational system, again accessible to all
without formal discrimination on the basis of racial membership or cultural diversity. In short, so long as the major central facilities are shared,
without regard to group membership, it becomes possible for various
groups to maintain fairly distinct cultural lives without serious conflict
with their different neighbors. From time to time the various ethnic or
racial groups act as if they are warring tribes whose peace treaties with
the other tribes seem fragile and ready to be disavowed after· one more
moment of hostility; but the fabric of central and coordinated government
somehow manages to survive. This is not to say that there is equality, in
the full sense of the word, among all these groups, for there is plenty of
prejudice and discrimination. But the formal laws do not permit these to
be exercised openly or without restraint; and over the years the different
origins of the various groups who make up these multi-national and
multi-ethnic countries tend to diminish in importance.

At the same time, one must acknowledge the very great problems of
race relations present in some of these countries, particularly the United
States and England. In each of these cases it is a group of distinctive
color — the West Indians and Coloured in England, the Negroes or
Blacks in the United States — that suffers the most serious class disadvantages and the greatest rejection in terms of social distance or prohibition of intimacy.

I

Professor Banton sorts out the difficulties in Southern Africa imposed by lack of research and the overlap of race relations and political power relations between Black and White. Although the two have much in common, and it was primarily power relations during the colonial period which conditioned the formation of post-colonial race relations, much could be lost by a failure to separate these two. Banton discusses a variety of social settings and interactions between Black and White; he is aware particularly of the self-imposed segregation of Whites and the suspicion and regret this breeds in Africans. He sees the continuity between the Whites' social roles of leadership and direction carrying over and "stiffening" their social interactions with Blacks. He is careful and precise in his description of differing racial attitudes towards the same sets of behavior — what the White sees in himself to value and what the Black African sees in this same behavior.

MICHAEL BANTON

Africa South of the Sahara

Contemporary Africa presents a magnificent laboratory for the student of human relations. There can scarcely be any other part of the world that offers a better opportunity for studying the factors which regulate relations

Reprinted by permission from *International Social Science Journal*, Vol. 13, No. 2 (pp. 197-214); Unesco, 1961.

between groups of contrasting culture when the group membership of individuals is evident at a glance. The analogy of a laboratory is more than a mere figure of speech, for Europeans and Africans (to consider first the two principal groups) are associated in varying proportions in different territories:[1] in Northern Rhodesia there is 1 European in every 32 of the population, in Angola 1 in 41, in Kenya 1 in 120, in Uganda 1 in 500, in Nigeria 1 in 2,000. Different territories illustrate different distributions of political power between racial and other groups, different systems of education, different patterns of employment, different religions. The variety is at first overpowering, but it gives the student an opportunity to control many of the variables which bear upon his problem and thus to isolate those with which he is most concerned. Then there are also important questions regarding relations with intermediary racial groups (Cape Coloureds, Sierra Leone Creoles) and with minorities who stand largely outside the political struggle (Indians, Levantines, Arabs) which present possibilities for critical comparison within the same territory that is often more valuable than comparison between territories. No less important are the opportunities to study patterns of behaviour associated with the growing social differentiation of the African population. At the same time, inquiries in the new urban centres into relations between Africans of different tribes can be particularly valuable as they exemplify categoric relations between groups of similar cultural background, outward appearance, and social status.

Compared with these opportunities the amount of research hitherto undertaken is pitifully small. For this two chief reasons may be advanced. In the first place, relations between persons of different race in Africa are much more than just racial relations — they are almost always also relations between people of different income levels, education, cultural background, access to political power, and economic interest. As these differences normally outweigh considerations of race, it has seemed premature to try and isolate any specifically racial factor. In the second place, an interest in the scientific study of intergroup relations has grown up only in recent years. The variety of circumstantial factors and the lack of good comparative material is still such that the student is induced to attempt a full description (often in part historical) of the position in a particular territory. If the scientific investigation of these problems is to progress it must diverge from the particular, descriptive and historical mode of inquiry and develop an abstract theoretical system which will help explain the inter-relations between the factors which make up any particular situation. The need for such a system is widely recognized but it cannot be devised to order; until greater progress has been made in this respect it will remain risky to attempt to abstract features of interracial

[1] See Table 1 . . . on page 26.

MICHAEL BANTON

TABLE 1. POPULATIONS OF THE STATES AND TERRITORIES OF AFRICA SOUTH OF THE SAHARA[a]

	Africans	(date)	Europeans	(date)	Others
Angola	4 147 000	(1955)	103 419	(1954)	30 240 Coloured
Basutoland	627 000	(1955)	1 689	(1946)	867 Asians (1946)
Bechuanaland	324 000	(1955)	2 379	(1946)	1 176 Asians (1946)
Cameroun	3 146 000	(1955)	16 020	(1955)[b]	
Central African Republic	1 177 000	(1959)[c]			
Chad	2 576 000	(1957)	4 900	(1957)	
Congo (capital Brazzaville)	795 000	(1959)[c]			
Congo (capital Leopoldville)	13 540 182	(1958)	109 457	(1958)	1 233 Asians (1958)
Dahomey	1 710 000	(1957)	2 633	(1955)[d]	
Gabon	399 800	(1957)	3 981	(1956)	
Gambia	285 000	(1955)	269	(1955)	
Ghana	5 049 000	(1955)	11 000	(1953)[e]	
Guinea	2 492 000	(1957)[f]			
Ivory Coast	3 200 000	(1958)	14 100	(1958)	
Kenya	5 815 000	(1955)	52 000	(1955)	180 800 Asians (including 144 100 Indians [1955] and 24 174 Arabs [1948])
Liberia	1 250 000	(1955)	5 333	(1959)	1 726 Asians (1959)
Madagascar	4 776 000	(1955)	74 085	(1956)[g]	10 092 Indians; 4 900 Chinese
Mali and Senegal	5 817 000	(1955)	50 000	(1955)[g]	
Mozambique	5 652 000	(1956)	65 798	(1956)	30 000 Coloureds (1956)
Niger	2 412 000	(1956)	3 040	(1956)	
Nigeria	31 254 000	(1955)	15 000	(1955)	17 200 Asians (1956)
Northern Rhodesia	2 280 000	(1959)	73 000	(1959)	9 600 (5 500 Asians; 1 500 Coloureds in 1956)
Nyasaland	2 750 000	(1959)	8 800	(1959)	5 000 Asians; 8 000 Coloureds in 1956
Portuguese Guinea	540 000	(1955)	2 263	(1950)	4 500 Coloureds (1950)
Ruanda-Urundi	4 689 065	(1958)	7 105	(1958)	2 320 Asians (1958)
Sierra Leone	2 050 000	(1955)	964	(1948)	2 074 Asians (1948)
Southern Cameroon	1 500 000	(1955)	700	(1955)	
Southern Rhodesia	2 770 000	(1959)	215 000	(1959)	15 400 (8 500 Asians; 1 200 Coloureds in 1956)
South West Africa	464 000	(1959)	69 000	(1959)	21 000 Coloureds
Swaziland	223 000	(1958)	3 201	(1946)	
Spanish Guinea	208 000	(1955)	4 436	(1953)	
Tanganyika	8 665 336	(1957)	20 598	(1957)	76 536 Indians and Goans; 19 100 Arabs (1957)
Togoland	1 080 000	(1955)	1 242	(1955)	
Uganda	5 300 000	(1955)	10 866	(1959)	71 933 including 69 103 Indians (1959)
Union of South Africa	14 500 000	(1959)	3 011 000	(1959)	1 036 000 Coloureds; 441 000 Asians
Uper Volta	3 222 000	(1957)	3 700	(1957)[h]	
Zanzibar	228 815	(1958)	507	(1958)	18 334 Indians; 46 989 Arabs (1959)

[a] 1955 and earlier figures are taken from ILO *African Labour Survey,* 1958.
[b] Includes Asians.
[c] Figures for different racial groups not available. There were 25,200 Europeans in French Equatorial Africa in 1956.
[d] Includes Levantines.
[e] Includes 1,930 Levantines.
[f] Total population; includes 4,538 French and 2,148 others (1951).
[g] Includes Levantines.
[h] Includes assimilated Africans.

behaviour from their context with any hope of ultimate justification. Nevertheless, sufficient progress has been made in the social sciences in recent years to permit an analysis in more objective terms than the earlier literature, which was largely restricted to the analysis of the distribution of resources among racial groups and to the discussion of problems immediately relevant to public policy.

RACE AS A STATUS SYMBOL

In most parts of Africa people respond differently to someone of another race because his appearance is taken to signify that he belongs to another social category and is therefore to be treated in the manner appropriate to that category. Race is thus interpreted as a symbol of a person's rights and obligations, that is, of his status. But systems of status based on race seem in general to be highly unstable over the course of more than a generation or two, so that it is advisable first to consider in general terms some of the factors affecting the equation of status with race.

The contacts with which we are chiefly concerned have mostly come about by Europeans invading and assuming authority over African territories. In these circumstances the superiority of the immigrant over the native race, and the distinction between the two, is unquestioned in every sphere of social life. Thus race is an unequivocal symbol of social status. But society abhors a vacuum, and the intrusion of Europeans triggers off a series of changes which make for a filling in of the gap between the groups and, later, for interchange between them. Some of the Africans adopt European ways, and they may well be encouraged to do so as there is a pressing need for interpreters, clerks, policemen, catechists, etc. if European skill is to be most effectively deployed. Some Europeans take native women as concubines, or a group that is biologically intermediate may spring up by immigration. Reactions to this situation depend upon whether the European group is a small one of administrators responsible to an imperial government and other temporary residents, or whether there is an appreciable population of European settlers. In the former case, immigration has been controlled and the European population, for a time at least, has consisted of skilled persons brought in to perform duties which could not be discharged by locally born people. This has facilitated the maintenance of a system of racial statuses. By keeping the gulf between the races fairly marked and preserving white prestige, a relatively small group of people has been able to exercise close control. In territories where proportionately large numbers of European pioneers have settled, the circumstances have been otherwise. As pioneers, these immigrants have been a much more mixed group; they have been less subject to outside control; and their economic interest has often been in conflict with that of the native peoples. In these circumstances the gap between the two races is less marked from the beginning and would soon be reduced further if the immigrant race did not use its political power to reinforce the criteria of race as a means of demarcating the groups.

In the long run the differences between the colonial administrator and the settler kinds of society are considerable. Where there is only a small European population Africans are trained to take over an increasing range of ancillary functions; a minority then acquire qualifications comparable with those of Europeans and the equation of racial with economic and cultural distinctions is challenged. In certain situations race is no longer a reliable symbol of status but, because both the Europeans and the illiterate Africans tend for a time to rely upon it as a guide, considerable irritation is provoked. It is at this stage that the different groups within the African population become aware that many Europeans regard all Africans as falling into one fundamental category; only then do the Africans perceive their situation in racial terms. It is, however, dangerous to build upon the notion of race consciousness in the African situation: the African élite soon decide that their political subordination is the key element in the situation and focus their attack upon this. In many circumstances it would be more accurate to speak of both European and African groups as being politically conscious but expressing themselves in the idiom of race because this is closer to the experiences of everyday life. The course of events in the newly independent territories certainly suggests that the function of race as a status symbol is changed more dramatically by the breaking of its association with political status than by changes in its other associations.

When a former colonial dependency becomes independent the basis of race relations is changed. The status claims of European immigrants derive from their potential contribution as evaluated by the native race. Race does not indicate a status relevant to all spheres of social life, but symbolizes a cultural difference which is of social significance in a limited range of situations. Yet recent history shows that while many colonial populations have been able to unite in expelling the imperial power, once this has been achieved they are troubled by internal divisions which may be identified with ethnic differences of a lesser order. The definition of racial problems may then shift to include these.

In the settler type of society the European group attempts to frustrate any changes within the native population that might disturb stratification along racial lines. Skin colour acquires tremendous emotional significance as a guarantee of the social order. But it would appear that even rigid forms of stratification cannot contain the forces generated by interaction between the groups, and that the effect of such policies is at best to delay the filling in of the gap between the races.

In practice, many colonial territories have shown both administrative and settler tendencies which have conflicted with each other. Influential groups of European settlers have sought to maintain strict racial distinctions while Africans have utilized the colonial connexion to try and increase their control over the political life of the country. As either side has gained a yard or two in the struggle so the significance of race as a status symbol has shifted. A vital factor here has been the influence of the Crown or the metropolitan Republic: all sections of the colonial society have acknowledged the overriding authority of the imperial government; the Europeans because it provided the justification and reason for their presence; the Africans, at times with touching affection, because they saw it as the ultimate guardian of their interests.

RACIAL STRATIFICATION
AND SOCIAL MOBILITY

Racial friction in colonial Africa has been associated much more closely with urban areas and centres of wage-earning employment than with the country districts. The effect of economic development is to diversify both groups and to make the system of stratification much more flexible. The diversification of the African group is the greater in extent and the more significant for the study of race relations for it is the African intellectual élite which more than any other group has forced the system of racial stratification to be modified. The emergence of such an élite is affected both by the level of economic development and by the policy of the colonial power. It has been strongest when, as in British West Africa, it could be based on the leadership of educated Africans who were members of the liberal professions — lawyers, doctors in private practice, etc. — and thus not dependent upon the colonial administration for their livelihood. The emergence of a group of Africans within the administrative service who possessed qualifications of this order posed a difficult problem [11].[2] If the administration gave them the same salary as expatriates from the imperial country who required an extra financial inducement to serve overseas, this was to introduce great inequalities of income within the African population and impose a taxation burden that was certain to increase: if, on the other hand, it fixed their salaries at a lower point, the administration laid itself open to charges of discrimination on grounds of race. Governmental policies might also tend either to separate this group from the mass of their fellows or to give them common political interests. Some writers [27] have emphasized the "spiritual confusion" of the educated African; others [26] while pointing out that "in his private life he is an African; in public a European" do not find that this duality gives rise to any serious psychological strains.

[2] The figures in brackets refer to the bibliography on page 44.

A clear-cut example of the position of an African élite isolated from the tribal population is provided by the Creoles of Freetown. Though they acted as agents of British expansion, the British scorned them for imitating white practices. More recently they have been under pressure from the numerically preponderant tribal people as they have never identified themselves with tribal interests nor, with one or two exceptions, did they try to offer tribal people political leadership in the days when it was still possible for them to do so [25, 5].

Contributors to a symposium on African élites in 1956 gave very different accounts of the élite in different territories. In the Portuguese provinces there were no élites agitating for political independence. Africans who measured up to the requirements for assimilated status — and these were by no means stringent — were pictured as an energetic minority working for the assimilation of their fellows and giving evidence of the missionary spirit of the colonial power. Africans might on occasion complain against a particular person but they never complained against the white community as a whole or about the Portuguese administration [33]. The intellectual élite in the Congo consisted of medical and agricultural assistants, clerks, ministers and priests, plus a few prospective graduates. It was noted that they were then reacting against the notion of cultural assimilation and trying to re-evaluate their traditional heritage. These groups had the opportunity of voicing their views in various consultative councils, but the native rural district councils were the exclusive preserve of the traditional leaders [7]. A later writer underlines the significance of this development, pointing out how, under the influence of African intellectuals in France and notably those of the Présence Africaine group, the Congolese élite began to react against the European assumption that Africans were in a process of development from an inferior to a superior stage, and to think instead in terms of the contact between two civilizations [44]. In the early 1950's an intellectual élite in British East Africa, composed of graduates of Makerere College, was also becoming established. Its members were still very conscious of the differences between themselves and the tribal population and were not very active in political organizations [15]. It has been generally observed that when young colonials pursue advanced studies in the metropolitan country they become more conscious of the subordination of their homeland and of the attractive elements in its traditional culture. This experience makes them much more conscious of racial and cultural differences.

A contributor to the 1956 symposium dealing with the position in Senegal stated that an intellectual élite based on the liberal professions had emerged before the war when it followed a policy of assimilation. After the war its numbers increased, competition with Europeans was intensified, and the group came to express an intense reaction against colonialism, drawing heavily upon Marxist theories and constructing a Negro mystique of the kind associated with Présence Africaine. Until just before the time of writing, members of this élite had remained aloof from the local political parties which gave them little opportunity for pressing the policies they favoured [31]. In Ghana the intellectual élite had by this time become a ruling class as the suffrage was restricted to literates. The conflict between this group and the Europeans was described as a bid by the former to oust the latter not only as wielders of political power but as a standard-setting group in the social sphere. Hence the African élite, particularly the politicians, aspired to bigger cars, more expensive clothing, and larger houses than the Europeans possessed [8].

The intellectual élite has often had to bear the brunt of European resistance to change which threatened the established social pattern. They have responded by concentrating upon moves towards a change in political relations. Thus an investigation in Uganda showed that young people there were in general radically opposed to any form of multiracialism in government, a characteristic which tended to be an expression of their better education, occupation and income; the more educated were far more opposed to non-African participation than were the less educated; and the better a man's job, especially if he were self-employed or in the very highest income group, the more clearly was he opposed to minority representation [18]. These results could probably have been confirmed at an earlier stage of West African experience where it was often affirmed by Africans that they had nothing against Europeans as people, but everything against them as rulers of their country. An experimental study in India has shown that attitudes towards the British became very much more favourable after independence and parallels for this might be found in Africa; certainly a very recent study dealing with Nigeria [41] concludes that mutual confidence between Europeans and Africans there is now greater than ever before.

In territories where a rapid growth in demand for skilled artisans, clerks, foremen, and others whose status is intermediate between those of the ordinary African and the colonial administrator, could not be met from the African population or from intermediary groups, Europeans have been introduced for this purpose [4, 30]. One East African study [45, 47] shows some of the consequences of such a development: the solidarity of the European community is seriously threatened and the image of "the European" presented to other groups is modified. The very considerable increase in the European proportion of the total population of many colonies after the war suggests that the diversification of the European racial group has been general. It has been said that antipathy toward Africans is strongest among the lower ranking classes of Europeans and that these resent the university-trained African's claim to a higher status [26].

Where, as in Kenya, there has been a stronger settler influence, European immigrants have been accepted without the occupational overlap between the groups being increased to any appreciable extent. It has been argued that in such circumstances the practice of racial segregation creates vested interests distorting the normal lines of economic interest. Thus European taxpayers in Kenya demanded economies in the administration but did not wish more posts to be filled by Indians — though that would have been a considerable economy — because the taxpayers had themselves propounded the race theory and were committed to it. The play of interests in this situation has been delicately analysed by Mary Parker [37].

In countries where racial segregation is more systematically developed, the contradiction between such practices and prescriptions of economic policy become increasingly apparent the greater the degree of industrialization. The productivity of enterprises is dependent upon increasing the productivity of African labour and that, in turn, requires the stabilization of the labour force in urban centres. If African workers are to have any incentive to work hard and save a proportion of their earnings, they must have a stake in the life of the town, a chance of improving their position, and some opportunity to press their views on matters of communal concern. The resulting conflict between economic pressures and the desire of a white minority to maintain their commanding position has been most clearly demonstrated in a study concerned particularly with Southern Rhodesia [17] but the principles are of more general applicability. The long-term economic interest of the society demands the expansion of the consumer market among Africans; it requires the optimum use of human resources and therefore entails the promotion of able Africans and the introduction of equal pay for equal work. Rigid social stratification along racial lines will be steadily eroded unless force is used to preserve it; in either event economic advance entails increased friction attaching to race as a symbol of status.

CULTURAL DIFFERENCES

The structure of relations between Europeans and Africans is influenced and tends to be maintained by the cultural assumptions of the members of the two groups and by their attitudes as individuals. It has been pointed out that in the colonial situation Europeans are relatively isolated from the institutions which have sanctioned the courses of conduct they value. Considerable willpower is required to maintain them in the face of what seem the laxer standards of those round about. The social institutions of European communities in the colonies are thus of crucial importance in preserving their identity as a group and the individual's sense of integrity. This would appear to be one of the factors responsible for their exclusiveness. The European thinks it only natural that he should keep his club for himself and his fellows, as a place where he can relax without any of the awkwardness which would arise if he admitted people who did not share these assumptions. This self-segregation on the part of Europeans has been bitterly resented because their circle has a wider significance in representing the social apex of the entire society. The successful African professional or business man has felt that he has made this grade and has been affronted over his exclusion in a way that he would never have been over rejection by Indian or Lebanese circles. Thus in colonies with a growing native élite the question of racial discrimination in club membership has acquired a significance out of all proportion to the real desires of the parties to obtain or avoid one another's company [5].

A consideration of the role of European women bears upon the same point. In the early years of many colonies the Europeans were an all-male group and, on the West Coast at least, they mixed fairly freely in African social life. When with the improvement of communications and medical services they brought their wives out, they withdrew into their own community [5, 14]. The women met Africans in very few roles other than those of servants and obtained a narrower view of them than their men did; for them the adjective "African" came to symbolize lower material and moral standards, and an encircling majority with whom they themselves had no direct relationships such as to give a sense of purpose to their residence there. This, together with the influence of sexual jealousy, may be responsible for the very general observation that European women express stronger prejudice towards Africans than men do. Among settler populations the women's role of bringing up children and transmitting the cultural heritage increases their resistance to contact with Africans on an equal footing because their influence — especially through the possibility of intermarriage — is seen as a threat to the purity of that heritage [14].

There has been relatively little research into the way cultural factors condition relations between Europeans and Africans. One study [5] emphasized in the first place the European notion of work as a moral obligation, coupled with the central significance of a man's vocation in deciding his social position and prospects. With this was contrasted the African conception of the "big man" as someone who had dependents to work for him. This observation is reinforced by the complaints of settlers and officials in other parts of the continent about the difficulty of getting Africans to undertake paid employment. In the second place, the European assumes that progress is possible and desirable. In a tribal culture based on subsistence farming, surpluses cannot readily be converted into capital; a premium is placed on tradition and a man is pleased to take his ancestors as models without considering the possibility of his improving upon them. In the third place, the European is used to a highly complex form of social organization in which very many relationships are of an impersonal character. The African is used to standing in personal relation to all the people with whom he regularly comes into contact, so it takes time for him to appreciate so different a set of social arrangements. Africans may feel the impersonal manner of Europeans as a form of rejection. Thus a writer on the Congo refers to a departmental head who did not tell his African colleagues that his father had died; they learned the news from another source and commented, "You see, he only regards us as workers, not as people." [44]

A Belgian missionary has demonstrated the significance of such cultural differences for relations between employer and employee [10]. He holds that an examination of tribal law in the Congo reveals contracts to be regarded differently from contracts in European law. An employer and a worker who accepts his offer enter into partnership; the employer is regarded as a somewhat special kind of clan chief and therefore has the chiefly functions of benefactor, guardian and protector. Thus the African worker at first regards the European employer as bound by obligations which the latter does not recognize; when he fails to observe them the African is embittered. The European, on the other hand, regards the African's expectations as evidence of his allegedly childlike nature.

THE STRUCTURE OF CHARACTERISTIC
SOCIAL RELATIONSHIPS

In one of the major contributions to research in this field, Cyril Sofer maintains that while friction arises in part from cultural differences between the racial groups, it stems also, and perhaps more importantly, from the structure of the characteristic social relationships which exist between the groups [46]. He starts from observations of the behaviour at work of Europeans, Asians and Africans in Uganda, and shows how this is influenced by the structure of social life outside the employment situation in the racially stratified total society. The influence, however, is reciprocal, in that patterns of inter-racial behaviour established at work can spread into other situations.

Asked whether they prefer to work under a European or an Asian, Africans show a clear preference for the European. The European, among other things is more interested in keeping Africans at a distance than keeping them subordinate. He owes his racial community an obligation to behave in a dignified and restrained manner. He has a prestige which induces an African to respond more easily and more graciously to his orders. An African is bound by an elaborately deferential etiquette in his interaction with a European. The European does not offer a reciprocal deference in return but he has implicit obligations towards the African to afford him leadership, protection and behavioural models. These obligations provide the justification for his presence in the country and are surrounded by a complex set of official and unofficial sanctions within the European community. The Africans, however, believe that the Europeans do not have African interests at heart, and they are most suspicious of any change proposed by them. Greatest friction arises between Africans and Asians. As the Asian has less prestige than the European, the African is slower to respond to his orders and it is necessary for him to be more vehement to achieve the same result. Squeezed between temporarily immigrant Europeans and the rising African mass, the Asian is anxious to show the European that he is superior to Africans and to disassociate himself from them. The African, on the other hand, knows that the power of an Asian supervisor is closely circumscribed by that of the European. He can challenge any order of his in the security that the European will arbitrate between them. Furthermore, the Asian group readily becomes a scapegoat for African discontents.

Sofer's work also shows how each group's position in the social system is reflected in, and supported by, its view of the society as a whole, of the other groups, and of itself. Thus the European views the system as harnessing European leadership to help Africans attain higher living standards and a greater measure of political autonomy. He thinks of the Asian as hard-working and clever at business, but crafty and devoted exclusively to the pursuit of material wealth. The African he perceives as ignorant, childlike, suspicious and unco-operative. In this way, a social system that in the long run is unstable develops, reinforcing mechanisms which tend to perpetuate existing practices and give the system a temporary equilibrium. A rough correlation between race, education and wealth remains. Europeans meet Africans at work usually in subordinate capacities and mix relatively little with them out of work hours though the comparison to bear in mind here is the extent to which, in a West European or American industrial society, a relatively rich man mingles with clerks and labourers.

A similar conclusion is reached by another sociologist writing from Uganda [16]. The author discusses legal differentiations and shows that in East Africa there are no laws which prevent, or even seriously hamper, informal social relations; while in recent years the exclusion of non-Europeans from the more expensive hotels and other discriminatory practices have been broken down. Informal interracial social life is, however, severely limited by the lack of common interests. Some Europeans, especially Christians of an evangelical inclination, entertain Africans, but, owing to their different housing, income and style of life, Africans do not often invite Europeans home. Both Africans and Europeans are inclined to display hostility toward Indians, mostly only in verbal form, though there are few Europeans who meet Indians socially unless they have business associations. Relations between people of different race are therefore largely, but not entirely, confined to situations in which people of one race are in a superior position and people of another race in an inferior position.

Governmental policy may affect the structure of characteristic relations by bringing members of different groups together in one kind of relationship and by minimizing contact in others. One such policy deserves notice here. When land was allocated to European farmers in Kenya, separate zones were established for the races. In Tanganyika, however, the entire country was regarded as native land. For Europeans, farm blocks of reasonable size were selected within the tribal areas in consultation with the chiefs. This interpenetration of racial settlement lessened the opposition between the races and may have contributed to the relative absence of racial friction in Tanganyika [16].

The patterns of deference behaviour on which Sofer comments have also been described in Swaziland. There every European male expects an African to greet him as *Nkosi* (chief) or *Baas* (master), and every European woman as *Nkosazana* (princess), or, if she be long married, *Nkosikasi* (queen) [23]. When a subordinate refrains from according one of these conventional titles, this is regarded as a repudiation of the customary status and therefore as a serious offence. There is very little material on such patterns, their variation between sections of the population and their changes over time.

EUROPEAN ATTITUDES

European minorities in tropical Africa are subject to considerable social and psychological pressures. This leads to the emphasizing of communal solidarity. Thus a Central African newspaper has been quoted as deploring the readiness of social anthropologists to live in native villages, continuing: "We do not ask sociologists to be Tories. They can be Communists if they like, but they should behave like responsible Europeans. . . ." [40] It also leads them to identify race with culture and to believe that their own way of life can only be maintained by people of the same skin colour: the pressure upholding this belief is far stronger than the authority of scientific evidence to the contrary. Where the political struggle is most severe this belief gives rise to an authentic racist ideology, which, though not yet systematized in any literary form, is evident in such statements as that of a former Prime Minister of the Central African Federation: "Africans, until they are very much advanced, are all liars."[3] It is also evident in the heavily paternalist attitude which has led paternalist employers to treat Africans, and to refer to them, as cattle [44]. However, it would appear that these pressures are the more coercive because the

---

[3] *Parliamentary Debates*, House of Lords (24 March 1959), col. 254.

Europeans are living in a society different from that in which they grew up. An immigrant can never internalize the values of his new culture so effectively as those of the culture of his birth. Thus it has been observed that second generation colonials, whose claim to membership of the society cannot be questioned, are frequently more favourably disposed towards the natives than are their parents, though no experimental study has been carried out in the region under review. Indians, and other intermediary groups, are inclined to avoid racialist arguments; they have suffered from Europeans using them against themselves [37].

Two studies of European minorities merit attention. One [29] deals with the conquest and settlement of Rhodesia, revealing very clearly the forces responsible for the climate of opinion in the white community. . . . [One] is chiefly concerned with Southern Rhodesia. . . . The other [30] is a preliminary report on the European population of Dakar. The author underlines the consequences of the diversification of both major racial groups, leading on the one hand to a concern with maintaining "white prestige" which is largely responsible for the disapproval of interracial marriage. This opposition is justified by a "shame-faced racialism" which people insist is the outcome of experience and not of any pre-conceptions. He emphasizes the importance of numerical relations; this accords with the position in rural areas where educated African civil servants often find that they can associate freely with European colleagues on a small station but are kept at a distance on a larger one [15]. Except for the African élite, European contact with Dakar Africans is very largely restricted to contacts at work, which is in line with Sofer's aphorism "race relations stop at half past four." An American anthropologist has attempted a brief comparison of the extent of racial discrimination under the different systems of colonial administration in West Africa in the 1940's [6]. But while the legal rights of Africans under the different systems have been compared, reliable data on differences in day-to-day conduct are unavailable.

A notable contribution to the study of the colonial situation and the unconscious motivations of the parties involved is to be found in a psychoanalytic study based on observations in Madagascar [28]. This constitutes a commentary from a particular standpoint on almost the whole range of factors discussed here; it offers the reader a new insight into the position rather than any concrete results. The author's argument is not easily summarized. He maintains that traditional tribal society conditions its members to a feeling of dependence upon one another; when they are confronted with people, like adult Europeans, having the independent personality associated with a competitive society, they have difficulty in adapting to the situation. At first they are apt to see in the European the master, the protector and the scapegoat. The Europeans who go out to the colonies are apt to be such as have inferiority feelings disposing them to aggressiveness and the domination of others, and when the institutional supports of social life in Europe are removed these tendencies become sharper. The European does not understand the native peoples' expectations of the relationship thus created or is inclined to distort what he does know in order to preserve the image of the native as someone on to whom he can project his own repressions. Their own predicament prevents the Europeans from weaning the native group from their dependence and consequently there comes a time when the latter feel harshly rejected; their dependence then turns to a sharp animosity and may result in armed uprising. As so many of these tensions are present in the triangular relationship between Prospero, Caliban, and Miranda, the European's conception of his position of domination has been well named the "Prospero complex."

AFRICAN ATTITUDES

One of the few studies to describe European-African relations in a rural district also casts light upon the position of Swaziland, one of the British-administered High Commission territories [23]. Swaziland is politically an island bounded on all sides by the Union of South Africa on which it is economically dependent as providing employment for migrant labour. Stereotypes similar to those found in other regions are reported. Thus the whites think of the Swazi as "just like children," able to imitate but not to reason for themselves, happy, stupid, ignorant of any notion of gratitude, etc., while at the same time there are preconceptions showing a mixture of envy and patronage. The Swazi also hold distorted ideas about the whites. They say that all Europeans look alike (this is a widely reported characteristic of interracial contact). By comparison with themselves, they see Europeans as more skilful but less kind, more powerful but less generous; their skill and power is described as something almost fortuitous — part of the white man and his heritage — not as the culmination of years of experiment by rational methods that the Swazi could themselves employ. Swazi parents frighten children with stories of the white bogeyman. The stories they tell emphasize European greed, and lack of manners and hospitality.

Colour, says Hilda Kuper, is a uniform that cannot be discarded. Some whites are proficient in Swazi culture and identify themselves more with the Swazi than with the whites but they are still described as Europeans. They can, if they wish, still enjoy the legal privileges of their colour group and, as soon as they move from the familiar surroundings, are treated by other people as white. Similarly Swazi may be educated, well dressed, practising Christians, admitted to the homes of some Europeans, but still denied the legal privileges, economic benefits and reciprocal courtesies of the white group. Interracial marriage is condemned from both sides so that Europeans married to or living with Swazi women have little contact with other whites. It is clear, therefore, that were it not for the exercise of political domination by the ruling minority, race would lose much of its significance as a status symbol.

The Swaziland study is concerned with relations in an area from which labour migrants go to the employment centres of the Union of South Africa, and has little to say of the effect of returned migrants upon race relations. Another study which concentrates upon the whole process of labour migration [42] shows how the absence of the men and the attachment to urban patterns of living have a disintegrative effect upon tribal life. This study, also, refrains from considering the effect of migration upon the development of African racial attitudes, and more recent work — which might be expected to show this effect more clearly — is lacking.

Labour migration is also an important feature of African life in the Central African territories. Research in Northern Rhodesia [49] draws attention to the fact that, in some circumstances, industrial employment does not appear to affect the retention by Africans of their tribal identity, nor their adherence to tribal chiefs. The returned worker resumes tribal ways because his claims to land are bound up with the whole nexus of relationships that form tribal society. He is content to recognize the authority of his traditional rulers, and if he is ambitious of political power, he seeks this within the traditional system. In such circumstances, Africans will cling to their rights in land and the tribal institutions that go with them. Most Africans say that they would prefer to stay in the reserves if they could earn sufficient money there, for this environment offers them a psychological security absent from urban life where social control is relatively slight. Where cash cropping is feasible, rural emigration is therefore reduced, but in most parts of Rhodesia (though not Nyasaland) cash cropping is made difficult for several reasons, chief among them being the inadequacy of transport facilities and the fact that the land closest to the industrial market is taken up by European farmers.

Two consequences of this situation merit attention. In the first place, Africans have seen recent political changes as threatening traditional rights in land, and the chiefs, as trustees for the land, have been forced to oppose the proposals for federation. Resistance has taken the form of refusal to observe agricultural, fishing and game regulations, so that recalcitrant chiefs have been deposed. In the second place, recent rises in African wages have forced employers to reconsider the advantages of a stable labour force. To bring this about, further changes will be necessary in order to encourage Africans to make their homes in the towns. In day-to-day intercourse with Europeans they are constantly reminded of how they are looked upon as inferior and all too commonly regarded with contempt. The discrepancy between African and European wages when related to the skills and productivity of the two categories remains striking and breeds discontent. As late as 1952 African wages in Southern Rhodesia were still on the average less than 7 per cent of those of Europeans and a similar discrepancy existed in Northern Rhodesia [50, 20].

A distinctive approach of considerable value in the study of race relations is that which seizes upon the observation of actual behaviour in social situations and seeks to explain it by taking account of the way the situation is structured both by large-scale socio-economic factors and small-scale ones such as the obligations of particular relationships. This approach has been particularly fruitful in analysing the problem of "tribalism" which has puzzled a number of commentators. While urban relations are often taken as evidence of the decline of tribalism, developments in some spheres point to a heightening of the sense of tribal identity and even in the towns tribal affiliation remains important in some circumstances. J. Clyde Mitchell has shown that two phenomena are often confused under the label "tribalism": tribal structure, as a total system of relationships in the rural area, and tribalism, as a category of interaction within a wider urban system [32]. Tribal allegiance has a different situational relevance in the two contexts. Where Africans find themselves associated with fellow tribesmen in opposition to other groups they express their unity in tribal terms; this occurs both in rural and urban areas. But where they find themselves associated with other Africans of different tribes in opposition to Europeans, they express their unity in racial terms and ignore the tribal differences. The same principle applies with class differences: where people are grouped on class lines they regard racial and tribal differences as irrelevant. However, it sometimes happens that tribal and class lines coincide, with the result that the interests of a socio-economic category are expressed as if they were those of a tribal group [12]. Racial friction is more frequent in industrial areas because it is there that social groupings more frequently form along racial lines and not because of the disposition of the parties as individuals, though psychological forces frequently reinforce the opposition. This analysis has been supplemented by a similar one concerned with the growth of industrial and political organization in an African urban community originally administered along tribal lines [12].

When African groups are continuously lined up in opposition to whites, a form of social demarcation becomes reinforced by a variety of psychological processes, leading members of each bloc to regard the other with great suspicion and to interpret ostensibly benevolent behaviour in terms of such preconceptions. One account of the clash of different assumptions in the classroom of a Uganda secondary school [34] underlines the prevalence in East Africa of the belief that Europeans are cannibals, the preservation of traditional beliefs about causation independently of the acceptance of scientific explanations, and the African schoolboys' suspicion that they might not be getting a completely genuine European education. The belief that Europeans are holding back from dependent peoples the last and most vital secret of their power is widespread; it is found in Melanesian cargo cults and the idea that the Europeans have removed the first page from the Bible they give to natives; similar evidence has been reported from Africa, like the story of the Belgian priest in the Congo who lost his breviary and discovered that a newly ordained African had borrowed it to compare it page by page with his own [44].

Essays written by African schoolchildren frequently reveal an ambivalence between emulation of the white man in certain specific connexions and a violent rejection of anything seeming to imply political subordination. One detailed study from Northern Rhodesia [39] found that boys identified themselves with Europeans more strongly than girls, and that they were more favourably disposed towards the whites. This was attributed to the greater contact African men have with Europeans in the course of their work. Because of the employment situation European culture has been in large measure transferred directly to African men, to the almost complete exclusion of African women. Though there is evidence that some tribes valued a light skin colour before European influence spread [2], the colonial order has in general enshrined white values and encouraged their dissemination.

In the development of African attitudes towards Europeans, the second world war had a tremendous impact throughout the colonies, quite apart from the stimulus it gave to economic development. African soldiers were taught to have no regard for the racial status of enemy Europeans. African soldiers had seen Europeans defeated in battle and as prisoners-of-war; they had seen other lands, come to appreciate that very many Europeans were of a very different kind from colonial administrators, and some had gone with white prostitutes. Such experiences removed much of the strangeness about the figure of the European and emphasized the common humanity of all races. A short study of developments in the Congo [44], while referring to this, also brings out very clearly a point which is fully in accordance with observations from elsewhere: that African demands upon the colonial administration have arisen out of the experiences of everyday life and have been very little influenced by more general considerations. In the Congo, as elsewhere, much of the fuel for nationalist fires has been supplied by discrimination in the salaries paid to the different races, by the contrast between the standard of living of the Africans and the Europeans, and by the incivility of the latter in their dealings with Africans. One political reaction to the feeling that they are scorned by Europeans which has been reported from several regions, but which has received little attention in academic writings, is the African claim that the Europeans who come to the colonies represent only the lower classes of their native country. This has been described as a feature of native racialism [28] but it would seem more justified to regard it as a belief that enables the subject group to retain its self-respect by denying that the aliens' criticism has any force.

RELIGIOUS MOVEMENTS

Religious institutions frequently provide an outlet of the expression of sentiments that are of a secular character. Thus it has been suggested that the success of Islam in West Africa is in part due to its presentation as an African religion providing a cultural foundation for an African grouping on a wider basis than that of tribal membership and standing in opposition to the Europeans [5]. In the early years of this century British writers sometimes saw African Muslims as more militant than pagans in their opposition to European influence. But it is doubtful if this proposition would find support today; nor does it appear that Christian groups are more apt to be nationalistic than pagan ones [11].

Relations between European missionaries and their African congregations are affected considerably by the balance of political power. A Protestant speaker commenting on his tour of mission stations has remarked: "In a few areas the social segregation of the Africans seemed to be conditioned largely by the social segregation and discrimination of government officials of the country. Settlers in some areas had passed on their colour-bar relations to the missionary groups and the two white groups reinforced one another by their acts of discrimination. Some of the missionaries seemed to have brought their prejudices with them to Africa. Their self-appointed superior roles were supported by a paternalism which had been established by their missionary predecessors." [38] Catholic and Anglo-Catholic missionaries have tended to lead a more primitive existence closer to their converts [35] but they have been certainly no less disposed to paternalism. However, missionaries mix more freely with Africans than do most other whites in their territories, and when the Africans have effectively challenged colonial rule the missions have been obliged to demonstrate their independence of the administration and of white authority. In any case, the interests of the administration and the missions conflict on a number of points. As the Swaziland study shows, the administration works through traditional leaders and maintains existing customs. The missions work through individual converts drawn from any stratum; they judge by reference to independent criteria and support their members in refusing to conform to customs they consider repugnant [23]. But any open break between the two is usually delayed because the missions are dependent upon support from the administration and the latter values the social services provided by the missions.

It is widely held that independent African churches serve as an institutional means of expressing nationalist, and occasionally anti-European, sentiment. Their churches have frequently seceded from a mission church: they have African ministers, a more colourful form of service, and make more concessions to such practices as polygyny.[4] Some of these churches seem to be largely of secular inspiration, like the National Church of Nigeria and the Cameroons which has functioned as a kind of ecclesiastical instrument of radical nationalism in eastern Nigeria [19]. In the messianic movements that have been so influential in the Congo [1, 3] it is more difficult to differentiate sacred and secular elements or to isolate the different social functions which the movements serve. Georges Balandier has argued with much justice that they transfer to the spiritual and ecclesiastical plane opposition to European authority in general. On this plane the reconstruction of African communities under African leadership can be effected: a process which is particularly liable to occur under an authoritarian colonial system where "religion is the only field within which emancipation is possible." [3] These movements frequently give expression to strong animosity against Europeans [1] and might be said to awaken racial consciousness amongst the illiterate masses. This view of messianic movements as a forerunner of political nationalism is reinforced both by Efraim Andersson's argument in his admirably documented survey that they are by no means the product of Protestant missionary work [1] and by more recent evidence of their role in the Leopoldville riots of January 1959 [22]. The religious factor also enters at several points into the analysis of the Mau Mau rising in Kenya. A psychiatrist has claimed that the Africans who hated the Europeans most intensely were those who had accepted Christianity but later found that white and supposedly Christian people had after all an exclusive group religion like the one the Kikuyu used to have themselves [9]. In Kenyatta's work separatist churches are presented as part of the nationalist movement [21]. The Mau Mau organization utilized many religious forms of expression and they seem to have played an essential role in building up mass support [24].

CONCLUSION

Recent developments in Africa prove the desirability of drawing a sharp distinction between those studies of race relations which seek to answer questions of public policy and those which concentrate upon scientific problems concerning inter-group relations. The foundation for studies of the latter kind has been laid by sociologists, psychologists and others working in America and Europe. Many fields of research, such as those

---

[4] The comparative evidence on the role of "Ethiopianism" has been reviewed at the conclusion of an analysis of the Nyasaland rising of 1915 [43].

dealing with the psychology of prejudice, social distance, normative influences upon industrial productivity, etc., could benefit if relevant findings were to be further tested in African contexts. Psychologists have recently elaborated procedures for attitude testing in Africa which could be used for inquiries into racial relations, but their results are not yet available [36, 41]. Sociologists and social anthropologists have provided illuminating analyses of conduct in situations of racial contact but more attention to general theoretical issues might assist them in pointing out which questions most require investigation and in organizing the diffuse experience which they acquire as parties to interracial relations.

Bibliography

1. Andersson, Efraim. *Messianic Popular Movements in the Lower Congo.* Uppsala, 1958. (*Studia ethnographica upsaliensia,* XIV.)
2. Ardener, E. "Some Ibo Attitudes towards Skin Pigmentation," *Man* 1954, no. 101, pp. 71-3.
3. Balandier, Georges. *Sociologie actuelle de l'Afrique noire.* Paris: Presses Universitaires de France, 1955.
4. ———. "Race Relations in West and Central Africa," in A. W. Lind, ed. *Race Relations in World Perspective.* Hawaii University Press, 1955, pp. 145-66.
5. Banton, Michael. *West African City: A Study of Tribal Life in Freetown.* London: Oxford University Press, 1957.
6. Bascom, William R. "West and Central Africa," in Ralph Linton, ed. *Most of the World.* Columbia University Press, 1949. See especially, pp. 377-86.
7. Brausch, G. E. J. B. "The Problem of Élites in the Belgian Congo," *International Social Science Bulletin* 8, 1956, pp. 452-7.
8. Busia, K. A. "The Present Situation and Aspirations of Élites in the Gold Coast," *International Social Science Bulletin* 8, 1956, pp. 424-31.
9. Carothers, J. C. *The Psychology of Mau Mau.* Nairobi: Government Printer, 1954.
10. Charles, Rev. P. Pierre. "Tribal Society and Labour Legislation," *International Labour Review,* 65, 1952, pp. 426-41.
11. Coleman, James S. *Nigeria: Background to Nationalism.* California University Press, 1958.
12. Epstein, A. L. *Politics in an Urban African Community.* Manchester University Press, 1958.
13. Fallers, Lloyd A. *Bantu Bureaucracy: A Study of Conflict and Change in the Political Institutions of an East African People.* Cambridge: Heffer, 1956.
14. Gann, L. H. *The Birth of a Plural Society.* Manchester University Press, 1958.

15. Goldthorpe, J. E. "An African Élite," *British Journal of Sociology* 6, 1955, pp. 31-47.
16. ———. *Outlines of East African Society.* Kampala, 1958.
17. Gussman, Boris. "Industrial Efficiency and the Urban African," *Africa* 23, 1953, pp. 135-44.
18. Gutkind, Peter C. W. "Some African Attitudes to Multi-Racialism from Uganda, British East Africa," *Pluralisme ethnique et culturel dans les sociétés intertropicales.* Bruxelles: Institut International des Civilisations différentes, 1957, pp. 338-55.
19. Hodgkin, Thomas. *Nationalism in Colonial Africa.* London: Muller, 1956.
20. International Labour Office. *African Labour Survey.* Geneva, 1958.
21. Kenyatta, Jomo. *Facing Mount Kenya.* London: Secker and Warburg, 1938.
22. Köbben, A. J. F. "Prophetic Movements as an Expression of Social Protest," *International Archives of Ethnography* 49, 1960, pp. 117-64.
23. Kuper, Hilda. *The Uniform of Colour: A Study of White-Black Relationships in Swaziland.* Johannesburg: Witwatersrand Press, 1947.
24. Leakey, L. S. B. *Defeating Mau Mau.* London: Methuen, 1954.
25. Little, Kenneth, "The Significance of the West African Creole for Africanist and Afro-American Studies," *African Affairs* 49, 1950, pp. 308-19.
26. ———. "The African Élite in British West Africa," in A. W. Lind, ed. *Race Relations in World Perspective.* Hawaii, 1955, pp. 263-88.
27. Malengreau, G. "Observations on the Orientation of Sociological Researchers in African Urban Centres, with Reference to the Situation in the Belgian Congo," *Social Implications of Industrialization and Urbanization in Africa South of the Sahara.* Prepared under the auspices of Unesco by the International African Institute, London. Paris: Unesco, 1956, pp. 624-38.
28. Mannoni, O. *Prospero and Caliban.* London, Methuen, 1956. (Translation of *Psychologie de la colonisation*, Paris, 1950.)
29. Mason, Philip. *The Birth of a Dilemma: The Conquest and Settlement of Rhodesia.* London: Oxford University Press, 1958.
30. Mercier, P. "Le groupement européen à Dakar: orientation d'une enquête," *Cahiers internationals de sociologie* 19, 1955, pp. 130-46.
31. ———. "Evolution of Senegalese Élite," *International Social Science Bulletin* 8, 1956, pp. 441-52.
32. Mitchell, J. Clyde. *The Kalela Dance.* Manchester University Press, 1956. (*Rhodes-Livingstone Paper*, no. 27.)
33. Moreira, A. "The 'Élites' of the Portuguese Tribal Provinces," *International Social Science Bulletin* 8, 1956, pp. 458-81.
34. Musgrove, F. "A Uganda Secondary School as a Field of Cultural Change," *Africa* 22, 1952, pp. 234-8.
35. Oliver, Roland. *The Missionary Factor in East Africa.* London: Longmans, 1952.
36. Ombredane, H. "Principes pour une étude psychologique des noirs du Congo belge," *L'année psychologique* 50, Paris, 1951, pp. 521-47.
37. Parker, Mary. "Race relations and political development in Kenya," *African Affairs* 50, 1951, pp. 41-52, 133.

38. Parsons, Robert T. "Missionary-African Relations," *Civilisations* 3, 1953, pp. 505-16.
39. Powdermaker, Hortense. "Social Change through Imagery and Values of Teen-age Africans in Northern Rhodesia," *American Anthropologist* 58, 1956, pp. 783-813.
40. Richmond, Anthony H. *The Colour Problem: Revised Edition*. Harmondsworth: Penguin Books, 1961.
41. Rogers, Cyril A. "A Study of Race Attitudes in Nigeria," *Rhodes-Livingstone Journal* 26, 1959, pp. 51-64.
42. Schapera, I. *Migrant Labour and Tribal Life*. London: Oxford University Press, 1947.
43. Shepperson, George; Price, George. *Independent African: John Chitembowe and the Nyasaland Rising of 1915*. Edinburgh University Press, 1959.
44. Slade, Ruth. *The Belgian Congo: Some Recent Changes*. London: Oxford University Press, 1960.
45. Sofer, Cyril. "Some Aspects of Race Relations in an East African Township." Unpublished Ph.D. thesis, London University, 1953.
46. ————. "Working groups in a plural society," *Industrial and Labour Relations Review* 8, 1954, pp. 68-78.
47. Sofer, Cyril; Ross, Rhona. "Some Characteristics of an East African European Population," *British Journal of Sociology* 2, 1951, pp. 315-27.
48. Ward, Barbara. "Research on Racial Relations: East Africa," *International Social Sciences Bulletin* 10, 1958, pp. 372-86.
49. Watson, William. *Tribal Cohesion in a Money Economy: A Study of the Mambwe People of Northern Rhodesia*. Manchester University Press, 1958.
50. ————. "The Social Background," in Colin Leys and Crauford Pratt, eds. *New Deal in Central Africa*. London: Heinemann, 1960, pp. 138-57.

II

In Brazil, race and class work together to form the distinctive pattern of race relations. There is little racial discrimination and little avowed belief in the importance of race in determining jobs and education. There are, too, a wide variety of racial categories, perhaps sixteen or more, and assignment is very unreliable. But racial differences seem to be important despite the rhetoric which denies this; the blackest in the population make up a disproportionate part of the lowest class. Regional differences are important, too; inland Negroes may be actively discriminated against. The factors of race, class, individual family, and region are carefully treated in this account by Charles Wagley.

CHARLES WAGLEY

From Caste to Class in North Brazil

In 1500, before the Portuguese arrived in the New World, the population of the area of South America which is now Brazil consisted of approximately 1,500,000 Indians divided into numerous linguistic and tribal groups. There was no unity among these peoples; instead each tribe,

From *Race and Class in Rural Brazil*, 2nd edition, edited by Charles Wagley, Unesco International Documents Service (New York: Columbia University Press, 1963), pp. 143-155, 157-158. Reprinted by permission of the author and the publisher.

sometimes each village, lived in a state of intense suspicion of its neighbours. Warfare was almost continuous between many tribes, and the native population did not offer any unified resistance to the Portuguese newcomers. After 1500, there was a rapid disintegration of organized Indian society under the constant pressure of the aggressive Europeans. The Portuguese did not come to Brazil to work. At first they were content to trade with the Indians for Brazilwood, but they soon turned to enslaving the native peoples in order to secure labour to make gardens which would provide them with food and to perform other tasks. Expeditions were organized to penetrate into the interior to capture Indian slaves. Despite the constant efforts of the Jesuits and other religious orders to protect the Indians from the slave-hungry colonists, and despite the laws promulgated by the Portuguese Crown against Indian slavery, the colonists continued to make slaves of the aboriginal peoples throughout the first two centuries of Brazilian history. The originally sparse aboriginal population was thus drastically reduced by slavery, by the wars made upon them by the Portuguese, and by European diseases against which they had no specific immunity. Whole tribes migrated inland to escape the ravages of the Portuguese and, by 1750, few Indians remained in the coastal fringe which was the effective area of the Portuguese colony.

It was soon apparent to the European, especially after the introduction of sugar cane in the middle of the sixteenth century, that they must look elsewhere for slaves. As early as 1538 the first African slaves were imported into Brazil. A period which lasted over 200 years began, during which there was a steady flow of Negroes across the Atlantic to Brazil. A very conservative estimate has it that approximately 3,300,000 Negro slaves entered Brazil in the seventeenth and eighteenth centuries alone, but the number was probably greater [2].[1] For a time, during the colonial period, there were more African slaves in Brazil than Europeans.

Brazil was founded as a society formed of two distinct castes[2] — namely, a caste of European masters and a caste of Indian or Negro slaves. Brazilian society, however, consisted exclusively of castes for only a very short time. Intermediate social groups began to take form almost immediately after 1500. In fact, when the Portuguese arrived to settle in Salvador (Bahia), which was one of the first settlements along the coast, they found Indian half-breeds. The famous Caramurú (Diego Alvares Correia), a Portuguese sailor who had probably been left there by a

[1] The figures in brackets refer to the references on page 61.
[2] The term "caste" is used in the sense that it is used by North American sociologists to describe "Negro-white" relations in the United States. "Caste" is used thus for an endogamous and hereditary group which in the two cases (i.e., North America and early colonial Brazil) were made up of racial groups. See Gunnar Myrdal, *An American Dilemma* (New York, 1944), pp. 667-69; and John Dollard, *Caste and Class in a Southern Town* (New Haven, 1937).

French boat as early as 1509-11, was found living with his numerous children by various Indian women [2]. Very few Portuguese women came to Brazil in the first days of the colony, and the Portuguese men are said to have found the Indian women exceedingly attractive. Miscegenation between Portuguese males and Indian women began almost at once; the *mamelucos*, the offspring of these unions, were raised as freemen and the European whites took wives from among the half-breed and quarter-breed women. A group of European-Indian *mestiços* were formed who stood midway between the European *élite* and the Indian slaves.

Race mixture continued with ever-increasing speed after the arrival of African slaves in large numbers. The Portuguese plantation owners, their sons and relatives took concubines from among the Negro slaves and the sons of these white fathers and Negro mothers were often given special treatment. They were taught to be administrators on plantations; they were made freemen; and they were often educated — a few were even sent to Portugal, where they attended the famous University of Coimbra. Soon mulattoes were represented among the professional classes as lawyers and physicians, they entered the priesthood and public life [3], and not only mulattoes but also Negroes gained their liberty and entered the economic and public life of the Colony during slave times. As Frank Tannenbaum has shown in his excellent essay entitled *Slave and Citizen* [4], one of the characteristics of slavery in Latin America which distinguished it from slavery in the English colonies and in the United States was the numerous methods provided in Latin America for manumission. By 1798 there were 406,000 free Negroes living in Brazil, and by the time of abolition in 1888 it is estimated that there were three times as many Negro freemen as Negro slaves [5]. These freemen — Negroes, mulattoes, and others of part Negro descent — formed a series of social strata between the European slave-owning caste and the lowly slaves.

Almost at once the relations between the Portuguese masters and their Indian and Negro slaves began to produce intermediary social strata between the two castes. By the end of slavery, the intermediate freeman class made up of people of Negroid, Indian and Caucasian racial stocks, and of a wide variety of *mestiços*, was numerically more important than the white *élite* or the Negro slaves. With abolition in 1888 the slaves entered Brazilian society as freemen, although at the bottom of the social hierarchy. Then in the late nineteenth and early twentieth centuries a relatively large number of European workers entered the country to join the ex-slaves and low-class freemen as labourers on plantations and in industry. Meantime, many land-holding families of "pure" European descent lost their aristocratic status and their dominant political position as they became less wealthy or even impoverished; many aristocrats have dropped in social status from the "white *élite* caste" to the level of the people who were descendants of slaves. Simultaneously, individuals who were descendants of slaves or low-class freemen have improved their economic and social standing; people of mixed racial ancestry and descendants of recent European immigrants have so prospered that they are represented among the financial and politically dominating class of the country. Especially since the formation of the Republic, politics has offered a road to social advancement, and many Brazilian families n v of high rank first came to the fore during the early Republic; the "old families" of colonial aristocrats have intermarried with this new upper class, and the old European caste has been broken down throughout most of the country. *Where Brazilian society was once formed by castes, it has now become a society of social classes which are themselves undergoing rapid change.*

Class lines are still rigidly drawn in Brazil. The descendants of the old white aristocracy with the new upper class which results from new fortunes and from relatively recent political success, form a small upper class which maintains many of the ideals of the old slave-owning aristocratic caste. These people follow a comfortable, even luxurious, way of life with all the educational advantages, the forms of recreation, and the technological equipment available to the economically well-off in any modern Western country. There is, however, a rapidly expanding middle class which is comprised of government employees, professional groups, commercial and industrial employees, owners of small business enterprises, and so on. The members of this Brazilian middle class generally identify themselves with the upper class, sharing to a great extent in their "aristocratic" values and ideals, and follow an upper-class pattern of life so far as their smaller incomes allow. They differ thus from the middle class of other Western countries which forms the numerical backbone of the nation and is proud of its values and way of life. Finally, in modern Brazil there is a large "lower-class," mostly illiterate, whose miserable standard of living offers a striking contrast to that of the contemporary upper class, even to that of the growing middle class. It is composed of the many subsistence farmers throughout the country, the workers on plantations, the industrial workers, the domestic servants, and the innumerable groups of people who perform manual labour of all sorts.

The numerical importance of these three contemporary social classes is difficult to estimate with precision. A study made of Brazilian national income a few years back, however, provides us with a basis for an estimate. According to Dr. Henry W. Spiegel, in 1944 a total of only 300,000 people, comprising only 2.5 per cent of those gainfully employed, received 30 per cent of the total national income, and another 2.5 per cent received 20 per cent. Thus, 5 per cent of those gainfully employed received 50 per cent of the national income; in economic terms, this 5 per cent represents the upper class. Urban workers contributing to the various social insurance organizations formed 24 per cent of those gainfully employed, but received only 20 per cent of the national income; although numerous groups are excluded from this figure, this seems to represent the situation and numerical importance of the middle class in modern Brazilian society. The agriculturalists (the small farmer, the sharecropper, the agricultural wage-earner) made up no less than 71 per cent of those gainfully employed and yet received only 30 per cent of the national income [6]. These latter, plus numerous others whose incomes are so insignificant that they are never recorded, make up the great lower class of modern Brazil.

Unfortunately, there are no similar studies which might allow us to estimate accurately the racial composition of these nation-wide class groups. However, most Brazilians and most foreign students of Brazil wonder that the upper class is composed almost exclusively of European whites or people "in whom the traces of Indian or Negro blood are infinitesimal." [7] The middle class is also predominantly Caucasoid, though numerous *mestiços* of various racial backgrounds have been able to ascend into this group. It is in the lower classes that the large mass of Negroes, of mulattoes, of people with American Indian characteristics, and of *pardos* (the convenient Brazilian term meaning "brown" which is used for people of all racial mixtures) are found. Although a process of "bleaching" — or progressive tendency of the Brazilian population toward a generalized Caucasoid appearance — is probably taking place, the homogeneous "Brazilian race" predicted by many authors is still in the future. Today, class lines generally divide the more Caucasoid Brazilians from those who might be called "people of colour." As yet, economic opportunities and educational advantages have not been extended to the rural masses nor even to all the urban poor; thus, the majority of the "people of colour" remain in the lower class. *It is thus still a general rule throughout Brazil that the people of the upper class are almost exclusively Caucasian in appearance, and the majority of the "people of colour" are found in the middle and lower classes.*

In the rural communities which have been described in this report, a shift from a caste society to a society based upon social classes has taken place, it has throughout the country. But the class system has not suffered the more recent influences of industrialization, of modern ideology, and of other innovations to the degree that other parts of Brazil have felt them. More is retained of the nineteenth century in these communities than in the large metropolitan centres on the coast.

All the social classes of a nation are never, of course, present in any one local community, and those described in the four rural communities of our study represent only a segment of the social strata present in the nation as a whole; yet they may be equated in a general way with those of the nation. Since all these communities are relatively isolated and are situated in agricultural areas, analogous social classes may be with one exception found in all four communities. The approximate relationship of the social classes in the four communities may be equated with those of the nation and with one another as shown in Table 1.

Only in the sugar-producing region of the Bahian Recôncavo are there representatives of the national upper class. In the community of Vila Recôncavo, sugar-producing has continued to provide an adequate profit since the early seventeenth century. Despite many fluctuations of price and despite the blow of abolition, the old landowning aristocrats have been able to maintain their hold on numerous plantations. Today, their existence is being threatened by large corporations which are establishing modern sugar mills in the area and purchasing plantations; but in turn the directors of these corporations, who are frequently of the new upper class deriving from political and financial success, tend to identify themselves with and to marry into the old plantation families.

The old aristocrats have disappeared from Minas Velhas and Itá, and may never have existed in Monte Serrat. There was a time in the past, however, when each of these communities had a traditionally wealthy

TABLE 1. BRAZILIAN SOCIAL CLASSES: IN THE COMMUNITY AND IN THE NATION

National	Vila Recôncavo	Minas Velhas	Monte Serrat	Itá
Upper class	Aristocrats	Not present Brancos-Ricos	Not present "Os Bons"	Not present
Middle class	Local upper class	(white-rich) Class A ⎯⎯⎯⎯⎯ Class B 1	(big shots) Class I ⎯⎯⎯⎯⎯ Class II A	"First Class" or "Os Brancos" (the whites)
Lower class	Local middle class	Preto-Pobre (negro-poor) Class B 2	"Os Pobres" (the poor) Class II B	"Second Class" (lower class town-dwellers) ⎯⎯⎯⎯⎯ "Farmers" (Rural lower class) ⎯⎯⎯⎯⎯
	Local lower class	Class C	Class III	"Collectors" (rural lower class)

N.B. The dotted lines represent social cleavages between important segments of a social class; the solid lines cleavages between social classes. Although the term "class" has been used by Hutchinson, Harris and Zimmerman to describe important social and economic segments of the prestige and status hierarchy of the communities under study, it is agreed that on the basis of multiple criteria for class placement Minas Velhas, Monte Serrat, and Itá are two-class societies, and that Vila Recôncavo has but three classes when considered in the broader perspective of the region or the nation. The functionally important classification of people as *branco-rico—preto-pobre* (Minas Velhas) or as *os Bons—os Pobres* (Monte Serrat) cuts across important social and economic groups present in each community. As each author has shown, however, it is this cleavage which is important in these communities in determining status and personal relations.

class. When mining was a more lucrative enterprise, during the eighteenth and early nineteenth centuries, Minas Velhas was the centre of a prosperous aristocratic class the members of which, although perhaps not as socially acceptable or as powerful politically as the sugar aristocrats on the coast, certainly belonged to the national upper class. During the period when there were enormous ranches in the *sertão*, some people were wealthy and well-educated enough to be recognized in the coastal cities as "traditional families" of the upper class. Even the small town of Itá had members of the regional and national aristocracy during the great rubber boom. There was a "Baron of Itá," a title granted by the Emperor Pedro II, and the wealthy rubber traders were recognized in the large city of Belém as people of importance in the region. In Minas Velhas and Itá, however, as the basis of their wealth disappeared members of upper-class families moved away, seeking to maintain their standard of living elsewhere and by other means. The individuals of this class who remained have been forced to stay and to earn their living as others in the community and have, so to speak, "lost caste" — lost their identity as a separate aristocratic group. This process was an important one; it has produced in three communities of our study — and in numerous others like them throughout rural Brazil — a less rigid class system than existed before, and one in which economic, educational and personal factors more often provide the means of social advancement. The absence of the old aristocratic caste in these communities has led to greater social mobility — to a local society without any absolute barriers to upward social ascension.

The "local upper class" of Vila Recôncavo, the "*brancos ricos*" of Minas Velhas, "*os bons*" of Monte Serrat, and the first class (or "*os brancos*") of Itá are, in each case, the local representatives of the national middle class. In lieu of the national upper class, these groups form the upper social and economic strata of the local community. The "local upper class" is a rapidly-growing group in rural Brazil including federal, State, and municipal employees, small landowners, business people, and professionals of all kinds. It is into this class that people of the lower class rise when they become educated or improve their economic condition; and it is in this class also that the competition for relative social rank is most intense.

Likewise, the lower classes of all four communities are generally equivalent to each other and to the lower class of the nation as a whole. Their occupations differ somewhat, although the small subsistence farmer is present in all four communities; in Itá there are rubber collectors; in Minas Velhas, artisans; in Vila Recôncavo, labourers on the sugar plantations, workers in the mill, and fishermen; and in Monte Serrat, *vaqueiros* (cowboys) and a few artisans. Everywhere this class is made up of people who do manual labour. Everywhere these people, like the industrial and manual workers of the cities, have a low standard of living.

The composition of these social classes in the four communities gives us important clues as to the nature of race relations in rural Brazil. First, the "aristocrats" of Vila Recôncavo contain not a single individual who is not Caucasian in physical appearance or who is known to have Negroid ancestors. This class, as stated earlier, is almost national in scope and has been enlarged by the addition of people who have been successful financially and politically in the recent past. With the addition of these people to the upper class, individuals who are known to have a Negro ancestor have been accepted by the aristocrats in other communities and in big cities; even members of the old aristocracy, such as those found in Vila Recôncavo, claim Indian ancestors in the distant past. But in the experience of the authors, there are no members of this class who are Negroid in appearance or who are even dark *mestiços*, although there have been exceptions to this rule in the past, and there must be a few exceptions even today. *With rare exceptions, the people of the upper class of Brazil are Caucasian in physical appearance.*

In the four communities studied the "local upper class" groups, representing the national middle class, are also predominantly white in physical appearance. But numerous people of mixed ancestry have entered these groups, and there are many cases of people with both Indian and Negroid physical appearance who are classed as upper-class in local terms. The people who make up these local upper-class groups are generally those who have climbed socially and economically, and it is noteworthy that fewer Negroes and dark *mestiços* have achieved this position than whites. The criteria for placing an individual in this group are numerous and vary somewhat from community to community; but *it may be said that in all the communities studied one's income, the kind of work one does, one's education, one's family (in varying degrees), and finally, one's physical appearance, are the main criteria used.* The individuals of each community might be graded in a separate prestige series according to each of these criteria, but the social position of any individual in the community derives from the total effect of all these principal criteria as well as from others which are less important and sometimes local in scope. Thus a man might be poor, but have a white collar job, a secondary education, be a descendant of a locally well-known family, be Caucasian in physical appearance and be placed in the local upper class; or he might be a Negro but have the other qualifications for membership in the local upper class and be so classified. These criteria for class are given different value — or different weight, so to speak — in the various communities; thus racial characteristics seem to have greater importance in Minas Velhas than in the other three communities studied, and a Negro who has all other qualifications is excluded from the upper stratum simply because he is a Negro. The position of an individual according to each of these criteria of rank tends in general to be more or less compatible; a person is white, has a good income according to local standards, has a "white collar" job, and comes of a "good family." *But since competition for membership in this local upper class, and the competition for social ranking within it, is relatively intense, it is at this point in the social hierarchy that the criterion of race becomes most crucial in determining social position.* If and when tension exists between people of these communities because of "race," it is between people striving to enter the local upper class who are competing for relative position within the class.

The lower-class groups in all four communities, as throughout Brazil, contain people of all racial types. Among these people, racial type is also a criterion for relative social rank within their class. In actual personal relationships, however, racial characteristics seem to be of little importance, being overshadowed by income, occupation, and other criteria both personal and social; though the existence of preferences as to racial type and even of derogatory attitudes toward people of different racial characteristics within this lower group does indicate that *a mild form of racial prejudice exists on all levels of society in rural Brazil.* But the lack of emphasis upon race within the lower class also indicates that this prejudice is so to speak latent, only becoming active when competition for the upper positions of the local social hierarchy is involved. That the majority of the "people of colour" in all four communities belong to the lower-class groups reflects the well-known fact about Brazil that, in the relatively short period since the end of slavery, opportunity for social advancement through education and economic improvement has not been provided for the descendants of ex-slaves. Negroid physical characteristics (and in the Amazon those of the Indian as well) are symbols of slave ancestry, and such people still have jobs involving manual labour in one form or another, which is another sign of low status since it was the slave in the past who did such work. Lack of education, the performance of manual labour, a low income, absence of family backing, and racial type, are all at work together to keep the "people of colour" in the lower rungs of society.

Yet, in these rural communities of north Brazil, this prejudice is mainly one of social class rather than one directly focused upon people having a particular set of racial characteristics.[3] Except in Vila Recôncavo, where the landowning aristocratic white caste persists, there are no positions in these rural societies closed to an individual because of "race." Despite the derogatory stereotypes expressed in each community regarding the Negro (and in Itá regarding the American Indian physical type also), the actual behaviour toward people of those physical types differs strikingly from the attitude as verbally expressed; actual interpersonal relations seem to be de-

---

[3] Pierson compares this prejudice to that existing within the Negro caste in the United States: *Negroes in Brazil* (Chicago, 1942), p. 341.

termined by other factors such as wealth, education, personal attachments and political position, rather than "race."[4]

Furthermore, actual physical segregation of people according to physical type (except in the satellite villages of Minas Velhas — see below) is absent. Segregation of people of any "racial" type in schools, residential districts, public buildings, or in other ways so common in North America and South Africa and some other parts of the world, is unthinkable to the people of these communities. The idea that people should be excluded from the right to vote because of "racial" type strikes most people as rather comical. That there should even be laws in some parts of the world which prohibit marriage between people of different racial groups would puzzle the people of these Brazilian communities profoundly. Never in the history of any of these communities, to our knowledge, has there since slave times been any violence resulting from tensions between people of different racial type.

Likewise, there are no organizations of Negroes or people of Indian physical type which are limited to people of that "racial" group. The Sociedade dos Pobres of Minas Velhas, although containing many Negroes and many dark *mestiços*, also contains people of other physical types, and its very name indicates that "being poor" is the qualification for membership. In Itá, the Brotherhood of St. Benedict was made up mainly of Negroes and led by the "old Negroes" but, like most Brazilian organizations founded on a basis of "race," the membership soon came to be representative of a wide range of racial types in the community.[5] In these rural societies, there are no associations based exclusively upon racial differences. In these communities, it is as people say throughout Brazil: "We are all Brazilians" (*somos todos brasileiros*). The Brazilian Negroes do not attempt to improve their social and economic position as a group, but as members of lower class and as individuals who are members of one society.

In a generally similar picture of race and class relations, each of the communities described in this report shows however certain variations. Of the four communities, Minas Velhas stands out as the one where prejudice, even discrimination, takes its strongest form. In the two satellite villages of Minas Velhas, residential segregation actually occurs and the force of the derogatory attitudes against the Negro, even overt exclusion of

[4] As a recent North American visitor to Brazil exclaimed: "Brazilians say they have race prejudice but act without it; we sometimes say we are free of it but our prejudice shows in our actions."

[5] In a recent Congresso Nacional do Negro held in Rio de Janeiro to consider the position of the Negro in Brazil, there were complaints by Negroes of the number of whites and mulattoes who seemed to be taking the leadership in the Congress. The Sociedade dos Homens de Côr (Society of Men of Colour), with headquarters in Rio de Janeiro, has never appealed to a large membership. Numerous organizations of Negroes have appeared in Rio de Janeiro, but most of them have had a short life. See Pierson, *op. cit.*, pp. 342-43.

Negroes from the Social Club, shows "race" as a strong factor in determining social position there. This situation may be due to the nature of modern economic adaptation in Minas Velhas, and also to the form of slave-master relationship which existed in that region. The slaves who worked in the mines did not have the close and intimate relations with the master which were possible on the plantations. The owners were often suspicious of their slaves, who they feared might secrete and sell precious stones. This was hardly conducive to warm relations between the two castes. Following the collapse of the mining industry and after abolition, the formation of an artisan class in Minas Velhas led to the social and economic ascension of numerous descendants of slaves; there was a simultaneous loss of social position (or exodus) of the mine-owning class. People of Negro and mixed ancestry rose to compete with the whites for social and economic position. In Minas Velhas, this led to the formation of a set of interpersonal relations and to attitudes toward people of Negroid stock which, compared to those in the other communities studied, are antagonistic and rigid.

In Vila Recôncavo, many of the patterns of race relations which must have existed on the sugar plantations along the north-east coast in the nineteenth century still persist. The plantation workers are usually Negroes, and the plantation owners mostly white. The artisans, the specialized workers in the mills and on the plantations, and the various special groups in the town are frequently of mixed ancestry. Although there is still a great social distance between the white aristocracy and the Negro workers, and even between the local upper class and the lower strata, relations between the racial groups and between social classes are tempered by the continuance of good personal relations between individuals. Despite the nearness of Vila Recôncavo to the large city of Salvador, it has changed less in this way than any of the other communities described. It is a society in which the Negro worker, the mulatto artisan or town-dweller, and the white upper class are fully aware of their obligations and rights. In other words, everyone knows his or her place. There is thus relatively little competition for social position, and Vila Recôncavo seems to have less tension between social classes and racial groups than the other communities.

In Monte Serrat the people are, on the whole, more homogeneous in physical appearance than those of Minas Velhas, Vila Recôncavo, and Itá, although individuals of all physical types are present. The percentage of Negroes is negligible and, though there are a number of people who are basically Caucasoid in appearance, the majority are of the *caboclo* type (mixed Indian ancestry). In addition, Monte Serrat, unlike the other communities, has never been the scene of a major Brazilian boom. Social and economic differences are noticeable, as they are in almost any rural community of north Brazil, but the majority of the people have a roughly

similar standard of living and way of life. This fact is reflected in race
relations, and in the relations between the social classes, which are neither
as antagonistic as in Minas Velhas or as fixed and personalized as in
Vila Recôncavo. Monte Serrat represents a case of but mild racial prejudice and of relatively fluid social classes and as such is characteristic of
numerous rural communities throughout north Brazil.

The Amazon community of Itá has certain characteristics unique in
Brazil. The Amazon is a backward and isolated part of the country, more
so than the regions in which the other three communities described in
this report are situated. After the rubber collapse in 1912, it was almost
forgotten by the nation until very recently. The American Indian has
figured much more largely in the historical background of the Amazon
than elsewhere; he was the slave, and the few Negroes who came to the
valley were most of them already freemen. Thus, the race situation in Itá
is marked by the low position awarded the descendant of the Indian and
the comparatively high prestige attached to Negro ancestry, although, as
everywhere, the Caucasian or white is given the highest place. Itá is the
smallest of the four communities, the poorest and the least influenced
by modern trends. In this community dark mulattoes are full-fledged
members of the highest rungs of the local upper class, and in the recent
past, the man of highest prestige was a Negro. In Itá the process of race
mixture and the breakdown of the old colonial social structure has taken
place slowly and unaffected by the recent social and economic changes
spreading from urban Brazil.

Finally, it should be said that the hypotheses set forth by Donald Pierson in the conclusions of his study of race relations in Salvador are generally reaffirmed by these studies of race and class relations in rural north
Brazil. Among the more important of these hypotheses are: (a) that Brazil
is a multiracial class society "distinct from Indian, for example, where the
social order is based upon the principle of caste and from those parts of
the world where a national or racial minority (or minorities) is in free
association with, but not accepted by, a dominant national or racial majority . . ." [8]; (b) "Prejudice exists in Brazil; but it is *class* rather than
race prejudice" [9]; (c) "This does not mean that there are no social distinctions in Brazil. . . . Neither does it mean that there is no discrimination or that blacks or mixed bloods are completely satisfied with their lot.
But it does mean (a) that a man of colour may, by reason of individual
merit or favourable circumstances, improve his status and even achieve
position in the upper levels of society and (b) that this position will then
be with reference not merely to the darker group whose colour he shares
but to the total community." [10] Thus Pierson's study, which had reference primarily to the city of Salvador in Bahia, seems to hold true generally
for a wide area of the rural north.

On the other hand, certain additions to Pierson's hypotheses seem to be suggested by the four studies here. These might be stated as follows:

1. In some communities of north Brazil, a remnant of a white aristocratic caste is found, membership of which is closed to the Negro, the dark *mestiço*, and even those who have Negro ancestry or marked Negroid features.

2. In both the cities and the rural communities of north Brazil, there is a decided preference for Caucasian physical features. People of mixed ancestry are considered physically attractive and, in fact, the *"morena"* is the ideal feminine beauty [11], but the features of these mixed-blood beauties which are emphasized are mainly Caucasian, with the exception of their darker skin.

3. The common Brazilian statement that "We Brazilians are becoming one people" seems to imply that Brazilians hope to become a nation more Caucasian in physical appearance. The process of absorption of the Negro into the white population discussed by Pierson, and the "bleaching" process mentioned by T. Lynn Smith, are both part of the unstated race policy of Brazil [12].

4. In the city of Salvador as in the rural communities studied, the Negro is considered the best worker (meaning in general, the most capable at manual labour), which is a rather doubtful compliment in view of the attitude of most Brazilians toward manual labour. Negro physical characteristics are universally considered ugly.

5. The attitude toward people of American Indian ancestry varies widely, depending upon the historical role of the Indian in the local scene. Among the aristocrats of the city and of the rural districts, Indian ancestors in the distant past are proof of a long Brazilian genealogy and thus a point of pride. But, in the Amazon, the attitude toward the *caboclo* reflects the former slave status of the Indian.

6. In rural north Brazil, people are acutely conscious of physical race. This is shown by the numerous categories of racial types used in all the communities studied. This consciousness of physical race is not related to discrimination, as it is in other countries. On the contrary, it is in Brazil (a) a system by which individuals are described; (b) a way of diagnosing a person's probable social rank, and (c) a mechanism by which "people of colour" can avoid the stigma of being classed as Negroes.

7. The expression of prejudice against the Negroes, the *mestiços* and people of Indian physical type is mainly manifested verbally and not in behaviour. Other factors (wealth, occupation, education, etc.) are of greater importance in determining the actual patterns of inter-personal relations than race.

8. Although rural Brazilian society has a rigid class structure, conflict

between social classes is relatively subdued. Instead, individuals strive to improve their status by moving — as individuals — into an upper class, without questioning the principle of the existing system of social classes.

9. Finally, the ability of "people of colour" to improve their status in rural Brazil varies considerably from community to community according to the possibilities open to them; everywhere it depends upon improving their educational level, their occupation, their economic situation, and their family connexions — factors which, combined with their physical type, give people their social position.

The system of inter-racial relations which has taken form in Brazil, with all its faults and its advantages, provides a comparatively favourable and fertile basis for the future growth of Brazilian society. Brazil has taken the form of a multi-racial society unlike that found in most colonial areas of the world where a rigid "colour line" is usual. [13] In most colonial areas, the intense and emotionally charged feelings of the native population (generally of Mongoloid or Negroid racial stock) toward the dominant European "caste," and the clash of economic interests between the racial castes, create numerous barriers to the improvement of social and economic conditions. Brazil has avoided developing a caste society such as that of the United States, where the strict line between the Negro and the white has been such a costly drain upon the nation and the individual. With the rapid economic development of Brazil, which is now under way, there should be more numerous opportunities for individuals to improve their economic status throughout the country, and Brazil should be able to make educational facilities available to its people on a much broader basis than at present. As the standard of living and the educational level of the lower strata of Brazilian society improve, the people of darker skin colour now occupying the lower ranks should take their place in the middle ranks of society. There are no serious racial barriers to social and economic advance and, as opportunities increase, larger numbers of people will rise in the social system. The great contrasts in social and economic conditions between the darker lower strata and the predominantly white upper class should disappear.

There are dangers, however, along the road to this ideal. There are indications both in the present studies and in reports from the great metropolitan centres of the country that discrimination, tensions, and prejudices based on race are appearing. As has been pointed out [14], when the number of individuals of Negro or mixed ancestry improve their educational and economic position, they challenge the dominant position of the white upper class. This might well result in emphasis upon "race" as a criterion for social position, in greater prejudice, in tension between racial groups, and even in discrimination. Furthermore, as Brazil becomes more closely tied to the Western industrial and commercial world, and develops its technological equipment, it will be exposed to the ideology of the more industrialized and technologically developed nations. The borrowing of cultural elements — of instruments, techniques, and concepts — is not a mechanical process. There is a tendency for new elements to be diffused from one culture to another in complexes or in clusters; attitudes, ideas, and even material objects often pass from one culture to another somewhat as appendages of a desired innovation. Both Brazilians and foreign observers have the impression that Western attitudes and concepts of racism are entering Brazil along with industrial and technological improvements. But there is no inherent relationship between Western industrialism and technology and Western racism, no necessary connexion between the widespread improvement of social conditions and the development, through competition, of tensions and discrimination between racial or minority groups. Aware of the dangers and pitfalls and taking care to avoid them, Brazil may enjoy the benefits of technological change, and of greater rewards for its underdeveloped potentialities, without losing its rich heritage of racial democracy.

References

1. Ramos (1944), p. 119.
2. Azevedo (1949), pp. 64 ff.
3. See Pierson (1942), Chap. 6, and Freyre (1946), especially Chap. 5.
4. New York, 1947.
5. Ramos, *op. cit.*, p. 119.
6. "Income, Savings, and Investment in Brazil," *Inter-American Economic Affairs*, Vol. 1, No. 1 (June 1947), pp. 116 ff.
7. Smith (1946), p. 174.
8. Pierson, *op. cit.*, p. 348.
9. *Ibid.*, p. 349.
10. *Ibid.*, p. 349. A complete list of Pierson's concluding hypotheses may be found on pp. 344-50.
11. *Ibid.*, p. 136.
12. *Ibid.*, pp. 125 ff., and Smith, *op. cit.*, pp. 173 ff.
13. Kennedy (1945), p. 308.
14. See Harris, *infra*, p. 47.

Bibliography

Azevedo, Thales de. *Povoamento da Cidade do Salvador*. Bahia, 1949.
Buarque de Holanda, Sergio. *Raizes do Brasil*, 2nd edition. Rio de Janeiro, 1948.
Bates, Henry Walter. *The Naturalist on the River Amazon*. London: Everyman Library, 1930.
Bilden, Rudiger. "Brazil, Laboratory of Civilization," *The Nation*, Vol. 128, 16 January 1929.

Calmon, Pedro. *Historia da Civilização Brasileira*, 2nd edition. São Paulo, 1935.

Carneiro, Edison. *Candomblés da Bahia*, Bahia: Publicações do Museu do Estado, No. 8, 1948.

Corrêa Filho, Virgilio. "Devassamento e Ocupação da Amazônia Brasileira," *Revista Brasileira de Geografia*, Vol. IV, No. 2, 1942.

Cunha, Euclides da. *Revolt in the Backlands*. Translated by Samuel Putnam. University of Chicago, 1944.

Delgado de Carvalho, Carlos. "Lectures on Brazilian Affairs," *The Rice Institute Pamphlet*, Vol. XXVII, No. 4, 1940.

Dollard, John. *Caste and Class in a Southern Town*. New Haven, 1937.

Diêgues Juniór, Manuel. *O Bangue nas Alagôas*. Rio de Janeiro, 1949.

Freyre, Gilberto. *Brazil: An Interpretation*. New York, 1945.

———. *The Masters and the Slaves*. Translated by Samuel Putnam. New York, 1946.

James, Preston. *Latin America*. New York, 1942. .

———. *Brazil*. New York, 1946.

———. "The São Francisco Basin: A Brazilian Sertão," *The Geographical Review*, Vol. 38, No. 4, pp. 658-61.

Kennedy, Raymond. "The Colonial Crisis and the Future," *The Science of Man in the World Crisis*. Edited by Ralph Linton. New York, 1945.

Koster, Henry. *Travels in Brazil*. London, 1816.

Landis, Ruth. *City of Women*. New York, 1947.

Lima Junior, Augusto. *História dos Diamantes nas Minas Gerais*. Rio de Janeiro, 1945.

Marchant, Alexander. *From Barter to Slavery*. The Johns Hopkins University Studies in Historical and Political Science, Vol. LX, Baltimore, 1942.

Myrdal, Gunnar. *An American Dilemma*. New York, 1944.

Oliveira Martins, J. F. *O Brasil e as Colônias Portuguêsas*, 3rd edition. Lisbon, 1880.

Pierson, Donald. *Negroes in Brazil: A Study of Race Contact in Bahia*. Chicago, 1942.

Ramos, Artur. *O Negro Brasileiro*. São Paulo, 1934.

———. *Las Poblaciones del Brasil*. Mexico D.F., 1944.

Rodrigues, Nina. *Os Africanos no Brasil*. São Paulo, 1935.

Smith, Herbert H. *Brazil: The Amazons and the Coast*. New York, 1879.

Smith, T. Lynn. *Brazil: People and Institutions*. Baton Rouge, 1946.

Smith, T. Lynn, and Marchant, Alexander, editors. *Brazil: Portrait of a Half Continent*. New York, 1951.

Spiegel, Henry W. "Income, Savings, and Investment in Brazil," *Inter-American Economic Affairs*, Vol. I, No. 1, 1947.

Tannenbaum, Frank. *Slave and Citizen*. New York, 1947.

Wagley, Charles. "Brazil," in *Most of the World*. Edited by Ralph Linton. New York, 1949.

Wallace, Alfred Russel. *Narratives and Travels in the Amazon and Rio Negro*. London, 1853.

Wanderley de Araujo Pinho, José. *Testamento de Mem Sá*. Rio de Janeiro, 1941.

Zarur, Jorge. *A Bacia do Médio São Francisco*. Rio de Janeiro, 1947.

III

Professor Banton's "stranger hypothesis" is a theory which sug-
gests that Whites in Britain react to Blacks as if Blacks were
strangers to their cultures. They experience the same uneasiness
in dealing with Blacks as in dealing with any man unfamiliar
with the unspoken social etiquette of Britain. There are several
attributes of the stranger which he treats in his hypothesis:
the man unknown, the man unfamiliar with his surroundings, the
unpredictable, and the outlandish figure. Banton's use of the
"social distance scale" to measure degrees of intimacy which
White Britains will permit with Blacks and the relative diffi-
culty which all experience in communication points to sources
of racial uneasiness within personal interactions. This article,
then, is an excellent treatment of the way in which group
ideologies become personal.

MICHAEL BANTON

White and Coloured in Britain

I: THE ARCHETYPAL STRANGER

The Englishman is no missionary, no conqueror. He prefers the
country to the town and home to foreign parts. He is rather glad and
relieved if only natives will remain natives and strangers strangers,
and at a comfortable distance from himself.   SANTAYANA[1]

From *White and Coloured*, by Michael Banton (New Brunswick, New Jersey:
Rutgers University Press, 1960), Chaps. V-VI, pp. 73-113. Reprinted by permission of the author and the publisher.
[1] George Santayana, *Soliloquies in England* (London, 1922), p. 32.

The network of relations that constitutes a society is maintained by a series of common understandings as to the rights and obligations of the persons who occupy positions in it. Social life can be seen as a sequence of relationships, each of them being defined by the rights and obligations of the parties to it. Norms of conduct in given situations may be explicitly stated in the law of the land, or they may be implicit in the conventions to which people subscribe. The continuance of social life is dependent upon the members of society observing these norms, and sanctions are applied against those who infringe them. Seen from this standpoint, strangers are people who do not know or will not accept the norms. They are not necessarily foreigners: the small child, the wealthy eccentric, the tramp, the village idiot, are all strangers to their society in that their behaviour cannot be predicted with any certainty, and the various informal pressures that usually produce conformity are not effective in their case.

In some societies little is left to chance, and a high proportion of the norms by which conduct is to be regulated are made explicit; if not in the constitution or the law, they are explicit in public discussion and are consciously taught to newcomers. Britain would appear to be one of the countries where the reliance upon implicit norms is particularly high. Britons, naturally, would be the last people to be aware of this, but American sociologists accustomed to the strenuous efforts made to turn varied groups of immigrants into patriotic American citizens are frequently impressed by this aspect of British social life. Thus Professor George C. Homans: "Any society rests on a set of unstated assumptions, British society more than most: that is, indeed, its strength."[2]. . .

These implicit notions about the proper way to behave, about the unannounced rights and obligations of people in particular positions, constitute the unspoken language of British social life. The Briton expects those with whom he has dealings to observe an unspoken code. If they deviate from it he will indicate by his tone of voice, a change of manner, or by silence, that he is unhappy about the turn events are taking, and if the other party fails to take the hint the relationship may be broken off. But Britons are aware of these codes more in breach than in observance: a variety of things are "not done," but there are relatively few positive regulations. Reliance upon the unspoken language is greater in the social classes near the top end of the scale than at the bottom. In the higher classes, acceptance of certain tacit standards is such that the minor social neglect of a person of inferior prestige can be a powerful sanction, and the more urgently someone seeks to climb the scale the more sensitive will he or she be to such pressures. In the rougher working-class districts, like

[2] George C. Homans, in *The Listener*, 16 August, 1956, p. 232.

those in the neighbourhood of the docks, sanctions of this sort have little effect and the resort to violence or the support of the police is far more frequent as a means of obtaining conformity. Thus it is easier for the stranger to gain acceptance in the lower social categories. The extent to which he is accepted by groups higher up the prestige scale will be partly dependent upon the extent to which he has learned their ways and is therefore subject to their controls.

The statement that a stranger may more readily gain acceptance at the bottom of the class hierarchy is subject to several qualifications. . . . It is our impression that working-class people more readily manifest hostility towards coloured people but are more readily induced to abandon it. If an upper-middle-class person dislikes coloured people he will conjure up an inexhaustible store of arguments to justify his views, for they do not spring to the same extent from a lack of information as is likely to be the case with a worker.

. . . How the various features of national behaviour cohere is a problem on which we have little information, but it may be suggested that one of the factors underlying insularity is the dependence upon the unspoken language. An actor must be able to interpret the other person's behaviour and convey his own sentiments fairly easily. This intuitive understanding of others is achieved more rapidly when a man is dealing with people who have a background similar to his own; he knows that they will see matters in much the same light as he does and that there is no great danger of his being misinterpreted. . . .

It is hard, very hard, for a stranger to become British. Feeling that the objective is virtually unattainable, and in any case scarcely desirable, Britons do not encourage him to try. The new norms of conduct round which the stranger would have to rebuild his personality were he to mix with complete freedom are the less easily apprehended because they are not made explicit; and for this very reason Britons are not sufficiently conscious of them to be able to teach them. Learning to be British is made even more difficult in that the newcomer has to learn, not a uniform national culture, but a class and perhaps regional culture appropriate to his position, which, while sharing many common features with the other subcultures, differs from them in important respects.

Though there are no sharp dividing lines in Britain between one class and another, and although many people pass from one class to the next, the characteristics of class remain relatively constant. For most English people the notion of class is an important reference group enabling them to "place" others, for though they may have widely different ideas about how many social classes there are, and how they are composed, most people think of themselves as belonging to a particular class, while nearly everybody tends to place most of his or her acquaintances in some class. Even if the individual is not sure about where he himself belongs in this scheme he is confident about the class membership of many other people.[3]

. . .

Even if it is rarely so marked as this nowadays, status-consciousness undoubtedly exercises a strong influence upon English behaviour. The acceptance of such differences and the alienation of the self from persons placed in other categories, is, from a comparative viewpoint, a remarkable feature. . . .

Are differences of colour comparable to "class stigmata" — as Orwell thought? Later on we shall contend that Britons view coloured men as strangers to their customary way of life in much the same way as they might view members of a different class, and parts of our analysis will be just as applicable to relations between classes as between any social groups which are regarded as possessing different rights and obligations from members of the actor's own group.

It has also been suggested that while the concentration of people in urban centres makes it easier for people to find some niche for themselves, the anonymity of city life makes it difficult for the newcomer to build up a truly satisfying role. . . . The newcomer who comes to live in a village is immediately forced into intimate relations with his neighbours and with those with whom he trades. The newcomer who settles in a large town often establishes only restricted relations with those about him. . . . This characterization of city life can easily be overdrawn and is certainly untrue of many neighbourhoods, but recent studies in urban sociology[4] have demonstrated that a large proportion of city-dwellers are afraid that their neighbours should learn anything of their private affairs. . . . It may be, as Thorstein Veblen suggested, that because of the emphasis upon showy possessions in contemporary civilization people save their best things for their public appearances and prefer to conceal the consequent shabbiness of their domestic life. While from another viewpoint it may be seen as expressing people's need to maintain control over the relationships they make when they have the freedom to choose their associates.

Mr. Gorer sees the question in terms of his theory of the English character, which he thinks potentially very aggressive but held under strict control.[5]. . . Dr. J. H. Robb [has] suggested that the characteristics ascribed to an out-group are likely to reflect some of the needs and repressed wishes of the hostile individual.[6] The images which Britons with

---

[3] Elizabeth Bott, *Family and Social Network* (London, 1957), Chap. 6.
[4] Cf. *Neighbourhood and Community*, Liverpool University Department of Social Science (1954).
[5] Geoffrey Gorer, *Exploring English Character*.
[6] James H. Robb, *Working Class Anti-Semite* (London, 1955).

strong colour prejudice have of the coloured man have not yet been the subject of scientific scrutiny, but if Mr. Gorer's theory is correct then it may well be true that the Negro is the white man's fear of himself. The Africans' and West Indians' capacity for letting themselves go, which some British people see as their most engaging characteristic, is for others one of the snares of the Devil. As Dr. Landes said: "I suggest that the Englishman's remarkable stress on personal and social discipline is deeply affronted by the Negro's incomprehensible and perhaps theatrical zest and spontaneity. To him this is possibly the most alien element of all, counting as irresponsibility and naked indulgence."

These various considerations suggest that in Britain the coloured man is not seen as a different sort of being but as the furthest removed of strangers — the archetypal stranger. . . .

Norms of conduct towards coloured people usually differ from those of conduct towards other whites not in kind, but in degree. Some evidence to support this inference may be obtained from the results of our racial attitudes survey.

From the survey it transpires that individual Britons are simultaneously well disposed towards coloured people and yet prefer not to be too closely involved with them. . . . Answers to a question regarding the restriction of colonial immigration suggested that public opinion on this topic was more favourable than might have been expected in view of the numerous proposals that had been advanced in 1955 and 1956 for limiting the influx from the West Indies. Respondents were asked: "Provided, of course, that there is plenty of work about, do you think that coloured colonials should be allowed to go on coming to this country?" — 72 per cent replied in the affirmative; 18 per cent were definitely opposed, and the views of the remainder could not easily be classified. Of those who were in favour of maintaining an open-door policy, nearly half emphasized the proviso as to the availability of work, or suggested that they should not be allowed to congregate in towns where there were difficulties in obtaining work. . . .

The distinction between individual friendliness and an acceptance of social distance came out clearly from two questions about discrimination in housing. People were told: "Sometimes landladies and hotels refuse to take in coloured people"; and were then asked: "Is this right or wrong?" — 12 per cent replied, unequivocally, that they were right in doing so, though a study of the answers suggested that in just over half the cases respondents were expressing tolerance of the landlady's behaviour rather than agreement with it; 52 per cent considered that refusal was definitely wrong. Most of the remainder gave qualified answers, indicating that circumstances vary and that the landlady or hotel manager must be allowed some latitude to decide for herself or himself; she or he must take into account the feelings of other guests, the neighbours and so forth. Many people would clearly prefer separate facilities if these could be provided without infringing coloured people's rights or hurting their feelings; they realize that this would be extremely difficult. Those who replied that discrimination was unequivocally wrong were later asked: "What if their business may suffer?" This question appeared to cause many of them some difficulty. A minority considered it irrelevant ("People come before money"), an imaginary fear ("This isn't true today as it used to be"), or a false distinction ("Why just them? Some Irish aren't fit to be taken in"). Rather more admitted that this was a very real difficulty, but the vast majority gave no clear reply; there seemed to be a tug-of-war between the feeling that it is unfair to exclude coloured guests without giving them a trial, and, on the other hand, the view that business is business, that other people must be considered, and that it is unfair to pass judgment upon landladies when there is a danger of their suffering on account of their adherence to a principle that bears so much less heavily on other sections of the community.

The other question ran: "Many coloured people from the colonies have difficulty in finding lodgings or accommodation. Which of these three things do you think we should do to get over these difficulties?" The interviewer then mentioned three possible measures: "Make it easier for them to get rooms in hotels and boarding-houses; ask more private people to have them stay in their homes; provide hostels for them." An overwhelming majority favoured the third of these suggestions: 71 per cent naming it by itself, and a further 10 per cent in association with one or both of the others. The reasons people gave for favouring hostels tended to fall into three categories: some people thought separate accommodation was in the immigrants' own interests as they were happier together and were protected from some of the unfriendliness of the whites, whereas others favoured segregation in the interests of the white population as they thought it would avoid trouble, and because they would not have wished to have coloured lodgers in their own home; the third set of reasons did not imply the interest of either group but featured the view that separation was preferable because the two groups have different customs, food, habits, etc., so that domestic mixing would be bound to cause friction. In general, respondents found it difficult to resolve conflicting sentiments, in favour of mixing and of keeping separate, or of distinguishing between the circumstances in which the different courses of action were appropriate. . . . Taking all the answers together, we find that 22 per cent expressed definite opposition to any possibility that might tend towards segregation; 26 per cent favoured hostel accommodation as a temporary measure or in the immigrants' interest; while 45 per cent chose hostels for reasons which appeared either to suggest a preference for separation or an acceptance of it as a necessary consequence of cultural differences.

Evidence from other sources supports the same general conclusion, though there are indications that the degree of social distance whites feel from coloured people has been declining in recent years. Miss Webster administered a Bogardus-type social distance test to girl students at an Oxbridge college and a teacher training college.[7] Certain differences between the responses of the two groups are apparent from Table [1]. The university women far more readily expressed willingness to marry Russians, Chinese and Indians. The teacher training college women were more ready to exclude entirely members of all groups, while the particular rigour with which they regarded the Russians and Chinese suggests that the responses reflected political as well as racial attitudes. The university woman — as Miss Webster points out in a more detailed analysis of the results — indicated a much smaller degree of distance, but, where she felt some, rather than suggesting complete exclusion indicated a course that would enable her to avoid intimate relations with strangers. But the most striking feature of the results is the relatively slight degree of social distance expressed throughout the test, compared with the data obtained by Professor Eysenck[8] from an earlier investigation based on a sample more representative of the total population. We may recollect, however, that young women such as those questioned by Miss Webster, and the university women in particular, would be more susceptible than most to the public protestations of racial equality and to ethical considerations. . . . Moreover, the subjects were not personally acquainted with the problems upon which the test bears and were themselves inclined to add "We've never really thought about it." The results may therefore not be a good guide to how they would behave in practice. Nevertheless, if we allow for the political loading in the teacher training college students' responses about the Russians there is a clear distinction between the subjects' willingness to accept members of the European nations as relatives by marriage, and their unwillingness to do so in the case of the coloured nations. This distinction is reflected more clearly in Eysenck's data.

The Bogardus-type test requires modification for use in different societies as the expression of social distance varies. Professor Eysenck came to the surprising conclusion that his subjects at least were more ready to admit a stranger to membership of their club than to British citizenship. "To us," he writes, "admission to citizenship and employment indicate a greater degree of acceptance than does admission to street or club." This question merits further investigation as it is not clear how such a finding is to be interpreted.

It is likely that the coloured man would appear less of a stranger were

[7] Sheila Webster, "Negroes in Bluebrick," unpublished manuscript in the Department of Social Anthropology, University of Edinburgh.
[8] H. J. Eysenck, *The Psychology of Politics* (London, 1954), pp. 84-87.

TABLE 1. THE SOCIAL DISTANCE OF FIVE STRANGER
NATIONALITIES

	I would marry one		I would allow my brother to marry one		I would allow into my club		I would let live in my street		I would allow to be employed in my occupation in my country		I would allow to become citizens of my country		I would allow as visitors to my country	
	Oxb.	TTC	Oxb.	TTC	Oxb.	TTC	Oxb.	TTC	Oxb.	TTC	Oxb.	TTC	Oxb.	TTC
Germans	72	69	87	77	96	91	98	94	98	95	99	98	100	98
Russians	54	16	71	27	87	42	92	50	94	52	100	75	100	97
Chinese	18	5	41	21	88	58	96	76	98	83	100	97	100	99
Indians	28	12	47	29	88	72	95	82	98	91	100	98	100	99
Africans	14	11	31	27	82	70	92	80	97	90	100	99	100	100

Subjects: 100 women from an Oxbridge college and 204 students at a women's
Teacher Training College. Responses have been reduced to proportions of 100; a few
were indeterminate.

British people better informed about the background and aspirations of
colonial immigrants. A relatively high proportion — 35 per cent — of
those interviewed had some connection, such as through friends or relatives, with one or more of the colonies and dominions. Yet no more than
36 per cent were able to give a rough indication of the difference between
a dominion and a colony. . . .

The suggestion that in Britain the coloured man is regarded as the
stranger par excellence may cast light on the problem of national differences in the reception accorded to coloured people. They themselves say
that the French, Italians, Scandinavians and others do not regard them as
being in any way peculiar. A typical remark is that of an East African
student: "I liked France very much and felt a load dropped off my
shoulders when I arrived in Paris. Everyone treated me normally and I
forgot I was coloured." In respect of colonial policies it would be difficult
to demonstrate that the so-called Latin peoples are more benevolently disposed towards their colonial charges than the British, while from the evidence available it is not likely that as individuals the Britons are so much
more antipathetic. The cause for the coloured man's complaint may well
lie in the British tradition of maintaining a greater social distance, and the
appreciation of cultural distinctiveness. It is as if they conclude that because the coloured man has his own cultural identity so there must be a
special way of behaving towards him.

· · ·

II: WHEN CUSTOM FAILS

Custom, as the embodiment of the unspoken norms, tells people how
they should behave in particular situations. It stipulates that persons

falling into a given social category are to be treated in a specific manner. . . .

Relations with members of a particular social group may be regulated by special norms. . . . [In the colonial period] special norms did not support any extensive system of discrimination, but pictured the coloured man as a colonial ward — a British subject in training and not a mature citizen. The position today has moved much closer to the situation in which there are no special norms for behaviour towards coloured people. . . .

According to the old norms, Britons, as a more advanced nation, were superior to the coloured peoples. They laid claim to special rights in their dealings with them. But there are no rights without duties, and their superiority — real or illusionary — imposed on Britons the responsibility of helping the backward peoples to advance. The assumption of this responsibility justified the claim to special rights. This pattern of thought remains important though it is now no longer of general validity. Thus, the obligation to help colonies was accepted without question by nearly all the people interviewed in the course of our attitude survey; 34 per cent considered that we ought to give more help to the colonies than at present, while only 6 per cent favoured a reduction; 71 per cent thought that coloured colonials, because they were British subjects, should receive preference over European foreigners in admission to the home country; 13 per cent did not agree with this suggestion, but their reasons were varied.

Relationships which conform to the old pattern of superiority and responsibility are still often regarded as providing a particularly appropriate setting for dealings with coloured men. In such relationships the Briton thinks he knows what is expected of him, and he feels more at ease. . . .

Relationships conforming to the generalized pattern of the superiority and responsibility of the Briton towards the colonial were once of a customary and generally accepted character. Colonials received tangible benefits in return for the deference they paid to the white man and the transaction was for a time advantageous to both parties. In Britain the coloured man who played up to British ideas of the "poor darkie" could do well for himself. . . . The converse of this has been that when whites have come into contact with coloureds occupying superior roles they have often been confused and sometimes resentful. Now, however, colonials challenge the patronizing attitude.

. . .

The question for an individual of how, in everyday situations, he is to act out his own appraisal of the racial issue is largely answered by the growth of customary practices. When custom requires that a coloured man be treated in a special fashion the actor must observe the norm or face the likelihood of being punished by his fellows. When the norm endorses equal treatment there is no problem. But when custom is changing the actor has to decide for himself how far he will go in upholding the old norms or in supporting the new ones, and to accept the consequences if he goes too far in either direction. No longer is there any clear guide to conduct; custom has failed him.

It is our thesis that the present position in Britain is one where the customary image of the coloured man and his place in society is changing. In some situations the old, special, norms are still valid. In others the new ones have triumphed. The actor's problem is to decide whether the situation that faces him belongs in the former category or the latter. . . . Often the general principle is clear, but there are special circumstances which make it difficult to decide. Because of this the Briton is often uncertain how he should behave towards coloured people. This uncertainty is frequently taken as evidence of prejudice when in fact it points to very different conclusions.

If the special norms are steadily being discarded, what hinders the pattern of relationships with coloured people from being assimilated to that obtaining among whites? One important reason may be the psychological one that it takes time for people to learn new norms and adjust to changed circumstances. Other influences may also be relevant, but it is our intention here to concentrate upon two of the sociological factors, namely the images of the coloured man as a stranger to British ways and of the coloured man as a stranger in terms of social class. We maintain — and this is perhaps the most important section of our analysis — that in many situations Britons are obliged to treat a relationship with a coloured man as requiring special care and perhaps a different approach (a) because he may not understand the norms governing the relationship, and (b) because onlookers may regard it unfavourably. The study of the variations from one situation to another can tell us something, not just about race relations but about social life in general.

We gain our knowledge of people by entering into relationship with them, and each relationship can be seen as a sequence of communications between the two parties. The actor interprets the other person's behaviour as having a particular intent and he responds to it so as to indicate his own views or to elicit further information from the other. This interplay between the two of them is built out of words, gestures, tones of voice and of the situation in which it occurs, and results in the two parties determining on particular courses of action or establishing a basis for further and cumulative interaction on another occasion. When the other person refuses to take up the messages that are being conveyed to him the commonest sanction is for the actor to break off the relationship. There is no one norm regulating the entire relationship, but a variety according to which of the parties' social personalities are brought into play. A seller may wish to keep his relations with his customers on strictly commercial terms and to exclude all norms except those relating to the rights and obligations of buyer and seller. His client may seek to introduce other considerations suggesting that theirs is also a friendship and recalling the norms of friendship. He may also draw attention to his personal circumstances, implying that he deserves special treatment and so forth. Social relations are, in Max Gluckman's term, multiplex;[9] every actor is several persons and he is linked to other members of his society through each of his social personalities. To enter into the life of a society it is therefore necessary not only to know the norms of relationship but also to be able to tell which of these norms are relevant. The stranger is not only uncertain of the norms: he cannot read the signals.

. . .

The Briton knows that awkward scenes may develop where people do not share the same customs and cannot take one another's hints; he feels the embarrassing scene acutely and avoids getting into a situation where it might arise. . . . Most people, at one time or another, will have had the experience of wishing to help someone, but being afraid that if they did so the other person might become too demanding and it would be difficult to shake him off. The occasional case illuminates what must be a general though usually unconscious principle of social behaviour. People fight shy of entering into the sorts of relationship which they feel are likely to get out of control. Their view of how such relationships should be conducted may be unfair to the other party, but it governs their behaviour nevertheless. The Englishman cannot be sure that the coloured man will recognize or accept the former's intention of extending to him only a limited acceptance. He cannot be sure, if he is kind to a coloured immigrant, whether that man will appreciate the limits of his gesture and not take advantage of his kindness. He does not want to be suddenly confronted with an inordinate demand for help, financial or otherwise, which is all too possible when the immigrants have such difficulty in finding work and housing. Consequently, where he suspects that the coloured man may not be familiar with the social norms to which he is accustomed the Briton is inclined to refrain from entering into relations with him.

These considerations suggest that the more a relationship is governed by unspoken norms, and acted out in accordance with signals that are known only to the initiated, the more necessary it is to ensure that the other party is familiar with these conventions. . . .

. . . Why should Britons be strongly opposed to any discrimination in the public treatment of coloured people and at the same time be so hesitant about treating them equally in private relations? The coloured

---

[9] Max Gluckman, *The Judicial Process among the Barotse* (Manchester, 1955), p. 19.

man has the same obligation as the ordinary Briton to pay taxes, serve his period of conscription if of the age which makes him liable for this, and to behave as befits a citizen. No one questions that in return he has a right to the same facilities as anyone else; a vote, a seat in the bus, a place in the queue, and the same consideration as one citizen shows another. To hold any other view would be to question all that successive Secretaries of State have said about our colonial "trusteeship." On the other hand, people who themselves subscribe wholeheartedly to these principles may prefer not to have anything to do with coloured people in their private lives. This is particularly true of marriage, the most private sphere of all. Not only do many find the idea of themselves marrying coloured people repugnant but they dislike the prospect of any of their relatives or countryfolk doing so either.

In the public sphere there are effective sanctions upon misconduct. The immigrant's rights as a citizen are defined by law: if he steps beyond them he can be punished by law. In the private sphere norms are implicit and sanctions weak. Relations between members of the same family cannot be satisfactorily based on legal requirements, but must stem from common understanding and shared aims. . . . If someone is admitted to the family who does not share their assumptions and cannot play his part in the life of the group, then the family bond may be broken. Hence, the more tightly knit a community the greater is the resistance to inter-marriage likely to be. . . . Whatever the psychological factors it is clear that resistance to intermarriage is an outlook traditionally transmitted and approved, and that social avoidance plays a part in the maintenance of this pattern of behaviour. . . .

. . . To the employer, a coloured workman appears as a risk, for he is unlikely to have the background of experience that a white worker has and he may need extra supervision. He is a risk in that if he is taken on other workers more valuable to the concern may protest. After all, any de-parture from the status quo is to some extent a risk. But if all employers draw the same conclusion a series of private decisions adds up to a public policy and to one contrary to the country's acknowledged duty to give all its citizens a fair chance.

The second of our two postulated sociological factors hindering the assimilation of relations with coloured people to the pattern obtaining among whites, was that because the coloured man is so extreme a stranger association with him is something out of the ordinary and is looked at askance. Unless some explanation is forthcoming the person who asso-ciates with a coloured man may suffer social disapproval or loss of prestige. . . .

A man's status within the local community depends to a considerable extent on the people with whom he associates. If he wants to be respected

he will be careful in his choice of friends, and if there is an identification
. . . then he will avoid entering into relationships with coloured people. . . .

People whose social position is secure relative to those about them will
not be so concerned about any unusual associations of theirs being the
subject of local tittle-tattle, but social climbers will be very sensitive
to such informal sanctions — and very many people are to some degree
would-be climbers. Women are, in general, more dependent upon the approval of their neighbours than are men, for, as has been said, "the man's
status is the status of his job, the woman's the status of her home."[10] The
landlady's house is both her job and her home, so she is more exposed
than most to the threats of gossip. . . . Association where the white person clearly stands in a superordinate relation to a coloured man evokes no
disapproval, but obvious subordination might harm a white man's standing among his fellows.

.   .   .

It is possible that people are more afraid than they need be of the
likely effects upon their reputation of being seen with coloured people.
But excessive caution in this respect is more easily understood when it
is seen how associations which most people would approve can sometimes
be interpreted in an uncharitable or malicious manner. Fear of what
others may think is more likely to weigh with a man in his private life
than at his place of work; there, he will be more concerned that the
stranger should understand the behaviour expected of him. In some situations only one of the two factors will be important, but in many there will
be a mixture of the two.

We would expect the Briton to be more likely to avoid association with
coloured men in the neighbourhood where he lives than at his work-
place. . . .

The observations of research workers and a poll conducted by the
British Institute of Public Opinion have substantiated this hypothesis.
Commenting upon the results of the poll, Dr. Clarence Senior remarks:
"Working relations were regarded [by the immigrants] as considerably better than off-the-job social contacts. Whereas 50 per cent of the outside
relationships were felt to be either 'all right' or better, 78 per cent of the
workshop contacts were so characterized. There is a four-to-one differential
in the 'very well, as a friend' category; 10 per cent outside work to 40
per cent at work."[11] The same conclusion, that "relationships in the factory are easier than across the apartment landing" has been drawn by

[10] Michael Young and Peter Willmott, *Family and Kinship in East London*
(London, 1957), p. 129.
[11] Clarence Senior and Douglas Manley, *A Report on Jamaican Migration
to Great Britain* (Kingston, 1955), p. 45.

other investigators who have either offered no explanation or have not seen it as constituting a problem. We regard this as just the sort of problem which should be meat and drink to the sociologist, for only he has the theoretical equipment to elucidate it.

Earlier . . . we maintained that avoidance of coloured people derived principally from two factors: the belief that coloured people may be unfamiliar with British norms and conventions of social intercourse, and the danger that onlookers may interpret association with them to the Briton's discredit. The first proposition was borne out by the experience of coloured people who found British reluctance to "speak directly" an obstacle to understanding. The second proposition also receives a measure of confirmation from the behaviour of coloured people themselves. With his own acquaintances a coloured man may be known as a doctor, as a student, as someone who has lived in Britain for many years and knows all the Briton's foibles — or he may even be someone born and brought up in this country. But to the man who does not know them each of these is as much a stranger as the latest arrival. It is their colour that is immediately noticed by someone meeting them for the first time, and that brands them strangers. Hence the way some coloured people prefer to keep to the circles in which they are known. Hence, too, the use by others of symbols indicating their social status. . . .

The third of our paradoxes referred to the way in which British people's behaviour towards the immigrants can suddenly change in quite a radical fashion when apparently nothing of importance has occurred to alter the situation. . . . Frequently, the slightest recommendation, a reference from an unknown source, or an appealing look, is enough to tip the scales and secure something for one coloured man that would be denied another.

· · ·

The absence of indicators as to a particular coloured man's merits is another facet of the difficulties of social intercourse with a stranger. Not only is he unable to read our signals but we cannot read his. An employer has various points to guide him when interviewing an applicant for a job — the man's appearance, bearing, previous employment, etc., but these criteria may be useless in the case of a coloured man. Stepney employers seemed sometimes to see the position in very simple terms: some coloured men were good workers, some bad, and the impression an applicant made in the first few moments decided in which category he was thought to belong. A new item of information might lead to an immediate switch-over. Many employers with some experience of the immigrants realize that they are at a disadvantage in this respect. They arrange for a coloured worker who has been with them for a fair time and in whose judgment they place some reliance to see coloured applicants and say what he thinks of them.

Men recommended by existing employees may be shown preference. This obstacle to communication occurs in a variety of face-to-face relations, so that employers often regard a senior coloured man as an unofficial chargehand who can speak to the employer for the others, and for the employer to the others.

Where conflicting norms are so evenly balanced the subordinate party can sometimes manipulate the relationship to his advantage, causing the other to redefine the situation as one calling for benevolence. Africans are usually better at this than West Indians. . . . Men who have been accustomed to subordination are more adept at such ways of winning round their superiors, whereas coloured students and those who most ardently desire political independence are more inclined to stand on their dignity. They have the justification that those who resort to such methods are exploiting and thereby keeping alive the old norms of superordination and responsibility which they would like to see replaced by norms of equality.

Another tactic sometimes employed by the immigrants when matters are going to their disadvantage is to accuse the white person of being actuated by colour prejudice. This can induce him or her to define the situation in a way more favourable to the coloured man. Landladies have recounted how any attempt to reprove some colonial students has drawn accusations of this kind. To prove to them that this was not the case they have at first given way, until they have found that their authority was being undermined.

This view of relations being so delicately balanced as to respond to slight variations in manner also helps us to understand another superficially puzzling phenomenon. Though so many coloured men complain of a colour bar in Britain there are a minority who quite sincerely say that they have never suffered any discrimination, and who aver that they have nothing to complain about. Sometimes such statements appear to be a psychological defence, for not everyone feels strong enough to admit to himself that he has been rejected when this is indeed the case; but this suspicion is clearly irrelevant to a considerable number of cases. Many coloured people do not demand complete acceptance from Britons: they may have too jealous a love of their own culture or they may quickly come to understand the Briton's viewpoint. Such people get on unusually well with their hosts. Others make demands that are considered unreasonable, so they are snubbed and in their resentment they repeat these demands all the more insistently, until they become incapable of sustaining harmonious relations with a member of the hated white majority. Violent political reactions and acute suspicion of any move on the part of British officials or representatives of voluntary associations have been characteristic of many coloured immigrant groups. Thus the coloured man's approach — cautious or aggressive — easily results in the white man's redefining the situation and acting in a different way — more friendly or less so — from that which his individual disposition might otherwise have rendered probable.

The more fluid the situation, the greater is the number of possible ways in which it may be defined and the greater is the scope for manipulation. One participant may succeed in getting another to take a different view of the matter in hand, or the general view of the whole community may be changed. Dr. Sydney Collins considers that immigrant groups in some towns are more favourably regarded because they have been "sponsored" by prominent citizens;[12] in effect, their view of how the newcomers should be dealt with has been accepted by other groups and members of the host society and, as a result, material assistance has often been forthcoming. The fluidity in the way Britons define relations with coloured people is also reflected in the results of public opinion polls; responses to questions about the desirability of continued coloured immigration can vary considerably. It was only to be expected that after the 1958 disturbances the polls should show a much higher percentage opposed to unrestricted immigration, for when opinion is fluid widely publicized events can stimulate people to adopt a more definite standpoint. Another factor of importance is that when questioned about something on which they have no set views people are apt to give the reply which they think the questioner wants — or the reply which seems safest. The interviews in our own attitude survey opened with five questions about the colonies and three about contact with coloured people, before the question of immigration was raised. This should have neutralized many of the extraneous influences. The fluidity of opinion and the uncertainty as to the correct course of conduct which underlie the rapid changes in attitude and behaviour make this the sort of issue on which determined leadership from individual Britons can have most effect.

British behaviour towards coloured people is characterized not by aggressiveness but by avoidance of them in relationships which might get out of hand. It is a response not to dark skin colour as a biological fact but to its social significance. If, as we have implied, the meaning of colour is slowly changing in an equalitarian direction as it is realized that the coloured man is not so much a stranger to our ways as was first feared, then such changes should be fairly easily detectable. James and Tenen, at the end of a detailed analysis of how adolescents think of foreigners, reach a conclusion which may be cited as evidence of this. They write: "It is when colour is disturbing that it is disliked. When it is not disturbing it may be liked or pass unnoticed. It is not disturbing when

---

[12] Sydney Collins, *Coloured Minorities in Britain* (London, 1957).

one feels safe and confident. When one has become accustomed to it, when the coloured person is known and liked."[13]

When the children discovered that coloured people were much like themselves their uneasiness subsided. Colour no longer had the same significance and they were not disturbed by it.

We may now turn to the last, and in some ways the most problematic, of our four paradoxes. Why should Britons believe their friends and neighbours to be less favourably disposed towards coloured people than they themselves? The facts at issue are not in dispute. For example, in our survey 71 per cent of the subjects replied that they would not mind working with a coloured man, or were positively favourable, whereas only 23 per cent of them believed that other people would not mind. Similar figures were obtained in an earlier investigation, and the responses to other questions bearing upon the distinction between the respondents' own attitudes and their assessment of other people's substantiate the general conclusion.

The kernel of the problem would appear to be the difference between antipathy as a state of mind and avoidance as a feature of behaviour. Army officers are supposed to refrain from discussing religion or politics in the mess because dissention ill accords with comradeship. It does not mean that they are not interested in these topics. Avoidance of coloured people, similarly, is a customary pattern of behaviour and is not to be interpreted as the outcome of the dispositions of the individual members of the nation. The reasons for it are to be sought first in the structure of British social life, which if it is to continue functioning effectively requires that those who participate in it shall understand what is expected of them in particular situations and that others shall be able to rely upon their filling these expectations. There are other factors, however, which lead into deeper waters. For example, not only do Britons regard others as less favourably disposed than themselves but they often seem to regard this imputed reserve as something creditable. Unwillingness to let down the barriers to the participation of coloured people in the more intimate British social activities, unless the newcomers have proved their eligibility beyond question, may be construed as an unwillingness to lower group standards. If groups are to be respected they must to some extent be exclusive. The more exclusive they are, the more membership of them is valued. If a foreigner could obtain complete social acceptance in Britain as easily as he can obtain naturalization papers, then being British would be of much less worth. To retain our pride we must exclude some people at least, and who is more clearly a stranger than a coloured man?

[13] H. E. O. James and Cora Tenen, "How Adolescents Think of People," *British Journal of Psychology*, Vol. 41 (1950), p. 170.

When people say that others of their acquaintance would dislike working with a coloured man, or having one as a neighbour or visitor, they are saying that this would be contrary to the group's norms of conduct, *not* that each of these people, individually, is unfavourably disposed. This crucial distinction is rarely appreciated. The maintenance of social distance is customary; it is not necessarily actuated by prejudice. It has been maintained that a tendency to consider others unfavourably disposed is in itself a sign of antipathy in the subject — as if he is claiming that others are hostile in order to justify his own antipathy. This argument, while overlooking the point we have been urging, also ignores an earlier finding that people who are very favourably disposed towards strangers are often most conscious of their own remaining antipathy, and thus tend to see more antipathy in other people than these would see in themselves. Others have been apt to conclude that the disapproval of association with coloured people is directed against the immigrants, when in reality it is a sanction applied to the whites who depart from group norms. People may be forced, by the relationships in which they are involved, to observe and even to support customs of which they disapprove, and which a majority of the group may also disapprove of. This is one of the brakes upon social change, but it is also one of the forces that holds a society together.

IV

Hawaiian race relations have been considered among the best in the world. Racial discrimination is virtually non-existent. Prejudice, when it does exist, is of little consequence because means do not exist to turn it into harmful action. Adams, in this paper, discusses the typical reactions of a newcomer to Hawaii and the way social pressures change these attitudes over time. He delineates three stages of socialization into Hawaiian society and into Hawaiian ideas about race: the newcomer, whose attitudes are immediately challenged, and who often experiences discomfort when his old stereotypes no longer work; the island resident, who is receptive and resists discrimination; and the "old timer," who may express some personal prejudices among friends but will make no effort to discriminate.

ROMANZO ADAMS

The Unorthodox Race Doctrine of Hawaii

. . . When a traveler familiar with race doctrines and practices in other places visits Hawaii, he is impressed with the apparent absence of what is commonly called race prejudice. One man said, "Humanly speaking, you have no race prejudice in Hawaii." The things observed relate largely to ritual. A man of any race is addressed as "Mister" in Hawaii. A man from Texas saw and heard a Negro in the legislature — a Negro treated with respect and as an equal — and he went away in disgust. If our visitor has traveled in China he knows that the Chinese are not admitted as guests to Shanghai hotels intended for whites. But in Honolulu a Chinese man or a man of any other race may be entertained in any hotel and white men may sit at the table with him. In cities of the United States, Negroes occupy a separate section in theatres, away in the rear. In Hawaii a man of any race may be seated in the best section. If our traveler were to visit the public schools he might find a Negro woman as principal of a school in which she is the only Negro, or he might find one whose principal is an American Indian. He might be shocked to discover that men of dark complexion can and do arrest white criminals and act as their jailers. If he goes to the governor's reception he will see men of all colors shaking hands and holding friendly conversation with each other. If he is entertained at the home of a leading citizen, and if he is believed not to have sentiments antagonistic thereto, he may sit at the table with guests some of whom are not of his own race. If he is taken to a university social affair he will see young men and young women of several races and mixed races dancing on the same floor and to the same music. Should our traveler visit the industrial or the commercial sections of the city, he might find a white man who takes orders from a man of some other race or a white man who deposits his money in a bank with a Chinese or a Japanese manager. If he consults the report of the Bureau of Vital Statistics he will find that men and women of all races are inter-marrying and that, in the general process of interracial amalgamation through marriage, the white race is taking an important part. Possibly our traveler may attend a church wedding to witness a white young woman marry a man of some other race, while the friends of both or several races give their sanction by sitting in the pews.

If our visitor talks freely with white men who have lived in the Territory long enough to have accepted the doctrinal implications of Hawaii's rit-ual of race relations he will hear expressions of opinion and sentiment consonant with the practices. When a white man familiar with a different ritual comes to Hawaii — if he comes into social contact with the local people at all — he is soon made to feel the pertinence of the old saying "when in Rome do as the Romans do," and he does, in a measure, con-form. One must do what "everybody" does — what is expected of him. It would not be in good form to do otherwise. There is a code for gentlemen. A man may observe the rules of the local code with his fingers crossed but he does observe them. In the Hawaiian language there is a name for such. A *malahini* is a newcomer not yet in sympathy with the local race mores.

If, however, the *malahini* remains long enough, and if he is normal in his social attitudes, desiring to be really a part of the society in which he lives and not a permanent outsider, he will, early or late, begin to readjust his theories or doctrines. One begins to feel humiliated at the thought of yielding to a code contrary to his doctrines — "principles." But he cannot change the code or yet violate it without some sort of penalty, the penalty involved in placing himself "outside." His doctrines are, therefore, reconstructed; and in this way he achieves a comfortable social status without violating his conscience or standing condemned by it as a coward. When he has made this adjustment he is no longer a *malahini*, but a *kamaaina*, an old-timer, a member of the "we-group."

Perhaps our *kamaaina*, if a white man and if not to be quoted, will qualify the doctrines somewhat. He may not accept all the implications of the ritual and he may have misgivings as to the future. In minor crises he may even manifest attitudes quite antagonistic to the code he commonly observes and, within the intimate circle, he may profess doctrines of a contrary character. But the existence of these contrary sentiments and beliefs is a matter of second-rate importance. The really important thing is the general body of tradition that inhibits the open and constant avowal of such attitudes. In the conflict between antagonistic mores, the sentiment that cannot be openly avowed, that cannot be expressed in slogans, and that cannot influence the civil law or the social code is ineffective or, at most, effective only in a rear-guard action to cover a retreat.

In short, the race mores of Hawaii are, or tend to be, the mores of race equality, and the doctrines are, therefore, unorthodox from the standpoint of white people, especially of most English-speaking white people.

At this point no question is raised as to equality of stature, beauty, strength, inborn mental ability, temperamental traits, education, or technical skill. It is just a question of what the social ritual symbolizes. The use of the title Mister, the front-door welcome, the sitting together at dinner, and many other things symbolize equality of social status in Hawaii, just as the denial of the title Mister, the back-door entrance, and other rules of similar import symbolize social inequality in other places.

In the long run, the ritual affects the relations of a more directly practical sort in a very important way. Under the code of racial equality, it is possible for men of superior character and ability to attain to positions of power and dignity and to exercise authority without limitation as to race. Personal status comes to depend more upon personal merit and less on racial antecedents.

Before undertaking to account for the special race mores that tend to prevail in Hawaii it is necessary to make certain admissions. In the first place, the opposing race doctrines and rituals of the white people, even of the English-speaking white people or of those who live in the United

States, are not strictly uniform in character. In some places there are so few colored people that they have not attracted much attention, and so there are no obviously well-established ideas and practices relating to race contacts. In other cases the experience of race contact has been too recent to permit the development of a definite set of mores. What is said relative to these mores must be taken to refer either to the somewhat undeveloped tendencies or to the doctrines and practices of those communities in which the contacts have been important for a long time. On the other hand, the experience of most of the actual residents of Hawaii with its system of race relations has been too recent to permit of the general and full acceptance of the code; and the number and influence of the people of more recent arrival, many of whom are but temporary residents, is not without influence on the general situation. For many, the local race mores are accepted only in a superficial sense; they are not supported by strong sentiment — they lack the sacredness suggested by the word mores. The term, then, must be understood as referring to the trend of attitude or to the attitude of the people of more stable residence. The race mores of Hawaii are still in the making.

If one wishes to discover the things that were most important in creating Hawaii's pattern of race relations he must turn to experience — to the experience of particular men and women as revealed in case studies. In the stories of the early white residents one sees the mores at the very beginning of their development.

Any explanation of the special sort of race relations that has come into existence in Hawaii must deal with the factors that have conditioned the development of ritual. It is not that the white people of Hawaii differed from the white people of Virginia in color, in character, in the religion professed, in temperamental traits, or in their initial theories or doctrines about race. Nor were they different essentially in their attitudes relating to economic affairs. Business always seeks a profit, and a high profit is preferred to a low. Nor has there been in Hawaii an absence of the sorts of personal attitude which in American colonial times contributed toward the development of slavery and its social code. The problem is to discover the things that, in Hawaii, favored the development of one sort of code and tended to inhibit behavior consonant with the other — the series of historic situations.

In the beginning the things that tended to favor a sort of behavior that was based on the assumption of race equality may be considered as accidents of history — a series of situations in which it seemed to the white people and to the Hawaiians to be advantageous to treat each other with respect and, sometimes, with deference, the respect and deference not being a one-way affair. Behavior of this sort became habitual. Custom was established. There came to be a normal expectation — an incipient tradition. The native Hawaiians, while representatives of a stone-age culture, were so far developed in this culture that they were able to produce in considerable quantity certain commodities — fruits, vegetables, meat, salt, and timber — which were desired by the masters of European and American trading ships. They were also of such cultural advancement that they wanted articles made of iron, cotton goods, and other commodities available for exchange. That is, they were of such cultural advancement that trade was possible and the trade was important to vessels operating in the Pacific in the early nineteenth century. The Hawaiians were under the rule of a strong and shrewd king or chief who was able to maintain order among his people and to control trade relations. It was advantageous to white traders to recognize his authority. Since the king symbolized the dignity of his people as a whole, the recognition of his authority, in a subtle way, involved for the people as a whole a status superior to what would have existed had there been no such chiefly authority.

The king secured the services of a number of white men, men who understood how to build and operate ships, to use firearms, to negotiate in relation to trade, etc. From such accounts as we have, it appears that they served him loyally and, while they did not symbolize their respect according to the native ritual, they did show it in a way that was understood and accepted. These men, because of the value of their services, were given positions of honor and were given native women of chiefly rank to be their wives. They were recognized as chief in the Hawaiian system and their half-blood children were, by the Hawaiians, accorded high rank. These early white residents were, by the nature of their services and on account of the rank and position they held and also by virtue of their family relationships, absorbed into the Hawaiian society. Through their services they added to the power and dignity of the king and to the ability of their society to command the respect of transient foreigners.

It is not necessary to inquire into the early upbringing of these men, whether they were taught to believe in the inferiority of the dark-colored peoples or were wholly ignorant of the existence of such peoples. Doubtless, if they had gone to Virginia to live they would have accepted the system of race relations that prevailed in Virginia. Coming to Hawaii, they found no pattern of race relations and so they had to establish one.

When men live among relatives and friends as members of a we-group they must observe the prevailing code. But when they are spatially and spiritually isolated from their old home people they may be free. These men had not come from their old homes directly to Hawaii with a fresh memory of the paternal benediction. They had knocked about over the

world and had met peoples of many varying customs and standards, so
that those of their old home did not seem to be so important. They were
emancipated men.

The case of a high-born Scottish lad who ran away from home may
serve as an example. He left home because he did not get along well with
his stepmother. He changed his name, taking that of his own mother's
father, thus symbolizing his ill will toward his father. According to the
story, he fought under Lord Nelson at Trafalgar. Eventually he reached
Hawaii, where he remained and probably never after had any communication with anyone in Scotland. Because of his qualifications, King Kamehameha desired his services and so he appointed him to positions of
dignity and gave him a Hawaiian woman of chiefly rank to be his wife.
As a man of special qualifications and as one closely associated with the
king he could not fail to have prestige among the Hawaiians. As a man in
the service of the king and as one taken into Hawaiian society he could
not assume the airs of racial superiority. His superiority, on the one side,
was a matter of personal qualification and, on the other, a matter of accepting honor under the Hawaiian system and at the hands of Hawaiians.
Through his children (there are over four hundred living descendants) he
was permanently identified with the Hawaiians. He inevitably had to support the doctrine of racial equality if he responded in a normal way to
the requirements of his situation.

Man is so fundamentally a social being that when he comes into contact
with strange peoples he tends to make such adjustments as are necessary
to the enjoyment of normal human relationships. It seems to be more important to a man to enjoy such relationships than to maintain the standards of his former people, and this is especially true if he is not only
spatially but also spiritually isolated from them. These men were free
from the control of the old home mores and they were in a practical situation that called for a special sort of behavior. Under the circumstances
they had to act as if the king was their superior and the other high chiefs
equals. They had to show respect and to accept the status given them by
the natives — a status which was, in fact, higher than they had ever enjoyed before.

Not only were the white men who thus early helped to set the pattern
of race relations men of the emancipated type, but in all periods, down
even to our own time, there have been in Hawaii considerable numbers of
white men of this sort — men away from home and, therefore, more or
less free from home standards. Sometimes these men contribute to the
strengthening of the race mores of Hawaii, not directly, by accepting them
at first, but as a result of an unintended commitment. Being nearly free
from all mores, they follow the course of least difficulty in their social
relations and cross the Rubicon by marrying Hawaiian women. Of course,

there are many such out-marriages by old residents who are under the mores, but the percentage of out-marriages is much higher among the new-comers, many of whom are merely emancipated, than among the white men of more extended residence who are more or less fully under the local mores. In such cases it is not at all certain that it makes any difference whether a man comes from a place where race standards are strictly maintained or from a place in which little attention is given to matters of race. For example, a young man from a southern state is said to have sung with the rest,

> "You may call 'em Hawaiians, but they look
> like niggers to me,"

when he first came to Hawaii, but within a year to two he was married to a Hawaiian woman and for years he has been working to support his wife and half-white children. When he was married he was merely emancipated from the mores of his old home, but gradually he tended to come under those of Hawaii.

Gradually, through the mixed marriages, there comes into existence a population of mixed racial ancestry and, since the mixed bloods typically have their origin in a socially sanctioned marriage relationship, they enjoy a status impossible where marriage is forbidden and where, consequently, the mixed bloods are supposed to have had their origin in temporary and unsanctioned unions. The influence of this group of increasing size and prestige is bound to be for a continuation of the mores of racial equality and they contribute not a little to the developing sentiment that makes custom sacred.

Within permissible limits it is not possible to refer to all of the significant situations in which the incipient mores were exposed to the danger of overturn. Suffice it to say that there has been a succession of challenging situations and that, in one case at least, the outcome seemed doubtful for a time. It was finally settled, thanks to favoring circumstances as well as to the strength of a partially established tradition, in harmony with the earlier practice.

The coming of the American missionaries, in just one aspect, repre-sented a possible influence for reversal. The missionaries tended to destroy the freedom of the emancipated white men in Hawaii. To a considerable extent they established communication with the outside English-speaking world and in that way tended to establish in Hawaii the standards of England and America. This was bitterly resented by some of the emanci-pated, but it could not be avoided. Moreover, the missionaries brought their wives and established white family life with New England standards. After a while the white wives of business men came. Here was a chance, at least, that there would grow up a strictly white social group with stan-

dards adverse to interracial marriage and hence to the type of social relations that normally leads to marriage. This would supply a theoretical
basis for a whole code of the typical American sort.

But when the missionaries applied for permission to reside in the
Islands and to teach, the request was referred by the chiefs to an old white
man of thirty years' residence who had served the king with honor and
who had a Hawaiian wife and a family of mixed-blood children. The
missionary cause rested on this man's advice. Since the advice was favorable, they were permitted to remain in the land. Being under such obligations to this old man, they were under the necessity of accepting his family
arrangements formally, even if there was some feeling adverse thereto.

But in any case the strategy of the missionary position was such that
they had to make concessions on matters of race. They saw many things
in the behavior of the Hawaiians which they disapproved. Even after
many natives were baptized as Christians, they did not commonly live up
to the standards set by the missionaries. Now if the missionaries had said
that these deficiencies of conduct were in consequence of certain racial
traits — of traits conditioned by biological heredity — they would have
found it hard to answer the question, "Why are you here?" But if the
defects of character were regarded as due to the lack of the Christian
religion, that is, to a cultural rather than to a racial trait, they could feel
that there was a reason for their presence.

The missionaries having accepted the incipient race traditions, at least
as far as the ritual symbolizing respect and good will was concerned, they
were destined to furnish a strong support for the Hawaiian social order at
a critical juncture. When, due to the multiplication of white residents and
transient sailors, there was danger of a complete overturn of all Hawaiian
authority, it was the missionaries who turned the scale. The old strong-
willed king Kamehameha was dead and the young king lacked resoluteness
and shrewdness. The transient sailors and some men of more permanent
residence manifested the common tendency of white exploiters and irresponsible transients to break down the native order. After such a breakdown
the next step commonly is for the foreigners to plead native incom-
petence and thus to secure the assistance of their national governments to set up a control of their own. At times the king of Hawaii was
forced to submit to unjust demands backed up by foreign warships. Sometimes these demands were of such a character as to suggest that they were
not expected ever to come to the attention of the civilized world.

The missionaries, because they had access to some of the agencies of
civilized public opinion and were able even to influence the foreign policy
of some of the great nations, played at this time a most important rôle.
Some of them resigned from their missionary connection and, as advisers
to the king, helped to reorganize the government so that it could maintain

order at home and so that it could meet its international obligations. As administrators they helped to maintain the king in a position of dignity and to protect the people against disorderly white residents and transients and also against cheating by shrewd traders.

All this automatically tended to favor the mores of race equality. It was necessary to treat the king, the members of his family, and other high chiefs in such a way as to symbolize respect. If one who thus treated the king and other Hawaiian dignitaries with respect did, at some other time, refuse social recognition to Hawaiians of lower rank, such discrimination had to be regarded as based on rank or class, not race. If white people commonly had their more intimate associations, according to preference, with each other, such association could not be made to symbolize what must be symbolized in a caste system of race mores. Their social relations with the king inhibited that.

If the whole story were to be told it would be necessary to refer to the new situations of each generation. At one time the Chinese were involved and, in a different way, the Portuguese immigrants. There is a Japanese and a Filipino chapter to the story and even the small groups such as the Korean and the Porto Rican have had a place in the developing situation.

If a superpatriotic orator in Minneapolis wishes to propagandize against the kind of people who live in Cicero, Ill., he must not refer to them merely as foreigners, lest the Swedes take offense. So in the height of the anti-Chinese agitation in Hawaii nearly fifty years ago, the whites could not use the terms necessary to make it a race issue without offense to their Hawaiian friends. They had to forego a most effective method of propaganda and, hence, the inferior status of the Chinese was of a less permanent character — so transient that no regular doctrines and codes were developed. With such modifications of behavior as came naturally with time and changing circumstance, the Chinese escaped from the early odium and were welcomed into the general community life and this, of course, committed them to the formal support of the race doctrines that worked in their favor.

So far, the tradition based on early practice has been maintained — maybe waveringly at times but, on the whole, maintained. The sentiment is coming to be more widely shared and the doctrines are being more definitely formulated. At each critical juncture there have been at least some factors in the situation that have favored a continuation of the early customs, and the developing traditions have been strong enough to cast the deciding vote.

The coming of comparatively large numbers of white citizens from the mainland, especially the men and officers in army and navy service, constitutes the most recent challenge to Hawaii's race mores. These men and officers belong to organizations with their own traditions; in their traditions, distinctions of rank are highly important. Such traditions make it easy for them to accept the traditions of a racial caste system, and most of those who have the greatest influence were brought up in, or have lived in, sections of the country in which the doctrines of race inequality are definitely professed and practiced. Naturally, they are irritated by the practices and attitudes of the local people, and in minor crises their opposing attitudes become manifest. Because of the very definite character of their traditions and because of the temporary character of their residence, there is no tendency to accept the local mores. Because of their access to the agencies of public opinion on the mainland their attitude constitutes a challenge of more than common importance. Hawaii's race mores are still in the making.

In the beginning the social contacts between the Hawaiians and the early white residents were between a people who had no memory of race relations, and hence no traditions relative thereto, and some white newcomers who were emancipated from the mores of their native lands. The situation came uncommonly near to one of absolute freedom from all predisposing tradition and, in effect, the early system of race relations was almost an unbiased response to the practical demands of the situation. These demands were such that behavior, dominated at first merely by a consideration of practical interests, was free from any implied assumption of racial superiority or inferiority. Out of the early practices came habit, custom, normal expectation. There were people of influence whose interests were best subserved by a continuation of the sorts of relationship that were becoming customary. In challenging situations there were, therefore, people who would struggle for the maintenance of custom, and in such struggle sentiment would be strengthened. The logical implications of the situation would come to the surface, receiving some more or less formal statement. That is, there came to be beliefs and theories and, when sentiment was sufficiently strong, these were doctrines.

The doctrines were, of course, in harmony with the habitual behavior, and as the doctrines came to be more clearly formulated the behavior acquired significance for what it symbolized; it tended to become a ritual. That is, the practices were becoming traditional. In later times these traditions, even the traditions of a not very well-established character, were able to cast the deciding vote in challenging situations and the early tradition tended to be self-perpetuating. In its struggle for self-maintenance it has, on the whole, been successful because there is a ritualistic code which supports the beliefs and theories and serves for the expression of sentiment. But also there has been, to some extent, a continuation of favoring circumstance.

V

Although in India there are no social groups formed on the basis of skin color, the hierarchies of caste are so rigid and the imputed differences between members of different castes are so great that the system is almost the same as a multi-racial one. Davis explores the meaning of the term "caste" and the existence or absence of "national" castes. He analyzes the associations among caste, religion, and traditional occupation, and considers values and norms within the traditional caste ideology which permit sub-castes through excellence or occupational change to gain caste status. He also discusses the influence of a changing economic and legal system on this traditional hierarchy. The dimensions of physical mobility and industrial mobility are empirically observed and analyzed.

KINGSLEY DAVIS

The Demography of Caste

DEFINITION AND ENUMERATION OF CASTE

. . . The common features, or tendencies, which together distinguish Indian castes from other types of groups are as follows:

1. Membership is hereditary, and is fixed for life.
2. Choice of the marriage partner is endogamous.

From pp. 162-176 in *Population of India and Pakistan*, by Kingsley Davis (Princeton University Press, 1951). Reprinted by permission of Princeton University Press and the author.

3. Contact with other castes is further limited by restrictions on touching, associating with, dining with, or eating food cooked by outsiders.

4. Consciousness of caste membership is emphasized by the caste name, by the individual's identification with his caste in the eyes of the community, by his conformity to the peculiar customs of his caste, and by his subjection to government by his caste.

5. The caste is united by a common traditional occupation, although it may be united also by the belief in a common tribal or racial origin, by adherence to a common religious sect, or by some other common peculiarity.

6. The relative prestige of the different castes in any locality is well established and jealously guarded.

In practice, of course, considerable variation is found. There are a few rare castes that admit new members; there are some that are not strictly endogamous. But any group that is called a caste will exhibit most of these features. The whole can therefore be regarded as a caste complex, and as such, in all its completeness, is peculiar to India.[1]

Although this definition seems clear for theoretical purposes, it is by no means so for statistical purposes. The main trouble is that there are different layers of caste. The word *caste*, for example, "translates two vernacular terms with different meanings. The first [in Northern India] is *zat* (breed), with *qaum* (tribe) as a synonym; the second is *biradari* or *bhaiband* (brotherhood). The *zat* is the caste as a whole; the *biradari* is the group of caste brethren who live in a particular neighborhood and act together for caste purposes. The *biradari*, quantitatively considered, is a mere fraction of the *zat*; qualitatively considered, it is the *zat* in action."[2] At any time an observer is likely to be faced with several ways of grouping people in a caste context — moving from a class of castes (e.g., Brahman), down to more narrowly delimited caste groups, to subcastes, sections, and sub-sections. It is often hard to draw a line between these different modes of grouping, and the matter has to be decided arbitrarily.

In Mysore, for instance, the so-called Neygi caste embraces half a dozen subcastes. Between these subcastes there are differences of language, sect, and custom, and barriers against interdining or intermarrying. On the other hand, some groups in Mysore that are less different from one another than these "subcastes" are entered as *separate* castes.[3]

Additional confusion arises when the name of an occupation, a locality, or a language is given instead of the proper name of the caste. Errors of

[1] Sir E. A. H. Blunt, *The Caste System of Northern India* (London: Oxford University Press, 1931), Chap. 1; L. S. S. O'Malley, *Indian Caste Customs* (Cambridge: Cambridge University Press, 1932), Chap. 1.

[2] Blunt, *op. cit.*, p. 10.

[3] *Census of India*, 1931, Vol. 25 (Mysore), Part 1, pp. 319-20.

spelling and accidents of nomenclature also cause confusion. A similar name in different localities may not indicate the same caste; and two apparently different names may not indicate separate castes but merely two spellings or two synonymous titles of the same caste.[4] Finally, there is widespread effort by caste groups, and often by individuals, to adopt either a new name (not having the invidious connotations of the old one) or the name of a higher caste.

. . .

THE PERVASIVENESS OF CASTE

Caste has been virtually universal in India. The people who are not members of some particular caste have been extremely few. Some reform groups, such as the Brahmo Samaj and the Arya Samaj, profess to repudiate caste, but these have only tiny followings.[5]

. . .

The Sikh religion, which began in part as a protest against caste, is today almost as caste-ridden as Islam. Indeed, there are many castes that have three branches — Hindu, Muslim, and Sikh. In the Punjab, for example, there are 58 castes important enough to be listed in the Imperial Caste table. These 58 fall into the following categories with reference to the three main religions of the Punjab:[6]

Hindu	8
Muslim	12
Sikh	—
Hindu-Muslim	9
Hindu-Sikh	10
Muslim-Sikh	—
Hindu-Muslim-Sikh	19

There are thus 29, or half of the 58 castes that have Sikh branches, despite the fact that the Sikhs constituted only 14 per cent of the total Punjab population. Yet there are no numerically important castes in this area that are exclusively Sikh. Furthermore, there is still a recognition that Sikhism is somehow opposed to caste. For one thing, it is known that the Sikh population has been growing in the last few decades by virtue of conversion from Hinduism.[7] Most of the converts are from lower Hindu castes, and one of the reasons for their conversion is to get away from their erstwhile caste status. "Except in the case of higher castes such as Jat and Rajput, converts to Sikhism do not as a rule return any caste, being con-

---

[4] Blunt, *op. cit.*, pp. 208ff.
[5] *Census of India*, 1931, Vol. 19 (Baroda), Part 1, p. 397.
[6] *Ibid.*, Vol. 17 (Punjab), Part 2, pp. 282-302.
[7] *Ibid.*, Part 1, pp. 304-09.

tent with the entry of 'Sikh' in the column of caste. . . . Many members of low castes such as Chuhra and Chamar adopt Sikhism in order to escape the inferiority complex. In regard to Sikhs the instructions to enumerators were that they should not be pressed to return their caste."[8]

Even Christianity has not been able to extirpate caste distinctions among its converts. Speaking with reference to southern India, the Madras census report has this to say:

> Intermarriage is practically no more possible between a Christian ex-Vellala in Tinnevelly (or as he would call himself, a Vellala Christian) and a Christian who had come originally (perhaps one or two generations ago) from the depressed classes, than it would be among Hindus of like origin, and boycott would be as sure a consequence if such a union did take place. It is common, among Roman Catholics at least, for a segregation to be made even within the church. . . .
>
> There are wide variations in the degree to which these prejudices exist along with alleged Christianity. They are stronger among Roman Catholics than Protestants, possibly because the former have a larger proportion of adherents of higher caste origin; they are worse in the south than in the north or west and in rural areas than in towns. Everywhere, they are present in some degree.[9]

However, there is evidence that, as with Islam and Sikhism, the doctrinal opposition to caste does exert itself to some extent among the Christians. This is indicated by the fact that the largest proportion of converts is drawn from the low and depressed castes. It is also shown by the fact that a large number of Christians, at least in some parts, do not return their caste. In Baroda, for example, 65 per cent of the Christians did not return their caste in 1931. This compared quite favorably with the Muslims (4 per cent not returned) and with the Aryas (14 per cent).[10]

In conclusion, it seems clear that the caste system is extremely widespread and pervasive in the subcontinent. It is present in all regions. It applies to nearly every person, regardless of his religion. It pervades even those religions, even those reform groups, which have as one of their tenets the social equality of man. It is this pervasiveness that still makes a person's caste one of his most salient characteristics, despite the numerous forces that are now working against the caste principle.

NUMBER AND SIZE OF CASTES

Because of the uncertainty of classifying castes, subcastes, and sections, and because of considerable confusion in names, it is impossible to say

[8] *Ibid.*, p. 308.
[9] *Ibid.*, Vol. 14 (Madras), Part 1, p. 328.
[10] *Ibid.*, Vol. 19 (Baroda), Part 1, p. 397.

exactly how many castes there are in India. In 1901, which was the last year in which an attempt at a complete tabulation of all castes was made, the number of "main" castes and tribes was found to be 2,378.[11] Some of these groups had numbers running into the millions, others had a mere handful. The average number per caste was approximately 120,000, although such a figure is virtually meaningless.

The figure of 2,378 main castes presumably did not include subcastes. How many of these there are cannot even be guessed, but it is safe to assume that any caste whose members run into the hundreds of thousands or millions is divided into a large number of subcastes. In 1891 the subdivisions of caste were recorded in detail, and the resultant lists contained thousands of names. "The Jat and Ahir, for instance, were each responsible for over 1,700 entries; the Kurmi for nearly 1,500."[12] In 1931 Tehri-Garhwal, a tiny state in the United Provinces with an area of 4,180 square miles and a population of only 350,000, had no less than 387 subcastes of Brahmans and 1,025 subcastes of Rajputs.[13] Between subcastes . . . the social barriers are nearly as strong as between castes, little interdining and intermarriage being permitted.

In the 1931 census over 15 million Brahmans were returned. Theoretically they form a single caste, but in practice they are split up into an immense number of separate groups and sub-groups. These separate groups even differ markedly in social standing. Some of the exalted Brahman castes rank at the top of the social scale, but others rank so low that even their own clients, members of low castes, will not take food in their houses. Clearly, then, the term *Brahman* designates a very loose class of castes, not a caste in itself.[14]

No caste, strictly defined, is diffused over the whole of India. The Brahmans, as a general class, have an extremely wide distribution, but any particular Brahman caste is more limited as to area. As noted above, the effective caste group is a local group. "The caste council can only act for a limited area, an area small enough for the members of the council to assemble and for members of the caste within the area to have some knowledge of each other."[15] It can be expected, therefore, that the total caste — that is, the widest intermarrying and interdining group — will not ordinarily cover a very extensive territory. . . .

Since the effective caste group is a local affair, one place to look at the

[11] *Census of India*, 1901, Vol. 1, Part 1, p. 537.
[12] Blunt, *op. cit.*, pp. 37-38.
[13] *Census of India*, 1931, Vol. 18 (United Provinces), Part 1, pp. 9, 572-87.
[14] Sir T. W. Holderness, *Peoples and Problems of India* (New York: Holt, 1910?), p. 98; *Census of India*, 1901, Vol. 1, Part 1, p. 540.
[15] J. H. Hutton, *Caste in India* (Cambridge: Cambridge University Press, 1946), p. 86.

number and size of castes is in the village. For this the census does not
help us much, but we are fortunate in having the results of a survey of
over 50 villages in the middle Ganges valley.[16] This study found that in
the area surveyed there were 52 castes. Not one of these castes, however,
was represented in every village. The Chamars, one of the most pervasive,
were found in only 32 and the Ahirs in only 30 villages. "And yet, *a priori*,
the Chamars should be represented in all villages, as they are the commonest type of *razil* population, supply all the labour in the village and
are indispensable to village life." There were Brahmans in 40 per cent of
the villages. The Nai, or barber caste, was represented in less than half
the villages.[17] The average number of villages in which each caste, taken
altogether, was represented was only 9.3.

In most instances the village, if it had any members of the caste at all,
had only one family of the caste. The number of instances in which a caste
was represented by a given number of families were as follows:[18]

1 family of caste in village	340
2 families of caste in village	80
3–5 families of caste in village	60
6 or more families of caste in village	32

It seems clear that the rural village has by no means a full complement of
castes, and that the castes it does have are generally represented by only
one or two families. The first fact means that each village must depend to
some extent upon the services of persons in other villages, and the second
that relations between caste members must be maintained by contact between villages. In this light, the common practice of marrying outside the
village can be understood. In short, the rural village is not an isolated
social entity, but is intimately linked with others in the immediate area.

Changes in the size of castes are hard to determine, because alterations
of name, reversals of tabulation policy,[19] and problems of classification introduce extraneous factors. Therefore, no figures on this are given here.

[16] S. S. Nehru, *Caste and Credit in the Rural Area* (London: Longmans,
Green, 1932).
[17] *Ibid.*, pp. 23-31.
[18] *Ibid.*, pp. 37-39, Table C(1).
[19] Since 1901, when a full tabulation was made, not all castes have been
tabulated. In 1911 those castes falling below a certain percentage of the provincial
population were not included in the tables. In 1921 the percentage necessary was
raised, and it was figured on a district basis. (See *Census of India*, 1921, Vol. 1,
Part 1, p. 224). In 1931 the percentage was raised again, from 2 to 4 per cent.
Always, however, the exterior castes and primitive tribes have been given full
tabulation, at least in the provincial reports. (See *Census of India*, 1931, Vol. 1,
Part 1, pp. 432-33.)

CLASSES OF CASTES

So many castes jostle each other in India that they must somehow be grouped. Otherwise, neither the scholarly nor the lay mind could find its way through the maze. In practice the people themselves adopt a rule-of-thumb mode of classification and subclassification — a system that makes the caste structure look much more like our own class order than we would otherwise expect.

Caste vs. Outcaste

The chief line of distinction runs between the twice-born, or "clean," castes on the one hand, and the once-born, or "unclean," castes on the other. The line is by no means uniform from one locality to another, but in some form it seems to be everywhere present. It persists almost independently of religion. It is the deepest cleavage in Hindu society.

Several criteria of membership in the depressed castes are available. If a caste suffers all of the following restrictions, for example, it is certainly depressed:[20]

1. Inability to be served by clean Brahmans.
2. Inability to be served by barbers, water-carriers, tailors, etc., who serve the caste Hindus.
3. Inability to serve water to caste Hindus.
4. Inability to enter Hindu temples.
5. Inability to use public conveniences, such as roads, ferries, wells, or schools.
6. Inability to dissociate oneself from a despised occupation.

Although these criteria would seem to be clear, they do not serve very well for statistical purposes, because they admit of degrees and vary somewhat independently. A caste that suffers food and water restrictions may nevertheless be served by Brahmans of good standing. In Bengal there have been castes whom the barber would shave, but whose toenails he would not cut and whose marriage ceremonies he would not attend.[21] Also, castes are not uniform with reference to particular criteria. "A caste may be untouchable in one district and not in the next; and there are untouchable castes with touchable sections." Finally, the attitudes toward a caste may vary according to which of the twice-born are being dealt with; for "a caste may be regarded as untouchable by some of the twice-born and not by others."[22]

.   .   .

---

[20] *Census of India*, 1931, Vol. 1, Part 1, p. 472.
[21] *Census of India*, 1901, Vol. 1, Part 1, p. 541.
[22] Blunt, *op. cit.*, pp. 334-35.

Bearing in mind possible errors and differences of interpretation, one can cautiously mention some figures on the number of outcaste persons in India (excluding Muslims and Christians). In 1931 the total number came to 50.2 million, which represented a slight drop from the figure for 1921, which was 52.7 million.[23]. . . Figures for 1911 are apparently unobtainable from the general report. It would be unsafe to accept the apparently diminished figure for 1931 as representing a trend, not only because of lack of data for an extended series but also because of changing definitions. Be this as it may, it is worth noting that the number of outcastes is substantial. In a sense this seems to be the largest bottom layer of any class structure in the world. . . . The large number of outcastes in India attests the low standard of living in the country. It is the depressed castes that bear the brunt of the struggle for survival in an overpopulated, underdeveloped country.

The emphasis on the line between interior and exterior should not obscure the fact that within each of these groups of castes there are sharp differences of rank. "It is not to be imagined that within the circle of untouchability," for instance, "there are no subgradations, and that all untouchables are equals among themselves.". . . An address of Mr. Gandhi contained the following statement: "All the various grades of untouchables are untouchable among themselves, each superior grade considering the inferior grade as polluting as the highest class of the caste Hindus regard the worst grade of untouchables."[24]

Brahman vs. Non-Brahman

But as is the case in other societies, public interest does not center greatly on the gradations of rank in the lowest strata. It centers on those gradations at the top. For this reason considerable attention has been paid to the Brahmans at the top, as distinct from the Non-Brahmans. Although the traditional occupation of the Brahmans is the priesthood, they have been free to abandon this occupation for many centuries. In 1911 the percentage of Brahmans engaged in the traditional profession of the Brahman class was only 13, based on data from 11 provinces and states.[25] A

[23] The Census Commissioner for 1921 regarded the figure of 52.7 million as a *minimum* estimate, because many members of exterior castes tried to improve their status by changing their caste names or otherwise dissimulating. He estimated the real figure to be between 55 and 60 million. (See *Census of India*, 1921, Vol. 1, Part 1, paragraph 193; also 1931, Vol. 1, Part 1, p. 472.) . . .

[24] Reproduced in Shiva Rao, *The Industrial Worker in India* (London: Allen & Unwin, 1939), pp. 81-82.

[25] *Census of India*, 1911, Vol. 1, Part 2, pp. 358-72. The data on Brahmans by occupation were not presented as fully in 1921 and 1931 as in 1911, hence the use of 1911 data.

double influence has been exerted to give the Brahmans a wide occupational affiliation. First, the Brahmans, being at the top of the social ladder, were in a position to have no one gainsay them when they chose to take up a lucrative profession. Second, there is apparently a tendency for the lower castes, when they improve their position in some way, to try to call themselves Brahmans, sometimes with success. This would necessarily increase the variety of occupations practiced by so-called Brahmans. It would also have the effect of increasing the total number of Brahmans. However, the Brahmans, as the topmost class of castes, tend to have a lower fertility than do other Hindus. Also, the conversion of new Hindus is primarily at the bottom of the caste scale. Consequently the proportion of Brahmans among Hindus has not been increasing, as shown by the following percentages:

1891	7.14%
1901	7.19
1911	6.71
1921	6.58
1931	6.37

Certain other castes and classes of castes, all smaller than the Brahman, are near the top of the social scale. Their influence is restricted in the main to particular localities, but some of them have an all-India reputation, such as the Kayastha, Vaishya, Rajput, and Baidya. These would have to be classed with the Brahmans as among the aristocracy, but since they are not found over the whole territory, since their status often varies from one place to another, it is impossible to determine the exact number of the upper class by taking those castes that have the highest social precedence. This leaves the alternative of relying upon some more objective criterion — say occupation or literacy — as a method of grouping "clean" castes in a hierarchy of social strata. Suffice it to say, then, that in terms of social distinction, the Brahmans at the top, in 1931, constituted 8.2 per cent of the total *caste* Hindus. Of the rest, a certain number, an unknown percentage, ranked close to the Brahmans as part of the aristocracy, while the others constituted a broad middle class embracing many kinds and degrees of gradation.

Distribution of Classes of Castes

One would expect the Brahmans to be widely diffused, and this is the case. . . . They tend to be strongest in and around their original center, the United Provinces and the Punjab States, and weakest in the outlying tracts settled by non-Aryan peoples. . . . Southern India is relatively free of Brahmans. Madras has only slightly more than a fourth the proportion that the United Provinces have. The Brahmans are apparently more abundant in the prosperous and urbanized areas. . . .

The exterior castes, the menials and dregs, also show considerable variations of strength from place to place. In general they are more abundant in the North than in the South, although . . . there are some notable exceptions to this rule. The range varies all the way from 56 per cent in Travancore and 37 per cent in Assam (the result of labor migration into that province) to 0.2 in Baluchistan States. By district there is also found to be considerable variation. In the Central India Agency, for example, the percentage varies from less than 3 in certain minor states to more than 19 in others.[26] In the Central Provinces and Berar the figure varied from less than 1 per cent of all Hindus in some districts, to more than 30 per cent in other districts.[27] In the city of Bombay the proportion of depressed cast members in the Hindu population was 13 per cent.[28] In the Bombay Presidency as a whole the proportion was 11 per cent.

CASTE AND OCCUPATION

If the members of each caste all followed the same calling, it would be easy to group castes according to occupation. Actually this is seldom the case. The common belief that castes are occupationally specialized is due in part to the ideal theory of caste, in part to the patent fact that many castes do follow one occupation predominantly, and in part to the fact that even when a caste has no actual line of work in common it may nevertheless be identified with a *traditional* occupation. Since the so-called traditional occupation is easier to handle statistically than the mixed lines of work usually pursued, castes have often been classified according to traditional calling. Such a classification has little significance, however, unless the traditional occupation is also, at least to a considerable degree, the actual one.

. . . In general more than half the male workers are engaged in a line of work historically associated with their caste, and . . . in many castes more than 70 per cent are so engaged. Without a doubt the traditional caste occupation therefore still means something.

. . . Breaking the samples down according to the nature of the theoretical caste calling, one finds the following:[29]

[26] *Ibid.*, Vol. 20 (Central India Agency), Part 1, p. 215. The percentage is based on total population.

[27] *Ibid.*, Vol. 12 (Central Provinces & Berar), Part 1, pp. 383-85.

[28] *Ibid.*, Vol. 9 (Bombay Cities), Part 1, p. 40.

[29] Blunt, *op. cit.*, pp. 251-52. The figures are taken from *Census of India*, 1911, United Provinces volume. They refer to male workers only, and if the traditional occupation was given either as the primary or subsidiary occupation, the person was listed as following his traditional line of work.

	Percentage in traditional occupation
Dealers in food and drink	37
Agriculture	91
Laborers and village menials	14
Pastoral	20
Learned professions	20
Boating and fishing	9
Trade and industry	
Unspecified	70
Specified	51

In Baroda the sample of castes by occupation was classified according to degree of enlightenment, as measured by literacy. It turned out that 63 per cent of the members of the "Advanced Castes" were in the traditional occupation, while 72 per cent of the members of the "Intermediate Castes" were in it. This confirms our view that the higher castes take advantage of their position to enter new occupations.[30]. . .

THE PERSISTENCE OF CASTE

Although its precise form has changed from time to time, the caste system has endured for some thirty centuries. During most of this time the trend was in the direction of a more rigid, more unequal, and more finely stratified order. It reached its peak at roughly the same time that the feudal system in Europe reached its peak. In order to judge the current changes, and what the future may hold, one must weigh carefully both the forces tending to diminish caste and the forces tending to perpetuate it. Both sets of forces are always present, but it is the balance between the two that is crucial.

Forces Tending to Diminish Caste

Too often one thinks that the only forces opposing caste are those modern ones introduced from the West. This is not true. Long before the Muslims or the British there were factors in India that worked against the system. These were factors that will militate against a complete caste system in any society. If the Hindu social order could be summed up in a single sentence, it would be this: It is the most thoroughgoing attempt known in human history to introduce absolute inequality as the guiding principle

---

[30] This of course conforms to ancient historical tradition in India. In the Post-Vedic period the rule was that "in times of distress one might follow the occupation peculiar to the lower orders, but never that of the higher, and preferably the one prescribed for the caste next in status to one's own." G. S. Ghurye, *Caste and Race in India* (London: Kegan Paul, Trench, Trubner & Co., 1933), p. 74.

in social relationships. Such an attempt cannot completely succeed, any more than an attempt to introduce absolute equality.

Inherent Contradictions. In the first place, any system of stratification must have certain standards of excellence that form the basis of its invidious distinctions. Hindu culture, like any other, has such standards. It places a high value on restriction of women, celibacy of widows, purity of diet, cleanliness of occupation, freedom from manual labor, knowledge of sacred literature, and economic security. It follows that any group (be it a local caste brotherhood or even a family) that manages to improve itself with respect to any of these standards, will also improve its social status. Inevitably some groups will strive to improve themselves, because they and their fellows believe in their standards. But in so far as a group achieves a greater conformity to the standards and thus improves its social position, it overcomes the main principle of caste, the fixity of inherited status.

. . .

It seems clear, then, that the Hindu attempt to construct a system of absolute social inequality is inherently contradictory. The very scale of values, or standards, by which one stratum is judged better than another motivates people to try to improve themselves with reference to these standards; in so far as they succeed, the community is bound to recognize their achievement by giving them more or less prestige. . . .

In theory the caste system is a hierarchy of strata in which each makes a functional contribution to the whole, deriving its prestige from the nature of that contribution. But the idea of exclusiveness and ritual taboo has overridden this concept. Some groups are too exalted or too lowly to enjoy the services of other groups, despite the necessary nature of these services. The Brahmans, for example, are supposed to be the priestly class and to perform the religious functions. But they cannot perform these services for the untouchables. Consequently millions of depressed peoples must find priests in their own ranks. New castes of priests, having a much lower rank than the Brahmans, are thus created. . . . There is then a tendency in India for the idea of exclusiveness to create closed communities, each having groups that are functionally interdependent, the whole Hindu polity thereby acquiring a fundamental lack of unity. Again we see that there is an inherent contradiction in the theory of a social system built on the principle of absolute inequality.

Incompatibility with Change. In addition to inherent contradictions, it can now be shown that the ideal of absolute inherited inequality is incompatible with societal needs. To be practicable the ideal calls for a completely static social order. But there is, and can be, no such thing. Every society generates internal frictions that lead to change, and every society lives under conditions that themselves change. The moment there is social change there is also social mobility, and hence fixity of hereditary status becomes impossible.

To have each caste performing its own unique occupation and occupying the same rung generation after generation, a uniform rate of population replacement would be necessary for every caste. But the very notion of caste implies that there are different caste customs, and some of these customs will unavoidably affect fertility and mortality, and hence natural increase. . . .

In addition, there is the political variable. Political sovereignty is associated with territory, but a territorial basis of cohesion cuts across caste lines. Only when the entire caste society is embraced in one political entity are caste and sovereignty wholly compatible. India, however, has never been united as one political entity. The nearest it has come to it is under the hegemony of the British, a foreign regime. The very weaknesses of a caste society make it incapable of political unity over a large territory, and virtually helpless against an invader. As a result, political conflict develops, which not only turns caste against caste but also area against area. . . .

Geographical changes should also be mentioned. Hindu society has from its inception been agricultural and pastoral. The practice of these arts changes the physical setting. Forests are depleted and fields eroded. As the population reaches the limit afforded by the given organization and technology, new developments must take place or else the death rate will rise. In so far as the social system adjusts to changing necessities, it facilitates social mobility.

The conclusion emerges, then, that the caste system has never been perfect. It has had to fight for its existence. It has had to contend constantly with social forces inherently contradictory to the caste principle. So the theory that the loosening of caste came only with the advent of Europeans in India, is wrong. The system was already loose. What the Europeans did was give an impetus to some of the old factors opposing caste, and add some new ones of their own.

The Impact of Modern Conditions

The ways in which modernization is dissolving caste have been detailed by many writers. All that we shall attempt is a brief summary.

The Spread of Education. Two mainstays of the caste order are, first, the content of its learning — mystical, religious, and traditional — and second, the distribution of this learning, limited mainly to the priestly class. The mysticism helps to rationalize and strengthen the superstitions of the masses, thus holding them ideologically under control, while the monopoly of the Brahmans restrains competition for spiritual leadership. Both features of the system place an effective brake on technical and scientific process. Western education, on the other hand, is directed along technical lines and is meant for all the people. It serves as an avenue of individual advancement, on the theory that productive achievement is to be rewarded with enhancement of status. It is precisely contrary to India's medieval view of education. In so far as it has gained ground in the subcontinent, it has tended to upset the caste system.

Literacy, which in India tripled between 1881 and 1941, increased faster among the lower than among the higher classes. This trend indicates that education is spreading, and the history of Indian politics during the last half century shows that Western ideals and methods are being introduced by it. . . .

Political Democracy. One effect of British rule was to remove much of the local autonomy that once prevailed. Since the stronghold of caste is the isolated and nearly self-sufficient rural area, where the caste *panchayat* and the village *pachayat* govern most of life, the centralization of government inevitably affected caste adversely.

In addition, the British progressively allowed greater measures of representative self-government to India. . . . [But] it soon became clear that the lower castes were not wielding the power in elections that the upper castes were wielding, and the clamor arose for special electorates along caste lines.

· · ·

In some provinces the Depressed Classes wielded considerable influence, occasionally acting as a cohesive group and sometimes split up between various parties. Curiously, their first objective was not economic improvement but the removal of their disbarment from Hindu temples. . . .

The policy of special electorates and reserved posts cuts both ways with reference to the persistence of caste. On the one hand, by giving special favor to one class, it emphasized the separateness of that group as against the rest of the Indian polity. If such a policy had been pursued to its bitter end, the voting public would have been cut up into so many special groups that concerted action would have been utterly impossible. On the other hand, the avowed purpose was to give equality to people who were not equal — in other words, to make it possible for the scheduled castes to make their political voice heard and in this way to improve their social and economic position. In analogous fashion the laws of various lands protect children, wives, aments, and primitive peoples.

Legal Democracy. The British at first made no attempt to impose their entire legal structure on India. In the personal sphere, especially, they left things alone — the courts simply applying the Hindu and Muslim law as it stood. . . . After 1864, however, more interpretation became possible, and other changes became noticeable.

. . . Whereas the Brahmans, as sole custodians of the law, had presented it to the lower orders as a divine creation, the British treated it as a secular institution, made by man for the benefit of man and not to be monopolized by any particular caste. This had a powerful effect in undermining the power of the Brahmans and hence the caste system.

. . .

A greater blow to caste was the adoption of the Western principle of equality before the law. . . . The courts, by making the Brahman and the sweeper equal, are the agencies of change; they offer an escape from the restraints of the old social order.

. . .

The caste has lost legal control over the very essence of the caste system — intermarriage. Although the British courts at first supported the ban on intermarriage, they later reversed this policy. The Special Marriage Act of 1872 made it possible for an Indian or whatever caste or creed to marry a person of any other caste or creed. . . . The legalization of intercaste marriages was not entirely accomplished, but the law was far ahead of custom. Although in the cities there is a tendency for romantic love among the younger generation to break down caste barriers, the rule of endogamy is still observed more scrupulously than any other caste usage.

Another legal blow at the caste system is the effort to abolish untouchability. Some of the provincial or central laws along this line, as already seen, free the untouchables from particular disabilities — such as temple pollution or separate schools. The most drastic legislation, however, was that of the Indian Constituent Assembly on November 29, 1948, which adopted with acclamation an article in the Constitution making illegal *any* kind of disability for untouchables.

Western Economic Influence. Three aspects of caste are particularly susceptible to modern economic influence: (a) the association between occupation and caste, (b) the local character of caste unity, and (c) the joint family system. These will be discussed in turn.

(a) The caste order always held, but did not thoroughly practice, the principle of hereditary occupation. Modern influence, because of its fast rate of change, has made the principle much more difficult to practice. . . .

(b) It was the local area where caste found its function and its unity. Nowadays, however, even the remotest village of India must submit to economic developments far beyond its horizon. . . .

(c) Where hereditary status is strong the family also must be strong. But modern economic enterprise pulls people away from the homestead and pays them as individuals. . . .

Urbanization. The anonymity, congestion, mobility, secularism, and changeability of the city makes the operation of caste virtually impossible.

. . .

New Technology. Technological innovations create new situations not defined by the previous folkways. In reaching a new definition of the situation, people are likely to make convenience the guiding principle, even when, from a logical point of view, it conflicts with the spirit of the old laws.

.   .   .

Religious Conversion. The presence in India of proselytizing religions that do not in principle recognize caste has two effects. First, it affords a means by which members of lower castes can partially lose the stigma attaching to their status. Second, by virtue of this possibility, it forces Hinduism itself to inaugurate certain reforms in order to meet the competition of the more liberal religions. . . . Of course, it is easy to exaggerate the role of conversion as an escape from low caste status. As has been mentioned before, the caste identification may persist after conversion.

Forces Tending to Maintain Caste

So many forces oppose caste in India that one may wonder how it ever got started and why it persists. But we know that certain conditions facilitate a caste organization. One of these is a settled agricultural economy. India has seen the growth of cities and industry to some extent, but it is still an agricultural area. As long as the village predominates, caste will be hard to eradicate, especially since it is now deeply rooted in the religion and mores of the Hindus.

In addition, castes are showing a certain amount of adaptability to modern conditions. Since about 1900 they have been forming associations that use modern methods in pursuing the interest of the caste. The associations consist of caste members who speak the same language. Their purpose is "(1) To further the general interests of the caste and particularly to guard its social status in the hierarchy from actual or potential attacks of other castes; (2) to start funds to provide studentships for the needy and deserving students of the caste, . . . ; (3) to help poor people of the caste; (4) and sometimes to try to regulate certain customs of the caste by resolutions passed at the annual meeting. . . ."[31]

.   .   .

Allied with the formation of caste associations is the tendency toward consolidation of sections and subcastes. Such a movement is noteworthy, because the thing that has been evident in the past is the ease with which new subdivisions are formed. . . .

The fusion of subcastes, if carried far enough, will tend to alter the caste system. Like caste associations, it is a movement to strengthen the caste in its competitive fight with other castes, and like them it disturbs the fixed hierarchy. If carried to the point of fusing castes rather than

[31] Ghurye, *op. cit.*, pp. 177-78.

merely subcastes, it will tend to create broad classes, and thus the caste system will be transmuted into a class system.

The Balance of Forces: The Decline of Caste

Our discussion indicates that the forces now opposing caste are more numerous and definite than those favoring it. This conclusion can be reached in another way — namely in the actual evidences of the decline of caste. Foremost among such evidences are these: (1) the noticeable loosening of restrictions on interdining; (2) the widespread violation of food taboos; (3) the slight tendency to ignore intermarriage barriers; (4) the gradual removal of untouchability; (5) the pronounced growth of social mobility.

. . .

Mobility is prevalent all up and down the caste hierarchy. There is growing up today a new middle class, based on professions such as law, medicine, and business. This new middle class is drawn from all castes, some more than others to be sure, but certainly from no particular caste.

Though the balance is in favor of the dissolution of caste, it should not be thought that the caste system is disappearing rapidly. An institution that has endured for thirty centuries is not likely to pass overnight. The central and most essential trait — caste endogamy — remains almost as vigorous as before, being nibbled at only slightly by the modern notion of romantic love and individual choice. Moreover, the caste system is adapting itself to new conditions; it has a certain fluidity. "A fluid takes the shape of the vessel within which it is contained but does not alter in volume or quality. Much the same applies to Hinduism and the Hindu caste system. . . . It is this fluidity which gives [them] their strength and which has ensured and will ensure their survival."[32] Yet, when adaptation is carried beyond a certain point it ceases to be adaptation and becomes change. The modes of caste adaptation — the growth of caste associations, the tendency toward fusion, the adoption of needed reforms — presage the end of caste. It shows every sign of turning into a system of classes, "rather more rigid perhaps in the beginning than their prototypes in modern European countries,"[33] but similar nonetheless.

Doubtless there will be remnants of caste in Indian life for centuries. On the other hand, some aspects may be gone before another generation has passed. The separation of Pakistan will probably eliminate caste from that large area of what was once India. The importance that government planning must assume in the new Union of India will doubtless hasten the decline of caste there. If industrialization proceeds rapidly in that nation, the caste system will have essentially disappeared by the end of this century.

[32] *Census of India*, 1931, Vol. 14 (Madras), Part 1, p. 339.
[33] *Ibid.*, Vol. 19 (Baroda), Part 1, p. 412.

VI

The Burakumin are physically and ethno-historically indistinct from the majority population of Japan. Yet there exist between these two groups all the intense emotions of highly visible racial conflict. Donoghue explores with care the dynamics of their interrelations; the changing factors in law and social organization which have divided the Burakumin communities into two groups; and the factors of occupational discrimination, limited access to education, and extreme stereotypes which still keep the Burakumin "in their place." Much attention is given to the problems of self-appointed membership in the community, passing, and Burakumin community control and direction in both cases. The importance of community and language in an otherwise fragile system is emphasized.

JOHN DONOGHUE

The Social Persistence
of an Outcaste Group

This [article] summarizes field research in which the major objective was to determine some of the factors contributing to the social persistence of

From *Japans's Invisible Race: Caste in Culture and Personality*, edited by George DeVos and Hiroshi Wagatsuma (Berkeley and Los Angeles: University of California Press, 1966), pp. 137-152, 393-394. Reprinted by permission of the author and the publisher.

Shin-machi — an outcaste community located on the outskirts of Toyoda City[1] in the Tōhoku District of northeast Japan. The following description and analysis is directed to the two questions: Why do the outcastes remain a distinct subgroup in Japanese society? Why do Burakumin remain in overpopulated substandard communities, rather than migrate to large cities where their pariah stigma may be lost?

. . . The outcastes are not racially distinct nor do they have major overt cultural characteristics that might differentiate them from the majority society. They are not required to live in segregated villages, and the hierarchical social structure of the feudal period no longer exists. Moreover, Buddhist religious taboos against the taking of life and Shinto conceptions of pollution associated with blood, dirt, and death, both of which contributed to the early formation and development of the Eta, have undergone essential modifications. Most Japanese people now eat meat, and majority butchers, tanners, and shoemakers, occupations formerly held only by Eta, are found throughout the nation. The primary distinguishing feature of the outcaste is residence in a socially segregated and isolated community. What follows focuses specifically upon the dynamics of intergroup and interpersonal relations, and upon the socioeconomic organization that influences the social persistence of this community.

At present, the special communities, traditionally located on river banks and other marginal lands, maintain a perceptible distinctness because of substandard, slum-like dwellings and serious overpopulation. Although many of the Burakumin are employed in the customary Eta occupations of butchering, leather and fur processing, begging, and other menial tasks, the largest percentage are farmers, fishermen, and unskilled laborers. They are further differentiated from the majority by an income far below the national average, and by their tendency toward local and caste endogamy.

ATTITUDES OF NON-BURAKUMIN IN TOYODA

A great deal of misunderstanding concerning the Eta exists in Toyoda in the Tōhoku District of northeast Japan. Most citizens prefer to avoid the subject of the Burakumin even in conversation. Most informants, although unaware of the location of Shin-machi, are familiar with the term *Shin-machi-nin* (people of Shin-machi), which is applied to the outcastes of Toyoda. Few city residents have ever been to Shin-machi and most have never knowingly met an outcaste. Buraku dwellers do not affect the lives of the Toyoda people, and do not constitute a recognized social problem. This lack of concern, however, in no way diminishes the atti-

[1] All place names in this chapter are pseudonyms. The nature of the community and its relationship to the majority society makes this necessary.

tudes of prejudice and hostility; rather, it propagates ignorance, obscurity, and even mystery. Four of the most general attitudes held by Toyoda informants toward the pariah caste are offered below.

Disgust is the most widely held and commonly verbalized attitude. Individuals who are unwilling even to discuss the outcastes distort their faces and exclaim, *kitanai* (dirty). These feelings are sometimes manifested more directly. For example, after one of the customers in a small wine shop noticed blood on the hands and shirt sleeves of a young outcaste he shouted disparagingly at him and was joined by several others: "You are dirty, you animal killer! Look at the blood all over you! You are a filthy *yaban* (barbarian, savage)!"

Fear is another commonly found attitude of the Toyoda people. Outcastes are considered dangerous and capable of inflicting bodily harm. There are exaggerated stories of physical prowess and fighting skill and they are likened to the gangsters and hoodlums portrayed in American films. There is also the fear that surrounds the unknown. Burakumin are believed by some to be sinister characters with evil powers, and mothers sometimes frighten their children with gruesome tales of the "eta" bogeyman. It is said, too, that the outcastes are afflicted with such contagious diseases as syphilis, gonorrhea, tuberculosis, and leprosy.

Because the Burakumin and their village are forbidden, the attitude of *erotic curiosity* prompts such questions as: "Do the 'eta' look different? Are the women really beautiful? Are they rough, like gangsters? Do they actually speak a different language? What kind of food do they eat?" Many wonder if Buraku girls are "better" than ordinary women, some young males have erotic desires for outcaste women, and restaurant hostesses often joke about an imputed enlargement or distortion of the genitals of the male "eta."

The spread of the final attitude, which might be termed *objectivity*, seems to be increasing steadily among the younger generation, but it has the fewest adherents in Toyoda. This attitude is not widespread because it depends primarily on observation.[2] "Look at the 'eta' and their houses — they *are* dirty, they have dirty occupations and they are diseased." "The 'eta' always marry each other, so their strain is weak. They are an exclusive, intimate group that rejects outsiders and any form of aid." "I feel sorry for the 'eta' because of their lowly position, but I will have nothing to do with them until they learn to live like other Japanese, that is, give up their occupations, marry outside their small community, clean up their villages, homes, and themselves, and drop their hostile clannish attitudes." Such beliefs are based less on legend than others but,

---

[2] Such viewpoints exist, as Merton states in another context, not as prejudice or prejudgment, "but as the irresistible product of observation. The facts of the case permit no other conclusion." Merton (1949), p. 182.

as with dominant Negro-white relations in the United States, they operate as a self-fulfilling prophecy in maintaining the outcaste status.[3]

The beliefs and myths of the Toyoda citizenry preserve majority group exclusiveness by associating the Burakumin with violations of some of the most fundamental and sacred Japanese values — those centering around purity, lineage, and health. The following are two of many popular legends heard in the city.

A young man met a beautiful girl in a restaurant. After a short courtship they were married against the wishes of the boy's parents. They lived happily for awhile, but when their children were born idiots with spotted complexions, it was discovered that the girl was a Burakumin.

It was customary prior to the turn of the century for Burakumin to wash the bodies of deceased commoners in return for an offering of *sake* but after the outcastes began to realize their emancipation, they frequently requested money for their services. Sometimes the demands were exorbitant. When the sum was refused, the Burakumin would threaten the family by vowing to drink the water used in bathing the body. The people were usually frightened into relenting to the Burakumin demands.

The general theme of the first story is the unhappiness of anyone who marries an outcaste, and the physical and mental deformity of the offspring. This is probably the most widespread myth, as it is employed by parents to discourage children from affairs that might result in a "love marriage." Even the most informed Japanese balk at the thought of marriage to an outcaste because of the popular notion of their "weak strain" from long intermarriage. The second legend illustrates the supposed barbaric quality of the Burakumin; not only were they mercenary, but they profaned the sacred, defiled the dead, and imbibed the impure and dirty.

SHIN-MACHI

Shin-machi's 347 inhabitants are housed in 43 dwellings, some including as many as ten households, located on a narrow dead-end road on the southeastern edge of Toyoda. Several relatively new houses dot the village, but the majority are old and dilapidated. Windows are covered with newspapers, and holes in the roofs are patched haphazardly with cardboard and paper held in place by large stones.

Family genealogies indicate only 18 surnames in Shin-machi, and seven of these account for the majority of the 78 households. Sixty-two per cent of the marriages are between residents of the community, and 79 per cent between individuals with Eta occupations and status. Thus, almost every individual is either consanguineously or affinally related to every other individual. Adoptions are frequent, especially between siblings, and illegitimacy is common; few families have no illegitimate births recorded in the city registration book (koseki).

[3] Merton (1949); Myrdal (1944); MacIver (1948).

The traditional outcaste occupations support 30 per cent of the households. Another 35 per cent are day laborers or claim no occupation. The remainder are dependent upon menial, low-income occupations such as begging, rag collecting, knife-grinding, peddling small confectioneries at festivals, and collecting food and clothing left at graves after certain religious festivals. Only four residents hold jobs that might be construed as ordinary occupations.

Analysis of the social and economic structure of Shin-machi reveals two clearly defined status groupings, with marked differences in prestige, power, attitudes toward outcaste status, and systems of interpersonal relations. Individuals identify themselves with the group to which they objectively belong (in terms of occupation, wealth, education, house type, and kinship orientation) and they are rated by others as belonging to one group or the other. The terms "upper class" and "lower class" are used here to differentiate them. (The Burakumin themselves make the distinction between "the people down there" and "the people up there," which are not altogether accurate references to the geographical location of lower and upper class dwellings.)

The upper class is composed of 13 households with a total of 75 members, 46 female and 29 male. The residences, many of which are clustered in one section of the village, are typical modern Japanese houses, each owned by its occupant. The heads of the households are usually literate, and several have reached high school. Upper class children have attended school regularly since the end of the war, and most will probably finish high school. Constituted authority in Shin-machi is vested in the upper class, with the headman and his assistant being members of this group.

There is a high degree of occupational stability in this class. All of the trades have been practiced in the households for at least three generations and, typically, a household has only a single occupation, such as drum-maker or shoemaker. In some instances, however, secondary income may be supplied by the employment of unmarried sons and daughters in wine factories and in offices outside the community.

The lower class has a total of 272 persons, 137 males and 135 females, residing in 65 households. The makeshift lower class dwellings, none of which is owned by the occupants, are overcrowded and poorly heated and lighted, thus sharply differentiating them from the upper class houses. Only two lower class individuals have completed the third grade. Though recent educational reforms have tended to increase the school attendance of lower class children, it still remains sporadic, primarily because of inadequate clothing, irregular diet, and prolonged illnesses. Also, ridicule by both teachers and students in the public schools reduces incentives for education; postwar hostility against Buraku children in schools is apparently directed at lower class students, who are distinguished by shabby clothing and dirty appearance.

In contrast to the upper class, the low-income occupations of the lower class are marked by diversity and irregularity. Of those interviewed, 43 of the families receive the major part of their incomes from fur cleaning and processing (12), day labor (17), begging (4), peddling (7), and relief (3). Another ten families claim no employment. Since these jobs are seasonal and part-time, lower class families are generally supported by more than one occupation.

The class division is a fairly recent phenomenon in Shin-machi. Prior to the depression of the 1930's, the Burakumin had been a rather homogeneous and economically prosperous group. Although overt discrimination had been more severe, the monopoly in the fur and leather crafts had assured them an adequate income. During the depression, however, many of the outcastes, especially the animal slaughterers and fur workers, suffered a marked decline in income. The demand for leather goods declined, the prices of traditional handicraft were depressed, and opportunities for outside employment were virtually eliminated. Few Burakumin starved during this crisis, partly because of their reliance upon the meat from slaughtered animals, but many were reduced to begging. Some sold all personal belongings, including houses, household equipment, and clothing.

The demand for fur goods never again reached a pre-depression level, so the majority of those engaged in the fur business have not been able to regain their former living standard. But all outcastes were not equally affected by the depression and many have since become prosperous, so that there are now two sharply differentiated groups, the relatively wealthy and the poor.

At the outset of the research in Shin-machi, it was believed that all the residents were forced to remain in the outcaste community because of the discrimination and prejudice of the larger society. But as our study progressed, it became increasingly apparent that the problem was not simply the relationship of the outcaste group to the larger society, but also relationships within the Buraku. Although the Burakumin are despised and discriminated against, the attitudes, beliefs, and fears of the outsiders do not fully explain the persistence of the community. In response to the external forces and outcaste subordination, Shin-machi has developed internally a distinct socio-religious identity and unity, and a strong set of social, economic, and psychological restraints upon individual mobility.

Community Organization and Social Solidarity

Although Shin-machi is a subdivision of Toyoda City, it is the only district that elects its own headman, holds town meetings, and maintains liaison with the municipal government. These are extra-legal functions, not provided for in the postwar city charter. However, they indicate that both the city officials and the Burakumin recognize the "special" (*toku-*

shu) character of Shin-machi. They also tend to stimulate community identity and cohesiveness by directly involving community members in local Buraku problems.

The village headman (*sonchō*) and his assistants (secretary, treasurer, fire and health commissioners, and shrine attendant) handle disciplinary matters within the community, cases of discrimination by outsiders, and such issues as the raising of money for special purposes, collecting taxes, and arranging religious festivals. General meetings, held in the village shrine and attended by at least one member of each household, are called by the headman to discuss village problems and, if possible, to reach decisions by agreement among the villagers.

In addition to sounding out opinion and disseminating information, the town meetings reinforce community solidarity. Few issues are settled at any meeting, but individuals become involved in the problems of the whole community. The town meetings generate feelings of belonging primarily because the problems are unique to the community and, in most instances, directly related to outcaste status. Except for religious celebrations, these meetings are the only occasions when all members of the community assemble for business and entertainment. Large quantities of *sake* are consumed, and status differences and special interests are subordinated to the greater general interest.

The pattern of social control that has developed in Shin-machi is related to its system of self-government. The Burakumin, particularly those at the apex of the power structure, are intent upon concealing from outsiders every aspect of their mores, especially those believed to violate or differ from majority Japanese standards. Stringent controls are therefore exerted upon community members to restrict relationships with the majority society. Public disturbances, lawbreaking, or any behavior that might bring disrepute to the Buraku are discouraged by ostracism, ridicule, and criticism, and even by threats or acts of violence. A person who discusses community affairs with an outsider is treated as a "fink" with pressures comparable to those employed by criminal groups and juvenile gangs in America. These measures obviously stimulate ingroup exclusiveness and set the Burakumin off as a closed subgroup.

Religious affairs also function to integrate the community. These observances, like all public community activities, are held at the Shinto shrine in the center of the Shin-machi graveyard, and are presided over by the headman. Religious celebrations are of two kinds: Buddhist festivals to commemorate the dead, and Shinto or shrine festivals in honor of the local tutelary dieties. While the themes differ, the rites are identical, and the overall unifying symbols are those of common ancestry, common territory, and common problems.

On Buddhist holidays the close kinship ties among the members of the community are made explicit by the homage rendered to common ancestors. These bonds are reinforced by community decoration of the graves, and prayers and speeches at the shrine make constant reference to relationships between the behavior of the living and expectations of the dead. Perhaps the most dramatic suggestion of kinship unity occurs during the spiritual interaction between the old men of the village and their common ancestors through a medium at the celebration of *Higan* (a Buddhist holiday commemorating the dead).

At the Shinto festivals, major emphasis is on cooperation and community welfare. The headman reviews past accomplishments and failures of the community, suggests ways to bring about greater realization of community goals, and asks the gods for their protection and good will. The principal concern is the continued well-being of the Buraku.

In every speech and in every prayer mention is made of the community in its relation to the world outside. Some are pleas for greater cleanliness in the village, or for curtailing the slaughter of dogs; others center on the outcaste's low position in Japanese society, or on the cruelty of the world as signified by a particular instance of discrimination. Some orations invoke the intercession of the gods for the attainment of economic success, for the marriage of daughters, and for less discrimination by majority society members. Clearly, the shrine and its gods are the locus of community identification; the religious rites express a system of relationships that differentiate this group from those surrounding it, and gave it a distinct socioreligious identity and unity.

During the drinking sprees accompanying the festivals, conversation invariably turns to the common enemy, the outsider. Occupations and poverty, family difficulties and poor living quarters, are all discussed in the context of relationships with the majority. All the fears and hopes expressed in the ceremonials are reiterated in conversation at the *sake* parties. Songs are often sung in a secret traditional Eta vocabulary (a kind of Japanese pig-Latin used frequently when outsiders are present) with an enthusiasm that reflects the intensity of the individual's identification with the community. The subordinate relationship of the community to the larger society, then, is an essential aspect of the social and religious life of Shin-machi, and it is an important mechanism for maintaining social solidarity.

Social Organization and
Patterns of Stability and Mobility

Individual members of Shin-machi are torn between the desire to emigrate and so lose outcaste identity, and the desire to remain in the community, thereby assuring a degree of social and economic security. Since the Eta emancipation in 1871, and probably before, individuals have passed into the larger society. However, the opportunities for leaving the Buraku have become greater since World War II, and this has intensified the ambivalence about remaining in the community. Remaining in the community has so far been the stronger sentiment, and the community has even increased in population from 310 in 1920 to 347 in 1954. A brief analysis of the socioeconomic organization of the two classes may reveal some of the factors underlying this situation.

Upper Class Burakumin

The household is the basic social and economic unit of the upper class. Each household is ideally composed of a man and wife, their eldest son and his wife, and unmarried children. The eldest son inherits the family property, debts, obligations, and occupation. He is also obligated to support his aged parents and to maintain the lineage, and at the death of the head of the household he is bound indefinitely to the residence and trade of his father.

Junior sons in the upper class are encouraged to migrate and seek employment in one of the larger cities. This accomplished, all obligations between the migrant and his family are terminated by mutual consent. When such emigration occurs, outcaste identity presumably is lost and the individual may be assimilated into the general population. Although the position of the younger sons appears advantageous insofar as it enables them to escape the outcaste stigma, considerable anxiety results from the situations into which they are thrust. Outside the community, migrants live in constant fear of discovery, and the consequences for those detected in their attempts to pass are usually disastrous. Several disillusioned persons have returned to Shin-machi after such failures; breakup of marriage, loss of family and job, and sometimes suicide, result from detection in an attempt to pass.

However, one of the greatest sources of frustration for the émigré stems from the still undeveloped wage-earning economy, combined with the pressure of overpopulation. Employment opportunity in Japan is still largely regulated by kinship affiliation and its extension — "The society is no more than an organization of families."[4] The migrant outcaste has no family connections; he has no sponsor and no reference in the society outside his community. Furthermore, in order to lose his stigma it is almost essential that he move to the urban centers, the major underemployment areas of the country into which a vast number of persons from rural areas flow daily.

The social and economic factors that arouse anxiety in the junior sons also tend to reduce mobility aspirations of the eldest sons, whose duty is to remain in the community. Those of upper class families are highly

[4] Stoetzel (1955), p. 57.

skilled craftsmen as a result of years of apprenticeship in the family trade. If they remain in the community, as they must in order to practice the inherited occupation, they are assured a degree of economic security. The choice therefore lies between abandoning a means of livelihood in order to erase the degradation of caste, and remaining a low-status Burakumin with an assured means of subsistence. The psychological dilemma is never solved.

The precarious economic balance in the upper class depends upon the regular out-migration of junior sons. The household economy is unable to support an additional individual or family, and the overcrowded housing conditions in Shin-machi make it impossible to shelter new members. Moreover, the Buraku occupational monopolies are so marginal that the addition of a single competitor would seriously depress individual incomes. Although mass production in the leather industries has reduced the market for handicrafts, the Shin-machi tradesmen still have a steady if limited outlet for their goods; if these conditions remain unaltered, the upper class Burakumin are assured a regular and relatively high income. The system of out-migration may therefore be viewed as a conscious attempt by the craftsmen to limit competition from junior sons who are potentially new members of the guild. Consequently, both the guild and the separate families have a vested interest in maintaining the continual flow of individuals from the community.

The upper class attitude toward the elevation of outcaste status also bears upon the emigration pattern. The intensity of their desire to erase all caste barriers cannot be overemphasized. They believe that they have acquired the material symbols and social skills necessary for recognition as members of the Japanese middle class but that they remain in the community because of family obligations, because of the order of their birth. Their interest and effort is focused upon raising the collective status of the Buraku. Members of this class believe that the outcaste stereotype held by the majority society will be modified by changes in the condition of the community. And as the deplorable physical environment of Shin-machi results in part from large population and low income, Buraku leaders feel that a stable population is a major factor in the status enhancement of the whole community. The notion of total caste mobility does not spring from a deep-rooted sympathy with the Burakumin and their problems, but has developed because the leaders feel that they will be able to enhance their own status only by elevation of the entire caste.

The fervor with which the upper class now seeks social and economic equality has coincided in general with the rising educational standard and the decrease in direct discrimination. Prior to World War II, the aspiration of community leaders of Shin-machi was predominantly for simple acceptance by the majority; the role the outcastes were destined to play in the society was conceived as immutable. With the return of the war veterans, the character of the upper class and the pattern of community leadership underwent significant changes. The young returnees were literate, optimistic, and experienced. They were unable to accept the inferior outcaste status based upon tradition, ignorance, and prejudice; rather, they felt that the majority society must eventually regard them as equals.

The recent decrease in the incidence of overt and direct hostility toward the Burakumin has tended to reinforce the new upper class beliefs, since it appears that majority attitudes are now shifting toward greater tolerance. This apparent trend has impressed upper class members with the proximity of their goal of equality, but psychological anxiety has been magnified because the actual status of the Burakumin has not changed significantly, and there are still sporadic cases of discrimination and out-group hostility.

In order to facilitate changes in majority attitudes, upper class leaders have instituted an improvement program designed to eliminate conditions within Shin-machi believed to be at variance with the prevailing standards of the larger society. Specific improvement is sought in the dirty physical appearance of the community, and in the "barbarian" behavior of certain Shin-machi residents. The former is difficult to eradicate because it is largely a consequence of inadequate housing and overpopulation. However, periodic inspections are made by the health and sanitation officers, and suggestions offered for the improved use of existing facilities. Communitywide cleanup days are held several times a year; and such practices as killing animals within the community and littering the area with garbage are discouraged.

The upper class Burakumin are at least partially aware of the outsiders' conception of them as immoral, criminal, irresponsible, and alcoholic, and they are also aware that such accusations are sometimes justified. There is promotion of such Japanese virtues as maintenance of family obligations, honesty in business dealings, moderation in drinking, and interest in child welfare. Failure to conform evokes gossip, ridicule, and condemnation.

Obviously, the specific improvements desired by the upper class require alterations in the living conditions and behavior of the lower class. But by and large, this class does not act in accordance with the new rules, thereby evoking hatred and disgust from their "superiors," attitudes similar to those expressed by outsiders toward the outcaste. In fact, upper class Burakumin often refer to members of the lower class as "those barbarians," "those dirty people," "beggars," and "Hinin."

Lower Class Burakumin

The social and economic life of the lower class is dominated by the fur and leather processing industry and regulated by a system of fictive kinship relationships: nearly two-thirds of the lower class households receive a proportion of their income from this industry. One wealthy and powerful individual, himself an outcaste, has an absolute monopoly in it, including the allocation of employment and the ownership of all lower class houses — the homes of his employees.

In this Buraku one finds a type of social-occupation-power relationship between this man and his tenants which is in effect a traditional set of diffuse reciprocal obligations known as the *oyabun-kobun* system, long an essential feature of the socioeconomic life of the lower class. Knowledge of this system is crucial to the understanding of community persistence.

The *oyabun-kobun* (literally, father role–child role) is a system "in which persons not usually related by close ties of kinship enter into a compact to assume obligations of a diffuse nature similar to those ascribed to members of one's immediate family."[5] It is a ritual kinship generally established by a special rite of passage. Members address one another by familial terms. Although it satisfies many of its members' needs, its primary function is the ordering of economic relationships. It operates in many spheres and on various levels in Japanese society, and there are a number of variations in its form, duration, and specific functions.

In Shin-machi the oyabun-kobun institution regulates two interrelated aspects of economic organization: landlord-tenant and employer-employee relationships. During the depression, a representative of a large Tokyo fur company loaned money to a number of Shin-machi inhabitants, as well as to the Toyoda butcher shop proprietors. In time, the borrowers became hopelessly indebted and were forced to sell their homes and businesses to their creditor, and a group of Burakumin thus became dependents of the new landlord, who required them to work for him to pay the high rents he exacted. Through his financial control over the local butchers he demanded the hides of all animals slaughtered in the Toyoda area. He now owns the large leather and fur stores in Toyoda as retail outlets.

By incurring obligations (*on*) to the oyabun, the followers are pledged to his service; in return, he assumes responsibility for their support. Because of his control over the supply of hides, his readily available labor force, and his system of distribution, the oyabun gradually forces the smaller independent furriers into the organization. At present, all but one of the furriers in the community are his employees, and he allocates the amount and kind of work done by each. Except for a few wealthy individuals, all are financially dependent upon him.

The oyabun is the most revered man in the community and there are innumerable stories of his kindness and generosity. He continues to aid the poor with favors and loans, and thereby reinforces his dominant position. The patron is committed to aid impoverished families, to assign jobs

5 Ishino (1953), pp. 695-707.

to clients in proportion to need, and to assure a certain minimum income to the families under his protection. Because of his wealth and record of generosity, he has created a kind of economic security for the lower class.

The obligations that characterize the oyabun-kobun relationship are a powerful deterrent to mobility, especially when reinforced by financial indebtedness. The oyabun is outside the community class structure because he does not participate in community affairs, and because he is not considered a member of Shin-machi by other members of the community. However, he lives on the periphery of the Buraku, and is regarded by Burakumin and non-Burakumin alike as an outcaste.

The obligation of the patron to assure his followers subsistence is an incentive for individuals to remain in the community. Although several lower class families must resort to begging, and others may occasionally go hungry, it is believed that no one will starve in Shin-machi as long as the oyabun-kobun system exists. The people have faith that any crisis can be met by resort to the patron's benevolence and there is also the possibility that some may gain more than mere subsistence. In addition to the opportunity for at least limited mobility within the occupational hierarchy, there are other possible advantages, such as loans for house repair, clothes, tools, and in one case, the initial investment in a confectionary and wine shop.

Although economic considerations are the major factors inhibiting lower class movement from Shin-machi, the same cultural and psychological conditions exist as those discussed in the preceding chapter. A large percentage of lower class Burakumin would be unable to pass into the larger society because they lack the ability properly to handle social relationships and speech forms outside the community.

Since the Japanese language is a highly respected art and an index of social class, people are most conscious of the variations in dialects and of the kinds of individuals who use them. Upper class urban dwellers, for example, use standard forms, while rural inhabitants speak local dialects, which immediately mark them as rustics. The lower class Burakumin in Shin-machi have a distinctive dialect similar to that spoken in isolated communities in the mountains nearby. They are also distinctive because they are illiterate in a society in which literacy and learning are valued skills. Additionally, their knowledge of correct Japanese behavior is insufficient. Since the way in which interpersonal relations are conducted indicates an individual's background, lower class outcastes are often branded as curious, different, or barbarous. The Burakumin are conscious of differences between themselves and outsiders and tend to withdraw from situations that might demand social interaction with majority people.[6] Members of the lower class generally regard themselves as truly in-

[6] An example is afforded by the following experience told to me:
A young man left the community to look for employment in Hokkaido,

ferior, believing that their position in Japanese society is predetermined and immutable.[7]

Outcaste status for lower class Burakumin is a matter of indifference and acceptance, except when specific questions are asked about it. In general, they are willing to discuss Eta problems, and are even flattered that outsiders will deign to speak to them. Similar questions about the Buraku could never be asked of upper class members, who vigorously deny that there is any difference between themselves and the majority and resent insinuations that such distinctions exist.

Intra-Group Relations: A Summary

In part as a result of the differences among outcastes in their attitudes toward their own status, hostility developed between the classes; the net effect of this has been to increase community solidarity by intensifying intra-group interaction. It has been suggested that members of both groups are constrained to remain in Shin-machi. However, the upper class is mobility oriented while the lower class is characterized by status acceptance and indifference. The upper class is committed to improving conditions in Shin-machi in order to raise the collective status of the Buraku, a program that requires total community participation. Since they are not mobile,

---

where there is little discrimination against Burakumin. Upon his arrival, he became lonesome because he had no place to go and had no acquaintances in the city. In an attempt to ward off solitude he stepped into a cabaret, but as he pushed open the doors, the hostesses began to laugh. Embarrassed, he immediately returned to Shin-machi. The young man claimed that "the girls laughed at me because they knew where I came from." (Obviously the girls would be unable to distinguish him from any other stranger.)

[7] The following excerpts from an interview with a lower class Burakumin convey this self-image clearly:

Q. Are you the same as common people (heimin)?
A. No. We kill animals. We are dirty, and some people think we are not human.
Q. Do you think you are not human?
A. (long pause, and then) I don't know.
Q. Are the common people better than you?
A. Oh, yes!
Q. Why?
A. They do not kill animals. They do not live here (in the Buraku). They are good people.
Q. Do you think you or your children will ever leave this district or change occupations?
A. No, we are new common people (shin-heimin).
Q. Do you think outsiders will ever come to this village and treat you as friends?
A. No, people on the outside don't like us. Things haven't changed for a hundred years.
Q. Do you believe this is right or fair?
A. (long pause) I don't know; we are bad people, and we are dirty.

persons of the lower class either do not comprehend or are unable to respond to the upper class innovations. This refusal or inability to conform to the standards dictated by the community leaders has separated the two groups. Members of the upper class feel disgust, hatred, and embarrassment because of lower class indifference, while lower class members believe that upper class policies are unnecessarily restrictive and unwarranted. If this situation were to exist in a society where both groups were really readily mobile, the differing orientations would either stimulate serious conflict or be eliminated altogether. But since both segments of this community are predisposed toward spatial immobility, the latent conflict is partially channeled into solidarity behavior.

The mechanisms described earlier for maintaining Buraku secrets have been designed and implemented by the upper class, and are directed specifically at the lower class. Cleanup days, sanitary inspections, town meetings, and religious ceremonials are also intended to educate the lower class to upper class conventions. These events, sanctions, and regulations require a high degree of interest and participation by the upper class. Therefore, leadership which might otherwise be directed away from the community and toward tasks more directly relevant to the individual or class mobility is oriented toward the internal affairs of the community. Although the motivations of the dominant group spring from a desire for individual status enhancement, the consequence of these drives is to solidify the community by focusing social action on problems of an intra-community nature. The integration thus achieved functions to maintain Burakumin as a distinct and unified subgroup of the larger Japanese society.

CONCLUSION

The social persistence of Shin-machi is determined by a variety of conditions governing both the internal and external social relationships maintained by Burakumin. A sanctioning system exists that is intended to conceal from outsiders many of the physical and social characteristics of the community. These controls engender exclusiveness and prohibit intercourse with members of the majority society.

The socioreligious organization, which is oriented toward the social problems of the underprivileged minority, stimulates ingroup unity and identity. The regular system of Japanese social relations, with its emphasis on obligation, loyalty, and duty, discourages migration.

True mobility aspirations have been inhibited by negative self-concepts, poor education, and the maintenance of traditional occupations. Because of vested economic interests in Shin-machi, the community leaders are oriented toward caste mobility, and are therefore predisposed to remain in the community, and to emphasize stability and unity. Although tensions have developed between the two classes within the Buraku, mutual hostility actually serves to increase the intensity of social interaction among community members.

We conclude therefore that the persistence of the outcaste in contemporary Japan cannot be explained simply by the discriminatory attitudes and prejudices of the majority. Attitudes toward self, the traditional system of Japanese social and economic relations, and the internal structure and organization of the Buraku itself are all essential in maintaining this continuity.

Economically marginal groups in Japan, such as the outcastes of Shinmachi, are often bound internally by close-knit systems of social and economic relationships and characterized by the prevalence of protective, hierarchical, and kinship-oriented institutions such as the oyabun-kobun system and the extended family. These traditional Japanese tendencies, which may develop as adjustments to precarious social and economic conditions, foster ingroup solidarity, dependency, and socioeconomic rigidity. However, a decline has been noted in the importance of "feudal" socioeconomic institutions that has been caused by the recent prosperity.[8] It is possible that if the employment capacity of the economy is expanded, the outcastes may gradually disappear as a distinctive subgroup of the society. But if they continue to remain an economically underprivileged group, they may also remain dependent upon "feudal," protective institutions and continue to reside in Buraku despite possible changes for the better in the majority society's attitude toward them.

Bibliography

Ishino Iwao. "The Oyabun-Kobun: A Japanese Ritual Kinship Institution," *American Anthropologist*, Vol. 55 (1953), pp. 695-707.

Ishino Iwao, and Bennett, John W. *Types of the Japanese Rural Community*. Interim Technical Report No. 6, Research in Japanese Social Relations, Ohio State University, 1953.

MacIver, R. M. *The More Perfect Union*. New York: Macmillan Co., 1948.

Merton, Robert K. *Social Theory and Social Structure*. Glencoe, Illinois: The Free Press, 1949.

Myrdal, Gunnar. *An American Dilemma*. New York: Harper and Brothers, 1944.

Stoetzel, Jean. *Without the Chrysanthemum and the Sword*. New York: Columbia University Press, 1955.

[8] Ishino and Bennett (1953).

VII

Japanese concepts of personal beauty have long included "white" skin and straight hair as important criteria. Although first contact with Europeans did little to undermine Japanese beliefs about their own superior beauty in terms of their own criteria, contact with Caucasian women in the late nineteenth century had an immediate effect. Wagatsuma discusses motifs in late nineteenth and twentieth century Japanese literature of inferiority to, and intimidation at the whiteness of Europeans. Stereotypes of extreme Caucasian sexuality which also developed are discussed. Attitudes towards Whites and Negroes among Japanese in California are compared with those among the Japanese at home.

HIROSHI WAGATSUMA

The Social Perception of
Skin Color in Japan

Long before any sustained contact with either Caucasoid Europeans or dark-skinned Africans or Indians, the Japanese valued "white" skin as beautiful and deprecated "black" skin as ugly. Their spontaneous re-

From *Daedalus*, Vol. 96, No. 2 (Spring, 1967), pp. 407-443. Reprinted by permission of the author and the publisher.

I would like to express my deep gratitude to my friend Professor Harold R. Isaacs, of the Massachusetts Institute of Technology, who urged me to write this article and gave me constant moral support. I am also indebted to my colleague

sponses to the white skin of Caucasoid Europeans and the black skin of Negroid people were an extension of values deeply embedded in Japanese concepts of beauty.[1] From past to present, the Japanese have always associated skin color symbolically with other physical characteristics that signify degrees of spiritual refinement or primitiveness. Skin color has been related to a whole complex of attractive or objectionable social traits. It might strike some as curious that the Japanese have traditionally used the word *white* (*shiroi*) to describe lighter shades of their own skin color. The social perception of the West has been that the Chinese and Japanese belong to a so-called "yellow" race, while the Japanese themselves have rarely used the color yellow to describe their skin.

I

"White" skin has been considered an essential characteristic of feminine beauty in Japan since recorded time. An old Japanese proverb states that "white skin makes up for seven defects"; a woman's light skin causes one to overlook the absence of other desired physical features.[2]

During the Nara period (710-793), court ladies made ample use of cosmetics and liberally applied white powder to the face.[3] Cheeks were

---

Professor George DeVos of the Department of Anthropology of the University of California, Berkeley, for his valuable advice. I am also grateful to my wife, Reiko Wagatsuma, who shared with me the burden of library research and interviewing. We are indebted to our Japanese friends in Berkeley, Tokyo, and Kobe, whose kind cooperation made the latter part of this paper possible.

[1] The word for skin in contemporary Japanese is either *hifu* or *hada*. *Hifu* is more or less a technical word and is used less frequently in daily conversation than *hada*, which is the abbreviation of *hadae*, originally meaning "vicinity of surface." *Hada* is also used figuratively in expressions such as *hada o yurusu*, a woman "permitting her skin" to a man when she gives herself to him. *Hada* is also used in the sense of temperament or disposition, as in *hada ga awanai*, the skin of two individuals does not fit due to the incompatibility of their characters. A dashing or gallant man may be described as a man of *isami hada* ("braced-up skin") and a research-minded man as a man of *gakusha hada* ("scholarly skin"). In describing one's skin color, the word *hada* is used more often than *hifu*, as in such expressions as *hada no shiroi hito* ("a white-skinned person"). A more common practice is to use the word *iro* ("color"), as in *iro no shiroi onna* ("a white-colored woman").

[2] S. Noguchi (ed.), *Koji Kotowaza Jiten* [Dictionary of Old Sayings and Proverbs] (Tokyo, 1963), pp. 40-41.

[3] Face powder, which in the Japanese is *o-shiroi* ("honorable white"), was invented, according to some legends, by one of the ancient wise kings of China, Shou of Yin, Wen of Chou, or Mu of Ch'in. Actually, graves of the early Han period (202 B.C. to about A.D. 25) have given up to archaeologists numberless lacquered vessels and metal boxes containing face powder, rouge, and other toilet preparations. Face powder, together with rouge, came to Japan via Korea in the third or fourth century. In 692, a Japanese monk named Kansei, or Kanjō, succeeded in making face powder from lead and was commended by the

rouged. Red beauty spots were painted on between the eyebrows and at the outer corners of both the eyes and the lips. Eyelids and lips were given a red tinge.[4]. . . Countless references were made in both illustration and writing to round-faced, plump women with white, smooth skin. Necessary to beauty was long, black, straight hair that draped over the back and shoulders without being tied.[5]. . . From the eighth to the twelfth century, the bearers of Japanese cultural refinement were the court nobility who idled their lives away in romantic love affairs, practicing the arts of music and poetry. The whiteness of untanned skin was the symbol of this privileged class which was spared any form of outdoor labor. From the eleventh century on, men of the aristocracy applied powder to their faces just as the court ladies did.[6]

In 1184, the warriors took the reins of government away from the effete courtiers and abruptly ended the court's rather decadent era. To protect the *samurai* virtues of simplicity, frugality, and bravery, the warriors set up headquarters in the frontier town of Kamakura located far away from the capital. The warriors maintained Spartan standards, as is evidenced in the many portrait paintings showing rather florid or swarthy countenances. Women still continued, however, the practices of toiletry established previously in the court. In 1333 the warriors' government was moved from Kamakura back to Kyoto, where the Ashikaga Shogunate family emulated court life and re-established an atmosphere of luxury among the ruling class.

Standards of feminine beauty still emphasized corpulence of body, white skin, and black hair, which in this period was worn in a chignon. Prefer-

---

Court and presented with "fifty lengths of cloth." A powder of glutinous rice and of millet was also used as face powder. Another substance, applied in liquid form, came from the floury seeds of the jalap plant (*o-shiroi-bana*). See T. Ema, "Keshō no hensen" [History of Toiletry], *Nihon Fūzoku Shi* [History of Japanese Customs], Vol. 4 (Tokyo, 1959), pp. 52-78; U. A. Casal, "Japanese Cosmetics and Teeth Blackening," *The Transactions of the Asiatic Society of Japan*, Third Series, Vol. 9 (May, 1966), pp. 5-27.

[4] *Beni*, made from the safflower and of a good but not too luminous red, was used as rouge. It was applied with a soft, short, round brush somewhat over an inch in diameter. It was distributed rather evenly with but slight shading. A more concentrated preparation, *kuchi-beni*, was rubbed on the lips with the third finger, which is still referred to as the *beni-sashi-yubi*, or "rouge-applying finger." The lower lips, rather fleshy with most Japanese, were from early times partly covered by white powder, and the rouge was applied so as to make them appear smaller. See Casal, "Japanese Cosmetics and Teeth Blackening."

[5] T. Adachi, *Yūjo Fūzoku Sugata* [Customs of Courtesans] (Tokyo, 1956); T. Endo, "Josei to Keppatsu" [Women and Their Hairdos], *Nihon Fūzoku Shi*, Vol. 12 (Tokyo, 1959), pp. 69-102.

[6] Ema, "Keshō no hensen," p. 65.

ence was voiced for a woman with a round face, broad forehead, and eyes slightly down-turned at the corners.[7] By this time, the old court custom of penciling eyebrows and blackening teeth had become incorporated into the puberty rites practiced for both boys and girls. . . . Following a chaotic political period, the Tokugawa feudal government was established in 1603. It was to last until the modern period of Japan, more than two hundred and fifty years. Changes occurred in the ideals of feminine beauty during this period of continuing peace. Gradually, slim and fragile women with slender faces and up-turned eyes began to be preferred to the plump, pear-shaped ideal that remained dominant until the middle of the eighteenth century.[8] White skin, however, remained an imperative characteristic of feminine beauty. . . .

The use of good water and the practice of steaming the face were thought to make skin white and smooth. Rings and socks were worn in sleep to stunt excessive growth of limbs since small hands and feet were valued attributes of feminine charm. The juice of the *sanekazura* root was used to straighten the hair. These practices all confirm the continuous concern with white skin and straight hair. . . .

Because Mongoloid skin shows a very quick tendency to tan and to produce "black" skin, the Japanese can maintain lightness of skin only by total avoidance of sunlight. Not surprisingly, Tokugawa women made constant use of parasols or face hoods to hide their skin from sunlight and assiduously applied powder to face, neck, throat, and upper chest.[9]. . .

From the beginning of the nineteenth century, the Kabuki actors set the standards of men's beauty. A rather feminine type of male with a slender figure, well-formed face, white skin, black hair, and red lips became a favorite object of feminine desire. . . .

[7] Adachi, *Yūjo Fūzoku Sugata*, p. 246.

[8] Adachi, *Yūjo Fūzoku Sugata*, p. 248.

[9] During the early part of the Tokugawa period, when the center of culture was in Osaka and Kyoto, and Edo was still very much a frontier, the Kyoto-Osaka custom of women thickly painting their faces and necks white did not reach Edo. Edo women, instead, tended to be proud of the natural smoothness and shine of their unpainted skin, and they used powder very sparingly. After the early-nineteenth century, however, under the influence of Kyoto-Osaka culture, the make-up of Edo's women became thicker. See R. Saito, *Edo no Sugata*, p. 223; Y. Ikeda, K. Hara *et al.*, *Sei Fūzoku* [Sexual Mores], Vol. 1 (Tokyo, 1959), p. 229; R. Nishizawa, *Koto Gosui* [Noon Nap in the Imperial Capitol], quoted in E. Mitamura, *Edo Jidai Sama Zama* [Various Aspects of the Edo Period] (Tokyo, 1929), p. 460. Edo women also came to paint their lips and fingernails pink and red. See S. Fujioka and K. Hiraido, *Nihon Fūzoku Shi* [History of Japanese Customs] (Tokyo, 1900), p. 133. Blackening women's teeth remained as an initiation ceremony at the age of thirteen or fourteen among the warrior class, but a woman of the commoner's status blackened her teeth and removed her eyebrows when she was married. See Ema, *Nihon Fūzoku Zenshi*, p. 179.

The word *white* repeatedly used in the quotations taken from various sources is the same Japanese word *shiroi* that is used to describe snow or white paper. There was no intermediate word between *shiroi* ("white") and *kuroi* ("black") used to describe skin color.[10] When distinctions were made, there would be recourse to such words as *asa guroi* ("light black").

II

Not long after the first globe-circling voyages of Magellan, Westerners appeared on the shores of Japan. Dutch, English, Portuguese, and Spanish traders came to ply their trade in Japanese ports. . . .

In several of the colored pictures of the day[11] that included both Japanese and Europeans, the Japanese artists painted the faces of the Portuguese, Spanish, and Japanese men in a flesh color or light brown, but depicted the faces of Japanese women as white in hue. In a few other pictures, however, some Portuguese are given white faces like Japanese women, while other Portuguese are given darker faces. . . . The faces of Negroes are painted in a leaden- or blackish-gray, and their hair is shown as extremely frizzled. The physiognomy of the Negroes is somewhat caricatured and in some instances closely resembles the devils and demons of Buddhist mythology.

. . . [One] scholar wrote:

> Black ones are impoverished Indians employed by the Dutch. As their country is in the South and the heat is extreme, their body is sun-scorched and their color becomes black. Their hair is burned by the sun and becomes frizzled but they are humans and not monkeys as some mistakenly think.[12]

. . . In 1853 Commodore Perry of the United States Navy came to Japan with his "black ships" and forced Japan to reopen her ports to foreign vessels. When Perry visited Japan for the second time in 1854, there were two American women on board. It was reported in a Japanese document:

> On board is a woman named Shirley, 31 years old and her child Loretta, 5 years old. Their hair is red. They have high noses, white faces and the pupils of their eyes are brown. They are medium in size and very beautiful.[13]

The portraits of Commodore Perry and five principals of his staff drawn by a Japanese artist show the Americans with noses of exaggerated size,

[10] The word *kuroi* ("black"), used to describe the swarthy skin of the Japanese, is also used to designate more black objects such as black charcoal or black smoke.

[11] B. Smith, *Japan — A History in Art* (New York, 1964).

[12] Ōtsuki, *Ransetsu Benwaku*, p. 16.

[13] E. Mitamura, *Edo Jidai Sama Zama*, p. 460.

large eyes, and brownish hair. Their faces are painted in a washed-out, whitish-ash color. In other pictures, however, both American and Japanese faces are painted with an identical whitish-gray, although the Americans are given brown hair and bushy beards. . . .

III

In the early Meiji period, the Japanese began their self-conscious imitation of the technology of the West. Less consciously, they also began to alter their perception of feminine beauty. In their writings, they referred with admiration to the white skin of Westerners, but noted with disapproval the hair color and the hairiness of Westerners. Wavy hair was not to the Japanese taste until the mid-1920's.

. . .

The subtle, not fully conscious, trend toward an idealization of Western physical features by the Japanese apparently became of increasing importance in the twenties. It remained a hidden sub-current throughout the last war while Japan, as the "champion of the colored nations," fought against the "whites." In spite of propaganda emphasizing the racial ties between Japanese and other Asians, the "yellowness" of the Japanese was never quite made a point of pride. The rapidity with which Western standards of beauty became idealized after the war attests to the continuous drift that was occurring in spite of ten years of antagonism and military hostilities.

IV

Older Japanese who have lived overseas have been astounded upon visiting postwar Japan. The straight black hair of the past is all but gone. Even most geisha, the preservers of many feminine traditions, have permanents and wave their hair. Among ordinary women, one periodically sees extreme examples of hair that has been bleached with hydrogen peroxide or, more commonly, dyed a purplish or reddish hue. Plastic surgery, especially to alter eye folds and to build up the bridge of the nose, has become almost standardized practice among the younger movie actresses and, indeed, even among some of the male actors. There were examples of plastic surgery to be found before the war, but its wide popularity is something new.[14]

[14] The writer failed to discover when the traditional preference for narrow eyes in a woman gave way to the new preference for round eyes with double-folded eyelids, which the Japanese must have learned to value from the Western aesthetics. There is a Japanese saying, "A woman's eyes should be bell shaped, and a man's eyes should be like thread," indicating the preference for round big eyes in a woman but for rather narrow eyes in a man. The time of the origin of this saying is unclear to us. Natsume Sōseki (1867-1916), one of the greatest novelists of modern Japan, seems to be among the earliest admirers of the charms of double-folded eyelids in women. For instance, in his first novel

Contemporary Japanese men interviewed in the United States and Japan all agreed in valuing the "whiteness" of skin as a component of beauty in the Japanese woman.[15] Whiteness is very often associated in their minds with womanhood ("Whiteness is a symbol of women, distinguishing them from men"), with chastity and purity ("Whiteness suggests purity and moral virtue"), and motherhood ("One's mother-image is white").

. . .

In interviews with both men and women, present attitudes toward Caucasian skin seem to fall into opposites of likes and dislikes depending, seemingly, upon the degree of an individual's receptivity toward or identification with Western culture. These two opposite attitudes may coexist within an individual, either appearing alternately or being expressed simultaneously. Somewhat more than half of both men and women interviewed in California and about two thirds of those interviewed in Japan considered Caucasian skin to be inferior to the Japanese from the standpoint of texture and regularity. This stereotype was among the negative attitudes expressed in the interviews.

> Caucasians' skin tends to be rough in texture, full of wrinkles, spots, and speckles.

> If you look at the neck of an old Caucasian woman with furrows and bristles, it reminds you of that of a pig.

> When I try to visualize a Caucasian woman, she is associated in my mind with skin of rough texture and unsmooth surface. Pores of her

---

of 1907, he describes one of the heroines: "Itoko with white, soft and full fingers and cute eyes with double-folded eyelids." He certainly mentions the whiteness of the girls: "White in color, born in the shadow of a setting moon, she was named Sayo"; "Fujiko's white face shone under her black hair." Natsume Sōseki, *Gubijinsō* [A Field Poppy] in *Zenshū* [Collected Works], Vol. 4 (Tokyo, 1963), pp. 74, 112, 119. One evidence of the Japanese woman's strong desire to acquire double-folded eyelids is the popularity of a small tool, widely advertised in the 1930's and 1940's. In shape it somewhat resembles an American eyelash curler, and it helps single eyelids to fold into a double crease. If such "folding" is repeated time after time, the eyelids, it is believed, will eventually become accustomed to a double fold. Sales of this instrument were revived after the war.

[15] The following section is based on a series of informal interviews, the first, in Spring 1965, with twenty-two Japanese men and women in Berkeley, California (graduate students, visiting scholars, their wives, one woman married to a Japanese American, another woman married to a Negro American; their ages ranged from 28 to 50; their stays in the United States varied from two to over ten years); the second, in Fall 1965, with thirty-six men and women in Tokyo and Kobe, Japan, who had varied ages, and educational and socioeconomic backgrounds. The second group shared one common factor: they had never been abroad; they had had little or no personal contact with Caucasians and Negroes.

skin may be larger than ours. Young women may have smoother skin, but older women have bad skin.

A Eurasian child will be very attractive if it takes a Japanese parent's skin and a Caucasian parent's facial structure, but the result of an opposite combination could be disastrous.

This notion concerning a Eurasian child seems to be fairly widely held among Japanese. The idea that Caucasian skin is "ugly" is also expressed in the following passage taken from the work of a contemporary Japanese novelist:

> When a kissing couple was projected on a large screen in a close-up, then the ugliness unique to Caucasian female skin was magnified. The freckles covering the woman's cheek and throat became clearly visible. . . . On the fingers of a man caressing a woman, gold hairs were seen shining like an animal's bristles.[16] . .

. . . For most of the Japanese without much personal contact with Westerners, skin is only one of several characteristics making up the image of a Caucasian. Other components of this image are the shape and color of eyes, hair, height, size, weight of the body, and also hairiness. Japanese feelings toward a Caucasian seem determined by all these factors. Many people interviewed in Japan talked of their difficulty in discussing their feelings toward Caucasian skin as differentiated from other Caucasian physical characteristics. An image of a Caucasian with white skin, deep-set eyes, wavy hair of a color other than black, a tall, stout, hairy body, and large hands and feet seems to evoke in many Japanese an association with "vitality," "superior energy," "strong sexuality" or "animality," and the feeling that Caucasians are basically discontinuous with Asians.

Positive attitudes toward Caucasian skin center on the idea that Caucasian skin is, in actuality, whiter than the so-called white skin of the Japanese and, therefore, more attractive.

It is interesting to note that Japanese who have spent time in the United States acquire the idea that Japanese are "yellow" rather than brown-skinned. Those we met in Japan, with only a few exceptions, hesitate or even refuse to describe their skin as "yellow." They know that the Japanese belong to the "yellow race" (*Ōshoku jinshu,* the technical term for the Mongoloid), but they cannot think of their skin as actually yellow, "unless," as some remarked, "a person comes down with jaundice." Having few occasions to compare their skin color with that of other races, the Japanese apparently do not have any words available other than *black* and *white* to describe their skin. In modern Japan, *shakudō-iro*

[16] S. Ariyoshi, *Hishoku* [Not Color] (Tokyo, 1964), p. 204.

("color of alloy of copper and gold") and *komugi-iro* ("color of wheat") are used to describe sun-tanned skin, but other words for brown and yellow are rarely employed. When I asked a thirty-year-old woman college graduate to describe the color of Japanese skin, she answered spontaneously, "Of course, it is *hada-iro* ['skin color']!" It is not known why the Japanese, after spending time among Caucasians, come to adopt the word *yellow* for their skin. This may be an attempt to adhere to common terminology, or it may be partially a continuation of a distinction between themselves and Southeast Asians, whom they consider to be darker-skinned.[17]

[An] informant who had told us about the "yellow skin" of her daughter was asked if she felt unhappy about her daughter's "yellowness." Her answer was an emphatic no, although she admitted that the white skin of Caucasian women is beautiful. A college graduate, married to a university professor, she suggested her solution to race problems:

> I think there should be three different standards of beauty to be applied separately to three groups of people of different colors. It is a confusion of these standards or the loss of one or two of them that leads to tragedy and frustration.

Many Japanese men, especially those in the United States, admit the beauty of white skin in Caucasian women, but also point out the sense of the inaccessibility of Caucasian women. Although the feeling of "basic discontinuity" between Japanese and Caucasians found among those without much contact with Westerners may become weakened as the Japanese spend time among the whites, it may sometimes persist in this feeling of basic remoteness and inaccessibility.

> Looking at the white skin I feel somehow that it belongs to a different world. People understand each other a great deal but there is something which people of different races cannot quite share. It sounds foolish and irrational, I know, but somehow this is the feeling I have, looking at the white skin of a Caucasion woman.

[17] The Japanese interviewed tended to be explicit about the physical differences they believed to exist between themselves and other Asian and Southeast Asian peoples; they also tended to be rather sensitive about Westerners mistaking them for Chinese or Burmese. Corresponding differential images may exist among other nations in the Orient: three American-educated Thai women told me, independently, the stereotypes of the Asian people held by the Thais: the Filipinos, Indonesians, Burmese, Laotians, and Cambodians look physically the same as the Thais, with big round eyes with double-folded eyelids and dark skin of rather rough texture, while the Japanese, Koreans, and Chinese look undistinguishably alike, all possessing narrow eyes and lighter skin of smooth surface. The Vietnamese, they said, fall between these two groups; some look like Thais and others like Chinese.

White skin suggests a certain remoteness. When I went to Mexico, where most women are not white-skinned like the American, I felt more at home seeing them. I felt more comfortable.

Sometimes I feel that the white skin of the Caucasians tells me that after all I am an Oriental and cannot acquire everything Western, however Westernized I might be. It is like the last border I cannot go across and it is symbolized by the white skin. Is this my inferiority feeling toward the white people — I often wonder.

. . . .

Though it seems somewhat painful for most Japanese to be frank about it (and many of them refuse to do so), there is among Japanese intellectuals a more or less unconscious, if not conscious, ambivalence toward the world of white people. Such an attitude is understandable if one takes even a brief glance at Japan's modern history. Japan, at first overwhelmed by an apprehension of the Western world's great power, caught up with the West in an amazingly short time. Then, feeling a sense of rejection over unequal treatment, Japan appointed itself a champion of non-white Asians. In this role, it boldly tried to win a place in the company of white imperialists. Failing disastrously after all, Japan found itself receiving a "democratic education" from its American teachers toward whom it felt the greatest rivalry mixed with admiration.[18]

The diffuse ambivalence toward Western civilization may very well be focalized in the admiration, envy, sense of being overwhelmed or threatened, fear, or disgust that are evoked in the Japanese mind by the image of a hairy giant[19] who, with his great vigor and strong sexuality, can easily satisfy an equally energetic and glamorous creature.[20] Consequently, actual sexual experiences with a white woman may help some Japanese to overcome such feelings of inferiority toward Caucasians.

[18] Minami Hiroshi, an American-educated social psychologist, writes: "For the Japanese, the foreigners are not only different people of different race and nationality, coming from outside, but they are also people of higher status and stronger power, coming from above. Japanese feel shy toward the foreigners as outsiders and feel inferiority-superiority complex toward the foreigners who come from above." H. Minami, "Nihonjin no Gaikokujin kan" [Japanese Views of Foreigners], *Ningen no Kagaku* [Science of Man], Vol. 2, No. I (1964), pp. 14-23.

[19] Japanese ambivalence toward a large body and large limbs is reflected in some proverbs: "Wisdom cannot fill up too large a body" (Big body, little wit); "A fool has big feet" or "Seeds of prickly ash are tiny but peppery" (A small man is shrewd and wise).

[20] When Japanese men feel a vague sense of annoyance or discomfort at the sight or notion of a Japanese woman marrying a white man, especially an American, the feeling may be related to their unconscious understanding that a Japanese woman, by choosing a white man, is challenging their worth as men and their masculine potency.

One of the persons interviewed remarked that his uncle once told him that during Japan's control over Manchuria many Japanese men enjoyed sleeping with white Russian prostitutes:

> My uncle said, having a relationship with a white woman made these men feel different, more masculine or something. The feeling is different from that one has after having a relationship with an Asian woman.

Generally, however, Japanese men, as authors of travel books suggest, seem rather overwhelmed and discouraged by the large physique of a white woman. . . .

In contrast to this complex of attitudes about Caucasoid racial traits, the Japanese attitudes toward the black skin and facial characteristics of Negro Americans encountered during the Occupation were generally negative, although a number of Japanese women married Negro men. The Japanese interviewed in California, being intellectuals and living in the United States, were all keenly aware of the recent racial issues. . . . These were the reactions of the Japanese to Negro features as a total *Gestalt* (eyes, hair, nose, and lips) but particularly to black skin.

> I think it is simply a matter of custom or habit. We are not accustomed to black skin. I have a Negro friend, very black. I respect him as a scholar and we are close friends and yet I still feel I am not yet used to his black skin. It's something terribly alien to my entire life. It is much better now than it was two years ago when I first met him.

> Coming to this country, I had not known that a Negro's palm was different in color from the back of his hand. I was playing cards with two Americans and one African student and I suddenly noticed the color of this African student's palm. I felt I saw something which I had never seen in my life. All that evening, playing cards, I could not help looking at his hands time after time. . . . I just could not get over it.

> A year after my arrival, I was introduced to an American Negro for the first time. He was a very friendly person and immediately extended his hand toward me. At that very brief moment, I hesitated. No. I did not hesitate but my arm did. My arm resisted being extended forward. Like a light flashing through my mind, I said to myself, "there is no reason why I don't want to shake hands with this black man." I did shake hands with him and I do hope he did not sense my momentary hesitation. Since then I have never hesitated to shake hands with a Negro.

The idea that black skin is something novel to the Japanese and only for that reason difficult for them to get used to was also voiced by a Japanese woman married to a Negro American.

> Frankly, I felt uneasy about it [black skin] in the beginning, but you see it every day, from morning to evening; there is nothing else you can do except to get used to it. I did get used to it. Especially since he was very nice and kind all the time. Once you get used to it, you no longer see it.

The same idea is stated in a novel by Ariyoshi Sawako, a contemporary Japanese author. . . . This novel, with the English subtitle *Not Because of Color*, is of special interest for us. Ariyoshi spent a few years in the United States as a Rockefeller Fellow. She then returned to Japan and wrote this novel, in which she describes the life of a Japanese woman married to a Negro in New York's Harlem. She also depicts a few other uneducated Japanese women married to Negro, Puerto Rican, and Italian Americans, as contrasted with a highly intellectual Japanese woman married to a Jewish college professor and working at the U.N. As suggested by the subtitle, Ariyoshi seemingly wanted to emphasize that — in spite of the prejudiced opinion of many white Americans and Japanese — laziness, apathy, lack of conjugal stability, and many other inferior characteristics attributed to Negro Americans are not racially inherent qualities, but the products of their degraded social status. The author accurately describes common Japanese reactions to Negro-Japanese marriages and their offspring. The heroine's mother, learning that her daughter wants to marry a Negro soldier, says:

> Our family has been honored by its warrior ancestry. Though we were not well-to-do, none of us has ever shamed the name of our family. And you, a member of our respectable family, wish to marry a man of such blackness! How shall we apologize to our ancestors? If you wish to marry an "American," that might be a different matter. But marrying that black man!

> Embraced by such a black one, don't you feel disgusted? I am afraid of him. Why don't you feel strange?[21]

. . . [Another] story to be mentioned here is the work of Matsumoto Seichō, a widely read author of numerous mystery and documentary stories. In this short story, two hundred and fifty Negro soldiers enroute to Korea break out of Jōno Camp in Northern Kyushu one night and attack civilian houses around the camp. Many women are raped. Two other companies of American troops are called out to subdue the disturbances; most of the soldiers are brought back to the barracks within several hours and sent to the Korean front a few days later. A Japanese man whose wife

[21] Ariyoshi, *Hishoku, op. cit.*

had been assaulted by a group of Negroes divorces his wife and begins working at the Army Grave Registration Service, as a carrier of corpses. One day, he finally finds what he has been looking for: the corpses of two Negro soldiers he remembered by their obscene tattoos. They were among those who raped his wife. Out of his anger, hatred, and desire for revenge, the man stabs the corpses with an autopsy knife. The Negroes in this story are frequently associated with animals and also with the primitive natives of the African jungle:

> Their bodies were all dark like shadows but their eyes shone like patches of white paper. . . . His white eyes shone like the inside of a sea shell but the rest of his face was black, his nose, cheeks, jaw and all. . . . His thick lips were pink and dull in color. . . . Hair was kinky as if scorched. . . . Their bodies exhaled a strong foul smell of beasts. . . . When he took off his shirt, his upper body looked like that of a rhinoceros, with rich heaps of black flesh. The skin looked almost ready to squeak when moved, like tanned leather of black color. . . . When naked, his body was swollen, abdomen hanging low. It was cylindrical like a monkey's body.[22]

·   ·   ·

Unlike the Japanese interviewed in California, those who were questioned in Japan expressed their feelings toward Negro Americans and Africans without reservation. They were undifferentiatedly seen by them as "black men, with inhumanly black skin, goggle eyes, thick lips, kinky hair, strong body odor,[23] and animal-like sexuality and energy." The feelings toward such an image were invariably negative. Many said that they felt indignation toward the white American discrimination against Negroes. Some were very fond of Negro musicians. Negro baseball players were well liked. And yet, as one said, their "basic feelings are repulsion and

---

[22] S. Matsumoto, *Kuro-ji no E* [A Picture on the Black Cloth] in *Tanpen Senshu* [Selected Short Stories] (Tokyo, 1965), pp. 70, 75-77, 81-85, 89.

[23] The strong body odor, actually perceived or imagined, of a Negro and sometimes also of a Caucasian was often considered by the Japanese to be a source of their repulsion. Fujishima Taisuke, a writer and one of the classmates of the Crown Prince at the Peers School, wrote a rather depressing essay with the title "We Cannot Marry Negroes" in a widely read and respectable magazine. He emphasized the strong body odor of the African Negroes. "When I arrived at Nairobi Airport," he writes, "I felt the air was filled with a striking smell. It was body odor of the Negroes. Unless one becomes accustomed to it, it is a sickening smell, really strong." After describing his other experiences with the body odor, Fujishima comes to his conclusion: "The real underlying thought upon which racial discrimination is based, I believe, is primarily derived from the physiological repulsion caused by this striking odor. All the other sophisticated thoughts and logics are justification added later. . . . Humanism is one thing, and the physiological repulsion of human being is another thing." T. Fujishima, "Kokujin to wa kekkon dekinai," *Bungei Shunjū* (February 1966), pp. 308-13.

disgust toward Negro features"; these feelings were frequently justified as a "physiological reaction, which one's reasoning cannot control."

Such strongly negative attitudes toward Negro physical characteristics certainly pose problems for the mixed-blood children of Negro American fathers and Japanese mothers, although nobody has yet made a systematic study of the lives of these children in postwar Japan. Three lower-class Japanese with less than six years of primary education independently voiced an astonishing notion when interviewed; they believed that if a Japanese woman gave birth to the black baby of a Negro man, her next baby, and probably the third one also, of a Japanese father would show some black tinge on the body. In other words, in the mind of these men, impregnation of a Japanese woman by a Negro man was associated with "blackening" of her womb as though by ink, so that the second and even the third baby conceived in it would become "stained."

The type of Negro the Japanese think attractive or handsome, or the least objectionable, is a light-skinned individual with Caucasian features. For this reason, they all find Hindu Indians with their Caucasoid facial structure generally more acceptable, even though the Hindus' black skin still groups them with African and American Negroes. The Japanese are not ready to appreciate a very Negroid Negro as attractive; the newly emergent trend among the Negro Americans[24] has not yet made any impression in Japan.

The Negro in the Japanese language is either *koku-jin* ("black person") or *kuronbo* ("black ones"); the former is a neutral word, but the latter has a definitely belittling, if not derogatory, tone. According to a philologist, the origin of *kuronbo* is Colombo, a city of Ceylon.[25] In the seventeenth century, Colombo was pronounced by the Japanese as "kuronbo" or abbreviated as "kuro," probably because of the association with the word *black (kuro)* since the servants on the Dutch boats, identified as "people from Colombo," were actually black-skinned. The word *bo*, originally meaning a Buddhist priest's lodge and then the priest himself, came also to mean a boy or "sonny." A suffix to certain words with the meaning of "little one," . . . *bo* also creates belittling or even contemptuous connotations in other words. . . . By the same token, *kuron-bo* ("a black one") carries the connotation of childishness.

Most Japanese born before 1935 first discovered Negroes by singing "Old Black Joe" and other Stephen Foster melodies in music classes at

[24] Harold R. Isaacs, *The New World of Negro Americans* (New York, 1963), pp. 90-96.

[25] A document from the late 1670's says, "In the country of Inaba there was a man of seven feet height. He was from the country of 'kuro.' He had been captured at the Korean war and brought over to Japan. His color was that of soot and people called him *kuron-bo*." See K. Ōtsuki, *Daigenkai* [Dictionary of Japanese Language] (Tokyo, 1956), p. 565.

school or by reading the Japanese translation of *Uncle Tom's Cabin*. Although they might have related the lot of Negro Americans to a vague notion of injustice, such a life remained for most Japanese children a remote world. Another sort of encounter with black people, with more direct reference to their color, was evidenced in a cartoon serialized for many years in a popular magazine for children, *Adventurous Dankichi*, and in a popular song, "The Chief's Daughter," dating from the 1920's. Dankichi was a Japanese boy who put to sea one day to go fishing and, while asleep, drifted to an island somewhere in the South Pacific. On the island, Dankichi outwitted the black natives by his cleverness and ingenuity and became their king. He wore a crown on his head and rode on a white elephant near rivers inhabited by crocodiles.

This fantasy cartoon blended ideas about South Pacific islanders and primitive tribes in Africa. Originally cannibalistic and warlike, these people could become loyal though somewhat simple-minded subjects when tamed and educated. It is worth noting that this was the kind of image of "black people" to which most Japanese children of the prewar period were exposed. "The Chief's Daughter" created an image of carefree South Sea islanders with black skin who danced away their lives under the swaying palm trees.

> My lover is the Chief's daughter.
> Though her color is black
> She is a beauty in the South Seas. . . .
> Let us dance, dance under the palm trees
> Those who don't dance, no girls will care to marry. . . .

V

Since a very early time in history, the Japanese have valued the skin color they consider "white."[26] The Japanese "white" skin is, above all, *unsuntanned* skin, while Mongoloid skin is, in actuality, very sensitive to the tanning action of the sun. Japanese, particularly the women, tried hard to remain "white," jealously guarding their skin from exposure to the sun. An old Japanese expression observes, "In the provinces where one can see Mt. Fuji, one can hardly see beautiful women."[27] The districts traditionally known for their white, smooth-skinned native beauties are, consequently, Izumo, Niigata, and Akita. These are all located on the Japan Sea coast where in long, snowy winter weather one rarely enjoys sunlight.

[26] The thousand years' practice of whitening a face with powder in the Far East might suggest universality of white color preference or the distant result of some past cultural diffusion of early European origin. An extremely. interesting subject of inquiry, it is beyond the scope of this paper.

[27] S. Shiroyanagi, *Nihon Josei Shiwa* [Stories from the History of Japanese Women] (Tokyo, 1934), p. 115.

Conversely, where one can see Mt. Fuji, one also enjoys a warm Pacific climate year-round and a certain continuous sunshine which can tan unguarded skin.

.   .   .

Still in search of their national identity,[28] the Japanese are experiencing some difficulties in maintaining and protecting the standards of Japanese beauty and handsomeness from the onslaughts of standardized images produced by the Western cinema. Preoccupied with changing standards, the Japanese may be slow to note a new convergent perception of beauty entering the West, which includes traditional Japanese aesthetic standards in art, architecture, and even in Mongoloid physical beauty. Physical attractiveness is gradually losing its unitary cultural or racial basis in most societies. Art or beauty cannot be maintained in a fixed, single standard. Each changes with the diversity of experiences.

[28] Harold R. Isaacs, "Group Identity and Political Change: The Role of History and Origin," a paper presented at the meeting of the Association for Asian Studies in San Francisco (April 3, 1965), pp. 31-36; R. Lifton, "Youth and History — Individual Changes in Post-War Japan," *Asian Culture Studies*, No. 3 (October, 1962), pp. 115-36; A. M. Rosenthal, "New Japan — Future Beckons to Timorous Giant in Search of an Identity," *The New York Times* (June 24-27, 1963).

VIII

Race relations in Malaya, as in so many states, revolve around the history of the state and its economic development. Tracing this history and tying it to changing economic organization, Silcock presents a picture of uneasy interaction and interdependence between Malayans, Indians, Chinese, and Europeans. The changing plantation economy, the different organizations of imported ethnic work groups, Malayan government, and Chinese entrepreneurial development combine to make race an important feature in education and in job opportunities. The influence of religion and the demography of politics are analyzed in this study of a pluralist state in which no group dominates any other, but in which jealousy and distrust are strong and contacts limited.

T. H. SILCOCK

The Effects of Industrialisation on Race Relations in Malaya

Malaya is a country in which race relations have been, traditionally, harmonious. It has passed through the process of achieving independence without, so far, encountering any major racial frictions. Though political

From *Industrialisation and Race Relations: A Symposium*, edited by Guy Hunter, published by Oxford University Press for the Institute of Race Relations, 1965. Reprinted by permission of the author and the publisher.

parties tend to be organised on racial lines, interracial alliances and fronts have been formed which have narrowly limited the range of electoral conflicts between the races.[1] The ruling party, the Alliance, is made up of three separate racial parties each covering one of the main racial groups,[2] the United Malays' National Organisation, the Malayan Chinese Association and the Malayan Indian Congress. One of the main opposition parties, the Socialist Front, is made up of the Labour Party, which is mainly Chinese and Indian, and the Party Ra'ayat which is almost wholly Malay. Racial parties fighting on their own are likely to be weak.

The demographic structure of the country, however, is not one that makes harmony easy. In the Federation of Malaya the Malays, who think of themselves as the indigenous race, form almost exactly 50 per cent of the population.[3] The Chinese (37 per cent) and Indians and Pakistanis (11 per cent) together make up about 48 per cent, while the other races — many of them economically or politically important though demographically negligible — make up the remainder. These include the Europeans and Eurasians, the Arabs, the Ceylonese and the Thais, and many other groups.

If the separate island of Singapore were included,[4] the Chinese and Malays would be almost equal, and the proportions of Indians and Pakistanis would fall very slightly.

By Asian standards Malaya is a prosperous country, with a gross national product per head of over US $200[5] without Singapore or nearly US $300

Part of the material for this [article] was presented as a paper in the seminar on Malaya at the Australian National University in 1962, the results of which have appeared as T. H. Silcock and E. K. Fisk (editors), *The Political Economy of Independent Malaya: A Case Study in Economic Development.*

This [article] was, of course, written before the creation of Malaysia.

[1] In the 1959 federal elections 100 seats were contested, and in 76 of these both the leading candidates came from the same community; in seven more, both candidates were non-Malays, though from different communities. In the local government elections of 1961 both candidates came from the same community in about 80 per cent of the contested wards. Count made from election reports: Federation of Malaya, *Government Gazettes* III, 16 Supp. 3 (4 August 1959), III, 22 Supp. 1 (22 September 1959); Federation of Malaya Elections Commission, *Local Authority Elections 1961, Results and Statistics of Voting.*

[2] T. E. Smith, "The Malayan Elections of 1959," *Pacific Affairs*, Vol. 33, No. 1 (March 1960), p. 39, note 1.

[3] *Population Census of the Federation of Malaya* 1957, Department of Statistics, Federation of Malaya, Kuala Lumpur, Report No. 1, p. 1.

[4] *Population Census of Singapore* 1957, Preliminary Release, No. 1, Cmd. 42 of 1958.

[5] Cf. Report of Miss D. Walters on the *National Income of the Federation of Malaya* 1955-59 (photostat copy, Department of Statistics, Kuala Lumpur).

if Singapore is included.[6] This prosperity is based mainly on rubber, which directly contributes about a quarter of the gross national product.[7] But the level of industrialisation is also reasonably high. The proportion of the work force in secondary industry and building in the Federation of Malaya is about 10 per cent,[8] or 12 per cent if Singapore is included.[9] This is not, of course, all modern industry, though the proportion of handicraft work is declining.[10]

It is impossible to say accurately how the gross national product is divided between the different races. The only attempt to analyse personal incomes was that made by Benham.[11] The information for 1947 by Benham gives some detail, but no attempt was made to break it down by race. It is possible, however, to do this approximately by referring to the 1947 Census.[12] A very rough attempt has been made, from which it appears that a crude division for 1947 of personal incomes for the whole of Malaya[13] would be Malaysians $650 million or just over 20 per cent, Chinese $1,700 million or just under 60 per cent, Indians $350 million and Europeans and others $300 million.

To bring this estimate more up to date, the household budget survey of the Federation of Malaya in 1957-8, together with the Inland Revenue Department's returns for 1958 give a rough guide, and indicate percentages, for the Federation only, in the order of Malaysians 30 per cent, Chinese 54 per cent. There is no good basis for comparing these figures with Benham's estimates, which included Singapore. But from knowledge of overall national income and the structure of population in Singapore, the

[6] F. Benham, The National Income of Singapore 1956, London, distributed for the Royal Institute of International Affairs by the Oxford University Press, 1959, p. 2.

[7] In the Federation of Malaya only. If Singapore is included the average figure is about one fifth. Cf. International Bank for Reconstruction and Development, Economic Development of Malaya (Singapore: Government Printer, 1955), p. 14; Walters, op. cit., Table III.

[8] Ronald Ma and You Poh Seng, "The Economic Characteristics of the Population of the Federation of Malaya, 1957," Malayan Economic Review, Vol. V, No. 2 (October 1960).

[9] Saw Swee Hock and Ronald Ma, "The Economic Characteristics of the Population of Singapore 1957," Malayan Economic Review, Vol. V, No. 1 (April 1960), p. 40, Table V.

[10] Second Five Year Plan, 1961-1965, Federation of Malaya (Kuala Lumpur: Government Press, 1961), p. 4, para. 15.

[11] F. Benham, The National Income of Malaya 1947-49 (Singapore: Government Printer, 1951), Chapter IV.

[12] M. V. Del Tufo, A Report on the 1947 Census of Population (Kuala Lumpur: Government Printer, 1949).

[13] Note that Benham is dealing with Malaya as a whole, while the Household Budget Survey does not include Singapore with its numerous, urbanised and wealthy Chinese population.

figures may be put in the following order of magnitude: Malaysians, 23-25 per cent, Chinese 60-63 per cent.[14] The effect of industrialisation on race relations has been complicated, at least in recent years, by the coming of political independence.[15] Political independence has had a marked effect on race relations, and at least some effect on industrial structure, so that direct effects of industrialisation on race relations are difficult to disentangle. We shall consider separately the pattern of race relations in Malaya and the pattern of industrialisation, and then attempt to trace the relations between them.

We need have little hesitation in describing the differences between the three main communities of Malaya as differences in race, using that term in a sociological rather than a biological sense. Differences in custom, language and religion are closely associated with observable physical differences, in features and pigmentation. It is true that individual differences are much less marked than those between the stereotypes that are commonly accepted. Pigmentation and features vary widely among all three groups, and not all individuals could be confidently placed in one group from physical appearance alone.

There is little intermarriage, because of the strong barrier of the Muslim religion. But where this barrier does not exist, Muslims who wish to conform to Malay custom and speak the Malay language are usually accepted as Malays, and intermarry with them freely. Colour prejudice, as such, is largely confined to the European community, and has diminished very strikingly since the Second World War. The main barriers to intermarriage are differences of religion and custom.

Language difficulties accentuate racial difficulties, but they do not create barriers only between the three main races.[16] There are at least five mutually unintelligible main Chinese languages and three main Indian languages spoken in Malaya. There is no one accepted mode of speech between people of different language groups. It is commonly said that Malay is the lingua franca,[17] but if this is to be true, the term must be interpreted rather narrowly. It is certainly the language — in a simplified form — for the essential minimum contacts: directions, commands to social inferiors, price inquiries. But because the main languages of education have, until very recently, been English and the Chinese national language, communication of ideas between people of different mother

---

[14] More detailed figures can be found in *The Political Economy of Independent Malaya*.

[15] F. H. H. King, *The New Malayan Nation* (New York: Institute of Pacific Relations, 1957), pp. 14-18; T. E. Smith, *loc. cit.*

[16] N. Ginsburg and C. F. Roberts, *Malaya* (Seattle: University of Washington Press, 1958), pp. 131-41.

[17] U. A. Aziz, "Political and Economic Books on Malaya: A Review Article," *Malayan Economic Review*, Vol. V, No. 1 (April 1960), pp. 26-27.

tongues is almost certainly commoner in these languages than in Malay. The situation is changing with the adoption of Malay as the national language, and the political importance of acquiring (or admitting) a knowledge of it. But one still could not assume, for any given attempt at conversation between people of two different languages, any one of the following conditions: that both parties would know enough Malay for any but the simplest conversation; or that both would try Malay first, when they found their languages were different; or that it would be socially acceptable to both to use Malay, even if it were the best common medium available.[18]

In the main, pressure to adopt Malay as a national language is a means of protecting the position of Malays against Chinese; to a smaller degree it reflects an anti-colonialist desire to move away from the use of English.

The background of British rule has had significant effects on race relations. In many spheres of activity the different races were more concerned with their relations to the British, who co-ordinated the whole system, than with relations to one another. In economic life there was specialisation of function, with the British manager controlling the plantations, the mines, the railways, the engineering firms and commercial houses, and organising their different kinds of labour through different intermediaries.

Sometimes the British so-ordinator could speak one or more of the local languages; planters often knew some Tamil or Telegu and some Malay. Civil servants knew Malay. Few of the British knew Chinese, but they worked through English-speaking contractors and English-speaking clerks.

In most places the main retailers were Chinese. These men tended to be multilingual, doing business in Chinese with their suppliers, communicating in simple market Malay with their non-Chinese customers, and knowing enough English to negotiate appropriate monopoly conditions — premises, permits, transport — for their businesses, with managers or Government servants.

In the absence of self-government there was no political need for the different races in a neighbourhood to communicate with one another, except for the casual needs of daily life. Most cultural and social life, outside the English-educated group, followed communal lines, not so much because of exclusiveness as for convenience.

The Western-type, large-scale institutions, at least before the Second World War, made their impact on race relations by employing the differ-

---

[18] These three statements are all based on information supplied in Malaya by Malayans, but not on systematic research. There are many social groups that know very little Malay; and there is, or has been until very recently, some unwillingness between Chinese of different dialect groups, or people with some limited English education, to talk in Malay at any level of intimacy or sophistication.

ent races in separate occupations, enabling them to co-operate by overall management through intermediaries, and often keeping them apart in their living conditions. The employers accepted the situation in which different types of labour had different functions, and were bought in different markets, and they did not attempt to make them interchangeable.

In many respects the Second World War was a demographic watershed. Although, before it began, the different immigrant races were slowly beginning to become domiciled in Malaya, a sharp distinction can be drawn between a pre-war period, in which for some decades non-Malays had been mainly reckoned as transients,[19] and a post-war period, in which it was recognised that Malaya had become a permanently multiracial society, even though not all its immigrant people were yet fully settled.

Under pressure of war in China, and with restricted male immigration, but unrestricted female immigration from China, a flood of Chinese women came to Malaya just before the war.[20] At the end of the war most of these women had families in Malaya. Conditions in China were far more unsettled than in Malaya, and few of these families returned. A settled Chinese population, with homes and schools in Malaya, was now a basic fact of the situation.

In the immediate post-war period there were a few isolated outbreaks of interracial violence.[21] It was easy, immediately after the Japanese surrender, for armed Chinese guerrillas to pay off old scores against Malays who had worked with the Japanese; and for the local Malay majority then to react, on racial lines, against the Chinese living among them. These clashes frightened people in Malaya generally, and made them alarmed at the danger of racial strife in their country. Fortunately this fear has on most occasions proved stronger than the fear which each race may have of the others. Both in the Maria Hertog riots of 1950 and in the later race riots in Penang there was some danger of racial feelings running wild; but in both cases it proved possible for responsible leaders to mobilise opinion against violence and hostility.

This is not to say that any very successful steps have been taken towards removing the causes of racial tension.[22] The Malays envy the Chinese,

[19] In the early Administrative Reports of the Federation of Malaya the emphasis was on attracting a population to develop the country, and the tendency of non-Malays to return to their country of origin was not over-emphasised. Perhaps the strongest emphasis on the transience of the non-Malay population is found in C. A. Vlieland, *A Report on the 1931 Census* (London: Crown Agents for the Colonies, 1932), p. 9, paras. 35-36.

[20] M. V. Del Tufo, *A Report on the 1947 Census of Population* (Kuala Lumpur: Government Printer, 1949), p. 33.

[21] T. H. Silcock and Ungku Abdul Aziz, "Nationalism in Malaya," in W. L. Holland (ed.), *Asian Nationalism and the West* (New York: Macmillan, 1953).

[22] F. H. H. King, *op. cit.*, pp. 44-48.

who are often their creditors, and the monopolistic suppliers of their essential needs. They envy them their higher incomes, and their possession of most of the capital of a country which the Malays regard as their own. The Chinese envy the Malays their special scholarships in secondary schools and universities when better Chinese candidates are available. They envy the Malays' control of political power, for the numbers of the two races are much less unequal than their voting power under the constitution.

Nor does either race take any consolation from its own advantages, for each firmly believes a myth which makes these advantages seem its natural right. The Chinese firmly believe that their wealth and Malay poverty are the natural consequence of Chinese industry, thrift and adaptability to modern ways, and of Malay indolence, thriftlessness and conservatism. The Malays believe that they ought to control the country's political life because they are the sons of the soil; that Malaya is their country, and that the Chinese were brought in as a result of foreign rule, with which they collaborated to their own advantage and to the disadvantage of the Malays, until the Malays achieved independence.

Each of these myths has an element of truth. Neither will stand much detailed examination. The Chinese have certainly worked hard for their wealth. They are both more industrious and more enterprising than the other races of South-east Asia. But other qualities have also contributed. They are far more adept at using money and credit than the indigenous races,[23] and are also much more skilled at turning a social and political situation to their own financial advantage. In this respect their much greater prosperity in South-east Asia than in their own country is a result of their capacity to profit from Colonial rule by others.[24]

Malay poverty is certainly due in part to Malays' lack of interest in money-making and the tendency to give little respect to the successful entrepreneur. It is also partly due to their codes of hospitality and family obligation, which worked effectively enough to maintain capital as well as social cohesion, so long as credit was not available, but which have since become a source of indebtedness.[25] Malays are not particularly conservative in their way of life. It is difficult to measure change in a nation's way

[23] M. Freedman, "The Handling of Money," *Man* 59 (1959), reprinted in T. H. Silcock (ed.) *Readings in Malayan Economics* (Singapore: Eastern Universities Press, 1961), Part I, Chapter 4.

[24] The fullest survey is V. W. W. Purcell, *The Chinese in South-East Asia* (London: Oxford University Press, 1951). But cf. also an admirable Cornell University Press data paper, G. W. Skinner, *Report on the Chinese in South-East Asia* (Ithaca, N.Y.: South-East Asia Programme, Department of Far Eastern Studies, Cornell University, 1951).

[25] R. W. Firth, *Malay Fishermen: Their Peasant Economy* (London: Kegan Paul, Trench, Trubner, 1946), Chapters 4-6.

of life; but there seems to be at least as much change, since the early British accounts of life in Malaya, in Malay as in Chinese ways of life; for example, in housing, crops, transport, consumption, medical and social practices and education. Malays have absorbed Western education less than the Chinese; this was primarily due not to conservatism but to religious factors;[26] much of the Western education was specifically Christian, and, because of the treaties with the sultans, was directed mainly to non-Malays.[27] The system of rule through Malay sultans and the measures to maintain Malay rice-growing also discouraged Malay movement to the towns.

The Chinese economic myth is thus distinctly one-sided, but the Malay political myth is hardly nearer to the truth. It is true that, outside the Straits Settlements, those parts of Malaya which were settled were mainly ruled and inhabited by people of Malay race until the British brought them under control in the four decades from 1873 to 1914. Some areas were ruled by Siamese overlords[28] and some inhabited by Chinese miners,[29] but the general picture is one of Malay rule and occupation. This applied, however, only to the main river valleys. Much the greater part of Malaya was never occupied at all (though nomadic aborigines wandered over it) before the British opened it up and occupied it, mainly with non-Malay labour.

It is also necessary to examine in what sense the existing Malay population can base a claim to priority on the fact that Malays were originally there. A large part of the Malay population, at least of Perak, Selangor, Negri Sembilan and Johore, was attracted from outside Malaya by the prosperity introduced by the rubber boom in the early twentieth century. The existing Malay population is not therefore the indigenous population of Malaya; nor were Malays the first settled inhabitants of most of its present territory. On cultural and political grounds they have a rather better claim than the Chinese that it is their country, but certainly not an exclusive one.

[26] D. D. Chelliah, A *Short History of the Educational Policy of the Straits Settlements* (Kuala Lumpur: The Government Press, 1947), pp. 73-75.

[27] It is a punishable offence in Malaya to convert a Malay away from Islam. Mission schools are required to exempt Malays, if they wish, from religious instruction. Though they will usually admit Malays, their chief effort has obviously been directed to the Chinese, and many of the Methodist schools are actually called Anglo-Chinese schools.

[28] Kedah, Perlis, Kelantan and Trengganu were transferred directly from Siamese to British suzerainty.

[29] Before British intervention the greater part of the population of the main tin-mining areas was already Chinese, introduced originally for the sake of the revenue by Malay aristocrats, cf. C. D. Cowan, *Nineteenth-Century Malaya: The Origins of British Political Control* (London: Oxford University Press, 1961).

The policy of the Alliance followed an earlier agreement reached by the Communities Liaison Committee: to improve the political condition of the Chinese and the economic condition of the Malays. Both sides have some cause for disappointment with the progress so far made. The Chinese have lost the right to citizenship by registration, which was provided for in the Constitution.[30] Yet at least they have made some gains. They now have the right of citizenship for their children born in Malaya since independence,[31] a right for which they had been pressing since the Second World War, and which Chinese certainly do not enjoy in other ex-colonies — Indonesia, the Philippines, or Vietnam.

It seems doubtful whether the Malays have gained any improvement in their economic position, either relatively to the Chinese or absolutely. It is true that the top political and civil service appointments formerly held by Europeans are now largely held by Malays. Some Malays have also been introduced as executives and directors, in Chinese and European businesses, as a political gesture. But it is hardly possible that the increased wealth of these (at most a few hundred) could offset the decline in income per head among the great majority of rural Malays, which has resulted from increased rural population, delay in expanding roads and drainage, and falling productivity in some branches of agriculture.[32]

Inevitably the effect of industrialisation on race relations will largely depend on whether it promotes or retards the growth in Malay absolute and relative incomes. For the implementation of the promise to improve the economic position of the Malays is the key to greater Malay acceptance of Chinese political equality, and hence of Chinese commitment to Malaya.

In determining the extent of industrialisation in Malaya we must first consider the position of the rubber and vegetable oil industries. Both these industries are, in the main, primary producers. But both are fairly capital-intensive, and hence give scope for an advanced form of company-structure. Moreover both of them process the raw material by factory methods, using expensive machinery, on the spot. This might suggest that

[30] This applies only to those not born in Malaya. Clause 16 of the Constitution, allowing citizenship by registration to those born in Malaya before 1957, subject to five years' residence, good character, intention to settle permanently, and knowledge of Malay, is unaffected; but clause 17 was abolished early in 1962, Federation of Malaya Government Gazette, VI, 4 Supp. 2 (24 February 1962). Chinese resident in Malaya but not yet citizens must now seek naturalisation.

[31] Constitution of Federation of Malaya (Kuala Lumpur: Government Printer, 1957), clause 14 (1b); Report of the Federation of Malaya Constitutional Commission, 1957 (Reid Report), H.M.S.O. Colonial No. 330, para. 38.

[32] E. K. Fisk, "Special Development Problems of a Plural Society: The Malayan Example," The Economic Record, 1962, pp. 212-14.

the rubber and vegetable oil industries, at least where they are organised on a large scale, ought to be treated as specimens of industrialisation.

A further reason, noted by the Census of Manufactures,[33] is that many of the processes of manufacture carried out on estimates are also operated in independent units buying mainly from smallholders. This applies to rubber milling, latex processing, the processing of coconuts and oil palm products and also to the manufacture of tea.

In spite of this we should probably not reckon the plantation industries of Malaya as strictly examples of industrialisation. The number of workers employed in the factories is, in every case, an insignificant proportion of the total labour force; and in every one of the plantation industries the methods of employment and wage payment, and the conditions of life of the workers, are more affected by the rural nature of the work than by the firm's industrial structure. Nevertheless, an outline of labour conditions in this important section of the economy is desirable.

The Malayan estate industry was built up on immigrant labour, mainly recruited overseas as part of an organised work force.[34] Locally recruited labour was at first insignificant and casual. Malays were not interested in regular employment for wages, and the limitations on the British power in Malaya did not permit the kind of pressure that was employed in some colonial territories.[35] Moreover, abundant supplies of labour were available in South India and South China, and the estates were more interested in drawing on these than in organising a local labour force within the sparsely populated Malay peninsula.

But Chinese and Indian labourers were recruited and organised on very different systems. Indian labourers came from another British territory, and the system could be organised and controlled at both ends.[36] Chinese labourers were brought in by Chinese entrepreneurs and transferred to Chinese labour contractors, who continued to organise them for profit within Malaya.[37]

Limited recruitment of Indonesians under an indenture system was also used by the rubber estates.[38] This continued much longer than Chinese

[33] *Census of Manufacturing Industries in the Federation of Malaya*, Department of Statistics, Federation of Malaya (Kuala Lumpur, 1959), pp. 1, 65.

[34] J. N. Parmer, *Colonial Labour Policy and Administration* (New York: Published for the Association for Asian Studies by J. J. Augustin, 1960), p. 16.

[35] R. Emerson, *Malaysia: A Study in Direct and Indirect Rule* (New York: Macmillan, 1937).

[36] R. N. Jackson, *Immigrant Labour and the Development of Malaya* (Kuala Lumpur: Government Printer, 1961), Chapter 10.

[37] W. L. Blythe, "History of Chinese Labour in Malaya," *Journal of the Malayan Branch of the Royal Asiatic Society*, XX (June 1947), pp. 64-114.

[38] *Annual Departmental Reports of the Straits Settlements 1938*, Volume II (Singapore: Government Printer, 1940). Report of Mr. C. Wilson, Controller of Labour, Malaya, p. 8.

or Indian indenture systems, and was discontinued only in the 1930s, when it was not replaced by any alternative system.

From the point of view of race relations, the chief importance of these systems was that they compelled the estates to keep their Indian labour force, their Chinese labour force and their Malay labour force separate: to deal with them separately, pay them in different ways, and provide different living conditions.[39] Indian labour was normally paid directly, increasingly on a piece-work basis. Chinese labour was provided by contractors, who were nominally and legally the employers; and therefore it was usually impossible to enforce on them the obligations to provide housing, schooling for small children, etc., that were gradually enforced on direct employers under the Labour Code. Often the Chinese labour would not want the same conditions. Many of those who worked for the estates were also squatters, farming on the fringes of the jungle, on land which they had often cleared without authorisation.[40]

Indian labourers lived in labour lines on the estates, often with piped water and electric light supplied, and always subject to Government inspection. But almost their whole life was on the estate. Chinese labourers lived either in squatters' huts or in the nearby villages. Malays were normally employed on a casual basis, though regular employment increased considerably after the Second World War.[41] They continued to live in Malay villages, among their peasant neighbours, the rice farmers, the small rubber farmers, the fishermen and the landless workers on their farms, and so brought a more regular flow of money into the stable and traditional, but economically depressed, village economy.

The separation of the different races was aggravated by measures taken by the British Government to combat Communist terrorism after 1948.[42] The aim of the Communists, who were predominantly Chinese, was to build up a supply organisation within the Chinese community.[43] In this they were largely successful, even though they never won much active support from the Chinese community as a whole. The key to operations against the terrorist organisation proved to be food denial.[44] This involved concentrating the Chinese squatters in villages which could be protected.

[39] *Report of First Rubber Industry Arbitration Commission* (Kuala Lumpur: Government Printer, 1949).

[40] Federation of Malaya, *Committee Appointed by H.E. the High Commissioner to Investigate the Squatter Problem: Report* (Kuala Lumpur: Government Printer, 1949).

[41] *Annual Report of the Labour Department* 1947 (Kuala Lumpur: Government Printer, 1948), pp. 23-25.

[42] T. H. Silcock, *The Economy of Malaya*, "Background to Malaya Series," No. 2 (Singapore: Donald Moore, 1956), pp. 6-7.

[43] L. W. Pye, *op. cit.*

[44] H. Miller, *Menace in Malaya* (London: Harrap, 1954), pp. 188-90, 216.

Concentration was compulsory, and involved much hardship and often loss of income. To prevent this from generating active support for the terrorists it was necessary to provide considerable compensations in public services and community benefits, as well as legal tenure of land.[45]

The Chinese "new villages" so formed have mostly survived the Emergency that created them. But along with the creation of new villages went increasing concentration of estate labour for protection. This consolidated the separation of the resident Indian labour from the outside Chinese labour, so hardening the racial division that might otherwise, in the postwar period, have yielded to pressures for greater uniformity.

One of these pressures was the cessation of immigration. Indian immigration was cut off by the Indian Government in 1938, as a result of a dispute over conditions of immigrants, and was never resumed.[46] Chinese immigration was terminated as a result of Malay political uneasiness after the Second World War. Another pressure towards integration was the growth of trade unions cutting across racial lines, and in particular the National Union of Plantation Workers.[47] Originally an almost wholly Indian union, this organisation has had some success in enrolling Chinese members, and in negotiating more equal conditions for the different races.

In the mining sector of the economy there are two divisions, European mining and Chinese mining.[48] The Chinese were there first, at least in tin-mining. European industry was unable to compete successfully with the Chinese until the introduction of the tin dredge, a technology using much more capital.[49] Only European company structure can collect the enormous sums required for erecting tin dredges, and these now produce more than half Malaya's tin. In the other important mining industry, iron, ownership and management is exclusively organised on Western, company lines, either British or Japanese.

Chinese mines are financed by syndicates, usually of only a few families, helped out by trade credit from the ore buyers[50] and by profit-sharing ar-

[45] E. H. G. Dobby, "Resettlement Transforms Malaya," *Economic Development and Cultural Change*, No. 3, 1952, pp. 166-69.

[46] Lennox A. Mills, *British Rule in Eastern Asia* (Minneapolis: University of Minnesota Press, 1942), pp. 228-37; J. N. Parmer, *op. cit.*, pp. 74-77.

[47] This is much the best organised industrial union in the Federation of Malaya. See C. Gamba, *The National Union of Plantation Workers* (Singapore: Eastern Universities Press, 1963).

[48] Sir L. L. Fermor, *Report upon the Mining Industry of Malaya* (Kuala Lumpur: Government Printer, 1940).

[49] For a very full account of the competition between European and Chinese miners see an (unpublished) Ph.D. thesis by Wong Lin Ken in the University of London Library.

[50] Yip Yat Hoong, "The Marketing of Tin Ore in Kampar," *Malayan Economic Review*, Vol. IV, 2 (October 1959), pp. 53-55.

rangements with their labour.[51] This financial structure keeps the labour force almost exclusively Chinese. There are therefore few racial problems within the Chinese part of the industry; but difficulties arise in its relation with the rest of the community, simply because it is necessarily exclusive. Tin mining competes for land with agriculture, which is mainly under Malay control. Tin tailings can cause flooding. Since Malays are not employed in the industry it is difficult to get the Malay state Government to allow enough prospecting.[52]

The Western division of the industry employs less labour, and a fairly high proportion of it is either mechanically trained or clerical. These skilled groups tend to be racially mixed, recruited from the English schools. The majority of the unskilled and semi-skilled labour is still Chinese, because mining was already a Chinese industry when the European tin mining began. More Malay labour is being recruited, partly because it is now more available, partly on political grounds. In the mining of iron, which was before the war a Japanese industry and had to be reconstructed after 1945, a successful effort has been made to recruit mainly Malay labour.

Before the war, much of the mining labour was recruited in gangs, through labour contractors, who worked on a profit-sharing basis, expecting higher payment when tin prices and yields were high, and accepting a bare subsistence if the mine was unsuccessful.[53] In recent years, direct employment has become more general;[54] but the labour is still more prepared to accept considerable wage adjustments than most other labour.

In some instances Western-owned mines are both far from any main centre of population and reasonably permanent, so that a small, semi-permanent interracial residential community grows up. These communities approximate to the other residential communities in the public services and in Western-style industry.

It is unfortunate that virtually no studies have been made of these interracial communities in Malaya. There is no general information about the policy when different races are provided with housing. Because of the background of immigrant labour, brought over for limited periods to do particular kinds of work, it is fairly common for employers in Malaya

[51] N. C. Siew, Labour and Tin Mining in Malaya (Ithaca: Cornell University, South East Asia Programme, Department of Far Eastern Studies, 1953).

[52] This is the reason for the allocation of a proportion of the export duty on tin to the state Governments in recent years, cf. Huan Tzu-Hong, "The New System of Revenue Allocation to the States and Settlements in the Federation of Malaya," Malayan Economic Review, Vol. II, No. 1 (April 1957); also Reid Report, op. cit., paras. 139 and 141.

[53] N. C. Siew, op. cit.

[54] Only ten per cent of labour on dredges was employed through contractors in 1960. Annual Report of the Ministry of Labour, 1960, p. 66.

to provide housing for at least a part of their labour force. This is bound to have some effect on race relations. But there have been neither comparative studies of the policy in different settlements of mixed race, nor sociological investigations of the way in which racially mixed communities behave.

Policy of employers with mixed racial groups is known to vary from deliberate segregation, for the sake of avoiding interracial friction (and also avoiding joint action by different races in industrial disputes), to deliberate standardisation and promotion of a common relation of all races to the company. Intermediate policies would include segregation for convenience only, or grouping for convenience only.[55]

Apart from the Western-owned mines, most of the industrial or semi-industrial establishments, in which these mixed communities are found, are in the public sector. One of the pioneers of industrialisation was the Malayan Railway, a State-owned enterprise with its main workshops at Sentul near Kuala Lumpur, and subsidiary workshops in several smaller centres. The Public Works Department, the Harbour Boards at Penang and Singapore, and the civilian establishments of the British armed forces, in Singapore and elsewhere, are other employers of an industrial type, with racially mixed labour forces, and providing accommodation for at least a proportion of their workers.

Outside the public sector, the greater part of the industry is Chinese-owned, and, like the Chinese mines, employs Chinese labour to the extent of 75 per cent or more. There are, however, a few industries, especially in Singapore, in which two or three large Western-owned firms employ an appreciable proportion of the labour force.[56] These include Engineering, Motor Repairing and Assembly, Soft Drinks Manufacturing and Printing. Generally speaking the Western-owned firms employ a more racially mixed labour force than the Chinese firms; though statistics are not given according to the race of the owner.

The Chinese-owned industry consists mainly of small family businesses. It is widely regarded as the most probable growing-point for industrialisation in the Malayan economy.[57] The output-capital ratio is almost certainly as high here as anywhere in the economy. Opportunities for technical progress are considerable. But most of the labour is still recruited on a basis of personal contact, trained by the existing employees and provided with food on the premises. This makes it difficult for Chinese

[55] There is some discussion of problems of housing Government daily rated workers in the *Final Report of the Joint Wages Commission*, Federation of Malaya and Singapore, 1948 (T. H. Silcock, Joint Chairman).

[56] J. J. Puthucheary, *Ownership and Control in the Malayan Economy* (Singapore: Eastern Universities Press, 1960), Chapter 5.

[57] International Bank, *op. cit.*, Chapter 6, Technical Report 8.

business to become a considerable employer of non-Chinese labour; and this in turn hampers effective development by creating antagonism between this sector of industry and the politically dominant Malays.[58]

Much of Malaya's deliberate economic development policy since the Second World War has been devoted not to industrialisation but to attempting to improve the economic condition of the rural Malays. A brief account of the measures taken is therefore necessary to an understanding of race relations.

The provision of village amenities — roads, piped water, electricity, schools, etc. — to the compulsorily resettled Chinese in the new villages was, as we have seen, a military necessity. But it inevitably created a demand that something similar should be done for the rural Malays. In 1950 a Rural and Industrial Development Authority was established on an interim basis, and from 1 January 1954 it was made a body corporate.[59] Its object was never sufficiently clearly defined. Officially it was to stimulate the development of the rural areas; and it was understood that it would give special attention to those areas occupied by Malay small farmers.

The Rural and Industrial Development Authority (RIDA) never had a real chance to tackle these problems. It has now been restricted to an organisation for giving loans and technical advice to small-scale industries; but the unspoken presupposition of preference for Malays still renders it costly and ineffective. In effect an industry which is to be aided by RIDA is one that Malays can be induced to undertake but that has not attracted Chinese. This virtually confines it to industries which are unprofitable, at least if some reasonable proportion of development costs is debited to them.

The general rural development functions of RIDA have now been taken over by a Ministry of Rural Development, headed by one of the most vigorous of the Malay Ministers, Tun Abdul Razak. As a result of his experience as Minister of Defence, he is attempting to plan rural development on the lines of a military operation; in each district a red book is prepared which challenges co-ordinated rural development, under each one of twelve headings;[60] and there is an operations room in every district and state, as well as at Kuala Lumpur. The plan has certainly generated haste, and a sense of urgency. But much of the necessary basic knowledge is simply not available to ensure that carrying out the plan will achieve the results intended.

58 E. K. Fisk, op. cit.
59 E. M. Fiennes, Report on Rural and Industrial Development Authority 1950-55 (Kuala Lumpur: Government Printer, 1956).
60 District Rural Development Plan, facsimile on reduced scale issued by Ministry of Rural Development (Kuala Lumpur, 1961).

Development of new land is usually regarded as the key to a satisfactory rate of growth. Owing to chronic delays in the alienation of land by State governments, block schemes are being adopted by nearly all states and also by the Federal Land Development Authority.

The schemes themselves, however, have had some direct effects on race relations. Nearly all the Federal and some of the state schemes are interracial; and the building up of mixed rural communities will do something to offset the hardening of racial segregation which the Emergency caused. But there are minor grounds for anxiety. The majority of settlers are Malays, and an effort has been made to appoint properly qualified Malay managers for the schemes. In many cases, however, this has proved impossible. A knowledge of modern planting methods is necessary, and several managers have been drawn from junior supervisory positions in the rubber industry. There are few if any Malays in these positions, and the rubber estates would — on political grounds — be very reluctant to lose any Malays. Experience in the schemes has shown the need for more and more direction, to maintain adequate standards. If the price of rubber should go on falling, so that the repayment of the sums advanced to settlers became very onerous, increasing resentment against non-Malay managers might develop.

We may turn now to trace the specific interactions between industrialisation and race relations.

First we may inquire whether race relations have been affected by any increasing tendency to counteract-relations and class structure, in place of traditional status-relations. On the whole the effects are unimportant except on the types of skilled work that are based on an English-language education. But, at least until the achievement of independence, industrialisation was increasing the importance of this type of work; and in the last few years before independence the junior managerial class was being increasingly admitted into positions formerly kept for Europeans, so partially eliminating a surviving distinction based on race.

Among the English-educated, junior executives and clerks were transferred between different positions, virtually without regard to race, and came to constitute a more or less homogeneous middle class. Artisans, in industries like the railways, where apprenticeship was based on education in English, formed a moderately homogeneous group at work, though their manner of life at home was less influenced by a Western pattern, and less homogeneous as between different races.

These English-educated groups were not particularly numerous in the industrial sector of the economy. They were far more important in the commercial houses, the banks and the Government offices. The development of these businesses was in part a result of industrialisation, but in the main they were ancillary to the entrepôt trade of Singapore and

Penang. The growth of an English-educated class, which tended to cut across racial lines, was therefore only loosely related to industrialisation. In the Western-style industry, however, the influence of an English-educated group in an intermediate position had some tendency to standardise the goals which the different racial groups sought to achieve as their standards of living rose. The artisans aspired to conditions of housing, dress, schooling and general consumption patterns like those of the clerks instead of setting separate racial patterns. As separate housing units replaced the Chinese *kongsi* houses or Indian labour lines, the pattern tended to be a poorer version of the housing supplied to clerks or other responsible workers, which in turn had been a very much smaller and cheaper version of the housing provided for assistant managers.

It is, however, doubtful what norms of behaviour will be generated by any future extensions of industrialisation. Much of the policy in relation to foreign capital, pioneer industries, etc., appears to postulate a continuing social structure not very different from that which prevails at present, with an English-educated middle class rising to management positions and eventual partnerships in overseas undertakings, and an infra-structure of clerks, skilled artisans, etc., expanded to fill corresponding positions in new industries.

The projected education policy, however, may not continue to produce such a middle class. The aim is to convert education increasingly to Malay, which will be the medium of instruction in secondary schools, and to some extent even in the University. The effect of this will inevitably be to promote a Malay-speaking middle and professional class as the country's *élite*. Some education through the medium of English will no doubt survive, particularly in mission schools. Its products will find lucrative work in the firms undertaking overseas business, particularly in the ports of Penang and Singapore. But it is difficult to foresee how the pattern will develop in industry as industrialisation grows. It is at least possible that industrialisation will accentuate divisions between groups that would have racial characteristics, though not following quite the present racial lines.

Much will depend on future developments in two special fields. How far will the Malay language in fact become an instrument of deliberate cultural assimilation? And how far will it in fact prove possible to provide technical education and training in Malay?

The Malays of the Alliance are on the whole moderate Malay nationalists, anxious to co-operate with those non-Malays who can be induced to co-operate with them, and unwilling to adopt measures that would exclude the great majority and include only a small minority of non-Malays. Their political tactic is in fact to underemphasize Malay political demands which other races find difficulty in accepting, such as Islam as the state religion, or the use of the Arabic script, and to assimilate their way of living to that of the Western-educated middle class, except in terms of language and a limited amount of royal ceremonial. But they are undoubtedly under some pressure from their Malay followers to behave in a more distinctively Malay way.

The Malay language has preserved, under British rule, many of the courtesy-inflexions of an aristocratic society; and so long as its use is fostered under a monarchical form of government it may well become an instrument for incorporating the upper levels of the professions and civil service into a structure of respect and social gradation, to which the leading non-Malays could be persuaded to conform, and which the Malay public could be induced to accept.

Many of those who support Malay as the national language, because of opposition to the present leadership of those most assimilated to Europeans, would no doubt strongly oppose any such aristocratic tendency. But most of these are non-Malays, and the implementation of Malay language policy will not be in their hands.

Success or failure in fostering technologies through the medium of Malay will also have some bearing on this problem. At present there is insufficient willingness to divert a high proportion of the educated Malays into translation and educational work, by suitable salary inducements or in other ways. Technical progress in this field has been wholly insufficient. Little more than a nucleus of Malay secondary schools and some limited University lecturing in Malay is likely to be achieved by 1967 when Malay is due to become the country's official language.

Meanwhile a structure of apprenticeship is being built up in existing industries in which the medium of instruction is still commonly English. This is at present confined to Selangor for most trades, but the aim is to establish formal apprenticeship in all industrial areas. It is interesting that the scheme is making some headway even in the building industry, where formerly training was almost wholly done by informal Chinese methods.

Over the greater part of Chinese industry, skilled workers are still trained on the job by the existing skilled workers. The labour structure remains traditional although enterprise is always available to try out new openings, and new machinery is readily adopted.

In these conditions, though it is difficult to project trends, there seems every likelihood that industrialisation will create two distinct groups, both culturally separated from the ruling *élite*. Large-scale industry, run on Western lines, may perpetuate an interracial group which continues to be technically trained through the medium of English, but is increasingly differentiated from the culturally dominant Malay-speaking middle class. At the same time small-scale low-cost industries may continue to be organised on a Chinese basis, with contacts throughout South-east Asia,

using the Chinese language, but equally separated from the politically
dominant group in Malaya.

A multiracial society of this kind might retain some political stability,
with some of the wealth derived from Western and Chinese industry
being used to extend rural development and build up a more prosperous
Malay peasantry. But it is difficult to imagine it being sufficiently successful industrially, in the long run, to achieve a rising standard of living,
especially if population continues to grow at present rates.

This raises the question of the reverse influence, of race relations on the
process of industrialisation in Malaya. For the fact that Malaya is a particular kind of multiracial society influences the way in which it can
promote industrialisation.

First we must take account of the fact that the Malays are politically
the most powerful group, but the group least inclined to industrialisation.
The Alliance, as a predominantly Malay party prepared to co-operate with
the financially dominant section of Chinese society, tends to take a tolerant and indeed encouraging attitude to capital, but not an active interest
in fostering the growth of either the Chinese or European types of industry found in Malaya. Facilities, tax exemptions and tariff concessions are
offered to capitalists who will set up establishments in Malaya[61] and will
offer a limited number of positions, and sometimes limited share-
participation, to Malays. But there is no Malay industrialisation to foster,
and no real inducement to prefer local Chinese to outsiders. This has
made Malaya an attractive country for investors. But it is hardly a policy
to encourage rapid growth of a locally-owned industry.

The same passive attitude to industrialisation is apparent in the alloca-
tions of public expenditure to industry under the first and second development plans. In the first plan just over 1 per cent was spent in
industry, nearly all on site development. In the second plan, under which
total expenditure will be more than double, expenditure on industrial site
development is actually reduced, and proportional expenditure on all industry, except rural industry, is less than before.

It is arguable that on economic as well as political grounds it is desirable
to concentrate most of Malay's public expenditure on transport and agricultural development. However this may be, an expenditure on industrial development (other than rural industry) of less than 1 per cent of
the total public expenditure is clearly disproportionately small for a
country as wealthy and underindustrialised as Malaya.

The above analysis suggests that the interaction between industrialisation and race relations in Malaya since independence is not too hopeful.
One section of industry was tending to create a fairly homogeneous and

[61] *Income Tax Ordinance* 1947, and *Pioneer Industries Ordinance* 1958
(Kuala Lumpur: Government Printer, 1961).

gradually expanding middle class, based on general and technical education through the medium of English; but this was never more than a part of the industrial structure. Linguistic and cultural policies are now creating a different political and professional *élite*, without necessarily creating the possibility of an industry based on training in Malay. An increasing tendency for industry to become an enclave of Western or Chinese culture within a predominantly Malay society may well preserve cultural heterogeneity, even if it does not follow strictly racial lines.

It is sometimes claimed that a policy of developing industry by nationally owned corporations would make it possible to retain Malay control and train more Malays in management. Here we may consider separately large organisations, on a scale to pay the salary of a university graduate or person of roughly equivalent training, and small organisations, employing a score or less of employees.

For the larger undertakings a case could be made out, if enough educated Malays were available for all important uses for them. Malaya should certainly be surveying the opportunities for such undertakings while it is expanding the supply of educated Malays. Industries particularly worth fostering would be those which would create demands for other small-scale industries.

It is much more difficult for the Government to enter into the field of small-scale industry described by the International Bank Mission Report, in which market skills are relatively important, and in which risk-taking, long hours of work and thrift are the main conditions for success. There are many examples of reasonably successful Government industries on a large scale; Government incursions into the field of small-scale industry have usually been costly failures. Effective national control hampers the flexibility which is the small-scale firm's chief defence against economies of mass production.

In the short run it will therefore be very difficult to prevent the continuation of two separate enclaves of industry, operating in ways which make assimilation difficult.

A heterogeneous society of this kind, even if it remained stable, would find difficulty in promoting rapid economic growth, and without rapid economic growth the present demographic pressures will make it difficult to improve Malay incomes, and hence difficult to grant non-Malays political equality.

It is important for Malaya to achieve a sense of common nationality. It is a fairly wealthy and strategically important area, inhabited by three races that can all claim affinity with larger and more powerful neighbours overseas.[62] Racial rivalry in Malaya can therefore be dangerous externally as

[62] T. H. Silcock, *Towards a Malayan Nation* (Singapore: Eastern Universities Press, 1961), pp. 76-77.

well as internally. But unfortunately the achievement of a sense of common nationality demands more than forgetting overseas links and accepting a common destiny.

Each of the two main races tends to feel that it occupies an inferior position because of the colonial past, which ought to have been brought to an end with independence. Chinese have lived in Malaya for decades and adapted themselves to, and prospered in, the multi-racial colonial society they found there; they regard the survival of Malay political rule as a dishonest trick of the colonial power. Malays find, on achieving independence, no escape from the Chinese, who came in under the umbrella of colonial rule, and made money and got the Malays into their debt by adapting to the colonial economy; to them the claim of a Chinese, born in Malaya, to retain rights there after independence seems only slightly less absurd than would be a similar claim by a Malayan-born Englishman.

Because the Malay grievance is mainly economic, economic progress might remove it, until no real obstacle to full Chinese participation would remain. But this progress is not taking place; and the interactions of race relations and industrialisation make it difficult to hope for much improvement.

IX

In the Middle East, race relations are exceedingly complex: this is not an area where two easily recognizable racial groups interact within a stable governmental setting. Instead, the Middle East has seen a series of empires incorporating people of different ethnic and religious groups rise and fragment. Muslim theology places no emphasis on race, so conflicts in the periods of imperial stability were interreligious. But as Ottoman power declined, one nation after another was formed by ethnically similar religious groups with European sponsorship. It was primarily then that race relations grew in importance. National boundaries divided tribes and divided ethnic groups, creating minorities and majorities everywhere. The varieties of conflict and the issues around which they focus are the subject of Professor Hourani's article.

ALBERT HOURANI

Race and Related Ideas in the Near East

RACES IN THE NEAR EAST

Very roughly, a "race" may be defined as a group of which the members share certain physical characteristics, such as color, or have a common biological origin. By extension, the term may also be applied to groups

From *Race Relations in World Perspective*, edited by Andrew Lind (Honolulu, Hawaii: University of Hawaii Press, 1955), pp. 116-143. Reprinted by permission of the author and the publisher.

of which the members are held together by the *idea* of common physical character or origin, even when the latter is fictitious. "Racial conflicts" arise when the physical differences, real or supposed, are blended with other forms of difference between the groups — differences of status or function or interest or conviction; the physical difference may come to symbolize the other forms, and may itself play a part in making the conflict more bitter and the separation more rigid than it would otherwise have been.

In the sense here defined, there are no clearly separated "races" in the Near East, and no "racial conflicts." Throughout history, the greater part of the Near East has been subject to a succession of great empires, and some regions of it have been stages on the great trade routes of the Old World; there has been a continual moving and mingling of peoples, with the result that in almost every part of the area, and within almost all of its national communities, there can be found, to a greater or lesser degree, a mixture of people of different physical types, and of varying origins. Moreover, the idea of physical difference has almost never assumed in the Near East the importance which it has had in some other parts of the modern world. The direct rule of the European nations was never imposed on all parts of the Near East; where it existed it did not last long or lead to the establishment of European settler communities; and when the European powers sought to justify their predominance, they did so not so much in terms of "race" as in terms of civilization or material progress or religion. Before they came the tensions which existed in Near Eastern society did not run along the lines of physical difference (except for the conflict, in the first centuries of the Caliphate, between those of Arabian tribal origin and other converts to Islam); and the idea that "racial" difference was the most important division between human beings — the cause or symptom of the racial problems of the modern world — did not exist. There may have been, in certain places, a certain social prejudice against those of black complexion, and that identification of "fair" with "beautiful" or "noble" which is to be found in many cultures; but where it existed it was due more to the association of blackness with slavery than to the color itself, and it was never formalized into a doctrine, or taken so seriously as to become itself a cause of conflict. For this there were many reasons, and one of them was the domination of Islam over a great part of the Near East. For Islam teaches that while races exist, they, like all human distinctions, are of no importance in the last analysis; in the eyes of God, and therefore of man also, the only real hierarchy is that of virtue, and there is neither black nor white, neither Arab nor Persian.

While Islam limited the consciousness of racial difference, however, it gave rise itself to other forms of human difference. The primary divisions inside the Near East are, as they have been for over a thousand years, religious: whether a man is Moslem, Christian, or Jew, and which branch of the Moslem, Christian, or Jewish community he belongs to. The secondary division is that into ethnic groups, that is to say, communities of which the members have shared a historical experience long ; nd profound enough to give them a significant degree of identity: in language, and all that is bound up with it; in modes of thought and feeling; and, within the limits already indicated, in physical characteristics (the product of a common environment and intermarriage). It is at this point, in the conflict between ethnic groups, that we may find a certain analogy with the racial conflicts which exist in other parts of the world. For racial conflicts, as we have said, are not just conflicts about physical difference. They are conflicts in which the fact or image of racial difference becomes a symbol of something else; behind them there lies the struggle of groups for power in a complex society, and they may end in the breakup of that society. There is a sense in which such conflicts, by the mere fact that they use "racial" symbols, are different from other conflicts; but there is another sense in which they are analogous to other conflicts for power in a complex society, even when the racial idea is absent or unimportant. The Near East has seen such a conflict in the past century. There has been a struggle between different ethnic groups — a struggle into which political and economic rivalries and religious differences have entered no less than ethnic differences, but of which ethnic identity has been the symbol and the rallying point; which has been given its shape by the Western nationalist idea, that ethnic identity should be the basis of political consciousness and organization; and which has led to the breakup of the political system which held the Near East together for many centuries. What follows is an attempt to describe and explain this process.

RELIGIOUS COMMUNITIES
IN THE OTTOMAN EMPIRE

For more than four hundred years, most of the Near East was ruled by the Ottoman Sultans, and until the reforms of the nineteenth century, the Ottoman Empire was primarily a religious state. The dominant element was Moslem, and, indeed, it was this element alone which constituted the political community. The Empire *was* the community of believers living in common under the authority of the sacred Law; and the Sultan was there to administer the Law, to extend its sway in the world, and to protect the Moslem community from external dangers. There was, it is true, another great Moslem Empire adjacent — that of Persia — but its differentia was religious and not ethnic. At one time the Turkish Sultan was Persian by culture while the Persian Shah was Turkish in language;[1] but

---

[1] Sultan Selim II wrote Persian verse, while his contemporary Shah Isma'īl wrote only in Turkish. A. J. Toynbee, *A Study of History*, Vol. 1 (London: Oxford University Press, 1934), p. 353.

the former was Sunni Moslem while the latter was Shī'i and it was this difference which separated them (apart from the natural tendency of a power-system to maintain itself).

Living under the protection of the Sultan, but not regarded as members of the political community, were the non-Moslems — the Christians and Jews. They were organized into communities or "millets," each regulating its communal life in accordance with its own religious law, and each recognized as a civil entity dealing with the government through its ecclesiastical head. There was a Jewish millet under the Grand Rabbi of Constantinople, an Orthodox millet under the Greek Patriarch of Constantinople, and an Armenian millet under the Armenian Patriarch of Constantinople.[2] Here again, the differentiation between the communities was religious. Membership of each group was defined by acceptance of its doctrinal basis, regardless of origin or language: all the Jews of the Empire formed one millet, whatever their provenance, and all the Orthodox formed one, whether they were Greeks, Arabs, Rumanians, Bulgarians, or Serbs.

.   .   .

THE EMERGENCE OF NATION-STATES

The last century and a half have seen the breakdown of this social system, a breakdown due to factors working from both inside and outside. The keystone of the whole system was the supremacy of the Sultan and of the Turkish Moslem element which he represented; but from the seventeenth century his power decayed and with it the whole organization of the Empire. The constituent elements fell apart, and the collective will of districts and communities reasserted itself. In the nineteenth century, the European idea of nationalism began to spread, partly through schools, books, and travel, and partly through the example of successful European nationalism. At the same time, the growth of European power and the rivalries of the Western states intertwined themselves with the emergent aspirations of the Near Eastern races. Sometimes those aspirations might conflict with the interests and policy of a Great Power; at others, they might be encouraged by a Great Power, granting its protection to churches or wealthy families, or supporting claims to independence, in pursuit of its own interests; at others again — and they were the most tragic — a Near Eastern people might find itself torn between the rivalries of powers, alternately encouraged and abandoned, or simultaneously

[2] These were the only three "millets" fully recognized before the changes of the nineteenth century, but there were others with a different basis of doctrine or religious practice and which enjoyed spiritual and, to some extent, civil autonomy: Copts, Syrian Orthodox, Assyrians, various Uniate groups. Some of these were officially recognized in the nineteenth century.

supported by one and opposed by another; and all the time, whether it succeeded or failed in its desire for a separate political existence, it found itself circumscribed, its political life dominated by the diplomacy or force of the powers, its material life changed by Western processes and products, its inmost thoughts molded by Western ideas of how men should live together in society. In particular, Western economic processes and education molded two new dominant groups: the commercial and industrial middle class, and the professional men — lawyers, teachers, engineers, and army officers. As these groups developed and came to power, they took as their own the new idea of nationalism, both because of their Western education and because their interests led them to want a government they could control.

Such influences have been at work since the beginning of the nineteenth century, and have gradually communicated themselves from one group to another. The process began when the Sultan's Greek subjects broke out in revolt in 1821. From the beginning, the revolt had a nationalist coloring, derived from the new Greek schools (both in the Empire and in the towns of settlement in Russia and Europe) and from the example of Napoleonic rule in Italy and the Ionian Isles. But side by side with the nationalist aims of establishing an independent state in Greece, there was the different aim of establishing Greek domination in the Empire as a whole, and so overturning the balance between Moslems and Christians; and behind this there lay not the Western idea of the nation so much as the Near Eastern idea of the millet.

. . .

It was significant that although the impulse behind the nationalist movements was religious as well as ethnic, the successful establishment of the Christian states encouraged the national idea and made them as eager to be independent of one another as they had been to be free from the Turks. They wished to be independent of the Greeks in religious matters no less than of the Turks in political — although there was no religious, but only an ethnic, difference between them and the Greeks. The Serbian Orthodox Church proclaimed its independence of the Patriarch of Constantinople in 1830, and restored its own Patriarch in 1920. The Church in the Kingdom of Greece declared itself independent in 1833, the Rumanian Church in 1865 (its Patriarch was restored in 1925), the Bulgarian Church under an Exarch in 1870. In 1899 the Patriarchate of Antioch once again received an Arab Patriarch, thanks to Russian diplomatic help.

Each Christian victory increased still further the tension between the Turks and the Christians left inside the Empire. The Turks looked with suspicion on any Christian group which grew in prosperity and culture, since its desire for independence would also thereby increase; and they reacted ever more violently as each nationalist success brought nearer the dissolution of the whole Empire. This process reached its climax when the success of the Bulgarians encouraged the Armenians to hope for independence. Since 1821 they had largely taken the place of the Greeks in the economic life of the Empire, and as the element on which the Turks relied to help them. With prosperity there came education, and with education the idea of independence, articulated and organized largely by Armenian students in France and Russia. . . . There was no Turkish province in which the Armenians formed a compact majority. Those regions which they claimed as theirs contained more Moslems (Kurds, Turks, Circassians) than Armenians; and the Moslem population was willing to go to any lengths, in co-operation with the Turkish government, to prevent Armenian independence. Thus, there began a series of civil conflicts, massacres, and deportations which, between 1894 and 1922, virtually destroyed the entire Armenian population of Asia Minor.[3]

It was largely as a consequence of these events that the chain reaction now spread from the subject peoples to the dominant people. Throughout the nineteenth century, successive Ottoman reformers had tried to cure the disease of rebellion by transforming the Empire from a Moslem state to a multinational association based on equality. But sooner or later such attempts involved them in a contradiction: while equality might be desirable if the Empire were to prosper, inequality was necessary for it to exist at all. Its very existence depended upon the supremacy of the Turkish or Turcized Moslem element, which provided the political and military toughness that alone could save it from disintegration.

When the reformers obtained unlimited power after the Revolution of 1908, a conflict broke out between those who placed the principle of equality first and those who placed Turkish supremacy first. The latter group seized power; but what did they mean by "Turks"? The idea of a Turkish people had been developed by European Turcologists and Turkish intellectuals from Russia, but it was still mixed with the idea of religion. The first Turkish nationalists thought of all the Moslem peoples of the Empire as potential Turks, and when once they had the power they tried to Turcize all Moslems by force. This, in its turn, aroused a defensive nationalism among those peoples which, while being Moslems and having been loyal to the Sultan, did not wish to become Turks. The Albanians, who had been pillars of the Empire as long as it was a religious Empire, revolted against it when it gave signs of turning into a Turkish state, and proclaimed their independence in 1912; the Kurds, who also had played a large part in defending the frontier against Persia and holding down the

[3] See W. L. Langer, *The Diplomacy of Imperialism, 1890-1902* (New York: Alfred A. Knopf, 1935), pp. 145 ff.

restless peoples, began to organize as a national group;[4] and the Arab national movement, which had previously been merged in the general movement for Ottoman reform, now began to separate itself and aim at autonomy if not independence.[5]

The revolt of the Moslem subject peoples in its turn pushed Turkish nationalism to its logical conclusion: the final rejection of the idea of the multinational Empire for that of the national State. Every state should contain only one nation; and the whole of a nation should be included in a single state. The second ideal could not be realized, since a large proportion of the Turkish people lived in Russia; but the first was almost wholly realized by Kemal Ataturk. By 1923, the Kemalists, while withdrawing from the Ottoman territories which were not Turkish (and which not became the Arab "nation-states" of the Fertile Crescent), had succeeded in eliminating almost all the non-Turkish elements in the Turkish "homeland" of Asia Minor; and this was far more than a political revolution, for by so doing the Turks freed themselves from their economic dependence on their subject peoples and mastered those professional and commercial activities which they had always left to Greeks, Armenians, and Jews.[6]

NEAR EASTERN NATIONALISM

The process by which national states came into existence is now virtually complete, but, far from ending the tensions which broke up the Ottoman Empire, it has given them a different form. Instead of a struggle for influence among groups inside a single Empire, there has appeared a struggle for land and power among groups controlling different independent states. For the groups had been so intermingled in the Empire that it was impossible to say where each national territory ended. Each nationalist movement made its act of faith in a divinely given "natural territory" with "natural frontiers." This led at least to frontier troubles, at worst to two groups trying to set up a nation-state in the same territory. The "natural Kurdistan" of the Kurdish nationalists was not very different from the "natural Armenia" of the Armenians; both Greeks and Turks could put forward a historical claim to Western Anatolia; both Arabs and Jews thought of Palestine as their inalienable birthright; Greeks, Bulgarians, and Turks all thought their national states incomplete without Constanti-

---

[4] See W. G. Elphinstone in *Journal of the Royal Central Asian Society* (January, 1952), p. 91.

[5] See George Antonius, *The Arab Awakening* (London: H. Hamilton, 1938).

[6] For the subject of this paragraph, see U. Heyd, *Foundations of Turkish Nationalism* (London: Luzac, 1950), a study of the ideas of Zia Gokalp, the leading theorist of the movement. It is not without significance that he himself was probably not of Turkish, but of Kurdish, origin.

nople.[7] Moreover, it was not always easy to say to what nation a particular group belonged. In a region so mixed, many groups possessed the secondary characteristics of more than one nation, and multilingualism was common. Several national movements might claim such groups and the territories where they lived. Thus in Macedonia, Bulgarians, Serbs, Greeks, and Turks all claimed a majority, whereas in reality the population was a cross of all these "pure" strains. Similarly, during the Alexandretta crisis (1937-1939) the Turks were able to claim a majority by counting as Turks all those whose mother tongue was Turkish, whereas in fact this number included many Arabs and Armenians who for various reasons spoke Turkish, but who nevertheless did not regard themselves as Turks or wish to be incorporated in the Turkish Republic.

Even when frontier questions had been settled, there remained the question of minorities. While in a supranational Empire several ethnic groups could live side by side in the same territory without asking whose it was, once the nation-state was set up, those who did not belong to the nation in whose name the state was established also did not belong in the full sense to the political community. However long their ancestors had lived there, they were now regarded as strangers. At best they lived on sufferance; at worst they might be looked on as economic rivals by the new indigenous *bourgeoisie*, or as potential traitors by the new government, dangerous either because of their own strength or else through the use to which they might be put by a Great Power.

The idea of the nation tended also to destroy the unity of the millet. In some instances, it is true, the nation was more or less coterminous with the millet: for example, the Armenians, although even here there were Armenian Catholics and Protestants who belonged to the national but not to the religious community.[8] But this was not true of the Moslem or Eastern Orthodox communities. If the nation was the object of final loyalty, what became of the ties which bound its members to those who shared their faith but spoke other languages? Religious ties might still be strong enough to create a certain fellow feeling; but the national idea, if carried to its logical conclusion, dissolved the *political* bond between men of the same religion. That the Balkan peoples were all Orthodox did not make them the friendlier to one another once they became indepen-

---

[7] See section on the present situation, p. 171.

[8] In 1915-1916, when the Young Turk Government forcibly deported and massacred the Armenian population of Asia Minor, the Catholics and Protestants were exempted. But on the other hand, the American Protestant mission schools had helped to spread the idea of nationalism among the Armenians; and even earlier the Catholics of the Mekhitarist Order had been largely responsible for that revival of Armenian culture, which, here as elsewhere, had preceded the nationalist movement.

dent; Arabs and Turks, although both Moslems, regarded each other with political suspicion once the Empire was destroyed.

But, by what might seem almost a paradox, while the religious link between one nation and another vanished, the relationship, *within* each national community, between religion and nation still persisted. Even in Turkey after the lay revolution of Kemal, the "ultimate identification" of Moslem and Turk continued.[9] Thus the theorist of Turkish nationalism, Zia Gokalp, although he advocated the separation of temporal and spiritual powers, nevertheless defined the Turkish nation as consisting only of Turkish-speaking Moslems; Jews and Christians, even if Turkish-speaking, were Turks only in respect of citizenship and not of nationality, while Moslems living in Turkey but not Turkish by language and tradition would gradually be assimilated. In practice, too, the new government discriminated against Jewish and Christian citizens of the new Turkey; for example, when called to do military service they were not allowed to bear arms, in accordance with a prohibition of the Islamic law.

Again, when the Turkish and Greek populations were exchanged after the Greco-Turkish war,[10] the criterion adopted was religious. Turkish-speaking members of the Greek Church were sent to Greece, and were welcomed by the Greeks as true Greeks, and felt themselves to be such. . . . Many of the Moslems exchanged from Greece were, on the other hand, Greek-speaking."[11] "Although from the Turkish point of view the object of the exchange was the eradication of Greek nationalism from Anatolia, Greek Catholics and Protestants were not expelled."[12]

A special case was that of Arab nationalism. While the majority of the Arab people are Moslems, a substantial minority are Christians, and many of these last are Arab by long tradition and culture, and national loyalty as well as language; but, on the other hand, the whole culture and history of the Arabs are inextricably bound up with Islam. Thus, in the theories of the nationalist writers and the practice of political groups there was a certain ambivalence. At one extreme point were those Christian Arab nationalists who tried to formulate a nationalist concept without reference to Islam; at another were those who advocated an Arab revival, not for its own sake but as the key to Islamic revival and unity; at another, again, were those Lebanese nationalists who denied that the Arab-speaking Christians formed part of the Arab nation, and wished to create a

[9] Bernard Lewis, "Islamic Revival in Turkey," *International Affairs* (January, 1952).

[10] See section on the present situation, p. 171.

[11] C. A. Macartney, *National States and National Minorities* (London: Oxford University Press, H. Milford, 1934), p. 9.

[12] Sir John Hope-Simpson, *The Refugee Problem* (London: Oxford University Press, H. Milford, 1939), pp. 15-16.

Lebanese and essentially Christian nation. But in the middle were those who tried (at different levels of understanding) to hold together the two facts stated above. Thus the advocates of "Pan-Islam," Jemal ad-Din al-Afghani and Muhammad Abdu, worked closely with such Arab Christian writers as Adib Ishaq, and never doubted they would have a place in the new national community they wished to form; again, in Damascus in the 1940s, a Christian writer founded a new nationalist party based on respect for the prophet Muhammad, not as a founder of a religion but as father of the Arab nation. In Lebanon, too, the majority of Christians were permeated to some extent by Arab feelings and knew they must try to cooperate with the Moslem Arabs, both inside the country and in the surrounding region.[13]

The development of Egyptian nationalism also was special. It was not Egyptian nationalism which created the Egyptian nation-state, as elsewhere in the Near East; it was rather, as in the old states of Western Europe, that nationalism grew up inside a state already established by a dynasty. But in the virtually independent Egypt created by the family of Muhammad Ali there were important groups other than the Moslem Arabic-speaking Egyptians: the Turkish ruling group; the Levantine Christian and Jewish commercial middle class; and above all the Coptic Christians, who formed over 10 per cent of the population and were Egyptian on any conceivable definition. The presence of these groups raised a question: which of them belonged to the Egyptian nation? In the first phase, nationalism tended to be cosmopolitan and all-embracing, in this reflecting the aims of the ruling family even when it was opposed to them; among the earliest nationalists was a Jew, Yaqoub Sanua, and it was a Lebanese Christian who gave currency to the slogan "Egypt for the Egyptians." If the Nationalist Party became anti-Coptic after 1908, that was for political and not doctrinal reasons; and when nationalism revived after World War I, with the foundation of the Wafd, it upheld the sacred union of Copts and Moslems no less emphatically than it excluded the Turks and Levantines. Some writers, in order to justify this union, went back beyond Islam to the Pharaonic origins of the Egyptians; and some Copts in their nationalist fervor declared that they could be both Moslems and Christians.[14] In the last twenty years the sacred union has worn rather thin. Although successive governments have behaved with formal correctness toward the Copts, and although few Egyptians outside the Moslem brotherhood would wish to revive the medieval Islamic concept of a Moslem theocracy with Christians living as "protected persons"

[13] See George Antonius, op. cit.; E. Rabbath, Unité Syrienne et Devenir Arabe (Paris: Rivière, 1937); A. H. Hourani, Syria and Lebanon (London: Oxford University Press, 1946).

[14] See M. Colombe, L'Evolution de l'Egypte (Paris: G. P. Maisonneuve, 1951).

within it, nevertheless it is more difficult now than it seemed a generation ago to be both Christian and Egyptian.

. . .

THE PRESENT SITUATION

. . . Apart from the unending problem of Palestine, there does not seem to be any national question in the Near East today which is likely to lead to war, massacre, or displacement.* The typical national questions today are those of a relatively small and powerless minority living in the national state of another people with a large compact majority; and the typical relationship is one which, while falling short of complete harmony, also falls short of open hostility. We shall now give examples of such situations as they exist in six Near Eastern States.

Turkey

According to the census of 1950, 88 per cent of a total population of approximately 21,000,000 are Turkish-speaking, 7 per cent Kurdish, 1 per cent Arabic, and 0.5 per cent Greek. Ninety-eight per cent are Moslems, the rest Jews and Christians. According to the constitution, all have equal rights of citizenship, regardless of race or religion. But in fact the policy of the Turkish government toward those of religions other than Islam and nations other than the Turkish remains what it was in the days of the Young Turks: to assimilate those Turkish citizens who are Moslems by religion but not Turkish by nationality, and to treat as foreigners those who are not Moslems. This is not due to mere prejudice; it is partly a logical deduction from the nationalist principle, partly a matter of national security. Thus the Greeks, Armenians, and Jews are neither regarded as Turks nor regard themselves as such. In 1942 a tax on wealth, made necessary by the expense of keeping the army mobilized, was assessed in such a way as to discriminate against the non-Moslem merchant communities, and those who could not or would not pay were sent to forced labor in Anatolia. In the last few years such acts have not been repeated, and the non-Moslems have been treated correctly, but still as being outside the national community.

Of the non-Turkish Moslems, the most important are the Kurds (at least one and one-half million). A considerable part of them revolted

---

* [Conditions have changed greatly in the Middle East in the fifteen years since this article was written, and much of the description of the "Present Situation" here is no longer applicable. The immediate post-war period of which this article speaks is still extremely important as a study in itself and as background to later developments. For a more current treatment the reader should see: Albert Hourani, *A Vision of History* (Beirut, Lebanon: Khayats, 1961), particularly Chapter III, "Race, Religion, and Nation State," pp. 71-105. — Ed.]

against the government in 1925 and again in 1930 and 1937, both because their desire for a national state had been encouraged by the abortive Treaty of Sevres (1920), and because of opposition to the "Westernizing" reforms and to the extension of regular administration. Their revolts were suppressed with a severity which was the more understandable as, lying as they did on a distant frontier across which lived others of their nation, they could threaten the whole existence of the Turkish State. Until 1946 they were subject to a special regime. Law and order were strictly maintained; better communications made revolt more difficult; control by government officials replaced the traditional authority of the local chiefs; only Turkish was taught in the schools; the seminomads were induced to settle; and whole populations were deported and replaced by Turkish peasants. In the last years some restrictions have been removed, and there appear to have been no overt troubles; but it is doubtful if the Kurdish national idea has been killed.

Iraq

Four-fifths of the population is Arab (roughly four out of five millions); but there are also Kurds (between 800,000 and 1,000,000), Turks, and Turcomans in some of the northern towns, and Persians in the Shi'i Holy Cities. Of the 100,000 Christians, some are Arabs or Arabized, but others in the north conserve something of their Syriac language and tradition.

The Iraqi constitution declares that there shall be no differentiation in legal rights on grounds of language, race, or creed, and grants to the various communities the right to maintain schools in their own languages, subject to the general laws regarding education. There are some extreme Arab nationalists who no doubt would wish to ignore these provisions, and to pursue a policy of rapid and, if necessary, forceful assimilation of the Kurds. They have not, however, been able to impose their ideas because of the continued presence and influence of the British, because of the existence of a monarchy which stands above the different elements and symbolizes the unity of the country, because the Kurds are too powerful and inaccessible to be repressed, and because all moderate and responsible opinion recognizes these facts. On the whole, successive governments have respected the principles embodied in the constitution, and have recognized the existence of the Kurds as a separate element in the country. In the northern provinces where most of the Kurds live, their language can be used in local administration and the law courts; it is used also in primary schools, but — because of lack of books and technical terms — not in secondary schools. Most officials in those provinces and some in the other provinces are Kurds, and there are Kurdish ministers in every government (although often they are Arabized Kurds from Baghdad).

The Kurds have not accepted the authority of the government willingly, for many reasons: because of the gradual spread of Kurdish nationalist ideas; because of the persistence of tribal loyalties and customs, making them oppose not only an Arab government but any government; and because so long as the Iraqi government was poor it tended to confine its constructive work — schools, hospitals, and roads — to the capital and surrounding districts, while the more distant provinces (and the Kurdish ones among them) were neglected.

Since the establishment of the Iraqi States, there have been several revolts — first under Shaikh Mahmoud, and later under Shaikh Ahmad of Barzan and his brother Mulla Mustafa; and in 1946, when under Soviet inspiration a short-lived Kurdish Republic of Mahabad was set up across the frontier in Western Persia, there was a danger of a more serious and widespread rising, but this did not take place.

Some Kurdish nationalists demand autonomy in the provinces with a Kurdish majority, but no Iraqi government would be prepared to consider this, because the whole experience of the Near East in the last century shows that autonomy is only a stepping-stone to independence. Most Kurds recognize this, and would be content if they were allowed to live fully as Kurds within the Iraqi State, enjoying full use of their language and full equality of opportunity. The increased royalties now coming to Iraq under the new oil agreements have given the government greater revenues for capital works all over the country, and this is bound to improve the situation in the Kurdish provinces sooner or later.

If the country were left to itself, one might expect the Arabs and Kurds to work out a *modus vivendi*, while the natural process of external assimilation of a minority to a majority would gradually soften ethnic differences. But it does not seem impossible that Russia will once more use Kurdish nationalism, as she tried in 1946, to weaken the existing political structure of the Near East.

In the early 1930s there was tension between the newly independent Iraqi government and one section of the Christians, the Assyrians, and it culminated in the massacre of 1933. There were two reasons for this: first, the claim of the Assyrian Patriarch that the Assyrians should still possess, in the modern centralized state of Iraq, the civil autonomy and isolation of an Ottoman millet; and second, the unfounded belief of both parties that Britain might back the Assyrian claims. Since then the tension has diminished; some of the Assyrians were settled across the frontier in Syria, and the rest have continued to live unmolested in Iraq, although mutual suspicion has not completely disappeared.[15]

[15] See S. H. Longrigg, *Iraq, 1900-1950* (London: Oxford University Press, 1953); A. H. Hourani, *Minorities in the Arab World* (London: Oxford University Press, 1947).

Until 1948 there lived in Iraq about 150,000 Jews who scarcely could be recognized as a separate ethnic element, so deeply Arabized were they and so long had they lived by the twin rivers. But the creation of the State of Israel wholly altered their position. The attitude of the Iraqi government and people toward them grew progressively more unfriendly; controlling as they did a large part of the commercial and financial life of Baghdad, they could no longer hope to live unmolested once political feelings were aroused; and the new Israeli government spread among them the idea that they should constitute part of the Israeli nation. In 1950-1951 all but 10,000 left for Israel. The virtual disappearance of this ancient Jewish community showed clearly how the Western idea of nationalism could evoke hostility where it had not existed, and disrupt an age-old symbiosis.

Syria

Here too the great majority of the population is Arab (perhaps three out of three and one-half millions). Of the religious minorities, too, the greater part are ethnically Arab (Druzes, Alawis, Ismailis, Christians). But there are also certain ethnic minorities. Some — Turcomans, Circassians, Syriac Christians — are of no great political importance, but two — the Kurds (about 250,000) and Armenians (about 100,000) — have played some part in political life.

Smaller in proportion to the total population than in Iraq, and without the same preponderance in any region of the country, the Kurds do not constitute a danger to the Syrian State. That many Syrians for a time thought of them as a danger was due to two reasons: first, the existence of a large Kurdish element in the population of the Jazirah province, which is important because it lies on the frontier and has been brought under effective government control only in the last generation; and second, the French government during its period as Mandatory always relied on the Kurds and Christians in order to offset the hostility of the Arab majority. Thus the Jazirah was always kept under direct French control, and the Kurdish nationalist party (the "Hoybun") was encouraged. Since the French left, there have been no serious disturbances; although not dead, Kurdish nationalism is quiescent; the educational and administrative policy of the government makes for assimilation. This is, indeed, a process which has been going on for centuries. Here, as in Iraq, there are half- or wholly-Arabized Kurds, who play a large part in political life. Of the five heads of the Syrian State since the French withdrew, two (Husni Zaim and Fawzi Sillo) have been of Kurdish origin.

The Armenians live mainly in Aleppo. Although many are refugees of the last generation, some belong to families long settled in the town. Mainly an artisan community, industrious and intelligent, they form an integral part of the economic structure. During the French Mandate some of them were tempted to rely upon French protection; but the majority, profiting from the bitter experience of their fathers, adopted the path of political assimilation. While preserving their own faith and culture, they tried to learn Arabic and play their part as citizens. They have two deputies in Parliament, and their relations with government and majority are correct. Any too obvious manifestation of their communal spirit still arouses opposition; but the process of assimilation could be expected to go on peacefully were there no danger that Russia would exploit their national feelings, as she did those of the Kurds. After 1945, several thousands were allowed to return to the Armenian Soviet Republic, but it is believed that they did not like what they found there.[16]

Lebanon

In Lebanon the main tensions are religious and not ethnic, and the State is indeed based on the religious communities. Parliamentary seats and offices are distributed among the different confessions according to their size. But on the other hand the constitution promises absolute equality for all without distinction. Almost all members of most confessions are Arabic-speaking; but there are two religious communities which are ethnically different from the rest — the Armenian Orthodox (67,000 out of a total population of one and one-fourth million) and Armenian Catholics (14,000). Mainly refugees from Turkey after World War I, from the beginning they were treated by the French Mandatory on a level with the other inhabitants of the country, and were able to fit into its political structure precisely because they formed a religious as well as a racial community. They have their own schools and communal organizations; and two out of the forty-four deputies are Armenian Orthodox.

At first they were not much welcomed by the population, both because they were foreign in language and customs, and because of the inevitable economic tension, in a poor country, between a destitute immigrant population, willing to work for starvation wages, and the existing population. Tension between Armenians and Moslems in Beirut reached a danger point on at least one occasion. But in the last ten years there has been a clear change for the better. They have made an effort to be assimilated; besides, the departure of the French has thrown the different communities together and given them a sense of responsibility toward one another. At the same time, here as in Syria they have not abandoned their traditions or given up their national loyalty, and some thousands returned to Armenia after 1945.

Egypt

The overwhelming majority in Egypt is Arabic by language and culture, and may be said to belong in some sense to the Arab "nation," although

[16] A. H. Hourani, *Syria and Lebanon.*

it is easy to discern differences of temperament and social organization which might justify one talking in another sense of an Egyptian nation. The only considerable ethnic minorities are to be found in the cosmopolitan trading towns — Cairo, Alexandria, and Port Said — where a mixed European and Levantine middle class (perhaps one-fourth million out of twenty millions) has controlled the commercial and financial life of Egypt for almost a century. They were always resented by the Egyptians because they were rich, because they were foreign, and because they enjoyed special privileges under the Capitulations. In the past generation they have been losing their position. They no longer have the Capitulations to protect them; and they are being squeezed out of their preserves by the growth of an indigenous Egyptian capitalism, and by the Law of 1947 which regulates the percentage of posts to be reserved for Egyptians in foreign companies. This process is likely to continue.

Israel

Since its establishment, the State of Israel has kept its doors open to all Jews who wish to enter it. But it has not yet defined the part which race and religion play respectively in constituting a Jew; and this is not only a theoretical question, but one with which is bound up the whole destiny of Israel.[17] Converts to Judaism have been accepted and welcomed, like the Italian village which was converted en masse and transferred to Galilee. Jewish converts to Christianity are allowed to enter, but there is a popular prejudice which makes it difficult for them to find employment.[18]

Out of the total population of 1,600,000, about 180,000 are Arabs, including 35,000 Christians. The Proclamation of Independence in 1948 promised them social and political equality, and some rights have in practice been given them. They preserve their religious organizations; education is Arabic in language, although its content is carefully controlled; Arabic can be used in the law courts, in administrative affairs and in Parliament; they have the right to vote, and at present eight deputies out of 120 are Arab. On the other hand, most of the Arab districts are still under military administration; movement is restricted (with some alleviation in 1954) and arbitrary acts of military authority occur from time to time. Under the Absentees Property Law of 1950, land can be confiscated (against compensation) not only from those who have left Israel but from those forced to move elsewhere inside Israel during the fighting, and subsequently forbidden to return home. The Nationality Law of 1952 grants Israeli nationality to Jews automatically, but to non-Jews only on certain conditions, and at the discretion of the minister of the interior.

---

[17] E. Marmorstein, "Religious Opposition to Nationalism in the Middle East," *International Affairs* (July, 1952).
[18] N. Bentwich, *Israel* (London: Benn, 1952).

Here again, such measures are not due to mere prejudice, but to the national basis of the State, and considerations of security.

CONCLUSIONS

The Near East is now divided into nation-states. The process cannot be reversed; and even if it could, we should have to balance against the sufferings it has caused, the benefits it has conferred. In more than one of the states, citizens with a new sense of self-confidence and responsibility are learning how to work together, and are trying to develop their human and material resources. But to what purpose? From national existence to national aggrandizement is not a necessary path to take, but it is an easy one; and it can scarcely be avoided if the nation sets itself up as the final object of worship.[19] A nation-state can be healthy only if its citizens are conscious of some loyalty beyond that to the state, and some realms in which their belonging to a certain nation is of no account. To make this statement is to become aware of the most grave and urgent questions of political philosophy — questions which could be answered only by a systematical investigation of the nature and purposes of Man in Society. Can there be a universal community, transcending the bounds of the national state, unless there is a bond between its members more lasting and stable than that of opposition to an external danger — either a positive common interest, or, at some level, an identity of political principle? Can such a community survive unless the smaller communities which compose it treat one another on a footing of equality? Is it possible in these days to preserve a sphere — of thought even more than of action — in which the government cannot impose uniformity upon its subjects? Inside that sphere, how can the individual preserve the true inner freedom of not regarding himself as determined by one only of his characteristics?

[19] E. Marmorstein, "The Fate of Arabdom," *International Affairs* (October, 1949).

X

Race relations between Maori and European in New Zealand are ambiguous. Although there is some evidence of unfavorable stereotypes of Maoris among Europeans, there is little direct evidence of discrimination in actual interactions between groups. There is some intermarriage and some exchange of residence between Maori and European. Class, as well as conflicting value systems, obscure interracial behavior, but Thompson's exceedingly well-documented essay removes much of this obscurity.

RICHARD THOMPSON

Race Relations in New Zealand

MAORI AND EUROPEAN

. . . Rapid social change is seen as the principal characteristic of the postwar situation [in New Zealand]. Maxwell,[30] Metge,[31] McCreary,[26] and Borrie[9] [10] have all discussed the social and economic implications of the growth of Maori population first analyzed by Buck forty years ago[47] and the consequent movement to the cities and particularly to the city of Auckland.* McCreary[24] and Morris[34] found that Maori crime was dispro-

From *Race Relations in New Zealand*, by Richard Thompson, National Council of Churches in New Zealand (Christchurch, New Zealand, 1963), pp. 20-35, 53-56. Reprinted by permission of the author and the publisher.

* [Superior numbers in the text refer to numbered bibliographical entries at the end of the article.—Ed.]

portionately high, even when the youthful nature of the Maori population was taken into account, but no consideration was given to socio-economic status. Hunn drew attention to the under-representation of Maoris in sixth forms, apprenticeships, skilled trades and professions and provided recent figures on such matters as population, education, health, housing, immigration and crime.[21] As Ausubel pointed out, factors known to increase racial tension overseas are present in New Zealand.[3]

European Attitudes to Maoris

A number of studies of European attitudes to Maoris have been reported, the two most interesting being literary in character. Erwin examined the ideas that travellers and residents formed of the character and attitudes of the Maori people (1642-1840).[16] The material for the study was drawn from printed sources — official accounts of voyages, reports by early travellers, letters and journals of residents, Parliamentary reports and missionary registers. Erwin concluded that the views of the earliest visitors came to be accepted as the conventional stereotype of Maori character. With the decline in the objective reporting which characterized early explorers like James Cook, favourable traits in the stereotype of Maori character were given less emphasis than the unfavourable and this trend was reinforced by occasional violence, often provoked by Europeans. In many respects, Erwin declared, the stereotyped picture of Maori character found in the early nineteenth century differed very little from that reported in the present day. Pearson surveyed the attitudes to Maoris expressed in some of the more easily accessible novels and stories.[37] In twentieth century literature the Maori was seen in a variety of roles, as a romantic character, a comic figure, an object of contempt and hostility, and as a symbol of all the virtues missing in the pakeha. The attitudes Pearson described were not only representative of common contemporary pakeha attitudes, but they revealed nuances and a complexity that had previously been neglected.

An account of the general picture of the Maori people and their affairs as presented by the newspaper Press of the Dominion was given by Thompson.[48] A content analysis of all items of Maori news in a sample of the New Zealand Press was undertaken for a twelve-month period. The picture of Maori affairs projected by the Press was grossly distorted by its concern with "news value" and the preponderance of attention given to crime, sport and accidents. The practice of race labelling Maori crime news was widespread and the reporting of Maori political news by newspapers was not only unsympathetic, but on occasion revealed such serious discrepancies as to lay the newspapers concerned open to the charge of editorial interference in their news columns. Certain themes with regard to the Maoris ran persistently through the news items of the period. Themes favourable to the Maoris asserted that they were: generous and hospitable, good rugby players, good artists, musicians and craftsmen and good soldiers. Themes unfavourable to the Maoris asserted that they were: lazy and irresponsible, abusing social security benefits, content to live in dirty and overcrowded conditions, morally and socially irresponsible, political opportunists, ignorant and superstitious, and holding large areas of land irresponsibly.

Using a Thurstone-type attitude scale, Fitt reported that the attitudes of his students towards Germans and Japanese became less favourable during the Second World War, gradually improving after the cessation of hostilities, and that the Maori measures showed a similar fluctuation, but at a more favourable level.[17] Thompson described attempts to develop a projective picture-story approach after the style of the Thematic Apperception Test, for the purpose of exploring European attitudes to Maoris,[49] and Vaughan and Thompson used this same type of projective approach in a study of the development of the attitudes to Maoris of 8, 12, and 16-year-old pakeha children in Christchurch and Auckland.[61] This study was continued by Vaughan in an investigation of the development of ethnic awareness and attitudes among 520 Maori and pakeha children between the ages of 4 and 12 years in Wellington.[59] Developmental patterns were examined in relation to: chronological age, sex differences, socioeconomic differences, variations in skin pigmentation and parental "race," and the effect of a Maori or pakeha experimenter on the subject's test performance. Vaughan concluded that the evidence pointed to the existence of ethnic attitudes and awareness in young children, the stabilizing of this awareness with increasing age and the beginnings of attitude differentiation with the approach of adolescence. The "own-race" preference of older pakeha children was less marked than that reported of white American children, possibly an indication that the penalties of being a Maori in New Zealand were less than those attached to being a Negro in the United States. Differences of sex and socio-economic status did not appear to be significantly related to the pattern of development of attitudes and awareness in the children, but skin pigmentation and parental "race" in Maoris proved to be significant as did the ethnic background of the experimenter. Maori children tended to favour pakeha figures to a significantly greater extent when the experimenter was pakeha. Vaughan and Quartermain used the projective pictorial approach to study the acceptance of Maoris by white students.[60] They concluded that either the students made fewer acceptance responses to situations in which Maoris were involved or they assumed that such responses represented the behaviour of other white New Zealanders.

European Attitudes to
Maori-Pakeha Intermarriage

The question of Maori-pakeha marriage is a deeply emotional one and Baxter suggested that the ultimate question in Maori-pakeha relationships for many people is still: "Would you want your daughter to marry a Maori?"[6] There are numerous passing references to this aspect of the relationship. Thompson reported that the T.A.T.-type picture depicting Maori-pakeha intermarriage often brought an emotional reaction.[49] The Beagleholes reported the responses of a group of 57 students to a question on intermarriage and concluded that only a minority were prepared to approve of a Maori-pakeha marriage and that the minority was smaller for women than men.[7] The Beagleholes also described the complex attitudes regarding Maori-pakeha marriages in Kowhai* and the strong condemnation by both Maoris and pakehas of Maori-Chinese marriages or informal sex-relations.

A significant study in European attitudes to pakeha-Maori marriages was reported by McCreary as part of a project carried out for Unesco's research programme on "Tensions Affecting International Understanding."[23] A factorial analysis of the results of a Bogardus social distance scale suggested that the racial and national groups listed fell into three categories; first, the most preferred the Anglo-Saxon peoples (English, Australians and Americans), second, the least preferred, the coloured peoples (Negroes, Hindus, Japanese and Chinese), third, the others (Maoris, Pacific Islanders, Germans, Jews, Russians and Italians). When the closest relationship considered was that of citizenship, Maoris and Pacific Islanders were welcomed together with Jews and Germans but Russians and Italians joined the coloured and least preferred category. When the relationship considered was kinship by marriage, the Russians and Italians rose to become acceptable and the Maoris and Pacific Islanders fell into the coloured and least preferred category. It was concluded that "colour here swamps all other considerations so that even the current disapproval of communism is ineffective."

Vaughan used a modified Bogardus social distance scale to examine the attitudes of a selected group of eighty students towards the Maoris and fifteen other racial and national groups.[58] The students' responses to the sixteen groups indicated that social distance was least in the case of North-western European groups, British and Protestant stock being preferred, and social distance was greatest in the case of Asians such as Chinese, Hindus and Japanese. More social distance was accorded to

---

* The names Kowhai and Rakau were adopted by the Beagleholes and by Ritchie to give some privacy to the communities concerned. They do not refer to places of that name in Canterbury and Nelson respectively.

Maoris than to members of North-western European stock and this distance increased when marriage preferences were considered. Social distance scores and marriage preferences correlated significantly with judged physical similarity to white New Zealanders and Vaughan concluded that among the subjects tested "race was the most important determinant of social distance."

Maori Character Structure

Studies of Maori-pakeha differences have been almost entirely dominated by the study of Maori character-structure. The classic statement of Maori character-structure is found in the Beagleholes' account of the Kowhai community.[7] The central fact in a Maori's character, the Beagleholes declared, it is that he is a "generous, friendly co-operative giver, one who is always ready to share what he has with his friends, one who always inclines to give back more than he receives." The desire to be generous and sociable was an expression, they believed, of anxiety arising from the time when after two or three years of parental indulgence, the child was largely thrown on its own resources and expected to be relatively independent. The adult Maori was committed to a search for the security, affection and companionship characteristic of his early life. For this reason, the Maori was no rugged individualist, he lacked the ambition, the aggressive competitiveness, the thrift, the individual responsibility, the long-range planning and the compulsive devotion to excessive work typical of the pakeha. The difficulties facing Maori youth arose from a character-structure virtually the opposite of that required for success in the pakeha world in which they must, to an increasing extent, earn their living. In a foreword, Buck expressed his own belief that the origins of Maori generosity were more likely to be found in the traditional co-operative tribal system than in a traumatic break in childhood affection.

The concept of character-structure has received detailed treatment in a series of studies of Rakau, a predominantly rural farming area in the process of industrialization. This large-scale project was outlined by Beaglehole and Ritchie[8] and resulted in a series of publications on the basic personality,[40] the early years,[38] the middle years,[15] and adolescence[35] in Rakau. The most recent report of the project is as yet unpublished.[42] The effect of these studies has been substantially to elaborate and refine the initial Beaglehold hypothesis without introducing any serious modification.

The Rakau studies were reviewed by both Metge and Campbell.[33] Campbell criticized the studies severely on methodological grounds, especially with regard to the undue dependence upon projective techniques and the lack of attention to sampling and control observations. In consequence, whether the Maoris tested at Rakau were representative of the

Rakau Maori population, whether the Rakau Maoris were a representative group of Maoris and whether there was even anything peculiarly Maori about the observations in the Rakau series are questions to which no answer can be given. The studies, Campbell asserted, provide a series of "interesting and ingenious speculations" the value of which will depend on how they stand up under investigation.

Maori Achievement Motivation

Several studies have done something to test the adequacy of the Rakau hypotheses, particularly in connection with achievement motivation. The Rakau studies suggested that Maori scholastic underachievement was due to the transmission of a non-achieving pattern arising from the child's experience of rejection by his parents in early childhood and leading to a readiness to conform to group expectations which oppose individual achievement. Williams explored the problem of achievement motivation in Maori Teacher Training College students.[64] There were, Williams suggested, two kinds of Maori among his subjects — those who were Maori by enculturation and upbringing and those who were Maori by conscious choice and learning, who, though largely pakeha in upbringing, had chosen to identify themselves as Maoris, learning about Maori ways, language and culture later in life. Tests were made with three modal personality hypotheses suggesting that the Maori character-structure had an inhibiting effect on the need for achievement, but in only one case was the difference from the pakeha control group statistically significant. Sapsford attempted to test the possibility that Maori personality lacked the controls which enabled young Maoris to defer immediate impulse gratification in favour of long-range goals.[44] An experimental study using pupils from an urban school serving an area where Maori and pakeha children were both exposed to the same over-all social and economic conditions, revealed no significant difference between Maori and pakeha children in the capacity to delay impulse gratification.

A study of the educational and vocational aspirations of two groups (urban and rural) of Maori secondary school boys, contrasted with those of pakeha control groups, was reported by Ausubel.[5] The Maori and pakeha groups, Ausubel reported, showed a remarkable overall similarity first, in educational and vocational aspirations; second, in the underlying motivations for achievement, supportive traits, their perception of prevailing opportunities and the pressures towards achievement exerted by family and peer group. The main finding of the study, Ausubel declared, was that the similarity in the first case was greater than in the second. Weaknesses of method and interpretation, however, prejudice his conclusions. Brown, in a study of Maori underachievement, used a battery of tests including the Rorschach.[11] He concluded that there did not appear to be any really significant factor which could be attributed to a distinctively Maori personality or form of intellectual functioning. A distinctively Maori problem of scholastic underachievement, Brown declared, existed only in so far as it was more severe and involved greater numbers than was the case with Europeans.

Other Rorschach studies have been reported. Malcolm made a comparative study of groups of Maori and pakeha children of lower socio-economic status using this test.[29] The personality patterns of the two groups were essentially the same, but Malcolm pointed to what she believed were indications of a greater amount of free-floating anxiety in the Maori group. Adcock, McCreary, Ritchie, and Somerset described a series of studies designed to explore the major differences in personality traits between groups of Maoris and pakehas with particular reference to the relationship between constitution and temperament.[1] The authors reported that on the Rorschach test, Maoris rated lower on the factor of imaginative thinking and they attributed this to a temperamental bias towards a practical outlook and placid temperament together with cultural differences bound up with the lack of an academic and literary tradition.

Adcock and his colleagues,[2] Ritchie,[41] and Walters,[63] all pointed to the lower scores of Maoris as compared to pakehas on the Wechsler-Bellevue intelligence scale and suggested that this difference was a function of the tests rather than of Maori intellectual inferiority. The verbal tests especially were considered by the authors to place the Maori subjects at a disadvantage. Analyses of intelligence test results were reported in unpublished theses by Calvert,[12] Walters,[62] and Smith,[45] and a comparative study of reading achievement of Maori and European children was reported in a thesis by McClew.[22] McCreary made a study of the attainments of Maori school pupils and the differential effects of schooling on various initial deficiencies,[25] and there have been a few surveys of merely historical interest. To date, this would appear to be all the research that has been completed regarding the problems of the schooling of Maori children. In 1961 a conference was called to discuss the research needed in the education of Maori children and suggestions were made with regard to the problems of schooling, classroom practice, language and thought, and the development of attitudes and values.[36]

Maori-European Relations

McQueen offered an impressionistic sketch of what he believed were the mutual attitudes of the two peoples incidental to his study of the vocational problems of Maori youth.[28] Ausubel offered a similar sketch which drew upon his own nation-wide survey of Maori and pakeha opinion carried out without apparent regard for the conventions governing the conduct of opinion surveys since no information was given about the questionnaire, sample or results.[4] Fowler's account of his impressions of Maori and pakeha relations since the war is more balanced and better informed.[18] Evidence of the attitudes of Maoris and pakehas towards each other is found in the Beagleholes' study of Kowhai[7] and in Ritchie's briefer account of race relations in Rakau.[42]

Kowhai is a small community where Maoris live side by side with Europeans and Chinese. The attitudes governing Maori-pakeha relations in the district are seen as complex and varying from person to person. In so far as Maori and pakeha see each other impersonally, they see each other in terms of stereotypes; in so far as they see each other as individual persons, they respond to each other as persons. Maoris and pakehas do not, however, have much contact; the two groups live side by side with few contacts of a friendly informal nature. Indifference was perhaps the predominant pakeha attitude towards the Maoris and the predominant attitude by both pakehas and Maoris towards the Chinese. The most adequate way of describing Maori-pakeha relations, the Beagleholes declared, was to see them in terms of social class; the average pakeha classified himself as middle-class and the Maori as belonging to a lower social stratum.

Ritchie's description of the variety of attitudes characterizing the relations of Maori and pakeha in Rakau[42] is not unlike those in the earlier study of Kowhai. The Maoris socially were acceptable only at a low status level and felt themselves excluded by the pakeha community. As the Beagleholes had pointed to social class as the chief determinant of social relations, so Ritchie pointed to socio-economic status compounded of income, occupation, home standards, education and personal qualities.

The external circumstances of the Maori situation appear to be clearly established — the substantially lower average income for the head of the Maori household despite his more numerous dependents; the higher proportion of Maoris living in unsatisfactory and overcrowded conditions; the high incidence of disease; the low proportion of Maori sixth formers, apprentices and university students; the high crime rate; the small proportion in the skilled trades, in management and the professions. In all those aspects of social life which are normally considered to determine social status, the Maoris are badly placed relative to Europeans. This gives considerable substance to the Beagleholes' suggestion that, in Kowhai, the average pakeha saw himself as middle class and the Maori as belonging to a lower social stratum.

Some isolated pieces of information exist as to how Europeans see Maoris but nothing is known about the way Maoris see Europeans. There is some evidence that pakehas do not approve of intermarriage with Maoris. Studies of Maori character-structure, especially in so far as it concerns the motivation towards achievement, remain inconclusive despite considerable expenditure of research effort. It is hard to avoid the impression that studies of Maori-European differences, other than those of a social and economic nature, become less conclusive in their results, the more precise and controlled the investigation. Whether this reflects the crudity of the measuring instruments or the absence of personality differences remains to be seen. There seems to be agreement that while the Maoris as a whole record lower scores on intelligence tests, this reflects a variety of cultural, social and economic factors which place the Maori at a disadvantage.

How do Europeans think of Maoris? How do Maoris think of Europeans? What do Maoris and pakehas expect of each other on those occasions when their paths cross, and how far are these expectations met or disappointed? What is the pattern of social stratification in New Zealand and where do the Maoris fit into this pattern? If a disproportionate number of Maoris are to be found in the lower strata, how does this effect such aspects of social life as political allegiance, religious affiliation and intermarriage? Is the Maori crime rate disproportionate when contrasted with that of pakehas of comparable social and economic status? How far are such factors as the lack of privacy and study facilities at home, the lack of parental interest and experience, the lack of suitable books and intellectual stimulus at home, the small income and large family which in Britain and the United States are considered to place the working class child at a disadvantage in the middle class culture of the school, relevant to the Maori educational situation? How far are the problems of Maori school-children the problems of working class children rather than the problems of Maori children? At present these questions are unexplored. Questions which imply the existence of social stratification in New Zealand run counter to the ideology of both political parties, but much that is written about the Maori family and its problems is reminiscent of accounts of working class communities in Britain.

AREAS OF DISCRIMINATION

There is no reliable information as to the existence, the nature and the extent of discriminatory behaviour in New Zealand. Ausubel, a visiting American Fulbright scholar, asserted in general terms that discrimination existed in the fields of housing, hotel accommodation, employment, credit and ordinary social interaction. In a government publication, Hunn reported that very little evidence of race discrimination in everyday life existed in the files of the Maori Affairs Department or in the knowledge of the senior officers of the department.[21] Looking back over many years, Hunn asserted, only a few isolated instances were able to be cited, all of them in the area of employment and accommodation. The tendency for those of mixed Maori-pakeha parentage to opt for identification with the

Maori group certainly suggests an absence of gross discrimination. The literature devoted specifically to race discrimination in New Zealand is confined to housing and accommodation, the Bennett incident at Papakura, the segregation of Maori children from the school at Pukekohe and New Zealand's sports tours with South Africa.

Housing and Hotel Accommodation

Published reports of discrimination are found most frequently in the area of hotel accommodation and housing, although no studies specifically concerned with discrimination in either housing or employment have been reported. Hooper asserted that two-thirds of those advertising accommodation in Auckland would not accept Cook Islanders,[20] and Challis also referred to discrimination in this area in his account of Samoan, Cook Island and Niuean immigrants.[13] McGee linked what he believed was discrimination against Indians in Wellington to their residential distribution.[27] Metge asserted that Maoris in Auckland tended to blame colour discrimination for their difficulties in finding accommodation anywhere but in the poorer residential areas.[32] Metge, however, pointed to other factors which were influential in driving Maoris into the central city area: the housing shortage, the Maoris' reputation for over-crowding and not treating houses with care, their preference for living close to the centre of the city and their belief in the prejudice of landlords and the consequent uselessness of searching widely.

Evidence of discrimination in housing and accommodation is not confined to incidental reports within research projects devoted primarily to broader topics. It has been a common practice for classified advertisements in some daily newspapers to announce the availability of flats, houses or bed-sitting-rooms and then add the phrase: "Europeans only," "Europeans," or "Colour welcome."

Rice, O'Gorman, and Wauchop reported an attempt to check the existence of discrimination against Maoris in 92 New Zealand hotels graded four-star or better.[38] Letters of application for accommodation were sent from a "Mr Latimer" and a "Mr Te Hau" for almost identical dates some months ahead, "Mr Te Hau's" letter being sent two days in advance of the other. The existence of discrimination against potential Maori guests was argued on the grounds that 17% of the hotels either neglected to reply to "Mr Te Hau" when they had replied to "Mr Latimer," had refused accommodation to the Maori when they had offered it to the pakeha, or had demanded a higher deposit from the Maori applicant. However, the differences in the replies to the applicants were not statistically significant (X^2) and could not be attributed to more than chance. Probably some hotel managers did discriminate, but so many did not that the over-all results failed to demonstrate the existence of discrimination and certainly did nothing to substantiate Ausubel's assertion that, in most parts of New Zealand, Maoris can get hotel accommodation only if they are well known.[4]

Papakura and Pukekohe

In February, 1959, there occurred the well-known incident in which Dr. H. R. Bennett, senior medical officer at the local hospital, son of a former Maori bishop and brother of the New Zealand High Commissioner to Malaya, was refused service in the lounge bar of the Papakura Hotel because of his race. The Prime Minister and the Attorney-General both made statements on the legal impropriety of this discrimination and following action by the company owning the hotel, Maoris were permitted to drink in the lounge bar. After inspecting reports of the incident in three newspapers and the ensuing correspondence, Harre concluded that pakehas in general showed themselves to be unaware that such discrimination was practised in New Zealand, even though it had apparently been imposed in this area as a result of pakeha pressure, and that accounts of other instances of discrimination in the same area, especially in Pukekohe, indicated that race discrimination was "fairly widespread, particularly in hotels, cinemas and barbers' shops."[19]

The negotiations leading up to the creation of the segregated Maori school in Pukekohe were described by Sage.[43] As the Maori population of the district increased, particularly during the period 1941-45, a demand arose for the separation out of the state school of all Maori pupils. Although it was the opinion of Maori school inspectors that separation was unnecessary and although Auckland schools had as great a proportion of Maori pupils as Pukekohe, the Minister of Education yielded to pakeha pressure and in 1952 a separate Maori school was established which all Maori children attended under local pressure. Sage emphasized that pakehas exerting pressure in favour of segregating Maori pupils declared themselves concerned only with the best interests of the Maoris, but recorded that such expressions of pakeha disinterestedness were viewed with considerable suspicion.

Sport

In 1958, the New Zealand Rugby Union admitted that Maori players would not be eligible for selection in the All Black representative rugby tour of South Africa in 1960. For twenty months a substantial section of the community protested against the Rugby Union's decision. Shortly after the Sharpeville shooting and the declaration of a state of emergency in South Africa, an all-white All Black team was given a state farewell at Parliament buildings by the political leaders: its representative status and informal ambassadorial functions were officially recognized. An account of this controversy up till the middle of March, 1960, as it related to the exclusion of Maori players was given in a booklet by the Citizens' All Black Tour Association.[14]

Thompson described the controversy as a clash of loyalties[50] — nearly all New Zealanders were devoted to rugby, which many Maoris play well, and nearly all New Zealanders disapproved of a colour bar in the Dominion. The prospect of a South African tour dependent on the exclusion of Maori players brought the two sentiments into collision. The power of the New Zealand Rugby Union as a political pressure group and the lack of institutionalized measures for the protection of civil liberties were two factors leading to the crushing defeat of the Rugby Union's critics. Thompson described the role of the churches in initiating and maintaining the controversy[53] and in other articles suggested civil rights legislation as a possible remedy for the weakness revealed by the conflict.[51] He pointed out that New Zealand lacked both the legal and constitutional safeguards of the U.S.A. and the tradition of independence amongst members of Parliament which made effective the informal safeguards of Britain.

In the summer of 1961-62, a white New Zealand cricket team toured South Africa to play white South Africans. Thompson pointed to evidence of race discrimination in this tour.[52] Elsewhere he discussed the discrepancy in the attitude of the New Zealand Government which endorsed all-white sports tours with racially exclusive South African organizations, and yet professed its support, at the United Nations, for the very South Africans who protested against these tours.[54] [55] Thompson also introduced a discussion on apartheid and the cricket tour between the manager of the New Zealand team and the secretary of the non-racial South African Sports Association regarding the practice of race discrimination on this tour,[56] and in a further article indicated the kind of industrial, political and social links which commit New Zealand to support privately a racial policy abroad which it must condemn publicly.[57]

The published evidence regarding the existence of discrimination, or the lack of it, is slight. There is some evidence to suggest that discrimination exists, but no adequate study has been made of the Pukekohe situation or the incident at Papakura. No study appears to have been directed specifically to the question of discrimination in the areas of accommodation or employment. In the absence of independent and systematic investigation, the lack of any but anecdotal evidence regarding discrimination is inevitable. The study of discrimination against Maoris in securing hotel accommodation did not reveal evidence which could not equally be accounted for by chance factors. It is in the field of New Zealand's sports tours with South Africa that the evidence of race discrimination against non-white New Zealand and South African players is most fully documented.

Does race discrimination against Maoris or any other ethnic group exist in New Zealand? If discrimination does exist in what areas of social life is it to be found? How extensive is it? Does it vary from one part of the country to another? Which groups are discriminated against and by whom? What is the underlying motivation — is it determined by considerations of social class, of race prejudice, of both, or by other factors yet to be identified? There are some clues but as yet no answers to these questions. In the meantime, statements either claiming or disclaiming the existence of discrimination in New Zealand are premature unless carefully specified.

· · ·

CONCLUSIONS

1. The Lack of Research

The most striking feature of the literature on race relations in New Zealand is the paucity of empirical research. Relatively few of the studies mentioned in this report were empirical in character and a high proportion of these were theses carried out in partial fulfillment of the M.A. degree. These fledgling efforts at research were of mixed quality and their results should be accepted with considerable reservations. Very little reliable information about race relations in the Dominion exists at present. The few facts available do not speak for themselves; nothing is obvious, nothing is self-evident.

2. The Ideology of Equality

The ideology of race equality has been a persistent theme in New Zealand's history. The belief that Maori and pakeha were "one people," destined to live together in friendship and equality, goes back almost to the time of the first European contacts with the Maori, and became symbolized in the Treaty of Waitangi which for one hundred and twenty years has stood as the charter of Maori rights. The spirit of this Treaty has become a very powerful psychological factor in conditioning the relations of the two peoples towards mutual respect and equality and it is constantly reinforced by official statements as well as by private action. The belief in Maori-pakeha equality has not always been sustained in practice, nor have Maori rights always been successfully championed when they have clashed with pakeha interests, but these are deviations which can only be understood by reference to the underlying ideology.

The ideology of equality appears to extend beyond the issues of race to an equalitarianism which regards all social inequalities as unjustifiable.

The possible existence of social stratification appears to be only a little less objectionable than the possible existence of racial discrimination. It has been recognized that the number of children in Maori families is larger, that in general the standards of Maori housing, health and education, the size of income and the occupational status, are all significantly lower than that of the Europeans. It does not appear to be recognized, however, that this consistent pattern of social and economic inequalities significantly affects the nature of Maori-pakeha relations. The same drive to uphold the equalitarian ideal has led to an attempt to close the social and economic gap between Maori and pakeha and to an inability to consider the possibility that Maori-pakeha relations are in many respects determined by the Maori position in a lower stratum of society. The inability to accept the possibility that aspects of the problems of the Maori people look suspiciously similar to those of working-class communities abroad, obstructs the attempts to explore and modify the existing pattern of social inequality.

3. The Ideology of Cultural Homogeneity

At present, race relations in New Zealand are seen as a serious problem. Not that the pattern of such relations is unusually discriminatory or undemocratic — on the contrary. It simply appears difficult for people to live together and take differences of colour and culture for granted. Such differences are a constant source of anxiety.

The approach to race relations as a whole seems to have been essentially ethnocentric. New Zealand problems have not generally been viewed in the light of similar problems abroad; indeed the assumption was more likely to be made that the problems of people meeting and living together in New Zealand were altogether different in kind as well as degree from problems in those countries where race relations have not been without incident. Nor has much interest been taken in the viewpoint of the Maori people or the immigrant groups themselves. It would appear that the future of race relations is felt to hinge on whether the Maoris become pakehas rapidly enough and whether European immigrants become quickly assimilated to the New Zealand culture pattern. The solution is felt to lie in the elimination of differences rather than in the willingness of differing groups to accommodate themselves to each other. There seems to be a deep distrust of nonconformity, an inability to visualize a plural society in which the "otherness" of a different cultural group is accepted as a matter of course.

The disapproval of cultural in-groups and the constant pressure upon the Maoris to renounce their cultural identity may have reduced the likelihood of inter-group conflict in the Dominion. At the same time, by imposing goals upon them and insisting that these be reached by pakeha methods they have almost certainly hampered the Maoris' attempts to work out their own salvation. They have almost certainly inflated the Maori crime rate by undermining Maori communal life with its built-in supports and restraints, thus accentuating the problems of social disorganization and personal maladjustment in Maori communities.

4. The Fortuitous Character of New Zealand's Reputation for Racial Tolerance

New Zealand has a relatively small, homogeneous population with an overwhelmingly large white majority and a high standard of living in which all sections of society have been able to share to a greater or lesser degree. It is this combination of circumstances generally considered to favour racial harmony, allied with some happy accidents of history, that has enabled New Zealand to acquire a reputation for racial tolerance and equality. The early bitterness towards Asian immigrants is a reminder that New Zealand's record of racial harmony does not rest on having met and resolved the problems with which other countries have wrestled with varying degrees of success and failure, but on a situation, the result of a variety of factors including restrictive immigration, which has in large measure enabled the Dominion to avoid having to encounter the problems at all.

Race relations in New Zealand are politically important. The rise of African and Asian nations and the consequent importance of racial equality has made the Dominion's reputation in this respect a diplomatic asset. As the world draws closer together and the racial problems of one country become the concern of all, domestic harmony in a relatively simple racial situation, though important, is unlikely in itself to maintain the Dominion's reputation abroad. This will depend to an increasing extent on the sensitivity shown by New Zealand in its external relationships with the peoples of countries where so straightforward a situation does not prevail. Issues such as immigration and the acceptance of racial restrictions on non-white sportsmen in sports tours with South Africa may well become the touchstone by which the genuineness of the Dominion's reputation for racial tolerance is judged.

5. The Fluid Character of Maori-European Relations

A feature of Maori-pakeha relations in New Zealand is their fluid quality. There is mobility between these groups. Maoris can to a large extent move across and be regarded as pakehas, and part-Maoris can be fully accepted as members of the Maori community. As the Maori people have until recently been to a large extent isolated in rural areas, this fluidity may reflect the possibility that there has not yet been time for a pattern of relations to set firmly. This is an untidy situation from an administrative point of view, but so long as relationships do not set into prematurely fixed forms, so long will society be able to regain its equilibrium with relative ease in the face of rapid social change. Emphasis on assimilation and integration as distinct policies is unnecessarily restrictive. A more permissive attitude would give the Maori people freedom to choose courses of action in accordance with their needs and wishes regardless of whether these fall within the approved pattern of Maori-European relations as denoted by one or other policy label. It could well be that the maintenance of a fluid pattern of relationships is the most important task for insuring the future racial harmony of the Dominion.

Bibliography

1. Adcock, C. J.; McCreary, J. R.; Ritchie, J. E.; Somerset, H. C. A. *Personality and Physique: A Rorschach Study of Maori and Europeans.* Victoria University of Wellington, Publications in Psychology, no. 12, 1958.
2. Adcock, C. J.; McCreary, J. R.; Ritchie, J. E.; Somerset, H. C. A. "An Analysis of Maori Scores on the Wechsler-Bellevue." *Australian Journal of Psychology*, vol. 6, no. 1, June 1954.
3. Ausubel, D. P. "Race Relations in New Zealand: Maori and Pakeha: An American View." *Landfall*, vol. 12, no. 3, September 1958.
4. Ausubel, D. P. *The Fern and the Tiki: An American View of New Zealand: National Character, Social Attitudes, Race Relations.* Angus & Robertson, 1960.
5. Ausubel, D. P. *Maori Youth.* Victoria University of Wellington, Publications in Psychology, no. 14, Price Milburn, 1961.
6. Baxter, J. K. "Is There a Colour Bar in New Zealand?" *Student*, no. 5, September 1953.
7. Beaglehole, E.; Beaglehole, P. *Some Modern Maoris.* New Zealand Council for Educational Research, 1946.
8. Beaglehole, E.; Ritchie, J. E., "The Rakau Maori Studies," *Journal of the Polynesian Society*, vol. 67, no. 2, June 1958.
9. Borrie, W. D. "The Maori Population: A Microcosm of a New World," in *Anthropology in the South Seas.* Edited by J. D. Freeman and W. R. Geddes. Thomas Avery, 1959.
10. Borrie, W. D. "Some Economic and Social Implications of Maori Population Growth in New Zealand." *Journal of the Polynesian Society*, vol. 70, no. 4, December 1961.
11. Brown, D. W. F. "Maori Scholastic Under-Achievement as a Challenge to Methodology." Unpublished M.A. thesis, University of Canterbury, 1962.
12. Calvert, C. G. "A Preliminary Enquiry into the Language and Other Difficulties of Maori Adolescents and the Extent to Which These Are Apparent in English Attainment and in Intelligence Test Scores." Unpublished M.A. thesis, University of Auckland, 1950.

13. Challis, R. L. *Social Problems of Non-Maori Polynesians in New Zealand.* South Pacific Commission, Noumea, Technical Paper no. 41, n.d.
14. Citizens All Black Tour Association. *"No Maoris No Tour": New Zealand Protests 1959-60.* Citizens All Black Tour Association, 1960.
15. Earle, M. J. *Rakau Children: From Six to Thirteen Years.* Victoria University of Wellington, Publications in Psychology, no. 11, 1958.
16. Erwin, R. N. "The 'New Zealanders': European Opinion 1642-1820." Unpublished M.A. thesis, University of Canterbury, 1961.
17. Fitt, A. B. "A Study of Racial Attitudes during and after the War by the Thurstone Technique." *British Journal of Psychology*, vol. 46, no. 4, November 1955.
18. Fowler, L. "New Zealand since the War: Maori and Pakeha." *Landfall*, vol. 16, no. 1, March 1962.
19. Harre, J. "A Case of Race Discrimination in New Zealand." *Journal of the Polynesian Society*, vol. 71, no. 2, June 1962.
20. Hooper, A. "Cook Islanders in Auckland." *Journal of the Polynesian Society*, vol. 70, no. 2, June 1961.
21. Hunn, J. K. *Report on Department of Maori Affairs.* Government Printer, 1961.
22. McClew, A. "A Comparative Study of the Reading Achievement of Maori and European Children in an Urban School." Unpublished M.A. thesis, University of Auckland, 1958.
23. McCreary, J. R. *The Modification of International Attitudes: A New Zealand Study.* Victoria University of Wellington, Publications in Psychology, no. 2, 1952.
24. McCreary, J. R. "Maori Age Groupings and Social Statistics." *Journal of the Polynesian Society*, vol. 64, no. 1, March 1955.
25. McCreary, J. R. *A Report on the Administration of A.C.E.R. Attainment Tests to the Children of Ruatahuna.* Victoria University of Wellington, School of Social Science, 1958.
26. McCreary, J. R. "The Challenge of the Maori Population." *Pacific Viewpoint*, vol. 2, no. 2, September 1961.
27. McGee, T. G. "Indian Settlement in New Zealand: 1900-1956." *New Zealand Geographer*, vol. 18, no. 2, October 1962.
28. McQueen, H. C. *Vocations for Maori Youth.* New Zealand Council for Educational Research, 1945.
29. Malcolm, O. Y. "A Comparative Study of Personality Patterns of Maori and Pakeha Children as Revealed by Rorschach Technique." Unpublished M.A. thesis, University of Canterbury, 1951.
30. Maxwell, G. M. "Some Demographic Indications of Population Movement among New Zealand Maoris." *Journal of the Polynesian Society*, vol. 70, no. 1, March 1961.
31. Metge, J. "The Maori Population of Northern New Zealand." *New Zealand Geographer*, vol. 8, no. 2, October 1952.
32. Metge, J. "Continuity in Change: Urbanization and Modern Maori Society in an Urban Area and a Rural Community in Northern New Zealand." Unpublished Ph.D. thesis, University of London, 1957.

33. Metge, J.; Campbell, D. "The Rakau Maori Studies." *Journal of the Polynesian Society*, vol. 67, no. 4, December 1958.
34. Morris, A. "Some Aspects of Delinquency and Crime in New Zealand." *Journal of the Polynesian Society*, vol. 64, no. 1, March 1955.
35. Mulligan, D. G. *Maori Adolescence in Rakau*. Victoria University of Wellington, Publications in Psychology, no. 9, 1957.
36. New Zealand Council for Educational Research. *Research Needed in the Education of Maori Children*. Bulletin no. 9, G. M. Maxwell (reporter), N.Z. Council for Educational Research, 1962.
37. Pearson, W. H. "Attitudes to the Maori in Some Pakeha Fiction." *Journal of the Polynesian Society*, vol. 67, no. 3, September 1958.
38. Rice, S. M.; O'Gorman, B. P.; Wauchop, R. J. S. "Race Discrimination in Hotels." *Comment*, vol. 1, no. 4, Winter 1960.
39. Ritchie, J. *Childhood in Rakau: The First Five Years of Life*. Victoria University of Wellington, Publications in Psychology, no. 10, 1957.
40. Ritchie, J. E. *Basic Personality in Rakau*. Victoria University of Wellington, Publications in Psychology, no. 8, 1956.
41. Ritchie, J. E. "Some Observations on Maori and Pakeha Intelligence Test Performance." *Journal of the Polynesian Society*, vol. 66, no. 4, December 1957.
42. Ritchie, J. E. "Values in Social and Personal Change: A Case Study of a New Zealand Maori Community." Unpublished Ph.D. thesis, Victoria University of Wellington, 1960.
43. Sage, C. B. "A Study in Community: Elements of Racial Discrimination in the Township of Pukekohe, New Zealand, with Particular Reference to the Present Construction of a Segregated Maori School." Unpublished M.A. thesis, University of Auckland, 1951.
44. Sapsford, S. "Delayed Reinforcement: An Experimental Study in an Urban School." Unpublished M.A. thesis, Victoria University of Wellington, 1961.
45. Smith, L. M. "An Investigation into the Influence of Reading Achievement in English on Intelligence Test Performances of Maori Children." Unpublished M.A. thesis, University of Auckland, 1957.
46. Sorenson, M. P. K. "The Racial Conflict over Land in New Zealand." *Journal of the Polynesian Society*, vol. 68, no. 3, September 1959.
47. Sutherland, I. L. G. "The Maori Population" (abstract). *Proceedings of the Seventh Pacific Science Congress of the Pacific Science Association 7*. Pegasus Press, 1953.
48. Thompson, R. "Maori Affairs and the New Zealand Press." *Journal of the Polynesian Society*. Part I, vol. 62, no. 4, December 1953; Part II, vol. 63, no. 1, March 1954; Part III, vol. 63, nos. 3, 4, September, December 1954; Part IV, vol. 64, no. 1, March 1955.
49. Thompson, R. "European Attitudes to Maoris: A Projective Approach." *Journal of the Polynesian Society*, vol. 68, no. 3, September 1959.
50. Thompson, R. "Community Conflict in New Zealand: A Case Study." *Race*, vol. 3, no. 1, November 1961.
51. Thompson, R. "Race Relations in New Zealand." *The Press*, 14, 15 November 1960.

52. Thompson, R. "Racial Issue: New Zealand Cricket Tour of South Africa." *The Press*, 4 February 1961.
53. Thompson, R. "The Church and Community Conflict." *Theology*, vol. 65, no. 502, April 1962.
54. Thompson, R. "Double Game in Africa." *N.Z. Monthly Review*, vol. 2, no. 22, April 1962.
55. Thompson, R. "Apartheid and Our Sporting Ambassadors." *Comment*, vol. 3, no. 3, April 1962.
56. Thompson, R. "Double Diplomacy." *Church and Community*, June 1962.
57. Thompson, R. "Cricket, Club and Commerce." *N.Z. Monthly Review*, vol. 4, no. 34, May 1963.
58. Vaughan, G. M. "The Social Distance Attitudes of New Zealand Students Towards Maoris and Fifteen Other National Groups." *Journal of Social Psychology*, vol. 57, First half, 1962.
59. Vaughan, G. M. "Ethnic Awareness and Attitudes: A Developmental Study of Maori and Pakeha Children in New Zealand." Unpublished Ph.D. thesis, Victoria University of Wellington, 1962.
60. Vaughan, G. M.; Quartermain, D. "Students' Acceptance of Maoris: A Structured Picture Test." *Perceptual and Motor Skills* 13, 190, 1961.
61. Vaughan, G. M.; Thompson, R. "New Zealand Children's Attitudes Towards Maoris." *Journal of Abnormal and Social Psychology*, vol. 62, no. 3, 1961.
62. Walters, R. H. "An Investigation into the Intelligence Test Performance of Maori Children." Unpublished M.A. thesis, University of Auckland, 1955.
63. Walters, R. H. "Wechsler-Bellevue Test Results of Prison Inmates." *Australian Journal of Psychology*, vol. 5, no. 1, June 1953.
64. Williams, J. S. *Maori Achievement Motivation*. Victoria University of Wellington, Publications in Psychology, no. 13, 1960.

XI

Puerto Rico is a society in which people recognize three skin-color categories, white, mulatto, and black, and in which they can assign themselves and others to skin color categories, yet most adamantly insist that these color differences are of no major importance in any area of life. There is a tendency for people to feel that white skin color is most preferred and that black skin color is least preferred, but these attitudes are neither as uniform nor as important as they are in the United States. This lack of importance of skin color is correlated with the insignificant role that skin color plays in access to education and to jobs. Not even within class are racial ascriptions highly important.

MELVIN M. TUMIN with
ARNOLD FELDMAN

Social Class and Skin Color in Puerto Rico

Throughout Puerto Rico one encounters the widest imaginable variety of skin colors, ranging from pale white to pitch black, with every intermediary shade. For the Mainland visitor, accustomed to responding sensitively to differences in skin color, the question immediately arises whether in

Reprinted from *Social Class and Social Change in Puerto Rico.* Copyright © 1961, by Princeton University Press, pp. 227-246, by permission of the authors and the publisher.

Puerto Rico, too, men are heirs to different social fates because of their colors.

It would seem that the average Puerto Rican, because his skin color is sufficiently dark, would encounter economic and social difficulties on the color-discriminating Mainland. The experience of Puerto Ricans who have visited or settled in the United States is not likely to give Islanders much reassurance. But more importantly, the prices of discrimination which have been paid in the States, by Negroes particularly and by the society as a whole, must certainly warn Island society that it too will suffer a considerable tax on its resources if it allows the same views, attitudes, and actions toward color.

We seek to understand, therefore, the way and the extent to which color does make a difference in a man's fate in Puerto Rico.[1] To press this inquiry, we must answer a number of questions:

1. What are the main recognized color distinctions?
2. Are skin color groups distributed unevenly in different educational classes?

[1] For a summary of recent research on the significance of attitudes toward "race difference," especially regarding educational opportunities, see Melvin Tumin, *Segregation and Desegregation: A Digest of Recent Research* (New York: Anti-Defamation League, 1957), and the supplement to that digest published in 1960.

For some recent estimates of the situations of Puerto Ricans on the Mainland, see Elena Padilla, *Up From Puerto Rico* (New York: Columbia University Press, 1958); and also Clarence Senior's Review of Padilla in the *American Sociological Review*, Vol. 24, No. 2 (April 1959), pp. 287-88. Also see Clarence Senior, *The Puerto Ricans of New York City* (Washington, D.C.: Office of Puerto Rico [n.d.]); Arthur Siegel et al., *Puerto Ricans in Philadelphia* (Philadelphia: Commission on Human Relations, 1954); C. Wright Mills et al., *The Puerto Rican Journey* (New York: Harper & Bros., 1950); and Joseph Monserrat, Issue Editor, *Education of Puerto Rican Children in New York City*, Special Issue of *The Journal of Educational Sociology*, Vol. 28, No. 4 (December 1954).

For various kinds of estimates of the significance of skin color in Puerto Rico, see Tomas Blanco, *El Prejuicio Racial en Puerto Rico* (San Juan: Editorial Biblioteca de Autores Puertoriquenos, 1942); Maxine Gordon, "Race Patterns and Prejudice in Puerto Rico," *American Sociological Review*, Vol. 14, No. 2 (April 1949), pp. 298-301; and the following works by Charles Rogler: "Some Situational Aspects of Race Relations in Puerto Rico," *Social Forces*, Vol. 27 (1948), pp. 72-77; "The Role of Semantics in the Study of Race Distance in Puerto Rico," *Social Forces*, Vol. 22 (1944), pp. 448-53; "The Morality of Race Mixing in Puerto Rico," *Social Forces*, Vol. 25 (1946), pp. 77-81; and *Comerio — A Study of a Puerto Rican Town* (Lawrence, Kansas: University of Kansas Press, 1940). Also see Renszo Sereno, "Cryptomelanism: A Study of Color Relations and Personal Insecurity in Puerto Rico," *Psychiatry*, Vol. X (August 1947), pp. 261-69; David Landy, *Tropical Childhood* (Chapel Hill: University of North Carolina Press, 1959); Eric Williams, "Race Relations in Puerto Rico and the Virgin Islands," *Foreign Affairs*, Vol. 23 (1945), pp. 308-

3. Do opportunities for the main rewards of the society — income, occupation, mobility, prestige, and others — vary with skin color? How do the classes view these differences in respect and opportunity?

4. Do the classes differ in their evaluations of the importance of skin color?

5. Overall, are there some average preferences for one color or another, and are these preferences variable by class?

We must first note three main color distinctions in Puerto Rican society: *Blanco*, or White; *Trigueno*, or Mulatto; and *Negro*, or Black. These terms seem to carry variable meanings, with no precise specifications. We have found that people of both light and dark skin, who in other places would be called White or Negro, call themselves Mulatto. Most curiously, and most importantly, there are quite a few Puerto Ricans who prefer to call themselves Mulatto rather than White, in addition to those who prefer Mulatto to Negro. For instance, when we asked the Puerto Ricans to describe their own skin color, we found that:

> 537 said they were White,
> 397 said they were Mulatto, and
> 55 said they were Black.

By contrast, when we asked our trained interviewers, all of them Puerto Rican and themselves very different in their skin colors, to describe the color of the respondents, they averred that:

> 608 were White,
> 307 were Mulatto, and
> 80 were Black.

In short, 71 of the 608 people called White by interviewers, or more than 10 per cent, insisted on calling themselves Mulatto; 25 of the 80 people called Black, or almost 30 per cent, preferred the category of Mulatto.

If White were clearly the preferred color category, we should have expected the figures to be quite different. We should have expected that

19; and the appropriate sections in Julian Steward *et al.*, *The People of Puerto Rico* (Urbana: University of Illinois Press, 1956).

Much of the literature on Puerto Rican race relations is controversial, because issues are not properly joined and cannot therefore be adequately settled by evidence. This is not the place to review the various estimates and stands made and taken. One thing is certain: because of the range of disagreement about how important skin color or racial differences are in Puerto Rico, without question, even if the maximum estimate is correct, there is considerably less significance ascribed to such differences in Puerto Rico than on the Mainland.

For an analysis of the differing implications for action of various portions of the "attitudes" about racial differences, see Tumin, *Desegregation: Resistance and Readiness* (Princeton: Princeton University Press, 1959).

many of the people called Mulatto would insist on calling themselves White. But they did not, and this is what gives some assurance that Mulatto does not carry nearly the invidious connotations which it does on the Mainland. But it is an open question whether this much can also be said for the Negro category. White may not be the nomenclature always preferred, but Negro is quite clearly not preferred.

If we assume that the skin colors are best classified as the respondents themselves see the matter, then we start with a population which is approximately 55 per cent White, 40 per cent Mulatto, and five per cent Black. . . . Within each of three residence groups, the per cent White generally increases with every increase in years of school completed. The sole exception is the decrease in per cent White from the high school to the college group in the San Juan and rural areas.

Only the differences between the high school groups in San Juan and the rural areas prove to be statistically significant. The other differences, though insignificant, should be kept in mind. In general, however, the more educated the group, the higher the percentage of White people. For instance, if we compare educational classes, ignoring the areas of residence, the same relationship holds: the 0-years people have 43.8 per cent White; the 1–4 years group has 49 per cent White; the high school group, 70.66 per cent and college group, 67.98 per cent.

These percentages suggest that the lighter the skin color, the better are the chances for advanced training in the schools. Nor does this seem to be a function only, or even especially, of the rural-urban distributions of skin colors. The White per cents in each of the three residence groupings do not differ in any patterned way, and none of the differences between individual pairs are statistically significant.

Because none of the differences between residence groups proved to be significant, and because there are no discernible patterns, the ecological distribution of skin colors can be called irrelevant to educational distribution. Confirmation of this point is provided by the distribution of the color groups in each of the residence groups. . . . Of all the Whites in the sample, 28.5 per cent are in the San Juan area, 34.1 per cent in the other-urban area, and 37.4 in the rural area. These percentages almost match what one would expect if there were no biassing factors: of the total sample, 26.3 per cent live in San Juan; 35.2 per cent in the other-urban, and 38.4 per cent in the rural areas. Residential differences, then, are of slight value in accounting for the differences in the per cent of Whites in the various educational groups.

Focusing alone on educational classes, we can compare the per cent of each skin color group actually found in each class with the per cent one would expect if the matter were purely proportional to population.

The above comparisons show that the Whites are most proportionately under-represented in the 0-years group and over-represented in the 9–12 and college groups. The size and direction of these deviations from expectation show some definite relation between the lightness of skin color and the years of school achieved.

Obviously, one's education doesn't "determine" one's skin color, except in those few cases where being educated makes it easier to establish and maintain a claim that one is White. Advanced education and social position may induce one to *desire* to claim the skin color of higher prestige. In general, however, the relationship works the other way, namely, skin color influences one's chances to secure an education.

In these terms, the color makeup of the various educational classes assumes added significance. If good education and White color each make a difference for life-chances, in combination they are likely to be that much more important. It becomes most noteworthy, then, that of the 530 people in the lowest education class some 248, or 46.8 per cent, are White, while of the 242 people in the high school and college groups combined, some 169, or 70 per cent, are White. These figures tell us that persons in the higher educational brackets are more frequently White than those in the lower brackets, having the advantage of the favored skin color in addition to higher education.

Some definite relationship, though hardly a matter for serious concern, exists between educational level and skin color. An analysis of this correlation yields a coefficient of only .16. Nor does skin color relate closely to other features of Puerto Rican life. Whether it is with religiosity, type of employment (by self, or others, or government), or any of the attitudes toward educational and occupational achievement, the correlation coefficient never reaches as much as .20.

Not even a more refined statistical analysis shows skin color to be significantly related to other class and non-class elements in Puerto Rico. The correlation between education and income, for instance, is .56. When skin color is controlled, this correlation is reduced by only a fraction to .55. In short, strong relations among other class variables persist whether we take skin color into account or not. Judging by these data, the unavoidable conclusion is that skin color does not make nearly the overall difference which was suggested earlier.

But testimony of common sense suggests something quite to the contrary. While Puerto Ricans will point with some pride to the relative freedom from color discrimination enjoyed on the Island as compared with the Mainland, they reveal a decided awareness of differences in skin color. This is especially true when intimate personal relations are under consideration. Which testimony is the more credible? The results of survey analysis, or the impressions of common sense and the feelings from talking off the record with a wide range of people? Probably both sets of facts can be harmonized without strain. It seems, on one hand, that skin color is among the facts least taken into account where ordinary life chances are concerned. But being Negro or White does matter, apparently, when dealing with status-conscious members of the middle and upper classes, and when personal and intimate relations are at stake. One can then say that on the main avenues of Puerto Rican life little attention is paid to skin color. But attention is heightened to critical awareness at the fringes and the interstices of personal relations, where public policy is not an issue, and where public controls are not available.

What then of the attitudes of the people themselves? How do people in different classes feel about the general and public significance of skin color? How do members of different color groups feel? How do members of different color groups *in different classes* feel? These are the three sets of views we now turn to examine. All the interviewed persons were asked the following questions:

1. Would you say that persons of your color are respected much more than, the same as, or less than persons of different skin colors?

2. Would you say that persons of your color have more, the same, or less opportunity to make their way in life than persons of other skin colors?

3. So far as opportunity in life, respect, and similar things, which color is best to have? Worst to have? Why?

COLOR AND RESPECT

A. By Class

The majority opinion of Puerto Ricans — that skin color has little or nothing to do with the amount of respect one receives — is shown in Table 1 below. Virtually no one from any of the five educational classes thinks that his skin color receives less respect. There are some differences in the numbers who think their color receives more respect, but there is no class patterning: the lowest and the college group have the highest per cent claiming more respect for their color.

TABLE 1. RESPECT FOR OWN SKIN COLOR, RELATIVE TO OTHER SKIN COLORS, REPORTED BY MEMBERS OF DIFFERENT EDUCATIONAL CLASSES

Years of School Completed	More No.	More %	Same No.	Same %	Less No.	Less %	No Information No.	No Information %	Total No.	Total %
0	43	17.6	189	77.5	4	1.6	8	3.3	244	100.0
1–4	24	8.4	254	89.1	3	1.1	4	1.4	285	100.0
5–8	22	9.8	194	86.6	5	2.2	3	1.3	224	100.0
9–12	19	11.9	134	83.8	2	1.3	5	3.1	160	100.0
13+	10	14.5	58	84.1	0	0.0	1	1.4	69	100.0
Total	118	12.0	829	84.4	14	1.4	21	2.1	982	100.0

B. By Color

In Table 2 below are the opinions of people in different color groups. Now some small differences begin to appear. The White group has the highest percentage claiming they receive more respect. The Negro group has a slightly higher percentage who say they receive less respect, though the number is so small — only 3 cases in all — that not much significance can be attributed to this datum.

In sum, when attitudes toward color are viewed through the eyes of people of different color, there emerge some slight differences in the per cent who feel they receive more respect, and these favor the White group. In all other regards, the color groups are much like the class groups in denying the significance of color for the accordance of interpersonal respect.

TABLE 2. RESPECT FOR OWN SKIN COLOR, RELATIVE TO OTHER SKIN COLORS[a]

Skin Color Groups	More No.	%	Same No.	%	Less No.	%	Total No.	%
White	85	17.6	395	81.8	3	0.6	483	100.0
Mulatto	20	5.0	369	92.9	8	2.0	397	100.0
Negro	5	9.4	45	84.9	3	5.7	53	100.0
Total	110	11.8	809	86.7	14	1.5	933	100.0[b]

[a] As reported by members of skin color groups.

[b] Of the 982 cases in which reliable information on self-rating of skin color is available, 49 cases could not be used in the tabulations above.

C. By Color Within Class

From Table 3 below we extract for special attention only that portion which shows how the persons who call themselves Negro view the importance of skin color. The interest here is whether Negroes of different class positions will take different views of the matter. Unfortunately, the

TABLE 3. RESPECT FOR OWN SKIN COLOR, RELATIVE TO OTHER SKIN COLORS, REPORTED BY NEGRO MEMBERS OF DIFFERENT EDUCATIONAL CLASSES

Years of School Completed	More No.	%	Same No.	%	Less No.	%	Total No.	%
0	4	33.3	8	66.7	0	0.0	12	100.0
1–4	0	0.0	23	95.8	1	4.2	24	100.0
5–8	1	14.3	5	71.4	1	14.3	7	100.0
9–12	0	0.0	6	85.7	1	14.3	7	100.0
13+	0	0.0	3	100.0	0	0.0	3	100.0
Total	5	9.4	45	84.9	3	5.7	53	100.0

total number of Negroes reporting is only 53. Any judgment made on the basis of the sub-categories within this group of 53 must be taken tentatively.

We note first the startling fact that only in the 0-years people is there a substantial per cent who claim more respect for their Negro skin color. Otherwise, the preponderant majority of Negroes in each class say that they receive no more nor less respect than persons of other color.

The tendency of Puerto Ricans at all class levels to claim equal respect has been noted frequently before. If there is any one special version of this tendency, it is for the lowest class to excel all others in its claim for high respect. The findings on color just presented bear out both tendencies. Respect is claimed regardless of class or color, and the lowest class tends more than others to claim greater respect.

COLOR AND OPPORTUNITY

A. By Class

There is a decided tendency, as Table 4 will show, for members of higher classes to claim more opportunity for people of their color. Almost one third of the college group asserts this claim. Only 15 per cent of the 1–4 people and 18 per cent of the 0-years group make the same claim. In the latter two groups there are also more people who feel their color brings *less* opportunities than are available to others. As the different classes see it, there is a closer relationship between color and opportunity than between color and respect.

TABLE 4. OPPORTUNITIES FOR OWN SKIN COLOR, RELATIVE TO OTHER SKIN COLORS, REPORTED BY MEMBERS OF DIFFERENT EDUCATIONAL CLASSES

Years of School Completed	More No.	%	Same No.	%	Less No.	%	Total No.	%
0	43	18.5	176	75.9	13	5.6	232	100.0
1–4	42	15.1	218	78.4	18	6.5	278	100.0
5–8	43	19.5	171	77.4	7	3.2	221	100.0
9–12	36	23.2	117	75.5	2	1.3	155	100.0
13+	22	32.8	45	67.2	0	0.0	67	100.0
Total	186	19.5	727	76.3	40	4.2	953	100.0

B. By Color

Table 5 bears out the conclusion just reached. In the group who call themselves White, two to three times as many members as in the Mulatto and Negro skin color groups claim their color brings them greater opportunities. Similarly, the Negro and Mulatto groups have larger per-

TABLE 5. OPPORTUNITIES FOR PERSONS OF OWN SKIN COLOR, RELATIVE TO OTHER SKIN COLORS, REPORTED BY MEMBERS OF DIFFERENT SKIN COLOR GROUPS

Skin Color	More No.	%	Same No.	%	Less No.	%	Total No.	%
White	133	27.7	341	71.0	6	1.3	480	100.0
Mulatto	38	9.7	325	83.0	28	7.2	391	100.0
Negro	6	11.3	41	77.4	6	11.3	53	100.0
Total	177	19.2	707	76.5	40	4.3	924	100.0

centages than members of other color groups who feel they get less opportunities.

As before, however, the large majority of each group feels that skin color does not matter in the opportunities to make one's way in life. Over three fourths of both the Mulatto and Negro groups feel they get an equal break.

C. By Color, within Class

Again, we select the Negro members of the different classes for their point of view on the relationship of color to opportunity. As can be seen in Table 6 below, the Negroes with no education excel all other Negro Puerto Ricans in their tendency to claim more opportunity for people of their color.

TABLE 6. OPPORTUNITIES FOR PERSONS OF OWN SKIN COLOR, RELATIVE TO OTHER COLORS, REPORTED BY NEGRO MEMBERS OF DIFFERENT EDUCATIONAL CLASSES

Years of School Completed	More No.	%	Same No.	%	Less No.	%	Total No.	%
0	4	33.3	7	58.3	1	8.3	12	100.0
1–4	1	4.2	20	83.3	3	12.5	24	100.0
5–8	1	14.3	4	57.1	2	28.6	7	100.0
9–12	0	0.0	7	100.0	0	0.0	7	100.0
13+	0	0.0	3	100.0	0	0.0	3	100.0
Total	6	11.3	41	77.4	6	11.3	53	100.0

Whatever the objective facts, there is little subjective feeling of discrimination among the Negroes. Nor does class impinge in the expected way. If anything, it seems that the lower the class, the higher the per cent who feel quite assured about the irrelevance of skin color for a chance to make their ways in life.

Once more, we must conclude that except for the small portion who feel that being White or Mulatto brings them greater opportunities, the majority of Puerto Ricans of all colors and classes do not assign much significance to skin color as it bears upon opportunities in the society. Lower class Negroes seem more assured than any others that their skin color is not a social obstacle.

REASONS BEHIND THE ATTITUDES

What will Puerto Ricans say in justification of their position on the importance of skin color? Asking each respondent to state the reasons for his opinion, we then classified many reasons given into a few major categories:

1. Whites/Mulattoes receive preference in jobs;
2. Whites/Mulattoes receive social preference;
3. Whites/Mulattoes receive preference in matters of education;
4. Whites have the power and they prefer to give opportunities to other Whites;
5. There are more Whites than any other color;
6. Whites/Mulattoes have greater intelligence and more educational preparation;
7. Whites/Mulattoes have more money and property;
8. We are all equal; there are no differences;
9. Opportunity has nothing to do with skin color;
10. Miscellaneous.

Table 7 shows the responses classified by color groups.

TABLE 7. REASONS FOR JUDGMENTS ABOUT IMPORTANCE OF SKIN COLOR[a]

Skin Color	1		2		(3, 4, 5, 6, 7, 10)		(8, 9)		Total	
	No.	%	No.	%	No.	%	No.	%	No.	%
White	75	15.8	23	4.9	36	7.6	340	71.7	474	100.0
Mulatto	39	10.1	8	2.1	24	6.2	316	81.7	387	100.0
Negro	5	9.8	1	2.0	4	7.3	41	80.4	51	100.0
Total	119	13.0	32	3.5	64	7.0	697	76.4	912	100.0

[a] Given by members of different skin color groups.

For the sake of simplicity, categories have been combined, so that [Table 7] contrasts categories 1 vs. 2 vs. (3, 4, 5, 6, 7, 10) vs. (8, 9). The last combination contains all the responses which deny that color is important. Almost 75 per cent of all the reasons fall in these two categories. Once again, three fourths of Puerto Ricans are clear in their denial that skin color matters. Nor does one's skin color seem to determine how frequently the significance of color will be denied. Over 69 per cent of the Whites say so, as do over 77 per cent of the Negroes.

Perhaps most interesting in all the findings is that discrimination in employment is by far the most frequently cited type of discrimination.

Nearly four times as many people call attention to this fact as to the obvious *social* discrimination which exists. Virtually no one seems to find it important to point out discrimination in *education*. Nor do any except the merest few assume that color groups receive different treatment because of native superiority in intelligence, superior preparation in education, or numerical superiority per se. The preponderant bulk of the complaints focus on job opportunities. Surely this emphasis reflects both the facts as they exist as well as the degree of importance attached to these facts. Educational discrimination is virtually nonexistent. Social discrimination exists, but it is relatively unimportant. Job discrimination exists and it is important. This is how the people see it; this is in effect how it is.

The evidence urges upon us the conclusion that skin color is considerably less important in Puerto Rico than in the United States; that it is virtually of no significance whatsoever in many important areas of life; that the majority feel that people of darker color are not blocked from major opportunities by their color; that only on job opportunity is there any serious question.

Since only a small minority — just over 12 per cent — talk of job discrimination, and the vast majority do not, it is fair to say that color discrimination in general is a subtle and minor theme in Puerto Rican life. Yet it is an insistent theme: its presence cannot be denied, however muted are the responses to it. Under such circumstances there should be an awareness in all color groups that color is a theme in Puerto Rican social life. This awareness should appear when we ask people to state whether it is better to have one color or another. Thus we asked the Puerto Ricans:

WHICH SKIN COLOR IS BEST TO HAVE?

A. By Class

As Table 8 below shows, the population is split between the judgments that it is better to be White and that color doesn't matter. Roughly one half of the people in each group express a preference for White color; roughly 40 per cent insist that all colors are equal; some, but only very few, say that Mulatto is best; and almost no one thinks it best to be Negro. The class differences are inconsequential. Though 39 per cent of the lowest group say that all colors are equal, 42 per cent of the college people make the same affirmation. And it is the 5–8 group with the highest per cent who insist that White is the best color to have.

B. By Color

When viewed through the eyes of the different color groups, the previous findings become somewhat clearer. Table 9 shows that the bulk of the 79

TABLE 8. BEST SKIN COLOR TO HAVE, REPORTED BY
MEMBERS OF DIFFERENT EDUCATIONAL CLASSES

Best Color	0		1–4		Years of School Completed 5–8		9–12		13+		Total	
to Have	No.	%	No.	%	No.	%	No.	%	No.	%	No.	%
White	105	44.2	138	47.8	125	54.8	84	49.4	38	53.4	490	49.5
Mulatto	28	11.7	24	8.2	14	6.1	10	5.8	2	2.7	78	7.8
Negro	3	1.3	5	1.7	1	0.4	4	2.3	0	0.0	13	1.3
All equal	92	38.8	119	41.2	82	36.1	69	40.7	30	42.5	396	39.5
Won't say	0	0.0	0	0.0	0	0.0	0	0.0	1	1.4	1	0.0
Don't know	8	3.3	1	0.3	5	2.2	2	1.2	0	0.0	16	1.6
Other	1	0.4	1	0.3	0	0.0	1	0.6	0	0.0	3	0.3
No information	1	0.4	1	0.3	1	0.4	0	0.0	0	0.0	3	0.3
Total	238	100.0	289	100.0	228	100.0	170	100.0	71	100.0	996	100.0

TABLE 9. BEST COLOR TO HAVE, REPORTED BY MEMBERS OF
DIFFERENT SKIN COLOR GROUPS

	BEST COLOR TO HAVE											
	White		Mulatto		Negro		All Equal		Other		Total	
Skin Color	No.	%	No.	%	No.	%	No.	%	No.	%	No.	%
White	322	58.9	18	3.3	7	1.3	193	35.3	7	1.3	547	100.0
Mulatto	148	37.7	61	15.5	1	0.3	173	44.0	10	2.5	393	100.0
Negro	23	41.1	0	0.0	5	9.0	26	46.4	2	3.6	56	100.0
Total	493	49.5	79	7.9	13	1.3	392	39.4	19	1.9	996	100.0

people who claim superior status for Mulatto color come from the
Mulattoes themselves. The Whites substantially outdistance all others in
saying that White is the best color. The Negroes and the Mulattoes have
significantly more people than the Whites who claim that all colors are
equal. A larger absolute number but a much smaller percentage of Whites
than Negroes say that Negro is the best skin color.

In sum, the color groups differ more than the classes in their views on
the merits of the different skin colors. Such sensitivity as there is to color
is found more among the lighter than the darker people. When the
latter deny the relevance of color more than the lighter-skinned people,
they may be insisting on their right to equal treatment, and expressing
their sentiment that in Puerto Rico this right is built into the structure
of the society.

C. By Color, within Class

That color more than class shapes the views and perspectives on the
color question is seen clearly in Table 10 . . . , where the respondents
are classified both by their class and their color.

Among the White 0-years people, 57.5 per cent say that White is the
best color to have, compared to 33.6 per cent of the Mulatto and 36.4 per

TABLE 10. BEST SKIN COLOR TO HAVE, REPORTED BY MEMBERS OF DIFFERENT EDUCATIONAL CLASSES, CROSS-CLASSIFIED BY SKIN COLOR

Years of School Completed	N	BEST COLOR TO HAVE									
		White		Mulatto		Negro		All Equal		No Information	
		No.	%	No.	%	No.	%	No.	%	No.	%
White											
0	(96)	61	63.5	4	4.1	1	1.0	28	29.2	2	2.1
1–4	(146)	93	63.7	6	4.1	2	1.4	44	30.1	1	0.7
5–8	(121)	70	57.9	4	3.3	0	0.0	44	36.4	3	2.5
9–12	(122)	68	55.7	3	2.5	4	3.3	46	37.7	1	0.8
13+	(52)	30	57.7	1	1.9	0	0.0	21	40.4	0	0.0
Total White	(537)	322	60.0	18	3.4	7	1.3	183	34.1	7	1.3
Mulatto											
0	(122)	41	33.6	24	19.7	0	0.0	52	42.6	5	4.3
1–4	(114)	34	29.8	18	15.8	1	1.0	60	52.6	1	1.0
5–8	(97)	51	52.6	10	10.3	0	0.0	34	35.1	2	2.1
9–12	(42)	14	33.3	7	16.7	0	0.0	20	47.6	1	2.4
13+	(18)	8	44.4	2	11.1	0	0.0	7	38.9	1	5.6
Total Mulatto	(393)	148	37.7	61	15.5	1	0.2	173	44.0	10	2.5
Negro											
0	(11)	4	36.4	0	0.0	2	18.2	3	27.3	2	18.2
1–4	(27)	11	40.7	0	0.0	2	7.4	14	51.9	0	0.0
5–8	(8)	5	62.5	0	0.0	1	12.5	2	25.0	0	0.0
9–12	(7)	3	42.9	0	0.0	0	0.0	4	57.1	0	0.0
13+	(3)	0	0.0	0	0.0	0	0.0	3	100.0	0	0.0
Total Negro	(56)	23	41.1	0	0.0	5	8.9	26	46.4	2	3.6

cent of the Negro 0-years groups. Or, where few Whites at any class level say that Negro is the best color, quite a few Negroes at the first three class levels (as many as 18.3 per cent of the 0-years group) express a preference for Negro color.

Other facts testify to the importance of one's own skin color in shaping judgments on color:

Only Whites and Mulattoes (and the Mulattoes are by far the more numerous) say that Mulatto is the best color.

The Mulattoes outdistance the other two color groups in their per cent who say that all colors are equal.

On the claim that all people are equal, there is less difference between the 0-years and college people *within* the Mulatto group, and *within* the White group, than between the 0-years people of the two groups, or the college people of the two groups.

This picture of the greater influence of color compared to that of class is by no means uniform; there are instances of the opposite in Table 10. For instance, the Mulatto 5–8 people affirm the superiority of White color to a significantly greater extent than the Mulattoes of any other educational level. Again, nearly twice as many 5–8 Negroes as 0-years Negroes say that White is the superior color. While there is a good deal of this interclass difference within skin color groups, there is no discernibly regular patterning. It is not always, or even most frequently, the 5–8 group who excel others.

Whatever difference class may make, it is not regularly patterned, at least not the data before us. The class differences are, in fact, so irregular that it would not be of much help to know a man's class when we are trying to understand his attitudes toward skin color. By contrast, it would help somewhat more to know a man's own skin color.

WHICH SKIN COLOR IS WORST TO HAVE?

A double check on the above information is provided by the answers to this question. Tables 11, 12, and 13 will give the responses first by class, then by color, then by color within class.

The major findings in these tables bear out the responses of Table 10. They are as follows:

1. Over 50 per cent of the total sample say that Negro is the worst color. The classes vary on this from the 46 per cent of the lowest group to the 58 per cent of the 5–8 group.

2. There is little class patterning here. The high school and college people resemble the 0-years people more than the 5–8 people on this issue.

3. Almost 40 per cent of the sample affirm the equality of all colors. The remaining ten per cent are distributed through the categories of White,

TABLE 11. WORST SKIN COLOR TO HAVE, REPORTED BY MEMBERS
OF DIFFERENT EDUCATIONAL GROUPS

Years of School Completed	White		Mulatto		WORST COLOR TO HAVE Negro		All Equal		Other		Total	
	No.	%	No.	%	No.	%	No.	%	No.	%	No.	%
0	8	3.3	10	4.2	110	45.8	99	41.3	13	5.4	240	100.0
1–4	9	3.0	6	2.1	146	50.2	125	43.0	5	1.7	291	100.0
5–8	3	1.3	5	2.2	133	57.8	80	34.8	9	3.9	230	100.0
9–12	3	1.7	7	4.0	83	48.3	72	41.9	7	4.1	172	100.0
13+	1	1.4	2	2.7	37	50.7	30	41.1	3	4.1	73	100.0
Total	24	2.4	30	3.0	509	50.6	406	40.4	37	3.6	1006	100.0

TABLE 12. WORST SKIN COLOR TO HAVE, REPORTED BY MEMBERS
OF DIFFERENT SKIN COLOR GROUPS

Skin Color	White		Mulatto		WORST COLOR TO HAVE Negro		All Equal		Other		Total	
	No.	%	No.	%	No.	%	No.	%	No.	%	No.	%
White	8	1.5	19	3.5	311	57.9	183	34.1	16	3.0	537	100.0
Mulatto	13	3.3	11	2.8	177	45.0	180	45.8	12	3.1	393	100.0
Negro	2	3.6	5	9.1	19	34.5	24	43.6	5	9.1	55	100.0
Total	23	2.3	35	3.6	507	51.5	387	39.3	33	3.4	985	100.0

TABLE 13. WORST SKIN COLOR TO HAVE, REPORTED BY MEMBERS OF DIFFERENT EDUCATIONAL CLASSES, CROSS-CLASSIFIED BY SKIN COLOR

Years of School Completed	N	WORST COLOR TO HAVE									
		White		Mulatto		Negro		All Equal		No Information	
		No.	%	No.	%	No.	%	No.	%	No.	%
White											
0	(96)	3	3.1	4	4.2	56	58.3	29	30.2	4	4.2
1–4	(146)	2	1.4	4	2.7	93	63.7	45	30.8	2	1.3
5–8	(121)	1	1.0	2	2.0	71	58.7	43	35.5	4	3.3
9–12	(122)	2	2.0	6	4.9	62	50.8	47	38.5	5	4.1
13+	(52)	0	0.0	3	5.8	29	55.8	19	36.5	1	1.9
Total White	(537)	8	1.5	19	3.5	311	57.9	183	34.1	16	3.0
Mulatto											
0	(122)	4	3.3	5	4.1	51	41.8	57	46.7	5	4.1
1–4	(114)	5	4.4	2	1.8	42	36.8	64	56.1	1	0.8
5–8	(97)	2	2.1	3	3.1	58	59.8	31	32.0	3	3.1
9–12	(42)	1	2.4	1	2.4	18	42.9	21	50.0	1	2.4
13+	(18)	1	5.6	0	0.0	8	44.4	7	38.9	2	11.1
Total Mulatto	(393)	13	3.3	11	2.8	177	45.0	180	45.8	12	3.1
Negro											
0	(11)	1	9.1	1	9.1	3	27.3	3	27.3	3	27.3
1–4	(27)	2	7.4	0	0.0	10	37.0	14	51.9	1	3.7
5–8	(8)	0	0.0	4	50.0	3	37.5	0	0.0	1	12.5
9–12	(7)	0	0.0	0	0.0	3	42.9	4	57.1	0	0.0
13+	(3)	0	0.0	0	0.0	0	0.0	3	100.0	0	0.0
Total Negro	(56)	3	5.3	5	8.9	19	33.9	24	42.9	5	8.9

Mulatto, no information, and so forth. Again there is no class patterning. The college and 0-years groups have identical percentages.

4. One third of the Negro group say that Negro is the worst color, compared to 45 per cent of the Mulatto and over 50 per cent of the White group. Almost no one in any of the skin color groups says that White is the worst color.

5. The darker the color, the fewer who say that dark color is the worst. There are class variations on this theme, but once again they are unpatterned.

In summary of the objective and subjective significance of skin color in Puerto Rico, we can say several things.

1. By any objective measure, there is only a small and relatively insignificant relationship between skin color and education, income, occupation, or any of the major indices of social and economic position. There is some tendency for the lighter skin colors to be more proportionately preponderant in the upper educational segments. But a more refined analysis of color-education relationships yields too small a coefficient of correlation to allow much of a case for this.

2. Skin color also seems to be only loosely and insignificantly related to differences in Puerto Rican attitudes toward education, occupational mobility, personal evaluation, positional evaluation, and other such indices of frame of mind and self images.

3. The majority of Puerto Ricans deny that skin color has anything to do with how much respect a man receives, with his educational opportunities, or with his chances for a job. If there is any one special tendency it is for Whites to feel there is preference for their color. But Negroes and Mulattoes do not join in this judgment.

4. On a most generalized test of color preference and color awareness, the population splits about 50–40 in favor of the proposition that White is the best skin color, as against the notion that skin color does not matter.

5. The major discrimination cited refers to job opportunities. Discrimination is almost universally denied in the field of education, and some mention is made of social discrimination.

6. There is, overall, a remarkably close correspondence between what objective analysis shows about the minor and insignificant role of skin color and what the people themselves subjectively perceive and feel. Perhaps the greatest sense that there is equality of color is expressed by the Negroes themselves.

7. *Trigueno* or Mulatto skin color enjoys nearly the same status as White, both on the objective measures and in the opinions of the population.

The implications of these findings for the population's readiness for rapid social change are great, and yet simple to state. Assuming that skin color remains as irrelevant as it was at the time of this study, it can be predicted that Puerto Rico can move toward its desired social goals without concern for the kind of trouble and conflict which the Mainland society has experienced in its attempts to assure equal opportunity for education and jobs. In view of the very great number of Puerto Ricans who would be called colored and treated as such on the Mainland, the absence of color bars and disabilities on the Island must certainly be counted as a positive asset. This is especially true when considering that the people of darker color are disproportionately concentrated in the lower economic and social levels. If, in addition to their present social obstacles, the lower classes had to face what people of color in Mainland society must face, it is dubious that the lower class segments would exhibit the high social morale, ambitions, and aspirations for the future which they now manifest.

If the future of Puerto Rico depends in some sense on an open class structure moving toward greater equality within a democratic government and an industrial economy, differences in skin color will not significantly affect the chances of realizing that future, if present attitudes toward color differences remain about the same.

XII

South Africa is a highly artificial society in which race exists by explicit legal definition. Internal passports are required for all Black Africans; and three analytically distinct forms of segregation are practiced and legislated: territorial segregation of some Blacks onto inland "native" reserves; segregation of urban Black living quarters in "locations"; and separate facilities for Whites and Blacks within urban areas. Whites, increasingly fearful of Black uprising, protect their supremacy more and more by arms and by restrictive legislation. The interplay between custom and law and between class and race, the destruction of the "Cape Coloured" as an intermediate racial category, and the strong Boer-English political antagonisms combine to make South Africa an interracial society without equality or intimacy and virtually without reciprocal interaction between the races.

PIERRE L. VAN DEN BERGHE

South Africa: The Culture and Politics of Race

THE SOCIAL STRUCTURE OF MODERN SOUTH AFRICA: CULTURE AND STATUS

. . . It is not surprising that as heterogeneous a country as South Africa should have an extremely complex stratification, and that, in addition, it should be segmented in ways that cut across the social hierarchy. For

broad descriptive purposes, the South African system of stratification can
be described in terms of caste and class, as Warner, Dollard, Myrdal, and
other authors dealing with the United States have done.[1] It is not my
intention here to reopen the debate on the use of the term "caste" in a
racial context, for the discussion is largely one of definition.[2] I shall therefore adopt a minimum definition of "caste" as an endogamous group,
hierarchically ranked in relation to other groups, and wherein membership
is determined by birth and for life. To avoid equivocation with Hindu
caste, I shall speak, where necessary, of "colour-castes" or "racial castes."

In most general terms, South African society consists of four racial
castes, and each of those is subdivided according to the usual criteria of a
Western class system. Such a description is only approximate, however,
insofar as many other lines of cleavage, some hierarchical, others not,
further subdivide the population. Let us begin, nevertheless, with the most
important criterion of status in South Africa, namely "race." Although
race gives rise to an extremely rigid division into four easily recognized
colour-castes, its social definition is oddly vague. There exist numerous
legal definitions of "race," adopting differing combinations of physical
appearance, ancestry, association with other people, and even "reputation"
(e.g., the testimony of witnesses can be accepted as evidence concerning
one's racial membership). Unlike statutes in the southern United States
which gave precise definitions of Negroes as any persons having more than
a specified percentage of African "blood" (1/16th, 1/32d, etc.), no such
precision exists in South Africa. This lack of formal precision about the
most basic single principle on which society is organized is only one of
the many paradoxes of South Africa.

In practice, however, there is relatively little confusion as to who belongs to which group, except in the Cape, where a long history of miscegenation allows many light-skinned Coloureds to "play White," and
where many "Whites" have "a touch of the tar brush." A number of
lighter-skinned Africans can also successfully pass for Coloured, but, in the
large majority of cases, physical appearance is a reliable indicator of race.
The four racial groups satisfy the minimum definition of "caste" given
above. They are hierarchized, almost entirely endogamous, and mobility
between groups is, with a few exceptions, impossible. Let us examine each
of these three characteristics in turn.

The Whites or Europeans numbering 19.4 per cent of the total population are clearly at the top of the hierarchy. . . . Not only do they enjoy

---

[1] See Gunnar Myrdal, *An American Dilemma*; John Dollard, *Caste and Class
in a Southern Town*; Allison W. Davies, B. B. Gardner, and M. R. Gardner,
Deep South.
[2] Oliver C. Cox is one of the prominent opponents of the use of the term
"caste" in the racial context. See his *Caste, Class and Race*.

a much higher standard of living, education, and health than the vast majority of the non-Whites, but they virtually monopolize all the occupations above the level of semiskilled workers; they are, for all practical purposes, the only group to have political rights, and they enjoy countless other legal and customary privileges. . . . By comparison, all three non-White races occupy a much lower status, and the differences between the three non-White groups are smaller than those separating Europeans and non-Europeans. The Coloureds (9.4 per cent of the total population) are nearest to the Whites insofar as they suffer under fewer vexations and legal disabilities than the other non-Whites, but, in terms of education and income, they stand perhaps a little lower, on the average, than the Indians, who constitute 3 per cent of the population. Indians and Coloureds occupy thus a nearly equal position in the hierarchy between the Europeans and the Africans, but nearer the latter than the former. . . . The Africans, more commonly referred to by the Whites as "Natives" or "Bantu," number 68.2 per cent of the population and constitute the broad base of the racial pyramid. . . . Their standards of living, occupational status, and education are the lowest, and they are the target of most discrimination. . . . The three lowest colour-castes are often referred to collectively as "non-Whites" or "non-Europeans" to mark the gulf that separates them from the Whites, so that it might be more appropriate to speak of two colour-castes, the lower one sub-divided into three subcastes. For purposes of simplicity, however, I shall speak of four castes.

Not only is the socio-economic gap between Whites and non-Whites wide and unbreachable, but, in some respects, the racial differential has increased until the mid-fifties, largely as a result of political restrictions. In spite of a tendency towards equalization of wages in developing economies, Africans then got a diminishing share of the National Income (less than 20 per cent), and were worse off in terms of purchasing power than before the War. . . . Educational statistics indicate that Africans are progressing proportionately faster than Whites, . . . but, since the passage of the Bantu Education Act, the quality of African schooling is steadily decreasing.

Endogamy, the second essential characteristic of caste, is likewise found in the four racial groups in South Africa.[3] Since 1949 marriage between Whites and all non-Whites is forbidden under the Prohibition of Mixed Marriages Act. There is thus complete compulsory endogamy between these two groups. Even miscegenation outside marriage is a criminal offense under the Immorality Act of 1927 as amended in 1950 and 1957.

[3] For a more detailed study of mixed marriages and miscegenation see my article: "Miscegenation in South Africa," *Cahiers d'Etudes Africains* 4 (1960), pp. 68-84.

Marriages between Indians, Coloured, and Africans are legally permitted, but actually rare. The same was true of White-non-White marriages before they were forbidden. In 1946, for example, only 1 European out of 714 married outside his racial group. The corresponding figures for Coloureds, Indians, and Africans were 1 in 20, 1 in 31, and 1 in 67 respectively. Of the total number of registered marriages in 1946, only 1.38 per cent were racially exogamous.[4] Among the Europeans, there exists now, contrary to the tolerant attitude in the old Cape, a strong taboo against miscegenation, and even more so against intermarriage. In the other groups, the racial taboo is not as strong as among Whites, but other factors such as religion, language, and education level effectively hinder exogamy.

The four racial groups in South Africa also satisfy the minimum definition of caste, in that membership in them is ascribed at birth, and mobility is practically non-existent, except through surreptitious passing. The offspring of racially exogamous unions is defined at birth as Coloured, regardless of the parent groups. In fact, a number of light-skinned Coloureds manage to be accepted as Whites, and brown-skinned Africans as Coloureds. A number of first-generation Coloureds also become assimilated in the African group. The extent of passing is, of course, impossible to determine accurately or even approximately, but, while passing has probably become increasingly rare during the last decade, the racial groups today are certainly anything but "pure" after three hundred years of miscegenation. Since the genetic situation remained relatively fluid until at least the first third of the nineteenth century, one can safely estimate that anywhere from one-tenth to one-quarter of the persons classified as "White" in the Cape Province are of mixed descent, and that almost every "old family" in White Cape society has genealogical connections with Coloured families. The passage of the Population Registration Act in 1950, however, intends to eliminate passing, and to make the four castes absolutely rigid. Indeed, the Act provides for the issue of identity cards where the race of the person will be indicated. Special boards are entrusted with the task of deciding once and for all the racial membership of marginal persons who contest their classification. While the task of these boards is still far from completed,[5] mobility between the colour-castes has become virtually impossible.

Besides the properties of the racial castes already mentioned, membership in a given "race" entails many other crucial consequences. We shall come back to various aspects of colour discrimination later, but, here, we must at least enumerate the main social correlates of skin colour in South

---

[4] *Ibid.*
[5] Some 21,000 borderline Coloureds have yet to be classified, according to a *Time* report of May 24, 1963.

Africa. To be White entails full humanity and citizenship plus a number of special privileges restricted to the master race. All Europeans over eighteen years of age (except convicted criminals) have the franchise at all levels of government. White workers are protected from non-White competition, insofar as they detain a virtual monopoly of skilled manual jobs, as well as of higher clerical, managerial, civil service, and professional posts, at rates of pay from *five* to *fifteen* times those of unskilled non-White jobs. They have the right to organize in trade unions, to go on strike, to bear arms, to own land in freehold in most of the country (except in the Native Reserves and in the few areas declared for occupation of Indians and Coloureds), to move freely in the entire country (except in certain African areas where they need permits), to change freely their place of residence, to buy and consume alcoholic beverages,[6] to stand for elective office, etc.

Technically, of course, the Europeans are subject to racial segregation, as are the non-Europeans, and a White person may not use facilities reserved for non-Whites, or live in non-White areas. In practice, such restrictions are only irksome to a small minority of liberal Whites who reject segregation in principle, and who resent the possession of racial privileges. For the vast majority of Europeans, these "restrictions" are, in fact, advantages, since the Whites monopolize the lion's share of existing facilities and resources, in terms of both quantity and quality. Whites own and occupy, for example, 87 per cent of the country's land. In many cases, a given amenity (e.g., park bench, swimming bath, golf course, cinema, etc.) is *only* available for Whites in a given community.

To be non-White means being deprived of most or all of the above advantages, and being treated as a helot and an unwelcome intruder in one's own country. Non-Whites are not only segregated, but almost invariably given inferior service and facilities, or no facilities at all, in practically every sphere of life, except in most shops (which have become sensitive to the threat of non-White economic boycotts). Racial segregation is the rule in restaurants, hotels, cinemas, hospitals, schools, waiting rooms, park benches, beaches, cemeteries, residential areas, ambulances, taxis, trains, buses, picnic areas, airports, entrances to public buildings, swimming baths, sport grounds, post offices, lifts, banks, toilets, bars, national parks, and many other places. Non-White servants accompanying their masters are, however, tolerated in many of these places, provided their servile condition is unambiguous. Some of that segregation is "customary" (i.e., imposed by traditional White prejudices), while some is compulsory under law. To avoid any ambiguity as to whether segregated amenities must be equal in their physical plant, a special law, the Reserva-

---

[6] Since 1962 this right has been extended to Africans.

tion of Separate Amenities Act, was passed in 1953, stating that facilities may not only be separate but also *unequal*.

All non-Whites (except foreign diplomats and the Japanese, who, for reasons of international trade, have recently been declared to be "White") are subject to the daily humiliations of segregation. No non-European may bear arms in the defence forces, stand as a candidate for Parliament, or live anywhere but in specially set-aside "Group Areas." Beyond these restrictions, there are differences between Africans, Indians, and Coloureds in the number and extent of disabilities and vexations. Africans are by far the most oppressed, and the Coloureds are the least underprivileged of the non-Whites, although their condition is rapidly deteriorating.

The Coloureds in the Cape Province still have a vestigial, though meaningless, franchise on a separate roll electing special White representatives to Parliament, whereas the Africans and the Indians have no franchise rights in the election of national, provincial, or municipal representatives.[7] The Coloureds still retain an increasingly precarious foothold in some skilled trades from which Africans and Indians are excluded. Unlike Africans who have to carry a "reference book" limiting their spacial mobility, and unlike Indians who are forbidden to enter or to stop in certain areas of the country (such as the Transkei and the Orange Free State), the Coloureds are relatively free to travel in South Africa. Coloureds have always had access to liquor, from which Africans, and to a lesser degree Indians, have been debarred by law until 1962. Where there is segregation between the non-White groups, as in schools, the amenities for Coloureds and Indians are generally better than for Africans, though considerably inferior to the White facilities. Coloureds and Indians still have a limited right to strike which is completely denied to Africans. Similarly, Coloureds and Indians have a right to own land in freehold in certain small areas legally set aside for their occupation. Africans, on the other hand, with a few insignificant exceptions, may possess land nowhere in their own country. Land tenure in practically all Native Reserves is communal, not personal; in practice this means that the right to use and occupy land can be granted and revoked at the whim of government-appointed chiefs. . . .

Although "race" is by far the most important criterion of status in South Africa, it is not the sole relevant factor in the system of social stratification, for each racial group is internally subdivided. We shall take in turn the Whites, Coloureds, Indians, and Africans. The Whites are first segmented into three distinct subgroups along linguistic and religious

[7] Since the establishment of the first Bantustan in the Transkei, Africans living in that area may elect a minority of the members of the Transkeian Assembly.

lines, namely the Afrikaners, the "English-speaking South Africans," and the Jews, not to mention much smaller groups such as the Germans. These divisions are not directly hierarchical but they are related to social status and to political and economic power.

The Afrikaners (formerly known as the Dutch or the Boers) are the Whites who speak Afrikaans. The vast majority of them also belong to one of the Dutch Reformed Churches. Afrikaans-speaking Coloureds are, of course, excluded from the *Volk*. Afrikaners number approximately 57 per cent of the Whites, and, under a practically all-White franchise, they have played a predominant role in the politics of the country. Since 1948 they hold a virtual monopoly of political power through the Nationalist Party which represents the vast majority of them. In terms of education and economic status, however, they still lag behind the other Whites, on the average, although these differences tend to disappear. Among Johannesburg Whites in 1952, for example, only 1.5 per cent of the Afrikaners compared to 10 per cent of the English families earned more than £1000 a year.[8] In Durban in 1951 the mean *per capita* income was £299 a year for English-speaking Whites and £187 for Afrikaans-speaking Whites.[9]

The Afrikaners are less urbanized than the English and the Jews, and their representation in big business, mining, and banking is still compared with that of the English Whites. In 1949 it was estimated that Afrikaners were in control of 6 per cent of South African industry and 25 to 30 per cent of commerce. However, the number of Afrikaner-owned firms increased from 2428 to 9585 between 1939 and 1949, and Afrikaner gains have continued since.[10] Yet, in the mid-fifties, Afrikaner capital in all branches of mining controlled only 1 per cent of total production.[11] The "poor Whites," who continued to be numerous until the depression of the 1930's, were practically all Afrikaners, but through government subsidies and the so-called "civilized labour policy," "poor Whites" have disappeared as a class.[12] In spite of this, Afrikaners are more heavily represented than the English or the Jews in the lower White echelons of the occupational, income, and educational scale. In the medical and legal professions, however, the Afrikaners are rapidly increasing. The vast majority of civil service posts reserved for Whites are held by Afrikaners, at all levels of administration. The 1957 civil service recruitment figures show

8 Stanley Trapido, "Political Institutions and Afrikaner Social Structures in the Republic of South Africa," *American Political Science Review* 57 (1963), pp. 75-87.

9 Heinz Hartmann, *Enterprise and Politics in South Africa*, p. 64.

10 Sheila Patterson, *The Last Trek*, p. 163.

11 Leo Kuper *et al.*, *Durban, A Study in Racial Ecology*, p. 89.

12 Of course, improved economic conditions in the late 1930's and during the Second World War also contributed to the disappearance of "poor Whites."

that of 100 White entrants at the professional level, 81 were Afrikaners; at the clerical level, 89 per cent of the new recruits were Afrikaans-speaking.[13]

The term "English-speaking South African" is doubly ambiguous, insofar as it is not only a linguistic label, but also a racial and a religious one. English-speaking non-Whites are not included in this category, since, in the eyes of most Whites, they are not citizens of the country. This label sometimes also implies membership in, or allegiance to, one of the Christian denominations. While most Jews are linguistically assimilated to the English Whites, they generally consider themselves, and are considered by the Christians, as constituting a separate group. Altogether, some 39 per cent of the Whites speak English at home. The English and the Jews share many socio-economic characteristics, as opposed to the Afrikaners. Both groups are predominantly urban, the Jews almost exclusively so, detain a virtual monopoly of large commercial, mining, and financial concerns, and are practically excluded from political power and the civil service, except in the Natal Provincial Administration and in the large municipalities of the Transvaal and the Eastern Cape. Compared with the Afrikaners, the other two White groups are wealthier and more highly educated. This is even truer of the Jews than of the English. Politically, the majority of the English support the United Party, but in recent years the English upper class and many Jews have turned to the less conservative Progressive Party.

The three main White subgroups cannot be called "castes," as the divisions between them are not rigid. Intermarriages are fairly common; many persons of Afrikaner origin have become Anglicized; and conversely a few originally English families are Afrikanerized. The 1951 Census classifies 73 per cent of the Whites as bilingual, though only 2 per cent habitually speak both European languages at home.[14] The main importance of the linguistic cleavage within the White caste is in the field of politics, as we shall see later.

The three White groups cannot be ranked hierarchically. While many Afrikaners have traditionally had a cultural inferiority complex vis-à-vis the English,[15] and while they are on the whole of a lower socio-economic status than the English and the Jews, the social class system cuts across linguistic and religious distinctions, and must be analysed independently. We shall presently turn to this task. In general, the White class system resembles that of the United States, Canada, or Australia, except for the virtual absence of a lower class. The class of impoverished farmers and

---

[13] Hartmann, op. cit., p. 62.

[14] Muriel Horrell, A Survey of Race Relations in South Africa (1958-1959), p. 279.

[15] See for example: Patterson, op. cit.

unskilled labourers known as "poor Whites," which numbered up to one-sixth of the European population in the depression of the 1930's, has almost disappeared. White artisans enjoy a legally protected position and a relatively high standard of living, and lack any consciousness of belonging to a proletariat opposed to the White bourgeoisie, or having any common interests with the non-White proletariat. . . . The absence of a White proletarian class consciousness accounts for the weakness of the South African labour movement. The latter has always been tainted by racialism in South Africa, and has always defined its function as that of protecting the White manual worker against non-White competition.

. . .

At the apex of White society, one finds small groups wielding considerable power. Like in many other "new" societies, there is no entrenched aristocracy in South Africa, but rather a number of distinct and conflicting elites or oligarchies competing for power. Of these, the most important are the big-business and the political groups. The relation between these two antagonistic groups will be examined later. The military is not a distinct power group in South Africa. The White intelligentsia is small, geographically scattered in the various universities and large urban centres, internally divided along political lines, largely excluded from direct participation in power, but nevertheless influential in certain spheres. Needless to say, these various White elites, while sharing a high socioeconomic status, differ widely in their tastes and modes of life, and do not, in any sense, constitute a unitary upper class.

. . . South African Whites view themselves, first and foremost, as members of the dominant racial group. Internal class differences become secondary, and the gulf that separates Europeans from non-Europeans serves to minimize class consciousness and the perception of objective class differences within the dominant White caste. As a corollary of the rigid system of racial castes, there exists among Europeans what might be termed "*Herrenvolk* egalitarianism." Not only does colour-consciousness create bonds of solidarity between all Whites regardless of class, but it also prevents the establishment of class ties *across* racial barriers. Colour overshadows and weakens class and class consciousness.

The Coloured group is stratified along lines similar to the Whites, but at a much lower socio-economic level. The Muslim Malays are slightly better off than the other Coloureds, but, because of their greater conservatism, they are less well represented in the professions. Whereas the lower class is almost non-existent among the Whites, the vast majority of the Coloureds constitute an impoverished proletariat of agricultural workers, domestic servants, and unskilled or semiskilled factory workers. Above this lower class, one finds a much smaller but sizeable lower middle class of artisans and petty clerks, and a tiny upper middle class of small businessmen and professionals, mostly schoolteachers. In economic terms, this Coloured elite lives at about the same level as the White petty bourgeoisie, because Coloureds earn much less than equally qualified Whites doing the same work.

The Coloured stratification system is, however, qualitatively different from the White system in one important respect. Of the four racial groups, the Coloured group is the only one to be internally differentiated on the basis of physical traits. All other things being equal, the more closely a Coloured resembles a White person in skin colour, hair texture, and facial features, the higher his status is. Coloureds are, on the average, at least as colour-conscious as the majority of the Europeans. In recent years socio-economic criteria have become more important than physical traits in determining status within the Coloured group, but appearance still plays an important role among older and uneducated people.[16] Educated Coloureds, for the most part, react strongly against status differences based on physical characteristics, and against the approval of concubinage with Whites among some members of the Coloured lower class as a method of "improving" the race. In practice, the two sets of status criteria are difficult to dissociate, because there is still a fairly high correlation between physical traits and various indices of socio-economic status within the Coloured group.

Racial consciousness among Coloureds has also entailed other consequences. As an intermediate caste, the Coloureds have traditionally been caught between their feelings of racial superiority vis-à-vis the Africans, and their constantly frustrated hope of acceptance by the Whites. This has led to ambivalent attitudes towards the Whites, to political passivity, and to a failure to identify with the Africans. The mass of the Coloured proletariat has, like the White manual workers, refused to identify with the African proletariat, which it views with feelings of superiority and hostility. We shall return to this marginal position of the Coloureds in the political context.

Of the four racial groups, the Indians are by far the most complexly stratified and segmented. They are first divided along religious and linguistic lines which are not hierarchical, but which are correlated with socio-economic status. . . . Western criteria of status, such as education, income, and occupation are of growing importance, and stratify the Indian group along increasingly distinct class lines. Contrary to European belief, most Indians are poor, and are either small farmers, agricultural

<hr />

[16] On this subject, see: W. van der Merwe, "Stratification in a Cape Coloured Community," *Sociology and Social Research* 46 (1962), pp. 302-311; and van den Berghe, "Some Trends in Unpublished Social Science Research in South Africa," *International Social Science Journal* 14 (1962), pp. 723-732.

labourers, or unskilled and semiskilled industrial workers. Above this poor working class, one finds a lower middle class of medium farmers, clerks, small shop-keepers, and skilled workers. The Indian upper middle class is divided into two distinct groups: a conservative, traditional elite of large merchants, some of whom are quite wealthy, and a Western-oriented, politically active intelligentsia consisting mostly of teachers, physicians, and lawyers. The White image of the Indian is largely based on the small merchant class which is anything but typical of the Indian community.

The African "race" is both stratified into emerging social classes and segmented into ethnic groups, but the two types of division are in an antithetical relationship to one another. In short, one can say that ethnic affiliation recedes in importance as social classes emerge from the process of Westernization. This statement is too schematic, however, and covers a more complex reality. Since practically all Africans still speak a Bantu language as their mother tongue, and retain other African cultural characteristics, they almost all belong to a so-called "tribe" in a formal sense. For most town dwellers and many rural inhabitants, this ethnic affiliation has become vague, however, and has ceased to be an important social reality. Such people are integrated into the Western economic system; they have lost all political, and even sometimes kinship, ties with traditional society; they are Christians, at least nominally so, and they live altogether outside of the traditional environment. They continue to speak their mother tongue at home, and they may preserve a sense of affiliation to their original national group, but many factors make for the rapid disappearance of "tribalism."

All urban centres are ethnic melting pots where Africans learn not only European languages, but also Bantu tongues other than their own, and common "pidgin" dialects. The disintegration of the traditional family through the migratory labour system favours interethnic unions, in the form of both marriage and concubinage. More and more Africans are thus of mixed stock. As members of Christian denominations, as neighbours in the "locations," as fellow workers in the mines or factories, Africans of various linguistic groups constantly mix with one another. Moreover, Africans are becoming increasingly conscious that they are subject to a common system of political oppression and economic exploitation. Political consciousness militates against ethnic particularism and leads people to think in terms of "we Africans."

All of these factors notwithstanding, a substantial segment of the rural population remains integrated, through kinship and local political ties, in the traditional way of life. This is particularly true of the Transkei and Zululand, the two principal remaining pockets of cultural conservatism in South Africa. . . . Traditional Southern Bantu society is unstratified in Western class terms, though there are, of course, wide differences in status between commoners and chiefs, and between various clans. . . .

Among Africans at various stages of Westernization, class distinctions following Western lines are becoming increasingly sharp. Prestige is closely related with the extent to which a person has acquired European culture, and the urge towards Westernization is strong. This is not to say that urban or Christian Africans want to be "White," as many Coloureds do, but rather that they have accepted the values of Western culture. The principal criteria of status among urban Africans are education, Christianity, occupation, clothing, and moral "respectability." Wealth does not play the role that it does in the White community, because the scope for capital accumulation among Africans is stringently limited. An African may not acquire land, or open a business except in a few small areas, and discrimination debars him from practically all better-paid jobs, no matter how well qualified he is. . . .

The majority of Africans live on or below the minimum standard for health, as domestic servants, mine workers, agricultural labourers, or unskilled workers in secondary and tertiary industry. Agriculture in the Native Reserves is almost invariably *sub*-subsistence, and must be supplemented by wage earnings. A small minority of petty white-collar workers live more or less precariously above the vital minimum as a *Lumpenbourgeoisie*, and an even smaller class of teachers, students, ministers, nurses, and other professionals constitutes the elite of the emerging African middle class. In 1959 there were 49 African lawyers, 67 librarians, 81 medical doctors, 73 chartered accountants, 176 laboratory assistants, and 61 analytical chemists in the entire country.[17] Even this elite lives at a material level inferior to that of all but destitute "poor Whites," in spite of the fact that many of its members have matriculated and hold university degrees. Literacy, knowledge of a European language, mostly English, membership in an established (i.e., non-"Zionist") church, and a certain standard of moral respectability are the minimum requirements for membership in the *Lumpenbourgeoisie*, and correspondingly higher requirements are necessary for membership in the tiny elite. It is largely from this last group that the political leadership of the liberatory movements is recruited.[18]

.   .   .

From the above description it can be seen that the stratification system of South Africa is far too complex to conform in detail to the American "class and caste" schema of Warner and others. The only principle which

[17] Hartmann, *op. cit.*, p. 43.
[18] For a more detailed treatment of the African urban middle class, see Leo Kuper, An African Bourgeoisie.

pervades the whole society is that of "race," leading to a rigid, fourfold classification imposed by the Whites, and rejected as illegitimate by the non-Whites. But each of the four colour-castes is internally subdivided and stratified according to criteria which differ from one group to the other. While there is a general tendency in all groups to develop social classes along Western lines, numerous other traditional factors continue to play an important role. Even when status is distributed according to Western class criteria, the standards of achievement are proportionately lower according to the position of the racial group in the colour-caste hierarchy. A middle-class African is, for example, not equal in status to a middle-class Coloured or White, because he belongs to a different "race" which is itself hierarchically ranked. Furthermore, the relative emphasis placed on the various criteria (such as wealth, education, and occupation) differs from one "race" to the other. Not only are the objective characteristics of class widely divergent from one racial group to another, but such class consciousness as exists is largely limited to one's racial caste. Because of the all-pervading racial barrier, each "race" constitutes at once a separate reference group in the status system and an autonomous subsystem of status with its own criteria. At the same time, the significance of "race" and the acceptance of racial criteria of status vary widely, being greatest among Whites and Coloureds, and minimal among Africans and Indians. Racial barriers are objective realities, but the vast majority of the non-Europeans are not accommodated to their lower status, and deny any legitimacy to the racial hierarchy which is ultimately maintained through the might of the White-controlled state.

SOCIO-POLITICAL CONFLICTS: "NATIVE POLICY"

We must now examine "Native policy," i.e., the theory and means advocated and implemented by the successive White governments to rule over the Africans and perpetuate European supremacy. From the following analysis, the essential agreement of all major European parties on the colour issue will become clear. In fact, the term "Native policy" is too restrictive for we shall also examine government policies towards the Coloureds and the Indians. The more inclusive term "race policy" is, therefore, more appropriate, although the numerical importance of the Africans has given them a choice place in the successive programmes of repression.

The following basic aims and principles of "race policy" have been shared by all South African governments since Union:

1. The maintenance of paternalistic White domination.
2. Racial segregation and discrimination, wherever there was any threat of equality or competition between Whites and non-Whites.

3. The perpetual subjugation of non-Europeans, and particularly Africans, as a politically powerless and economically exploitable group.

The Nationalist policy of apartheid is only the last phase in a long process of continuous strengthening of the system of White oppression. Apartheid differs from the race policy of earlier governments mostly in that its ideology is more explicit, its rationalization more elaborate, and its implementation more thorough and systematic. Before describing the implementation of race policy previous to and since the Nationalist regime, it is important to understand the philosophy which underlines that policy. The model of race relations which all South African governments have tried to maintain is one of old-style colonial paternalism. South African Whites have looked at themselves, like other settler minorities, as a superior group endowed with greater intelligence, initiative, and inventiveness. They have considered their language, religion, technology, and culture in general as unquestionably better than those of the "primitive savages" whom they conquered. Conversely, they have looked down on the Africans as backward, immature, stupid, irresponsible, uninhibited, grown-up children incapable of managing their own affairs. As carriers of a "higher civilization," the Whites cast themselves into the role of the stern but just master who has to look after the welfare of his childish and backward servants.

The "White-man's-burden" attitude is a useful rationalization of European domination, because the benevolent aspect of paternalism appears to reconcile despotism with justice. The fact that this benevolent aspect was rarely implemented in practice is irrelevant here. The ideology of paternalism allows the White group to believe in all sincerity that its domination is not only just, but beneficial to the people it oppresses and exploits. Paternalism has transformed the reality of the "Black man's burden" into the myth of the "White man's burden." The master-servant relationship is considered by the majority of Whites as the ideal and only conceivable relationship between Europeans and non-Europeans, and the successive governments have basically aimed at extending and preserving that model at the national level.

In South Africa, European ethnocentrism was combined with White racialism. Not only did the Whites consider themselves *culturally* superior, but also endowed with greater *innate* capacities than the Africans. Thus, the differences between Whites and Blacks were assumed to be permanent and immutable, or at best changeable only over extremely long periods of time.

Racial segregation and discrimination are at once logical developments from the policy of paternalism, and indices of its failure. The purpose of segregation is not to prevent contact between Whites and non-Whites.

South African Whites do not object to prolonged and intimate contact with non-Europeans, so long as the latter are in a servile capacity. Segregation aims clearly at preventing *egalitarian* contact between the "races."

. . . Racial separation has grown increasingly rigid over the years, as more and more non-Whites have risen in socio-economic status to a position where they could associate on equal terms with the Whites. Similarly, discrimination based on colour, whether legal or customary, is an attempt to prevent competition on the basis of merit between White and Black, and constitutes an avowal that the Whites need the protection of an artificial colour-bar in order to maintain their dominant position. Racial segregation and discrimination have been rationalized by the various governments as the best means to prevent racial conflict. In fact, they are attempts to perpetuate racial inequality, in a situation where the paternalistic master-servant relationship has ceased to be the only form of contact between the racial groups.[19]

· · ·

From the ideological point of view, the advent of apartheid meant the triumph of the stern frontier paternalism of the Boer Republics over the more benevolent and sophisticated paternalism of the Cape. In every essential respect, however, the race policies of the Afrikaner Nationalists represent a logical evolution from, rather than a rupture with, the traditional White South African *Weltanschauung*. As conditions of rapid urban, industrial, and social change increasingly endangered White supremacy and the paternalistic model of White-Black relations, White governments grew more and more repressive. They failed to adjust to changing conditions, and they clung to the old pre-industrial, colonial pattern.

The term "apartheid" (literally "separation") is an Afrikaans neologism first coined in 1929. It only entered into common usage in 1948, however, when it became an election slogan and, after the Nationalist victory, the official designation of government policy.[20] . . . As presented by its intellectual apologists, notably by the members of the South African Bureau of Racial Affairs (SABRA), the argument in favour of apartheid runs as follows: We, Afrikaners and White South Africans in general,

[19] On this point see also . . . P. L. van den Berghe, "Distance Mechanisms of Social Stratification," *Sociology and Social Research* 44 (1960), pp. 155-164.
[20] Among other works, see S. Pienaar and A. Sampson, *South Africa, Two Views of Separate Development*; N. J. Rhoodie and H. J. Venter, *Apartheid: A Socio-Historical Exposition of the Origin and Development of the Apartheid Idea*; P. V. Pistorius, *No Further Trek*; B. B. Keet, *The Ethics of Apartheid*; E. P. Dvorin, *Racial Separation in South Africa*; P. L. van den Berghe, "Apartheid, Fascism and the Golden Age," *Cahiers d'Etudes Africaines* 8 (1962), pp. 598-608; as well as the many publications of the S. A. Bureau of Racial Affairs and the S. A. Institute of Race Relations.

have no homeland other than South Africa. The country is ours, and we have no desire or intention to leave it. We have just as much right to be here as the "Bantu," and we have arrived in South Africa at about the same time as they. We want to preserve our superior "White civilization" and maintain our racial identity, but we are surrounded by an overwhelming majority of non-Whites who threaten to swamp us culturally and racially.

Integration, the argument continues, is unthinkable, because, no matter how slow and gradual, it must end in black domination, miscegenation, and swamping of "White civilization." . . .

The phrase "ideal apartheid" has been used by a number of people, but it is somewhat misleading in that it has two widely different meanings. Government officials often oppose "ideal" to "practical" apartheid; by the former they mean total geographical segregation by race, a goal which they deem desirable but unrealistic in the near future. As used by non-Nationalists, "ideal apartheid" means the "positive" or "benevolent" aspects of the doctrine, as contrasted to the repressive ones. . . . The extent to which the "positive" aspect of apartheid is translated into actual practice is open to interpretation. . . .

The proponents of "positive" apartheid claim that "parallel development" will eliminate White domination, and establish an equitable geographical partition, but Strydom, the second post-war Nationalist Prime Minister, stated categorically: "Our policy is that the Europeans must stand their ground and must remain boss in South Africa."[21] Verwoerd now speaks of "independent Bantustans," but in 1951 he said in Parliament: "Now a Senator wants to know whether the series of self-governing areas would be sovereign. The answer is obvious. . . . It stands to reason that White South Africa must remain their guardian."[22] . . .

In 1959 Eiselen, the Secretary for Bantu Administration and Development, declared: "The utmost degree of autonomy which the Union Parliament is likely to be prepared to concede to these areas [the Bantu homelands] will stop short of actual surrender of sovereignty by the European trustee."[23]

·   ·   ·

It is useful at this point to refine somewhat the analysis of segregation as practiced or advocated by the Nationalists. Depending on the actual physical distance between racial groups, one may speak of "micro-segregation," "meso-segregation," and "macro-segregation." The blueprint calls

[21] Quoted in *Africa Today* 11 (March, 1964), p. 2, from speech in the House of Assembly, January 25, 1963.
[22] Quoted in *Treatment of Indians in South Africa*, p. 5.
[23] Quoted in Horrell, *op. cit.*, 1958-1959, p. 50.

for maximization of segregation, but government policy is prepared to accept a lesser degree of physical separation when it is expedient. In the direct work situation, i.e., in factories, farms, shops and the like, *microsegregation* is acceptable to the Nationalists. In practical terms, this means that White and non-White workers associate on the job, but use separate dressing rooms, toilets, dining halls, elevators, waiting rooms, post-office counters, etc.

As soon as these non-Whites who work with Europeans leave the immediate job situation, the blueprint calls for *meso-segregation*. They board completely segregated means of transport to go to widely separated residential areas where they have virtually no contact with Whites, except for policemen, and "location" superintendents, but where they are within commuting distance of the White world for work purposes. Increasingly, the government attempts to suppress *micro-segregation* off the job, as, for example, in the case of domestic servants living on the premises of their employers (albeit in special servants' quarters). Apartheid calls for *meso-segregation* off the job, as this is the greatest physical distance compatible with any sort of economic activity at all. *Meso-segregation* is, of course, costly and wasteful in terms of transport costs, man-hours, fatigue, and frustration, but yet economically feasible, as the last fifteen years have shown. As the voteless non-White masses have had to bear the main cost of this *meso-segregation*, the Whites have only voiced minor protest at the inconvenience of not having servants live on the premises.

Finally, for those Africans not actually in the employment of Whites, apartheid calls for *macro-segregation*, i.e., round-the-clock separation in totally distinct regions, namely the Native Reserves, now in the process of restyling under the name of Bantustans. *Macro-segregation* thus becomes synonymous with the government's notion of total territorial partition, accompanied, of course, by White political paramountcy, even in the African areas. The three degrees of segregation can thus be considered as a scale wherein, according to Nationalist ideology, the greater degree is preferable to the lesser ones, unless practical economic contingencies make the introduction of a lesser degree of physical distance imperative.

. . .

It would be out of place here to refute the racist assumptions on which apartheid is based, or to take a stand on the ethical merits of that policy, or to discuss its practicability. Suffice it to say that the "ideal" form of apartheid as equitable partition is a convenient rationalization, which, accepted at face value, allows well-meaning paternalists to call themselves Nationalists, and serves as the ineffective basis of international apologetics, but that the government has never seriously envisaged its implementation. The implementation of "ideal" apartheid would entail the political and economic disruption of the entire country. "Practical" apartheid, on the other hand is simply a more systematic and internally consistent policy of White oppression. . . .

The segregation of rural Africans in Native Reserves was already an accomplished fact long before the time of Union. The establishment of the Native Reserves system goes back, as we saw, to the work of Theophilus Shepstone in the 1840's in Natal, and to the "Native policy" of the Boer Republics. That system was consolidated and expanded under the Native Land Act of 1913. In urban areas the diamond and gold mines led the way in racial segregation and discrimination by establishing special compounds for their African workers. The Mines and Works Act of 1911 was the first piece of legislation making for a compulsory colour-bar in employment. This Act excluded non-Europeans from skilled jobs in the extractive industries. Residential segregation of Africans in cities, which had hitherto been enforced by the mines and by municipal regulations, was made uniform by the passage of the Native Urban Areas Act of 1923. By the time Hertzog came to power in 1924, the basic pattern of racial discrimination in employment and of physical separation of Africans in urban and rural areas had thus been legislatively established.

Hertzog's rule from 1924 to 1939 was characterized by intensified racialism, and it foreshadowed the post-1948 apartheid programme. As a result of pressure from the White trade unions, and of the White labour revolt on the Rand in 1922, the Mines and Works Act was amended and made more stringent in 1926. Non-Whites were subjected to further disabilities in the field of labour through the Industrial Conciliation Act of 1924, amended in 1937, the Native Service Contract Act of 1932, and the Masters and Servants Amendment Act of 1926. These acts denied the right to strike to Africans, and made a breach of contract on the part of servants a criminal offence. In 1927 the Immorality Act prohibited extramarital and sexual intercourse between Europeans and Africans. Residential segregation of Africans was further entrenched by the Native Urban Areas Amendment Act of 1930, and the Native Trust and Land Act of 1936. The Native Administration Act of 1928 prohibited the sale of alcoholic beverages to Africans (except for "Kaffir beer"); and the Arms and Ammunition Act of 1937 practically restricted the ownership of firearms to Europeans.

As regards the franchise, the Hertzog regime steadily reduced the importance of the non-European vote in the Cape. The Women Enfranchisement Act of 1930 extended voting rights to White women only, and thereby reduced by half the relative weight of the non-White vote; the Franchise Laws Amendment Act of 1931 waived the property, income, and education qualifications for White voters but not for non-Whites; finally, the Native Representation Act of 1936 eliminated Africans from the common electoral roll in the Cape, and instituted a system whereby qualified Africans, on a separate voting list, elected three White representatives in Parliament. This act, together with its companion piece, the Native Trust and Land Act, was considered by Hertzog as the permanent solution to the "Native problem."

In one important respect, however, the Hertzog colour policies differed from present-day apartheid. The legislation mentioned above affected almost exclusively the Africans, and left the Coloureds almost untouched. Although Hertzog was opposed to miscegenation, he saw in the Coloured group a "natural ally" of the Whites against the "Black menace," and favoured a policy of economic, cultural, and political assimilation for the Coloureds. For obvious demographic reasons, this "softer" line towards the Coloureds still appeals to the more intelligent "moderate" Nationalists today.

Far from making a more liberal turn in racial policies, the second Smuts regime (1939-1948) further perfected Hertzog's colour policies. Indeed, Smuts was directly associated with them as the second most prominent member of the Hertzog cabinet from 1933 to 1939. As Prime Minister he continued to entrench "White leadership." The Native Urban Areas Consolidation Act of 1945 systematized further the provisions of the Native Urban Areas Act of 1923 and 1930. The Apprenticeship Act of 1944 further secured skilled manual jobs for the Europeans. . . .

When the Nationalists won the 1948 election, they only had to extend and systematize an already imposing structure. The Prohibition of Mixed Marriages Act of 1949 forbids any marriage between a White and a non-White. The Immorality Act of 1927 was made more and more stringent in its 1950 and 1957 amendments to the point where "immoral or indecent acts" between a White and a non-White of opposite sexes are punishable with whipping and up to seven years of prison. The process of disfranchisement of the non-Whites was pursued to its logical conclusion. After a five-year constitutional fight, starting with the Separate Representation of Voters Act of 1951 and the High Court of Parliament Act of 1952, the Cape Coloureds were finally eliminated from the common roll in 1956. In 1960 the last token representation of Africans by White M.P.'s was abolished.

A number of laws extended the scope of compulsory physical separation between the four main racial groups. The most important of them is the Group Areas Act of 1950, amended in 1952, 1955, and 1957, which provides for the establishment of segregated residential areas for each "race," and for the mass removal and expropriation of members of the "wrong" skin colour in any given area. This act affects mostly the Coloureds and the Indians, as the Africans were already rigidly segregated when the Nationalists came to power. . . . The principle of separate and *unequal* treatment is also explicitly entrenched in the Reservation of Separate Amenities Act of 1953. . . .

The Bantu Authorities Act of 1951 provides the blue print for the Nationalist "new deal" in "Native Administration." In theory, the government envisages the creation of "independent Bantustans" in the old Native Reserves, but, in practice, Bantu Authorities are a most efficacious version of the old system of appointed chiefs and advisory bodies, with somewhat increased local autonomy. The Native Building Workers Act of 1951 and the Native Labour (Settlement of Disputes) Act of 1953 put the African workers under further occupational handicaps. The Native Administration Amendment Act of 1956 and the Natives (Urban Areas) Amendment Act of the same year extend arbitrary powers of imprisonment and exile over Africans. So as to prevent the passing of Coloureds for Whites, the Population Registration Act of 1950, amended in 1956, provides for the issue of racial identity cards. Special White boards are to decide on the "race" of marginal persons who wish to contest their classification.

In the field of education, the Nationalists passed two important laws. The euphemistically named Extension of University Education Act of 1959 forbids all non-Europeans to attend the English-speaking universities . . . ; this act thus makes for complete racial segregation at all levels of education.[24]

. . .

Two recent laws overshadow all previous ones, however. The first, the 1962 General Law Amendment Act, popularly known as the "Sabotage Act," further extends the already wide limits of arbitrary government powers. It provides for a minimum sentence of five years of prison and a maximum sentence of death for "sabotage," and places the burden of proof on the accused. The concept of "sabotage" includes any attempt to promote disturbance, to disrupt any industry, to hamper the maintenance of law and order, to encourage any social or economic change, and to promote hostility between different sections of the population. Illegal possession of explosives or illegal entry into any building is considered sufficient evidence of an intention to carry out acts of sabotage. The act also extends previous government powers to ban newspapers, organizations, and gatherings, and to imprison any person for any length of time without due process of law, and without having to declare a state of emergency.

[24] Non-White students enrolled at English universities before the act was passed may complete their studies, however. The medical school of the University of Natal may continue to enroll non-Europeans, but that school has always been segregated *de facto*.

On May 1, 1963, an even more draconian General Law Amendment Act was passed, once more with the support of the United Party. The act provides for repeated detention of persons for ninety days at a time, for questioning; refusal to allow anybody, including legal counsel, to see detained persons; total prohibition on the courts to interfere with this form of detention; indefinite imprisonment without trial for persons having completed ordinary gaol sentences; powers to hold letters, telegrams, and parcels sent by post; death penalty, applicable also to juveniles, for receiving training in the use of violence outside South Africa, or for achieving the objects of a banned organization; and fifteen years of prison for entering a "protected" area without consent. . . .

. . . The government, and the White group which it represents, resort to at least five other major forms of discrimination besides legislation. These extra- or para-legal types of racial discrimination contribute even more to tension than legislation as such, and must therefore be mentioned at some length.

The first of them consists of the innumerable police and municipal regulations, ministerial orders, and government gazette proclamations which regiment almost every aspect of the lives of non-Europeans. These regulations and orders are based on legislation, of course, but the scope for arbitrary action in laws governing "non-European affairs" is so wide that the various branches of the executive practically constitute autonomous legislative bodies responsible only to the Prime Minister. By far the most important of these regulations is the vast and intricate system of "pass laws" and "influx control." The pass laws constitute the cornerstone of government control over the African masses, and are the most detested aspect of discrimination. More than any other set of measures, they harass the daily life of Africans. . . .

Under the system of pass regulations, any adult male African must carry at all times a "reference book" containing his employment history, as well as a number of documents such as tax receipts and various sorts of permits. In short, an adult African may not reside anywhere without permission, may not move outside his allotted place of residence without approval of the authorities, is subject to a curfew at night, may not live in any "White" area without being gainfully employed, may not own land in freehold (aside from some insignificant exceptions), and may be expelled from his residence and deported to any place, when the administration deems his presence to be "undesirable" or "redundant." . . .

The objects of the pass laws are to restrict African migration to the cities, to prevent the rise of a stable African urban middle class, and to keep the masses under the continuous control of the police. In all these objectives, the pass regulations have only met with limited success. Urban migration continues at a fast rate in spite of all influx control measures, the African middle class and intelligentsia are steadily growing, and the population is harassed and frustrated, rather than controlled, by the police. The main effects of the pass laws have been to disrupt countless African families, by separating for long periods the wage earner from his dependents; to promote violence, anger, prostitution, and juvenile delinquency; and to waste labour potential by maintaining the mass of the workers in the position of an unskilled, floating proletariat.

The second form of discrimination falling outside the strict scope of legislation is partial and unequal treatment of non-Whites in the courts. . . . [A] curious way in which the dual standard operates is in the more lenient punishment of Africans committing crimes against Africans, than of Whites against Whites. This seeming bias in favour of Africans does, in fact, mean that law-abiding Africans have no adequate protection against criminals. In most cases where non-Whites have been victims, the police does not investigate the crime with nearly the same zeal as when a White is involved. . . .

A third type of extralegal discrimination consists in the various forms of economic exploitation to which non-Whites, and particularly Africans, are subject. Contrary to the general belief that the Whites carry the financial burden for non-European facilities, the official government policy is that each racial group must pay its own way. In fact, the position is reversed, and one may speak of a "Black man's burden." Through artificially low wages resulting from "job reservation," the repression of non-White trade unions, restrictions on labour mobility, and other measures, the non-White worker subsidizes White industry, and contributes heavily to the high living standards of the Europeans. . . .

The fourth source of racial tension and extralegal control of the non-Whites by the government comes from the intimidatory role of the police and army. In the last few years the police and Defence Force are being reorganized and reinforced, in part to crush any internal disorders. Since 1960 the size of the Permanent Defence Force has increased from 9,019 to 15,288 men, exclusive of some 10,000 army reservists on active duty at any given time. . . . The military budget nearly trebled between 1961 and 1964 (from £40,000,000 to £104,000,000), making it the largest of any African state.[25] . . .

While the stage of large-scale terrorism has not yet been reached, the police is deliberately used as an instrument of intimidation and harassment of the African population. Under the cover of enforcing the pass and liquor regulations, the police constantly raids African locations at

[25] *Africa Report* 9 (January, 1964), p. 18; and *Africa Today* 11 (March, 1964), p. 6. Interestingly, the 1964 military budget is approximately as large as the sum proposed by the Tomlinson Commission for the development of the "Bantu homelands" over a ten-year period.

night, and carries out systematic house searches and mass arrests. . . . On the basis of official crime statistics, I would conservatively estimate that one African adult man out of three is arrested and convicted of an offence each year. Over the years few urban African men have escaped imprisonment for purely technical offences against discriminatory laws. The police arrest an average of 3000 Africans *a day*.

.   .   .

In short, in a country where the law-making and law-enforcing process has become a major means of political oppression, it is difficult for Africans to dissociate authority from its abuse, or "law and order" from the *status quo*. Denying any legitimacy to the state, the average African has basically the same negative attitude to law and law-enforcement as the psychopath or the criminal. . . .

The fifth and last type of extralegal discrimination would deserve a book by itself, and we can only deal with it very cursorily here. It concerns the private behaviour and attitudes of Whites towards non-Whites, or, in other words, the day-to-day race relations.[26] White colour prejudice is, of course, at the root of the racial conflict in South Africa. Legislation and the whole state apparatus reflect accurately the attitudes of the dominant White group. At the same time, however, official segregation and discrimination reinforce the already existing prejudices, and make for further increases in private discrimination. Private and public racialisms are thus the two mutually reinforcing elements in a vicious circle of ever deepening racial conflict.

.   .   .

. . . Where there is no legal provision for segregation, the "customary" colour-bar sets in to prevent egalitarian contact. Where such contact is unavoidable, the Whites expect and receive preferential treatment, such as being served first in shops. In other words, the potentially equal relationship of co-customer is made unequal by racial discrimination.

In general, "customary" discrimination and segregation (which the Whites often term "voluntary") have preceded and exceeded, by far, legal apartheid. . . . The presence of the "customary" colour-bar has led many English-speaking Whites to criticize apartheid laws as "unnecessary." Indeed, for most practical purposes, many of the apartheid laws

[26] I have dealt at greater length with this topic in *Caneville: The Social Structure of a South African Town* (Middletown, Conn.: Wesleyan University Press, 1964); and in "Race Attitudes in Durban, South Africa," *Journal of Social Psychology* 57 (1962), pp. 55-72. See also I. D. MacCrone, *Group Conflicts and Race Prejudice* (Johannesburg: South African Institute, 1947); H. Kuper, *The Uniform of Colour* (Johannesburg: Witwatersrand University Press, 1947); Thomas F. Pettigrew, "Social Distance Attitudes of South African Students," *Social Forces* 38 (1960), pp. 246-253; and Alan Paton, *Cry the Beloved Country*, 1948.

simply rigidified the *status quo,* and were intended to eliminate a few aberrant exceptions to customary apartheid, or to prevent organized campaigns by multiracial organizations from breaking down "voluntary" segregation. . . . The few liberal Whites are not only compelled to comply with apartheid laws if they want to stay out of gaol; they are also viewed as "quite mad," or, worse, traitors to their "race," if they transgress the colour *mores* of the White group. Many non-Europeans also regard the behaviour of White liberals as suspicious because it is unusual, and question the motives of such Europeans. At the same time, because his behaviour is not allowed to be consistent with his principles, the liberal White suffers under a constant burden of guilt.

Government policy towards the Coloureds and the Indians explodes whatever rationalizations the Nationalists have devised to defend apartheid. Apartheid, we are told, aims at the development of distinct ethnic groups, conscious of their cultural identity and eager to retain it. This development is to take the political form of ethnic nationalism, in that each of these ethnic groups is to constitute a "self-governing" nation-state, a "Bantustan." Verwoerd's "new deal" for the Africans has some superficial similarities with the above principles, and these have led some analysts to interpret apartheid as a move away from White domination and towards the political recognition of ethnic pluralism.

In my estimation, the Nationalist policy towards the Indians and Coloureds utterly refutes this interpretation. The Coloureds, as we have seen, are not an ethnic group in any sense of the word. If ethnicity were the criterion for separate development, then the "Coloureds" would become identified with either Afrikaans- or English-speaking South Africans. As to the Indians, apart from the fact that many of them are strongly Anglicized, they belong to five main traditional language groups, and to two main religions. In the case of both Indians and Coloureds, the criterion of group definition is obviously not ethnicity, but whatever nebulous concept the dominant group has of "race." The fiction of apartheid as envisaging territorial partition between ethnic groups is also exploded by the government's Coloured and Indian policy. The "national homelands" of these two groups have even less reality than in the case of the impoverished Native Reserves; they consist of hundreds of little ghettos termed "group areas." Any interpretation of apartheid other than that of a system of oppression and segregation based on race clearly conflicts with objective evidence.

XIII

In colonial South America three different policies of Spanish dominance were practiced: in some states the colonists exterminated Indians; in others, Indians, retaining some of their customs and social organization, were incorporated into the colony; and in a third group they were assimilated into a Spanish culture. These colonial policies set up the racial groups which interact in contemporary Latin America, and establish the basis for three styles of race relations today.

Skin color is not an important fact in any of these groups of states; instead, culture, as defined by language, custom, and place of residence, divides people. The persistence of severely disadvantaged Indian and Mestizo groups in such a system can only be explained in cultural and historic terms.

RALPH L. BEALS

Indian-Mestizo-White Relations
In Spanish America

The varied and complex patterns of race relations in the numerous nations of Spanish America and the incompleteness of existing data preclude a definitive and comprehensive analysis of the area. In this paper, the

From *Race Relations in World Perspective*, edited by Andrew Lind (Honolulu, Hawaii: University of Hawaii Press, 1955), pp. 412-432. Reprinted by permission of the author and the publisher.

Spanish-speaking countries of the Caribbean, Cuba, and Santo Domingo are excluded from consideration, partly for lack of data, partly because the race relations problems of these countries are Negro-mulatto-white relationships. Negro-mulatto-white relationships also have importance, often primary importance, in some of the mainland countries about the Caribbean, but for reasons of time and space are not considered in this paper.

SOURCES AND APPROACH

Despite the large amount of literature on Latin America, relatively little is useful for the analysis of race relations. The major sources of information come from tribal and community studies carried on by anthropologists, and from historical sources. Census data, as will be shown, are of little use for most countries, while sociological writing in most cases is nonempirical. Consequently, the author has in part relied upon personal observation and upon oral information.[1] Statements made in this paper are, in part, intuitive and must certainly be regarded as tentative.

Finally, even if wholly adequate theoretical frameworks were available in the field of race relations, the accessible empirical data lend themselves better to descriptive than to analytical treatment. Basically, the author of this paper views race relations as special cases of socio-cultural relationships which may not be studied in isolation from the more general phenomena of individual and group interaction. In this view, culture contact or social differentiation — to take only two examples — are basic areas of study which in some cases acquire the special dimension of race relations when real or *imagined* biological differences between groups are invoked by one or more of the groups under study to explain or justify sociocultural or behavioral differences, either between groups of differing cultures (in the case of culture contact) or groups of different social statuses or roles (in the case of social differentiation). Real or visible biological differences, it is suggested, may have more persistent effect upon social relationships than imaginary differences. The Latin American data, descriptive though they are, permit casting within this framework even though methodological rigor and fine discriminations must await more sophisticated and directed field studies.

LATIN AMERICA AS A LABORATORY

Latin America as a whole presents an important laboratory of race relations. For more than four hundred years people of mixed European origins have been in contact with American Indians of mixed, but predominantly Mongoloid, stock. Initially the two groups possessed markedly visible dif-

---

[1] I wish also to acknowledge the help of my assistant, Agnes Bierman, in assembling the data for this paper.

ferences in biological character as well as quite distinctive cultures. At the outset, then, there existed race contact as well as cultural contact, and for a brief time it might be argued that a true race problem existed. However, the nature of the *relations* between the two racial groups was determined even from the very first by the cultural and social equipment each group brought to the encounter. This view, if space permitted, could be amply documented by comparison of Spanish behavior with different groups as Spanish culture changed through time, or in the differing patterns that emerged as the Spanish encountered Indians of significantly different culture. The extermination of the Indians in parts of Spanish America versus the development of mixed societies elsewhere was not a function of "Indianness" or "non-Indianness" but of the differences in the Indian societies and in the experience and purposes of the Spanish at given times and places.

After the initial contact, relations between the two groups varied, although the white has been predominantly the invader, the conqueror, and the ruler throughout the area. Nevertheless, both genetic and cultural intermixture has taken place at varying rates throughout the period. From a biological point of view, then, we have three major groupings: the population of European ancestry, that of Indian ancestry, and a mixed group. Social and cultural significances attached to these biological facts have differed markedly in time and from country to country, as I shall endeavor to show. At the present time, biological significance tends to be attached to socially determined groupings rather than the converse.

The countries of mainland Spanish America fall roughly into three groups with respect to race relations problems: Group 1. Argentina, Chile, Costa Rica, and Uruguay, countries in which Indians are virtually absent or form insignificant distinct minorities. The majority group tends to regard itself as predominantly European in biological origin. Group 2. Colombia, Honduras, Nicaragua, Panama, El Salvador, and Venezuela, countries in which the Indian is numerically of relatively small importance but which recognize a strong mestizo component in the population. (In most of these countries, Negro and mulatto elements are more numerous than Indian and mestizo elements, especially in lowland coastal sections.) Group 3. Bolivia, Ecuador, Guatemala, Mexico, Paraguay, and Peru, countries in which the Indians as a distinct entity are numerous, and which also recognize a large mestizo class.

THE "EUROPEAN" COUNTRIES: SOLUTION BY FICTION

Our information is scantiest for countries from Group 1; nevertheless these countries are of considerable interest in view of the failure of biological realities to coincide with social interpretations. Consequently they represent one of the several types of adjustment to a situation of racial contact and racial mixture.

Argentina is of particular interest in this respect, for contemporary Argentinians tend to take pride in the biological purity of their European ancestry as well as to consider Argentina to be the "purest" representative of Spanish culture in the New World. Nationalism is high and expresses itself in antagonism toward North European culture, especially the United States version. Other countries in the Americas are looked down upon because of their racial mixture, with particular scorn being reserved for Brazil, which is frequently referred to as being a "country of Niggers." (At least, this was a common remark made to me by Argentinians in 1949 when they learned I had just come from Brazil.) The biological facts, on the other hand, are quite different.

It is quite true that the contemporary Indian population in Argentina is small. Except for the Andean region, the aboriginal Indian population was nonfarming and was relatively less dense than in many other Spanish American countries. Throughout much of Argentine history, extermination of the nomadic and unexploitable simple farmers seems to have been the informal if not the official policy. The sources dealing with the origins of the Argentina population have been reviewed by Carl C. Taylor.[2] The most careful estimates seem to be those of Ingenieros, who for 1700 estimated a population for Argentina of 600,000, divided as follows: 3,000 pure white; 50,000 mixed (i.e., mestizos); 530,000 Indians; 7,000 Negroes; 10,000 mulattoes. For 1800 he estimates a population of 720,000, as follows: 9,000 white; 421,000 mestizos; 210,000 Indians; 20,000 Negroes; 60,000 mulattoes. For 1852 the estimated total is 810,000, as follows: 22,000 white; 563,000 mestizos; 100,000 Indians; 15,000 Negroes; 110,000 mulattoes. The following years marked the beginning of the period of heavy European immigration into Argentina, and by the time of the first systematic census in 1869, the following classfication is made by Ingenieros: 350,000 white; 1,315,000 mestizos; 3,000 Indians; 15,000 Negroes; 120,000 mulattoes.

The few figures cited indicate that the Argentine image of the biological origins of the population is quite inaccurate. Before the period of heavy European immigration it is clear that the Argentine population was predominantly mixed, with the Indian and Negro elements being genetically more important than the European. "Old stock" Argentinians — i.e., people descended from inhabitants before about 1850 — are typically mestizos or mulattoes or some combination of the two. Biologically, therefore, Argentina is by no means of Spanish derivation, although its culture is.

[2] Carl C. Taylor, *Rural Life in Argentina* (Baton Rouge: Louisiana State University Press, 1948).

Argentina, then, represents an extreme example of one solution to race relations problems — namely, denying that race differences exist internally. A myth of racial homogeneity and purity has been created and accepted. Attention to the falsity of the myth is diverted by extreme nationalism, and strong anti-Semitic, anti-Negro, anti-Indian, anti-Anglo-American sentiments. These views are strongly held not only by the man in the street but also by some Peronist "socialist scientists" in the universities.

Similar historical information is not available for Uruguay, Chile, and Costa Rica. In Uruguay demographic development apparently was very similar to that in Argentina. In Chile and Costa Rica, the proportion of early Spanish settlers may have been somewhat higher and the proportion of Negroes somewhat lower, while recent European immigration has been comparatively much less or nearly absent (in the case of Costa Rica). Nevertheless, the bulk of the population by the end of colonial times was probably mestizo. There is somewhat more tendency to recognize this fact in Chile, and perhaps in Costa Rica. But, generally, the essential homogeneity of the population biologically is accepted, but without a nationalistic and race-conscious accompaniment.

Countries in Group 2 generally recognize the predominantly mestizo character of the population. Upper-class families may emphasize the purity of their European ancestry and tend to monopolize wealth, particularly in terms of large landholdings. Despite the existence of strongly defined class barriers, there is political participation by, and in some cases economic equality for, mestizos. It is true that lower-class positions are occupied primarily by mestizos and that upper-class families tend to claim European origin. Even when class conflict is sharp, or class exclusiveness strong, however, there seems little tendency to interpret these in biological terms.

In these same countries the recognized Indian population is still essentially tribal or communal in its living patterns. While the Indians are by some regarded as a nuisance, and by others as groups to be exploited, national policy increasingly tends to regard them as a national responsibility, requiring special attention and care. Insofar as the Indian is considered a problem, the Group 2 countries reflect, in less marked degree, the problems of the countries in Group 3.

THE "INDIAN" COUNTRIES: CHARACTER AND HISTORY

Countries in Group 3 present the most important and instructive problems. Sizable Indian populations, large numbers of mestizos, and recognizable white populations exist in each. It is with them that the remainder of the paper will be concerned.

Although the countries included in Group 3 possess certain characteristics in common, there is nevertheless a wide difference in race relations in the countries under consideration. The most significant common element is the recognition of the existence of separate Indian, mestizo, and white groups. The Indian in some measure is regarded as a group apart from the remainder of the national society, although attitudes toward this separation and the isolated group may vary. The mestizo group is generally regarded as intermediate and approximating the characteristics of the European group and of European culture, although attitudes toward the mestizo group vary considerably. The most marked and significant differences are concerned with the degree to which the Indian (and sometimes the mestizo) is regarded as biologically inferior, or to be indefinitely isolated from other groups, in contrast with countries where efforts are made to incorporate the Indian into full participation in the national culture.

Historically, in Latin America contradictory tendencies have been operative since the first European contacts. To the bulk of the colonists from Spain in the New World, the Indian was a legitimate object of exploitation. If he had the wealth, it was proper to take it from him. If his lands were desirable he should be dispossessed or converted into a rural proletariat, or, if not amenable to this procedure, he should be enslaved or exterminated.

In contrast, the Spanish Crown and the Spanish bureaucracy saw in the large Indian population an opportunity to create additional Spanish citizens. The restrictions placed upon land grants, such as the *encomienda*, or the *repartimiento* in its various forms, were designed to require the holder of these special temporary rights to prepare the Indian for Spanish citizenship. The efficacy of these efforts in colonial times is suggested by the disappearance of distinct Indian populations in many areas of the *encomienda* in Mexico and other countries.

A third trend was represented by the humanistic movement within the Catholic Church, which saw in the American Indian an opportunity for saving souls and for creating a stronghold of Christianity. In Mexico efforts were made to isolate the mission-controlled Indian from European culture by teaching in the native languages. Ideally, the Indian was to learn only such parts of the European culture as met with the approval of the Church. While some charges of exploitation leveled against the missionary establishments may be true, nevertheless there were many Utopian efforts to establish ideal Christian communities.[3] It is significant, moreover, that the heavy concentrations of surviving Indian groups today tend to be in areas once primarily under the domination of missionary orders.

One major problem requiring analysis in Spanish America is the degree

[3] For example, see Silvio Zavala, La *"Utopia" de Tomas Moro en la Nueva España y Otros Estudios* (Mexico, 1937), on Bishop Quiroga in Michoacan.

to which the Indian, the mestizo, and the white are defined in biological terms, and the extent to which definitions have reality. A second major consideration is the degree to which the cultural and social patterns involving these three groups operate on the basis of biological criteria and the extent to which they operate by social and cultural criteria. Put another way, we may ask, to what extent are social relationships determined by ideas of biological differences and to what extent are these differences real or imagined?

Historically, the attitudes toward Indian and mestizo have undergone several transformations. Comparison of the various stages with other contact and colonization situations might contribute to generalization. Initially, virtually all the Spanish coming to the New World were males who sought their sexual gratification among native women. In those regions where the Spanish conqueror encountered a highly stratified society, similar in many respects to his own, legal intermarriage was frequent in the native higher class levels. Many of the lieutenants of Cortez, for example, married women of the native nobility. In many cases, as with the daughters of Montezuma, the legal marriage implied rise in social status for the males, many of whom were of lower-class origin. It is also true that many of the women possessed, or were believed to possess, valuable landed properties.

THE SHIFT FROM RACE TO CLASS

With the increase in numbers of European women in the New World, and particularly with the growing conflict between the colonial Creole and the Spanish-born official, legal marriage between Indian and white was prohibited. Racial exclusiveness also developed in Spain with the expulsion or forced conversion to Christianity of the Moors and the Jews. In the New World, sexual contacts between European men and Indian women continued, but were now unauthorized and irregular in all cases.

The rigid separation and efforts to maintain purity of European lines soon became confined to only a few aristocratic family lines. Initially, efforts to classify the population rigidly on the basis of ancestry seemed feasible when only Negroes, Indians, whites, and first-generation hybrids were concerned. But with the appearance of trihybrids and backcrosses in the second-generation hybrids, terminology began to elaborate unconscionably. Moreover, despite efforts to establish distinctive dress and occupations for each hybrid type, a virtually continuous hybrid sequence developed which made identification of ancestry impossible. The forgery and sale of *fueros de sangre* by venal officials likewise made the *limpieza de sangre* requirements meaningless, not only in the colonies but at home too.

Yet, if Pimentel documents the racist attitudes in colonial and Republican Mexico, both he and the predecessors he cites are evidence of an eloquent opposition. For example:

> See what the Bishop of Michoacan as early as 1799 counseled the King of Spain. . . . "Eliminate the odious personal tribute; cease the outrage to justice created by laws unfair to people of color; declare them capable of occupying all civil employment that does not require a special title of nobility."[4]

Efforts to maintain distinctions on a biological basis soon vanished. The terms of classification used were reduced in number and increasingly reflected cultural and social characteristics. This situation is well described by Kubler, who says:

> In Peru the quantitative relationships between Indian and non-Indian groups have long been governed by the processes of caste formation and caste recruitment. "Racial" criteria intervene only by verbal confusion, when the biological terms of everyday usage such as "Indian" and "Mestizo" are made to perform double duty as terms denoting class status. Throughout the past century and a half in Peru, people have said "Indian" when they meant "rural proletariat." They said "Mestizo" when they meant the small farmer, the artisan, the industrial laborer, or the number of other low-income groups not attached to the land.[5]

Kubler's statement is perhaps oversimplified, but it has some measure of applicability throughout most of Spanish America.

PARALLEL CULTURES

John Gillin and others have pointed out in Mexico and Guatemala — and the Andean countries of South America might be added — the existence of parallel cultures, which are usually identified as Indian and are predominantly Indian in the biological sense as well. For the most part, such cultures exist either as tribal groups, or, more commonly, as village communities. Such communities in Mexico and Central America fall roughly into three types: (a) communities almost exclusively Indian, for example, Cherán in Michoacan;[6] (b) mixed mestizo and Indian communities in which the two groups maintain reciprocal relationships but have distinctive socio-cultural patterns (several of these have been

---

[4] Francisco Pimentel, *Memoria sobre las causas que ban originado la situacion actual de la raza indigena de Mexico* (Mexico, 1864), p. 195.

[5] George Kubler, *The Indian Caste of Peru, 1795-1940,* Institute of Social Anthropology Publication No. 14 (Washington, D.C.: Smithsonian Institution, 1952), p. 36.

[6] See Ralph L. Beals, *Cheran: A Sierra Tarascan Village,* Institute of Social Anthropology Publication No. 2 (Washington, D.C.: Smithsonian Institution, 1946).

described, for example, Gillin,[7] or Tumin[8]); (c) mestizo or Ladino communities constituting a political or economic center surrounded by satellite Indian communities.

Economically, the Indian communities produce most of the food consumed and participate only to a very limited extent in the market economy, even in situations where the Indians exist as renters or workers on land owned by the mestizo or Ladino. Such communities are relatively homogeneous and lack class differentiation. Each possesses its own social and political controls and religious ceremonial system, usually organized in hierarchical status positions open to anyone willing to make the effort and economic sacrifice to achieve them. Often the individual progresses by a series of regular steps, and by old age has achieved the highest possible status in the community. As Gillin's analysis points out, such a parallel culture may be far more gratifying to the members than is the culture of the mestizo or the Ladino to him.

In contrast, the Ladino participates in a larger society whose major orientations and goals are set in the urban centers of political power. He exists in a class-stratified society which also sets obstacles to his vertical movement within the larger society, both economically and status-wise. He is in a far more economically competitive situation; and wealth, family, and other factors over which the individual has little control tend to determine status and achievement.

To this situation also the term *caste* has been applied, notably by Gillin and Tumin. Without discussing the appropriateness of the term, within the restricted area in which a member of an Indian community normally exists, he is a part of a relatively self-contained system; however gratifying this system may be to its members, it occupies a low status position within the national society. The significant point, perhaps, is to what extent movement out of the parallel culture is restricted in terms of racial characteristics.

Gillin and Tumin, for the community they studied in Guatemala, apparently find it virtually impossible for the Indian to move into mestizo culture and to be accepted within the confines of the village. However, it is possible for the Indian who leaves his home community in Guatemala to transfer his position, providing his origin is not known in the new community.

Roberts, comparing the work of Gillin and Tumin on the one hand,

---

[7] John Gillin, *The Culture of Security in San Carlos,* Middle American Research Institute Publication No. 16 (New Orleans: The Tulane University of Louisiana, 1951).

[8] Melvin M. Tumin, *Caste in a Peasant Society: A Case Study in the Dynamics of Caste* (Princeton: Princeton University Press, 1952).

and of Robert Redfield and Sol Tax on the other, concludes that in Guatemala the caste situation is not universal.[9] The same conclusions are expressed in Tax.[10] The parallel cultures in all cases are noncompetitive to a considerable degree; they are integrated into a reciprocal relationship creating a degree of interdependence; and, while the Indian occupies and generally accepts a socially subordinate position, his culture provides sufficient gratifications that he is able to accept the situation with a minimum of resentment. In such communities as that studied by Gillin and Tumin, the Indian apparently is regarded as biologically inferior and cannot move into Ladino status; in communities studied by Redfield and Tax, the Indian is regarded as socially inferior and he is criticized, not for incapacity, but for failure to adopt Ladino ways. A measure of social mobility, consequently, is possible.

MEXICO: INDIAN POPULATION

In Mexico the situation seems more complex. Whetten points out that a considerable part of the Mexican population is indistinguishable from the Indian except in terms of self-definition.[11] The Indian lives in a community which is distinguished often by special dress, by participation in a distinct social organization, and, most importantly, by the primary use of a language other than Spanish. In other cases the dress is sufficiently similar and the physical characteristics so indistinguishable, that community affiliation, language, and self-definition are virtually the only bases for identifying the individual as Indian. In such areas whole communities may gradually shift through time from being regarded as Indian to being regarded as mestizo. This is certainly true of many of the communities in the general Tarascan area where all stages in the process may be observed.[12] Parenthetically, it is of interest that part of the process is the marrying of land-owning Indian women by mestizo or white men, just as in the early contact period.

The vagueness of the term *Indian* is particularly marked when purely objective material culture traits are used as criteria, as has been the case in a number of national censuses, particularly in Mexico. Many mestizos then become indistinguishable from Indians. Whetten calls this group "Indian-colonial." Other writers have used the term "Indian-mestizo culture." Whetten points out that by following the objective cultural criteria

[9] Robert E. T. Roberts, "A Comparison of Ethnic Relations in Two Guatemalan Communities," *Acta Americana* VI (1948), 135-151.

[10] Sol Tax *et al.*, *Heritage of Conquest* (Glencoe: Free Press, 1952).

[11] Nathan L. Whetten, *Rural Mexico* (Chicago: University of Chicago Press, 1948).

[12] See Tax, *op. cit.*, pp. 94 ff., for a discussion along similar lines of the problem of defining the Indian.

used by the 1940 census, 51.2 per cent of the total population of Mexico are found to be living on the Indian-colonial level.[13]

Nevertheless some distinction is made in Mexico between Whetten's Indian-colonial group and the recognized, or named, Indian. The Indian-colonials are a rural group in the main, and are regarded as lower-class. Assignment to this class, however, is purely on the basis of certain living habits and economic status. The parallel cultures of the Indian, on the other hand, represent either tribal or community-organized groups, self-identified in some measure, and offering self-contained social systems with their internal status and prestige mechanisms.

Attitudes toward identifiable Indians or Indian groups differ considerably in various parts of Mexico. However, the Indian who changes his way of life and no longer self-identifies as an Indian has relatively little difficulty in moving into at least the rural Indomestizo or colonial category. If he stays in the same locality it may take at least two or three generations until his Indian ancestry is forgotten, but very rarely is such a distinction really made on a racial basis.

Clearly, for the Indian to move into the rural mestizo culture involves mainly ceasing to speak the Indian language and ceasing to participate in the parallel social system. The basic patterns of subsistence and material culture change very little.

For the Indian who goes to the city in Mexico, the changes may be even less marked in some respects, for by definition a factory worker in Mexico is not an Indian. This seems to be regardless of whether he still speaks an Indian language or what his physical appearance may be.[14] Or, as the late Miguel O. Mendizabal once remarked to me, when an Indian can talk Spanish reasonably well, wears store-bought clothes, and has *n* number of pesos, he ceases to be an Indian.

It would be an error if I have created the impression that in Mexico Indians are not looked down upon and discriminated against by non-Indians. It is important, however, to recognize that in Mexico biological terminology is applied to culturally defined groups, for a given Indian may actually be more European in ancestry than is his mestizo counterpart. Rather, the classifications are based upon linguistic habits, self-identifications, community affiliations, and ways of living. It is further important to recognize that changes in these socio-cultural determinants result in a change of classification, although in many places — and apparently this is far more generally true in Guatemala — the individual may have to leave the community where he is known in order to make this transition.

Thus far the discussion of Mexico has concerned itself primarily with Indian-mestizo relationships. If we turn to the position of the mestizo

[13] Whetten, *op. cit.*, p. 361.
[14] Cf. Wilbur E. Moore, *Industrialization and Labor* (Ithaca: Cornell University Press, 1953).

group versus the European group, great changes have taken place in recent years. Officially Mexico regards itself as a mestizo country. The relatively few individuals who claim purely European ancestry are frequently from old families which often have conveniently forgotten an Indian ancestor in early colonial times. Such attitudes are confined to a relatively powerless remnant of prerevolutionary aristocracy. The holders of political power today are mainly mestizos, and reputed possession of some degree of Indian ancestry has long been a political asset in Mexico. The "mestizo problem" exists only for those few families who attempt to maintain the purity of a European-derived lineage, and a few intellectuals who confuse the results of biological mixture with the disorganization resulting from rapid urbanization and industrialization and mixed cultural heritages. Such literature is not of great significance in Mexico today.

MEXICO: FROM RACE TO CLASS

There are marked social divisions in Mexico, which are sometimes described in pseudobiological terms. These divisions clearly are class-derived, however, and consist of the dichotomies between urban and rural, and between the upper class and the proletariat in the city. Perhaps the clearest indication of attitudes emerges from a study of Mexican national students in the United States university. Virtually all Mexican students are disturbed by discrimination against the Negro in the United States. When asked about discrimination against people of Mexican origin in the United States, the almost invariable reply is that such people are of lower-class origin and, of course, would be discriminated against in Mexico as well. And, while "Indian" may be an epithet hurled at a lower-class person, "barbarian," "brute," "animal," "pig," and, above all, "goat," are more common.

The present situation in Mexico is by no means of long standing. Rather, it represents an aspect of the ideological and social transformations stemming from the revolution of 1910-1916. Clark, speaking of prerevolutionary Mexico, remarks that "the racial inferiority of the Indian and the mestizo had been for centuries an accepted fact."[15] When pseudo-industrialization began under the prerevolutionary Diaz regime, every effort was made to preserve the worker in the status he had occupied in the non-industrial society, i.e., to preserve the essentially feudal relationships of the colonial and agrarian economy and social structure.

Clark cites Pimentel to show the tendency to link Indian and mestizo:

> A portion of the native race is completely free, but another portion groans in slavery. In various parts of the country the workers on the

[15] Marjorie R. Clark, *Organized Labor in Mexico* (Chapel Hill: University of North Carolina Press, 1934), p. 4.

> *haciendas* are debtors to their masters for varying amounts and they
> cannot move to another location until they have paid. . . . . Even
> in the Capital the same system is employed with the workers in the
> bakeries, who never leave the workshops except to go to mass, al-
> ways accompanied by an overseer who does not leave them out of
> sight.[16]

The prerevolutionary attitudes, nevertheless, may have been confined primarily to the then controlling aristocracy. Taylor has described conditions
in a Mexican rural community predominantly Spanish in origin.[17] Arandas
in Jalisco was established in 1768 by a group of Spanish settlers with some
Indian and Negro servants and slaves. In the following six years, 69 per
cent of the children baptized were Spanish, 14 per cent mestizo, 10 per
cent mulatto, and the balance Indian or other mixtures. Data less than
half a century later show that between May 17, 1802, and May 16, 1906,
despite a strong tendency for Spanish to marry Spanish, more than half of
the marriages of other groups were mixed, and nearly half of the Spanish-
mestizo marriages were of mestizo men to Spanish women. Assuredly no
very strong prejudices could have existed then.

Taylor nevertheless records a persisting feeling of superiority on the part
of those with Spanish ancestry and a high value placed on light or white
skin. On the other hand, he presents as typical a quotation from a man of
Spanish ancestry:

> There is almost no mixing with Indians here; we are of the *raza*
> Espanola. But there is not race prejudice. Although of the white race,
> the people do not regard with prejudice the people who are *in-
> digenas*. There is a more universal spirit here — more a spirit of
> social distinction and class than of race. There is no prejudice here,
> we are all Mexicans — but individuals.
>
> The Spaniards came here with their families, they married with the
> *indigenas* but very little, because few *indigenas* were here; not because
> of race prejudice.[18]

The extent to which racial criteria are being rejected could be documented from many other sources. Typical is the insistency of the
demographers Leon and Alvaro that discussion of population quality
must be confined to purely socio-cultural factors such as educational
levels attained.[19] One of the few serious attempts to analyze race character-

---

[16] Pimentel, *op. cit.*, pp. 202-203.

[17] Paul Schuster Taylor, *A Spanish-Mexican Peasant Community: Arandas in
Jalisco, Mexico. Ibero-Americana*, Vol. IV (Berkeley: University of California
Press, 1933).

[18] *Ibid.*, p. 20.

[19] Alberto P. Leon and Aldama C. Alvaro, "Population Problems in Central
and Caribbean America," *The Annals* 237 (January, 1945), 34-44.

istics in relation to social differentiation merely underscores the relative meaninglessness of racial criteria in Mexico.

Williams[20] classified 828 rural Yucatecans (Yucatan, Mexico) on the basis of metrical and morphological characteristics into five groups ranging from most Indian to least Indian. He then correlated these groups with occupations according to prestige. Indians predominated in the low-prestige occupations of farmer or farm laborer, but this being a rural area, 58.9 per cent of the least Indian group were also farmers or farm laborers. In high-prestige occupations the most Indian group was almost unrepresented. No evidence is given to show whether lack of Indian representation results from exclusion or from adherence to differing traditional values or parallel culture orientations, for Williams' prestige rating of occupations is entirely culture-bound; i.e., it reflects the evaluations of European culture.

Williams also found a positive tendency, strongest on the *hacienda*, for light-skinned men to marry light-skinned women. With the break-up of the large estates in Yucatan in recent years one may suspect this difference is less marked. Williams gives no data on conditions in the cities where skin-color discrimination may be stronger. However, neither from Williams nor from other sources do we find evidence that strongly Indian appearance is a bar to upward social mobility, unless coupled with low social status of parents or with adherence to Indian cultural behavior. One exception probably is entry into the elite "forty families" of Merida, a group declining in power and whose exclusiveness even in marriage is crumbling. Some very distinguished Yucatecans of recent years have claimed to be of pure Maya ancestry and evidence could be presented for the existence of an inverse racism among some Maya groups.

To summarize, in Mexico discrimination as a rule is based upon class criteria, and, despite the use of biological terminology at times, fundamentally people are differentiated in terms of socio-cultural participation and not by racial criteria. The only partial exceptions to this are the homogeneous Indian communities, and it is clearly possible for the Indian to move out of his classification by a change of residence, or even for whole communities over time to lose their Indian character. Guatemala is similar, despite the more caste-like character of the situation. Even in the markedly rigid situation described by Gillin and Tumin, individuals are able to emerge from the Indian classification by changing residence and their socio-cultural behavior.

Fragmentary materials from elsewhere in Central America seem to support the class nature of conflict situations or inequitable distribution of wealth and power. Smith describes El Salvador as being 92.3 per cent Mestizo (according to the 1930 census), 5.6 per cent Indian, and only

[20] George Dee Williams, *Maya-Spanish Crosses in Yucatan*. Papers of the Peabody Museum of American Archaeology and Ethnology, Harvard University, Vol. XIII, No. 1 (Cambridge: Harvard University Press, 1931).

2.1 per cent white. Most land is owned by the whites who grow coffee, renting small areas to mestizos to raise the necessary food crops. In cultural characteristics the mestizos conform closely to the Indo-colonial pattern described for Mexico. No data are available on the position of the Indian, but Smith's analysis suggests strongly that El Salvador has a feudal-type social structure and that the historical accident of a total conquest by Europeans with aristocratic traditions accounts for the dominance of the white group rather than contemporary ideas of racial inferiority.[21]

THE ANDEAN COUNTRIES: RACE OR CLASS.

The Andean countries of South America — Ecuador, Peru, and Bolivia — are much less well-documented and studied than are Mexico and Guatemala. Most observers, however, feel that differentiations between Indian, mestizo, and European groups are much more strongly defined and rigidly enforced in this area. This is particularly true of Peru. Here again, however, the realities, in part at least, are socio-cultural rather than racial.

The 1940 census classes slightly more than 40 per cent of the population of Peru as Indian. In the main, people are classed as Indian by census-takers who often exercise rather individual criteria. In general terms, the Indian is identified by community affiliation and by language, dress, and economic status. Often he lives in separate communities with parallel social structures, much as in Mexico and Guatemala, which provide status ladders for members of the community based upon achievement rather than through class membership.

The Andean area also varies from Mexico and Guatemala in that numerous rural mestizo groups are as clearly defined in terms of community affiliation, distinctive costume, and other cultural attributes as are the Indian communities. The urban mestizo is less distinct but, especially in Peru, social and economic control tends to be firmly held by an upper class which claims European ancestry. For example, in the past relatively rigid barriers to the rise of mestizos above certain levels in government service have existed, a marked contrast to the predominantly mestizo control of government in Mexico.

Attitudes toward the Indian, and to some extent the rural Cholo (mestizo) class, in Peru today are not dissimilar to those existing in Mexico before the 1910-1920 revolution. Both in word and act it is clear that many Peruvians of the upper class, and even urban mestizo individuals, tend to regard the Indian as non-human. The Indian, therefore, may be exploited as mercilessly as one might exploit a mule. These comments are in part based on personal contacts and observation and have been

---

[21] T. Lynn Smith, "Notes on Population and Rural Social Organization in El Salvador," *Rural Sociology* IV (1945), 359-379.

little documented, but studies such as those of Castro Pozo in Peru[22] and Buitron in Ecuador,[23] indicate these attitudes.

Despite the strength of "racial" discrimination in the Andean countries, however, the actual criteria, again, are primarily socio-cultural, and the barriers are not impassable. Kubler points out that in 1586 Indians in Peru constituted approximately 95 per cent of the population. Except for a brief period between 1826 and 1854 there has been a steady decline in the percentage of Indian population in Peru. To suggest, however, that this is due to biological causes is untenable; rather, it has been due to "passing." As Kubler remarks:

> The evidence we have is that Peruvian population composition is a social process and not a biological one. In the course of this process the two dominant castes exchanged positions of dominance and increase at irregular and unpredictable intervals in the recent past, and in unexpected magnitudes. The governing factors in the process are probably economic and ideological, and in no case biological, where caste is involved. It is not unlikely that among the conditions favoring Indian increase and dominance are local conditions of economic disintegration and impoverishment and geographical isolation. Also relevant is the need of a society approaching industrialization, for a large reserve of cheap and rootless labor. Intervening here, a romantic ideology of Indian rural existence has the paradoxical and unintended effect of hardening the caste boundaries between the Indian and the Mestizo. Such is the literary, artistic, and political movement of "indigenismo" in Twentieth-century Peru, which, by lamenting and publicizing Indian dispossession and Indian misery, reenergized a racial concept of Indian status instead of dispelling it.[24]

Kubler's analysis suggests that in the colonial period, passing was actually more rapid than in republican times. This was particularly true in the period shortly preceding the independence movement, when the government apparently became increasingly liberal in permitting people to move from Indian to mestizo status and, hence, escape the tribute exacted of the Indian. This was a move to gain a wider basis of support in the obviously approaching struggle between the Crown Government and the Criollo class. In the republican period, a temporary reversal of trend occurred with the removal of the protective attitudes of the Spanish Crown and its officers toward the Indian.

It is, perhaps, too early to assess the effect of industrialization in the last

[22] Hildebrando Castro Pozo, *Nuestra Comunidad Indigena* (Lima: 1924).
[23] Anibal Buitron and Barbara Salisbury Buitron, *Condiciones de Vida y Trabajo del Campesino de la Provincia de Pichincha* (Quito: Instituto Nacional de Prevision, 1947).
[24] Kubler, *op. cit.*, pp. 65-66.

few decades in Peru, but there has been a large movement of Indians into the urban environment. In part this movement is an attempt to escape from the disadvantages of being classed as Indian, and it seems certain that, in large measure, migrants ultimately merge with the urban proletariat. That the full effect of this may not be entirely understood as yet is suggested by Kubler's reference to the influence of the *indigenista* movement in reinforcing the separateness of the Indian.[25] A second possible consequence is in the weakening of the position of the *latifundia* and the *hacienda* in the Indian areas, where inefficient technology plus loss of labor to the city has produced, in many cases, bankruptcy, with the consequence that Indian rural communities often have been able to expand their landholdings and to strengthen their economic position in recent years. It is conceivable, therefore, that the loss of a considerable percentage of Indian population into the anonymity of the city may at the same time have the paradoxical result of reinforcing the strength of rural Indian culture and its apartness from the mestizo and urban culture of the country.

INDIAN EMERGENCE?

True racial discrimination is implied to exist in Bolivia by Urquidi.[26] However, he lays most of Bolivia's difficulties to the fantastically large landholdings, leading to underconsumption and widespread and continuous malnutrition among a large part of the landless population. He does argue in favor of miscegenation as a means of eliminating differences and prejudices existing in the present social organization,[27] but elsewhere he insists that social *"mestizaje"* is more important.[28] This point of view has recently been challenged by Goins, who asserts that today "there are no Bolivian Indians but only Indian Bolivians."[29] Métraux similarly found Bolivia to be undergoing enormous changes in his recent visit.[30] It seems probable, therefore, that in Bolivia, as elsewhere, class conflicts and differences are the basic problems to which at times are attached biological terminology. On the surface it would appear that real race discrimination and prejudice exist. On the other hand, the large Indian and sizable rural mestizo populations both form parallel cultures, easily distinguished by community affiliation, language, and dress as well as other cultural attributes. Were these to disappear, classification of individuals by physical traits would become difficult except for the most extreme types.

[25] *Ibid.*
[26] Arturo Urquidi, "Aspectos Sociologicos de Bolivia," *Revista Mexicana de Sociologia* XV (1953), 67-82.
[27] *Ibid.*, 81-82.
[28] *Ibid.*, 73.
[29] John Goins in an oral communication, 1954.
[30] Alfred Métraux in an oral communication, 1954.

While unquestionably biological criteria and vocabulary have more potency in the Andean region than in Mexico and Central America, the major classifications are socio-cultural. Although strong class barriers exist, and the Indian tends to predominate in the lowest-class category, or to exist in a parallel socio-cultural milieu, barriers to passage are not insurmountable, and long-term trends suggest a gradual leveling of the population and the development of a more modern industrial-type class system.

The Paraguayan situation is somewhat obscure. Clearly recognizable Indians in tribal status do receive special and to some extent discriminatory treatment. Asuncion probably is the only capital city in the New World which enforces a curfew law against Indians, who must not stay in the city during the hours of darkness. On the other hand, the Paraguayans moved many of the Guarani-speaking Indians east of the Paraguay River where they were settled in established communities and their children sent to schools taught in Guarani.

But although Guarani is the most used language in Paraguay, the educational ladder leading to and through the university is all conducted in Spanish, while the dominant upper class makes some attempt to set itself off from the bulk of the Indian-mestizo population. One may, however, suspect that the operative forces are not an attempt to establish a racial dichotomy but to protect the economic and political power of an aristocratic group in a basically feudal society. If so, here as elsewhere, racial terminology when used is attached to socio-cultural classifications.

SUMMARY

To summarize, it is suggested that, as a result of over four hundred years' contact, extensive biological mixture has occurred. Except for countries with very large recent European immigration, the number of persons of pure European ancestry is very small, while the numbers of persons of relatively pure Indian ancestry vary from almost none to substantial portions of the population. In almost all countries, however, the bulk of the population is biologically of mixed ancestry, with the Indian genetic contribution to the mixture being in most cases the largest.

Europeans entered Spanish America as a dominant conquering group, bringing with them an essentially feudal outlook supporting a static class structure. As a result of this historic factor, higher social class or power positions tend to be occupied by individuals of more European type, while lower-class or lower-status positions tend to be occupied by persons of more Indian type. In many areas, however, the markedly Indian types are found to live in parallel cultures which afford them high social gratifications.

During part of the colonial and republican periods strong emphasis was placed upon biological distinctions. Biological inferiority was attributed to Indians and mestizos. Increasing mixture has made biological distinctions difficult and today differentiation is made primarily upon sociocultural criteria. Where terms of biological meaning are employed, they are used to identify socio-cultural groupings. General trends are to seek ways of eliminating both biological and cultural differences. In some cases where parallel Indian or Indian-colonial cultures do not exist, and cultural differences are clearly of a class character, myths of racial homogeneity and predominance of European origin have become firmly implanted. In others, both shifting attitudes, or violent (as in Mexico) replacement of a feudal-type society by a status and class-differentiated society characteristic of industrialized nations, are leading to increasing social mobility and the decreasing potency of biological symbols. Historically, Spanish America affords important materials for the study of both race and culture contacts. In contemporary societies, however, problems of social differentiation are of primary importance. Race relations are in varying degrees involved in the problems of social differentiation but are of secondary and diminishing importance.

XIV

The role of Negroes in the United States is changing in both the South and the North. Since the end of World War II, and particularly since the Supreme Court desegregation decision of 1954-55, Negroes have become better educated. Industrialization in the South is opening new jobs for Negroes. Civil rights legislation, much of it prompted by Negro agitation, has decreased discrimination in housing, jobs, and education. These factors and others have accelerated the formation of a Negro middle class, but its position is ambiguous. In some ways it represents an increase in racial equality and a solution to the problem of segregation. But middle class Negroes may feel more deprived than any other group: they are in part alienated from their own lower class heritage and from the members of their own race who have not changed class position; and they are also acutely aware of the very great disparities between their status and that of supposedly equal White groups. Race relations in America, particularly in the South, are changing, but change brings new confusion.

M. ELAINE BURGESS

Race Relations and Social Change

1

Long a dormant giant, the Negro community is now astir, and dramatic alterations characterize southern race relations. News media are saturated

From *The South in Continuity and Change*, edited by John C. McKinney and Edgar T. Thompson, sponsored by the Southern Sociological Society and

with discussions of the "Negro Revolution." Boycotts in Montgomery, sit-ins in Greensboro, riots in Birmingham, freedom rides in New Orleans, and marches on Washington fill the headlines, leaving little doubt of a quickening pace so far as Negro protest is concerned.

In spite of rising tension and intermittent violence, to date the drama has been played largely within the existing social order — legislative enactments, court decisions, executive decrees, and non-violent demonstrations. Martin Luther King states the dominant Negro position in this fashion: "We are a nation of laws, not of men . . . but we must present our very bodies, if necessary, to make certain our laws are just and that they are implemented."[1] Most Negroes leading the fight for change in racial patterns have not lost faith in the existing social system so much as in officials of the white community who have refused to provide equality within that system. They are seeking to make the nation aware of these inequalities, hopefully without a trail of blood. Indeed, one student of race relations has hypothesized that stress on non-violent resistance to segregation has developed among southern Negroes primarily as an effort to mediate between the conflicting traditions of the former accommodative patterns and the new militant protest patterns. For the rapidity of change in recent decades has caused most Negroes to be caught between two contradictory ways of life, the old second-class versus the new first-class citizenship. The underlying philosophy of the protest movement bridges the gap between these ways of life by legitimatizing "passive aggression" within the framework of our normative code.[2]

Thus far the Negroes' energetic push for equality, in spite of the fears of some alarmed whites and some voluble Negroes, is not so much a revolution as it is a fast-moving reform movement. Their goals do not seek to overcome the basic structure of government or other fundamental institutions. What they are demanding in ever louder voices is admission to a closed white society which has denied full access to its protection and benefits. In short, as scholars of race relations have emphasized, the American Negro is now striving to become a *Negro American*. Whether the present shifts in Negro-white relations remain at this level depends upon a number of complex and interrelated factors, but for now the patterns of change exist, in part, in social continuity.

the Center for Southern Studies, Duke University (Durham, N.C.: Duke University Press, 1965), pp. 337-358. Reprinted by permission of the author and the publisher.
[1] As quoted in: Louis Lomax, "What Mass Protests Can't Do," *Saturday Review* (July 6, 1963), p. 12.
[2] James Vander Zanden, "The Non-Violent Resistance Movement Against Segregation," *American Journal of Sociology* (March, 1963), 544-550.

The Negro is not simply becoming more and more a protagonist of change. He is now, and he has always been, a symbol of change. The new militancy in civil rights is a vital part of a generalized social transformation throughout the South, and the nation as a whole. Every major change in the status and role of the Negro in the past has been a reflection of important modifications in other parts of the social system.[3] And nothing. of what is happening today in race relations in the South and elsewhere can be understood apart from all of the small- and large-scale modifications taking place. The obvious legal changes of recent decades come into mind, but other changes, frequently unnoticed, have played a vital part in weakening the foundations of segregation. Demographic alterations, shifts in the economy, expanded communication, and increased urbanization, mechanization, industrialization, migration, and political participation have all wrought changes in Negro-white relations. . . .

We do not believe that changing racial patterns can be understood by studying the South alone. It is true that the southern experience with racial problems is in many ways unique, and that the focus of the "American Dilemma" has until recent years been primarily in the South. But the southern experience is unique only in detail and degree, and Negro-white relations have always been a national problem. This has become increasingly obvious as Negroes have moved out across the nation to settle in the ghettos of the large urban centers of the North and West. Furthermore, the South has grown less and less isolated from other regions of the country and ever more occupied with national affairs.

Yet despite these facts there remains a constellation of socio-cultural characteristics peculiarly southern. A sense of history and identity continues to set the South apart. The very fact that there has been, and still is, a special quality surrounding southern Negro-white patterns, and that it was here that the boycotts, the picketing, and the sit-ins began, means that we can deal with regional race relations. For, unlike other regions of the United States, much of what the South has been, is now, and is presently to become can be understood only in terms of its biracial nature. V. O. Key illustrates this idea most succinctly:

> In its grand outlines the politics of the South revolves around the position of the Negro. It is at times interpreted as a politics of cotton, as a politics of free trade, as a politics of agrarian poverty, or as a politics of planter and plutocrat. Although such interpretations have a superficial validity, in the last analysis the major peculiarities of Southern politics go back to the Negro. Whatever phase of the

---

[3] See: Charles U. Smith, "Race, Human Relations and the Changing South," *Phylon* 23 (Spring, 1962), 66-72.

southern political process one seeks to understand, sooner or later the trail of inquiry leads to the Negro.[4]

Thus, while our first concern is with race relations in the South, we are ever mindful that these relations influence, and in turn are influenced by, race relations throughout America.

The *South* as used throughout this analysis will ordinarily follow the definition of the Census of the United States, including the states of the South Atlantic, East South Central, and West South Central areas. Occasionally, we shall speak of the *Southeast,* following the delineation of Howard Odum. In such cases Louisiana, Tennessee, Virginia, Georgia, South Carolina, Arkansas, Kentucky, Mississippi, Alabama, North Carolina, and Florida are included in the definition. The time limits of this study will be somewhat narrowly drawn. To be sure, present trends in biracial patterns have their roots in the ante bellum period. A case can also be made for beginning with the events of the depression years and the New Deal. However, it is the very significant alterations in Negro-white relations that evolved during and following World War II which seem most pertinent. Therefore special attention will be paid to the changing status of the Negro from the decade of the 1940's to the present.

2

Students have observed that the central fact of social change appears to be alterations in the individual or group positions of members of a society. Consequently, what is presently happening in race relations in the South can best be understood in terms of changing status and power aspirations.[5] Without denying the cogency of these arguments we would remiss if we did not underscore a fundamental change in attitudes and values of Negroes which make these efforts toward status shifts possible. The objectives of every movement for change, whether or not such movements are revolutionary, have in common the fact that they represent interests and values that have failed to find full recognition in the existing power and status system.[6]

Segregation in the South and elsewhere has symbolized the inevitable

[4] V. O. Key, *Southern Politics in State and Nation* (New York: Alfred A. Knopf, Inc., 1949), p. 5.

[5] Edgar T. Thompson, "The South and the Second Emancipation," in Allan Sindler (ed.), *Change in the Contemporary South* (Durham: Duke University Press, 1963), pp. 93-118; Ruth Searles and Allen Williams, "Participation in Sit-Ins," *Social Forces* 40 (March, 1962), 215-220; M. Elaine Burgess, *Negro Leadership in a Southern City* (Chapel Hill: University of North Carolina Press, 1962); Daniel C. Thompson, *Negro Leadership Class* (Englewood Cliffs, N.J.: Prentice-Hall, Inc., 1963).

[6] See for example: Kurt Lang and Gladys Lang, *Collective Dynamics* (New York: Thomas Y. Crowell Co., 1960), p. 492.

inferiority of Negroes. It has "kept the Negro in his place," not only on buses and streetcars, in hospitals and restaurants, but to a great extent in the total socio-economic system. Resistance to any modification of this symbol of inferiority has been predicated, in many instances, on the fear that if the Negro were allowed to escape from his inferior position the status of the white man would thereby be jeopardized — the very prestige that "whiteness" has provided would be automatically abrogated. Nevertheless, the recent gains Negroes have realized as the result of shifts in the socio-economic structure have made many of them increasingly aware of the variance between the "ideal" values implicit in democracy and the "real" values explicit in discrimination and desegregation. They have become painfully conscious of the discrepancy between their ascribed status of race and their achieved status of high school or college graduate, skilled, white-collar, or professional worker.

Where has this status inconsistency[7] been felt more keenly? The answer seems to lie within the rising new middle and lower-middle class, nourished and trained within the urban black belts. The slow but steady gains made by middle-class Negroes have (as we shall discuss in more detail later), prompted more, not less, dissatisfaction with their position in the power and status system. It is here, we propose, that some explanation can be found concerning the agitation for change in patterns of race relations, particularly since the Supreme Court decision of 1954.

The above assertions give rise to two basic questions: (1·) what are the evidences of a significantly large and growing middle class among Negroes? and (2) why has this growth made a difference in expressions of racial conflict and change? Let us examine first the evidence attesting to an emerging Negro middle class.

3

While most students of race relations would agree that there is a sizeable Negro middle class in America today, the average layman may still find it hard to believe that most Negroes are not inherently lower class. It is, of course, difficult to define "middle class" with any exactness, and sociologists continue to disagree over the best means for differentiating social class in general. As in the white community, the class structure of the Negro community is fluid. There are no precise lines among strata, and social mobility is apparent. Yet we have continued to refine measures of class strata, and such measures provide some validity for the delineation of various class levels.

[7] For a discussion of "status inconsistency" and similar concepts, see Elton F. Jackson, "Status Consistency and Symptoms of Stress," *American Sociological Review* 27 (August, 1962), 469-482; Gerhard Lenski, "Status Crystallization: A Non-vertical Dimension of Social Status," *American Sociological Review* 19 (August, 1954), 405-413.

Among the current indexes of class position *occupation, education, class identification,* and *income* seem to be the most useful. Numerous revisions of earlier works place more or less emphasis on these variables as the most reliable measures presently available to the social scientist.[8] The relative importance of these symbolic characteristics of class status varies slightly between the white and the Negro community. A recent review of a number of studies done on Negro prestige and social class contends that while occupation is considered to be the single most important predictive class characteristic for whites, education continues to rank above occupation for Negroes.[9] Regardless of the weight attached to these criteria, however, there is ample support for their use as objective measures of class, and the author shall employ them to illustrate important advances made by the Negro middle class during the past two decades.

It was implied earlier that the emergence of the Negro middle class was concurrent with an expanding Negro urban population. A brief discussion of Negro urban migration is therefore pertinent, for it is in the larger cities of the South, and more especially the North and West, that we find unmistakable evidence of the growth of class divisions and a sizeable middle stratum.

Following emancipation Negroes began their slow migration into the cities, although in 1890 four out of five Negroes still lived in rural areas. Those who moved went largely to southern cities, and as late as 1910 nearly 69 per cent of the urban Negro population still resided in the South. Between 1910 and 1917 urban centers of the South experienced a new influx of Negroes in response to the demand for labor in railroad building and new commercial and industrial enterprises. Thereafter the large Negro ghettos throughout the country began a very slow process of occupational and educational differentiation. A small group of pre-war freedmen and a small number of business and professional men provided the nucleus for an upper and a middle class. The latter gradually came to be separated from the mass of lower-class Negroes by greater stability of family life and by closer integration with the institutional life of the

[8] August B. Hollingshead and Fredrick C. Redlich, *Social Class and Mental Illness* (New York: John Wiley and Sons, Inc., 1958), pp. 387-397; Robert A. Ellis and W. Clayton Lane, "The Index of Class Position: An Improved Intercommunity Measure of Stratification," *American Sociological Review* 28 (April, 1963), 272-277; Joseph Kahl and James A. Davis, "A Comparison of Indexes of Socio-Economic Status," *American Sociological Review* 20 (June, 1955), 317-325; Charles B. Nam, "Nationality Groups and Social Stratification," *Social Forces* 37 (May, 1959), 328-333.

[9] Norval D. Glenn, "Negro Prestige Criteria: A Case Study in the Bases of Prestige," *American Journal of Sociology* 68 (May, 1963), 645-657; Burgess, *op. cit.*

sub-community. Most of this group were skilled and semiskilled workers, and the more responsible domestic and service workers.[10] Still the climb up the class ladder was painfully slow and the middle class, as well as the upper class, remained very limited.

It was not until the decades of the 1940's and 1950's when we witnessed the most explosive growth of urban population in our history — particularly Negro — that a significant rise in the Negro middle class took place. While the native white urban population increased by 22.6 per cent (old urban-rural definition) between 1940 and 1950, the Negro urban population increased by 43.2 per cent (or at a rate almost twice that of whites) during this time. The rural South lost a million Negro residents in the years of the forties alone. Many migrated West or North, but a large number moved into southern cities as well.[11] A rapid rise in industrial employment facilitated this movement which continued through the 1950's. If we look only at the eleven states comprising the Southeast we find that 61 per cent of the nation's non-white population resided here in 1940; by 1960 the percentage had dropped to 44.8 per cent. In 1940 these southern states contained 32.8 per cent urban non-white population. In 1950 this proportion had risen to 42.9 per cent and by 1960 it was 52.9 per cent. By 1960 nearly 14 million of the approximately 19 million Negroes were living in urban areas of the United States.[12]

What do these migration patterns mean with regard to changing Negro class structure? Hylan Lewis explains their significance in the following way:

> The normal economic, political, and social imperatives of urban life are such that the Negro in the cities of the South gets an automatic increment in his struggle for status and power merely by the fact of being there. The urban premium on freedom, impersonality, effi-

[10] E. Franklin Frazier, *The Negro in the United States* (New York: The Macmillan Co., 1949), p. 190; Alvin Boskoff, "Negro Class Structure and the Technicways," *Social Forces* 29 (December, 1950), 124-131.

[11] Donald Bogue, *The Population of the United States* (Glencoe, Illinois: The Free Press, 1959), p. 127; George Simpson and Milton Yinger, "The Sociology of Race and Ethnic Relations," in Robert K. Merton, Leonard Broom, and Leonard S. Cottrell, Jr. (eds.), *Sociology Today* (New York: Basic Books, Inc., 1959), p. 385.

[12] Selz C. Mayo and C. Horace Hamilton, "Current Population Trends in the South," *Social Forces* 42 (October, 1963), 80. Because Negroes make up approximately 98 per cent of the non-white population of the Southeast, 95 per cent of the non-white population of the Census South, and 92.1 per cent of the non-white population for United States as a whole, Negro and *non-white* have been used here and throughout the rest of paper as roughly coterminous. U.S. Bureau of the Census, *United States Census of Population: 1960, Subject Reports, Non-white Population by Race*, PC(2)-1C (Washington, D.C.: United States Government Printing Office, 1963).

ciency and profits, voluntary organizations and participation by representation provides for Negroes and whites a new frontier for shaping of a common destiny.[13]

It is in the city that the greatest educational opportunities have become available to the Negro. It is here that expanding occupational opportunities have been possible, and that a rise in income and standard of living have gradually been realized. In the urban black belts, Negro institutions such as the church, the schools and colleges, business and professional associations, labor and political organizations, the Urban League, and the National Association for the Advancement of Colored People have flourished. These social institutions provided the breeding ground for a new kind of citizen and a new kind of leadership trained in the values and skills of the middle class. In what do they believe and what do they value? Primarily they believe in themselves and their future, in respectability, family stability, economic security, a "decent standard of living," and in responsible participation in community (i.e., Negro protest) affairs. Education and occupational achievement are highly valued. Education is the avenue to necessary training and skills for getting ahead, for inculcating the youth with the "right democratic values," the right motivations, the right commitments to the future, and the right patterns of behavior. A high school diploma is increasingly essential, and sacrifice to send children on to college is a positive good. Aspirations are for the professional, semiprofessional, white-collar, and skilled occupations — and the chance for a respectable style of life dictated by ability, not race. In sum, the new Negro middle class is distinguishable because it adheres to the predominant American value system of equality and is militantly determined to share in the "American Dream."[14]

Despite the characteristics we posit for the new middle class we do not assume that the members of this or any other stratum — Negro or white — are completely homogeneous. There is, of course, variation in behavior and in the degree to which they are committed to these middle-class goals and aspirations. Nevertheless, members of the Negro middle class, like other social class members, share significant traits in common and the social scientist can make generalizations about them.

A resumé of occupational shifts among Negroes during the past two decades illustrates important advances despite continued gaps between Negro and white attainment. Relatively little progress was made in permitting non-white workers to enter white-collar and skilled occupations prior to the 1930's. It was not until the labor shortages, the expansion of

---

[13] Hylan Lewis, "Innovations and Trends in the Contemporary Negro Community," *Journal of Social Issues* 10 (1954), 22-24.

[14] Joseph Kahl, *The American Class Structure* (New York: Rinehart and Co., Inc., 1957), pp. 193-205; Burgess, *op. cit.*, pp. 34-35.

many occupations, and the effects of mass urban migrations began to be felt in the early 1940's that the growing occupational differentiation in the Negro population began to appear. Between 1940 and 1950 Negro occupational gains were very large compared to gains of previous decades. Utilizing an intracohort analysis to measure changes in occupational status of Negro males relative to education, Nathan Hare found that significant gains were made in the occupational groupings of proprietors, managers and officials; craftsmen and foremen; clerical and sales workers; and operatives and kindred. White males evidenced an increase in proportion among the first two categories, but the Negro representation changed at a relatively faster rate than it did for whites. Among the latter two occupational groups Negroes increased rapidly while whites showed a net loss. While Negroes are still overrepresented in the lower levels of the occupational structure and underrepresented in the upper strata, they have succeeded in leaving occupations of overrepresentation. Negro male college graduates made greater strides toward parity with whites than did those at any other educational level during the period from 1940 to 1950, but during the 1950's, unlike the 1940's, education in general was found to be much more effective in helping Negroes leave occupations of overrepresentation.[15]

Although the most important modifications in Negro occupational status occurred in the decade of the 1940's, substantial gains have continued to the present. During the first eight years of the 1950's the number of non-white male farmers (largely sharecroppers in the South) was estimated to have dropped by 55 per cent, and the number of farm laborers dropped by 21 per cent. The proportion of Negroes in certain higher status jobs has increased since 1950 as follows: professional and technical workers, 49 per cent; clerical and kindred workers, 69 per cent; sales workers, 24 per cent; craftsmen, 20 per cent. Discussions of growth rates can be misleading, since they can exaggerate the amount of change if the number of Negroes in a given occupation is initially very small. Nevertheless, a comparison of the proportion of non-white workers in each occupation with the average per cent who are non-white among all workers does illustrate that important shifts have taken place. In no one of the upper and middle occupational groups is the proportion of non-whites negligible, and there have been concrete additions in the proportion who are non-white in almost all categories. In 1940, 10.0 per cent of the non-white labor force were in professional, managerial, clerical, sales, or craftsmen occupations;

[15] Nathan Hare, "Changes in Occupational Status of Negroes, 1930-1960: An Intracohort Analysis," paper read at the American Sociological Association, Los Angeles, California, August, 1963, pp. 9-13. See also: Norval Glenn, "Changes in the American Occupational Structure and Occupational Gains of Negroes during the 1940's," Social Forces 41 (December, 1962), 188-195.

12.2 per cent were operatives. By 1960 these proportions had almost doubled with 22.2 per cent non-whites in the top five occupational groupings and 24.4 per cent listed as operatives.[16]

Within the South the same general trend has taken place, although at a slower pace. While there remains a high concentration of Negroes in the lower-status "Negro" jobs and a low proportion in the high-status "white" jobs, in the *broad middle range* of the occupational system of the Southeast there has been convergence among Negroes and whites.[17] These and similar findings lend support to the contention that a clearly defined and sizeable Negro middle class has evolved during the last two decades.

The gap between educational attainment of Negroes and whites has also narrowed during the past twenty years. In 1940 white persons twenty-five years of age and over had completed 8.7 median years of schooling in contrast to 5.8 for non-whites. By 1960 the medians had risen to 10.8 for whites and 8.2 for Negroes. An analysis of the young adult Negro population in the United States shows where the most striking gains have been made in educational advancement. The average level of attainment has risen more rapidly among the young non-white than it has among the young white population. The median school years completed for the white population between the ages of twenty-five to twenty-nine in 1940 was 10.7, compared to 7.0 for non-whites of this age, or a difference of 3.7 median years. In 1960 the difference in median school years completed had narrowed to 1.5, with the whites having completed 12.3 median years of schooling in contrast to 10.8 for non-whites. Similar achievements were made for non-whites in the thirty to thirty-four age group as well.[18]

By observing the changing proportion of Negro high school and college graduates we find an analogous trend. Only 9 per cent of the non-white population in the United States twenty-five years of age and older had completed four years of high school or beyond, or received a college degree in 1940. By 1960, 25.3 per cent in this age category had done so. Among those twenty-five to twenty-nine years of age in 1940, 13.9 per cent had graduated from high school, gone on to college, or finished at

---

[16] Bogue, *op. cit.*, pp. 503-505, 506-507; U.S. Department of Labor, *The Economic Situation of Negroes in the United States, Bulletin S-3* (Washington, D.C.: U.S. Government Printing Office, 1960).

[17] Munro S. Edmonson and David R. Norsworthy, "Industry and Race in the Southern United States," (New Orleans, Louisiana: Tulane University, 1963), p. 3 (mimeographed).

[18] U.S. Bureau of the Census, *U.S. Census of the Population: 1960, Characteristics of the Population, United States Summary* (Washington, D.C.: U.S. Government Printing Office, 1964), Table 173; U.S. Bureau of the Census, *U.S. Census of the Population: 1940, United States Summary* (Washington, D.C.: U.S. Government Printing Office, 1944), Table 18; Bogue, *op. cit.*, p. 343.

least four years of higher education. The proportion had jumped to 44 per cent by 1960.[19]

Increased educational attainment is further reflected in data on school enrollment, as Table 1 illustrates.

TABLE 1. PERCENTAGE OF SCHOOL AGE YOUTH ENROLLED IN SCHOOL, BY COLOR: 1940, 1950, AND 1960

Census Year	7 to 13 Year Olds		14 and 15 Year Olds		16 and 17 Year Olds	
	White	Non-White	White	Non-White	White	Non-White
1940	95.5	91.3	91.0	82.8	70.6	52.9
1950	95.9	93.9	93.6	89.0	75.9	64.3
1960	97.8	95.9	94.7	90.1	81.9	73.3

Source: U.S. Bureau of the Census, *U.S. Census of the Population: 1960, United States Summary,* Table 169. U.S. Bureau of the Census, *U.S. Census of the Population: 1950, United States Summary* (Washington, D.C.: 1954), Table 110. Charles P. Nam, "Race and Educational Advancement," *Columbia University Seminar on Population and Social Change,* November 12, 1963 (New York: Columbia University Press, 1964), Table 1.

The South still lags behind other regions of the country in the median number of school years completed, in the proportion of persons completing high school, attending or graduating from college, and in the proportion of youths enrolled in school. Yet the same general trend of educational advancement for Negroes and whites is found. For example, the median number of school years completed for the total population of the South rose from 8.6 in 1950 to 9.9 in 1960. In southern urban areas the median number of school years attained by Negroes jumped from 6.7 in 1950 to 8.4 in 1960. Similar improvements were evidenced for rural Negroes of the South.[20]

One final note with regard to education and the Negro in America. Recent research provides evidence that the plans and ambitions of Negro youths are becoming more similar to those of their white peers. In one instance it was found that Negro high school student educational aspirations exceed those of whites, as do their mobility aspirations.[21] While such studies do not indicate what subsequent educational achievements actually are, a survey made by the Census Bureau on plans and actions of high school seniors reveals that a slightly higher proportion of non-white seniors indicate that they plan to attend college than do whites.

[19] Charles B. Nam, "Race and Educational Advancement," paper read at Columbia University Seminar on Population and Social Change, New York, November 12, 1963, Table 8.

[20] U.S. Bureau of the Census, *U.S. Census of the Population: 1950, Characteristics of the Population,* II, 363-364; *U.S. Census of Population: 1960, Subject Reports, Nonwhite Population by Race.*

[21] Noel P. Gist and William S. Bennett, Jr., "Aspirations of Negro and White Students," *Social Forces* 42 (October, 1963), 40-48.

But a slightly higher proportion of the white seniors who plan to attend college actually do so than do non-whites.[22] Such studies, although merely suggestive, do indicate that Negro aspirations have greatly increased in recent years, and although their actual achievement of further education remains below that of white youth, differences are diminishing.

The divergence in income contingent upon race has narrowed substantially since 1939 when the median wage and salary income of non-white primary families and individuals was only 37 per cent of that of the corresponding white group. Between 1947 and 1962 non-white families enjoyed about the same relative increase in average age income as white families did (although in absolute terms the rise was considerably larger for white families). The median income rose from $1,600 in 1947 to $3,300 in 1962 for non-white families throughout the United States, representing an increase of 106 per cent. For white families income rose from $3,200 to $6,200, or by 98 per cent. The relative gains made by non-white families were more substantial in the first part of this period. The highest ratio of non-white to white income came in 1952, when it was .57. In subsequent years the ratio has fluctuated between .51 and .56, and in 1962 it was .53.[23] Of special interest for our purposes, however, is the fact that in 1949 only 6.1 per cent of the non-white families in this country had incomes ranging from $3,000 to $6,999, while in 1962 the proportion having incomes in this range jumped to 25.5 per cent. Furthermore, in 1962 the proportion of non-white families in the middle income group of from $4,000 to $6,000 was 21 per cent, about the same as the proportion of white families within this range, which was 22 per cent. The great disparity in income distributions between whites and non-whites is now found in the lower and higher income brackets.[24]

Alterations in income distribution in the South over the past twenty years show a trend similar to that for the entire country, although it remains behind the rest of the United States in this index as it does with others. The relatively low income of the southern rural Negro population, as well as the continued heavy concentration of Negro workers in the lower paid service and labor jobs, and the hazards of irregular employment influence Negro family income in the South particularly. Yet median fam-

[22] Charles B. Nam and James D. Cowhig, "Factors Related to College Attendance of Farm and Non-Farm High School Graduates," in U.S. Bureau of the Census, Farm Population, ERS (P-27), 32 (Washington, D.C.: U.S. Government Printing Office, 1961).

[23] For regions outside the South, the ratio was approximately two-thirds in 1962, whereas in the South it was less than one-half. U.S. Bureau of the Census, Current Population Reports, Consumer Income: Income of Families and Persons in the United States: 1962, P-60, 41 (Washington, D.C.: U.S. Government Printing Office, 1963), pp. 5-11.

[24] Ibid., p. 33; U.S. Bureau of the Census, U.S. Census of Population: 1950, United States Summary, p. 298.

ily income as well as per capita income of the Negro has moved upward
here, too. In 1949 the median income per person fourteen years of age
and over was $739 for Negroes in the South. By 1962 it had risen to
$1,604.[25]
Another interesting permutation in the Negro economic position can
be seen in data on annual purchasing power. In 1939 Negro purchasing
power in the Southeast was less than $1 billion. By 1950 this figure had
grown to approximately $3.5 billion. For the United States as a whole
the Negro purchasing power was slightly less than $15 billion in 1950. A
recent market survey indicates that by 1964 this purchasing power will
pass $28 billion annually, not quite double what it was in 1950, and
approximately equal to Canada's entire consumer market.[26] These data
demonstrate in a slightly different way that the overall economic status of
the Negro has been improving.

We are not unmindful that the occupational advances made by Negroes
have been slowing down during recent years and that the majority of
Negroes remain at the lower levels of the occupation ladder, making them
particularly susceptible to unemployment and other problems created
by increased automation and technology. Nor are we unaware that Negro
youths continue to represent the highest proportion of school dropouts.
Their level of educational attainment and the quality of education for
large numbers is far below that of their white peers. We are also conscious
of the fact that 60 per cent of the Negroes continue to be represented at
the lower levels of income and that the median income of Negro families
is only about half of that for whites. Nevertheless, important changes
have occurred. Growing numbers of Negroes are securing high school and
college education; there has been a striking increase in professional,
managerial, white-collar, and skilled occupations; and there is ample evidence of a rising standard of living. These phenomena have had their
most dramatic influence at the middle levels of the Negro population,
testifying to the appearance of a sizeable Negro middle class within and
without the South.

4

Why has an expanding Negro middle class made a difference in the tempo
and tone of American race relations in general and southern race relations
in particular? The answer lies, I believe, within sociological theory on

[25] U.S. Bureau of the Census, *Current Population Reports, Consumer Income,*
P-60, p. 36; U.S. Bureau of the Census, *U.S. Census of Population: 1950,*
Table 162, p. 413.
[26] Lucile Chambers, *America's Tenth Man* (New York: Twayne Publishers,
Inc., 1957), p. 261; Richard L. Tobin, "The Negro and the Advertiser,"
Saturday Review (November 9, 1963), pp. 67-68.

change, collective behavior, and reference groups. Much of the literature dealing with social protest movements has given emphasis to the expressions of frustration and hostility felt by the deprived lower classes toward those in power, as well as toward themselves. Alienated from the larger society, they are driven by a sense of common fate into mass movements that provide release from the tension and psychological disturbance of their deprived status.[27] If this be the sole explanation one might well ask why then did not the militant activities of the Negro begin long ago when their conditions were, by present standards, much harsher. Kurt and Gladys Lang provide a partial answer when they observe that, although the alienated are composed of the "have-nots," they are not identical with the underprivileged lower classes. Rather, they may best be typified by the disaffected new middle classes and minorities whose expectations have been aroused but who somehow are blocked in the fulfillment of these expectations.[28]

Wilbert E. Moore holds a similar point of view but expands on it by turning to the concept of relative deprivation and reference group theory. He first makes the point that status and prestige systems may endure for considerable periods without causing rebellion because of the very nature of the differential distribution of power, resources, and knowledge. The question of how the poor and powerless will come to react against inequality can be answered only if we note that it is not always the most downtrodden members of the system that lead movements of protest or form the spearheads of discontent. Rather the overt manifestations of discontent are likely to occur among those who have not fared badly, but also have not fared well. Even Marx, whose capacity as a social analyst was frequently obscured by his political ideology, recognized the differences between "leading elements" and what he called the *Lumpenproletariat*. This characteristic of protest by those who have escaped the very lowest positions has been observed in the newly developing areas of the world such as Africa, and we derive from this evidence a kind of cross-sectional confirmation of dynamic processes of order and change.[29] Therefore, concludes Moore:

> The *"relative deprivation"* [italics mine] of those fairly fully incorporated into the values associated with new modes of social placement, but thereby more envious of complete success than their

[27] See for example: R. M. McIver and C. H. Page, *Society* (New York: Rinehart and Co., Inc., 1949), p. 372; Robert K. Merton, *Social Theory and Social Structure* (rev. ed.; Glencoe, Illinois: The Free Press, 1957), pp. 155-156.

[28] Lang and Lang, *op. cit.*, pp. 324-343.

[29] Wilbert E. Moore, *Social Change* (Englewood Cliffs, New Jersey: Prentice-Hall, Inc., 1963), pp. 83-84.

less fortunate compatriats provides the explanatory key to the source
of discontent in systems of social inequality.[30]

Neither the Negro lower class nor the upper class could have mounted
the resistance movement we are now witnessing throughout the South.
The former does not possess the resources, either internal or external,
essential for such a movement, and the latter is much too small and,
very frequently, too far removed from the masses to do so. Such activity
had to wait upon the development of an ample middle class that was
motivated to push for validation of a hard-won class position, thus far
denied by the white social structure. The question of unequal distribution
of status and power between Negroes and whites would consequently appear as a special case of the more basic problem of order and change. By
no means are we saying that all challenges to established social structures
or power distributions are class oriented, or directly concerned with relative social position. Nevertheless, it is true that one of the major sources
of tension and therefore of change and potential change in the South, as
in the broader society, stems from the new middle-class Negro's disbelief
in past rationales for inequality and the desire for substitution of new
rationales.[31]

Although the middle-class Negro has arisen in segregated urban subcommunities he has not been unmindful of his counterpart in the white
community. It is not simply a matter of his having been educated to the
democratic values of equality that has made him acutely aware of discrepancies in his status. The gradual changes in his occupation and other
socio-economic positions have permitted certain kinds of communication
and interaction with middle-class whites, at least on a formal level. Contact via community welfare and service agencies, professional contacts in
such fields as education, religion, government, and law, and interaction
within labor unions, the creative arts, the armed services, and other such
areas have grown considerably during the past twenty years. He no longer
looks about him and says "I am better off than my parents were," or "I
am better off than the mass of Negroes." Rather, he compares himself to,
and identifies with, persons of similar position and training within the
white community and finds his own position "wanting" in contrast to this
new reference group. Nor does the old reference group of the upper-class
Negro any longer obtain. With the changing networks of social relations
and his increasing integration into the larger community, the middle-class
Negro has sought to escape the obligations and pressures of "keeping up"
the requirements of upper-class behavior in the Negro group, while acting
in the role of middle-class white-collar worker in the community at large.

[30] *Ibid.*
[31] *Ibid.*

Instead he seeks to orient his behavior with reference to the middle class of the broader community.[32] As he observes his white counterpart he finds reason for feeling deprived, and this sense of relative deprivation has proved the catalyst for militancy and mass protest against segregation and discrimination. Recent alterations in Negro tactics from passive accommodation to active demonstration can be seen, therefore, as a direct consequence of a shift from evaluating his status primarily in terms of his own (Negro) membership group to evaluating it in terms of the (white) non-membership group.[33] Incidental to this permutation in reference group has been, of course, "creeping legal desegregation," culminating in the Supreme Court decision of 1954, which has provided legitimacy to his desire for equal rights. It has given him the self-respect and the moral support needed in his push for complete realignment of his place in the American social system.

Hence an articulate and responsible citizenry has evolved in Negro subcommunities throughout the urban South. A proliferation of Negro organizations has emerged, such as the Southern Christian Leadership Conference and the Student Non-Violent Coordinating Committee, to take their place alongside the Urban League, the National Association for the Advancement of Colored People, and a myriad of other local and national religious, political, economic, and educational associations concerned with racial advancement. From the ranks of the articulate citizenry and the various organizations in city after city has come a new kind of leadership. The traditional Negro leadership roles have been replaced by a spirit of equalitarianism. The new leader fights, not acquiesces. No more can a single spokesman, a "white man's Negro," an apathetic or fearful leader, exercise influence. In spite of occasional assertions by some within the Negro ranks that vital leadership is still lacking, at no time in the history of the Negro in America has there been such a reservoir of qualified leaders as those now heading the push for equal rights.[34] The fact that they do not always agree on the means and/or the short-term goals involved in their crusade for equality does not alter this fact. Some diversity of purpose, some specialization of function are to be expected here as in other areas of society. The various protest programs within and among various Negro communities must, of course, realize a degree of harmony in order to be effective. But here again, never before has communication and interaction among Negroes, North and South, been more evident.

---

[32] Frazier, *op. cit.*, pp. 299-300.

[33] Searles and Williams, *op. cit.*, pp. 216-217; Merton, *op. cit.*, pp. 242-269.

[34] See for example: Daniel C. Thompson, *op. cit.*; Lewis Killian and Charles U. Smith, "Negro Protest Leaders in a Southern Community," *Social Forces* 38 (March, 1960), 253-257; Burgess, *op. cit.*; Louis Lomax, *The Negro Revolt* (New York: Harper and Row, 1963).

It is true that in some instances leaders, such as those within the Black Muslim movement, reflect goals and employ means which run counter to the mainstream of Negro aspiration. Responsible southern leaders are aware of, and do not discount, the sentiments expressed by groups like the Black Muslims, but thus far they have rejected their tactics and goals and strive for "Christian" action in obtaining full participation in the larger society. Furthermore, a new generation of Negro leadership is now coming from the colleges throughout the South — young people already skilled in leading marching columns of protest. Their determination and freedom of spirit, made possible by the changes we have been discussing, pay honor to present day Negro leadership, many of whom the young Negro will soon shoulder aside. It would seem, therefore, that the stage has been set for increasingly aggressive leadership in programs geared to the removal of barriers surrounding the black belts in the immediate future.

5

One is tempted to search for parallels in the experiences of the Negro and early immigrant groups, parallels which may shed light on the prospective course of Negro-white relations. As wave after wave of immigrants came to America they brought with them aspirations for the future. Beginning at the bottom they gradually moved up the status ladder as they acquired skills, capital, land, and eventually acceptance. Each group, in time, added something to the culture and meaning of America. They repeatedly illustrated that the uniqueness of America is a common hope, not a common past. Eventually, as Edgar Thompson has so eloquently pointed out, each of the groups could look back and say "We Americans — we did it."[35] Now the Negro, breaking out of the ghettos as did the immigrants in time past, desires to say "We Americans — we did it." He yearns for a future America that he too will have a part in building, a part quite different from that allotted him until now. To this extent an analogy exists.

There are some important differences, however, between the aspiring foreign-born white and the aspiring Negro. It was the European peasant coming to America who held pride in achievement. Although his standard of living in Europe may have been nearly as low as the Negro slave's, he came to our cities better equipped to move upward. He had had an opportunity in the Old World to market his produce, to manage his small stock of goods and money. Contrarily, Negroes emerging from slavery, or later from sharecropping, had little experience with money and little occasion to develop skill in planning and saving. Furthermore,

[35] Edgar T. Thompson, "The South and the Second Emancipation," op. cit., p. 108. The author has benefited immeasurably from a number of provocative ideas present in Thompson's article.

Negroes have differed from European immigrant groups in that they did not develop the same kind of clannishness in the city. They did not have the same close family ties or strong family structure that in other groups provided a pool of resources upon which to rely, until such time as individuals "could make it on their own." It has been difficult for the Negro to develop the notion of "sticking together," of building a common life within the ghetto in order to get ahead in the broader society. Only gradually did Negro institutions gain strength to provide a cohesive force for the black belts.[36] Thus pride in achievement, aspiration for full participation in American life, did not begin with the oft-times hopeless lower-class Negroes. These had to await the development of the lower-middle and middle classes.

There is, of course, a more significant difference between the Negro and the European immigrant. The Negro, no matter how successful he may become, cannot hide his membership in a group that has for so long symbolized inferiority in the minds of whites. Desire for advancement does not erase color. Whereas European ethnic groups were easily assimilated, posing little lasting threat to the basic status system of America, the Negro is not, and thus continues as a threat. And so long as there remains a color line there is much the Negro must continue to fight for, including achievements that the offspring of white immigrants realized much more rapidly.

What then of the future of Negro-white relations throughout the South and the country as a whole? The walls of discrimination have not yet come tumbling down. Advances made have also brought new problems needing urgent attention. Changes in Negro rights have to date been more symbolic than revolutionary. The occupational and economic advancement of the Negro has, for the time being at least, slowed down. The mass of lower-class Negroes suffer most from the threat of automation and unemployment. The problem of housing for urban Negroes has yet to be faced squarely in most communities. School desegregation in southern and northern communities alike is complicated by tokenism, overcrowding, poor preparation, lack of equipment and teachers, lack of motivation, and housing segregation. A hard core of white resistance to Negro advancement has appeared, and must be met. The mass of Negroes must develop responsibility for implementing their new rights and privileges.

Truly, the concentration of multiple problems in the Negro sectors of our cities remains exceptional, but low income, poor housing, and lack of education can explain only so much. The uprooting caused by urban migration creates new problems from which even the best organized and integrated immigrant groups suffered. When the basic core of organiza-

[36] Nathan Glazer and Daniel Moynihan, *Beyond the Melting Pot* (Cambridge, Massachusetts: M.I.T. Press and Harvard University Press, 1963), pp. 32-33.

tion, the family, is still weak as it is for many Negroes, the magnitude of the problems can be staggering. What slavery began, prejudice and discrimination have continued to keep alive.

This, in essence, is the situation in many Negro communities today; it will likely remain so for some time. Hence the Negro middle class suffers greatly from the burden of its people's social problems. Frequently the dilemmas of the lower-class Negro are so great that the middle class is unable to deal with them. Too, their own image is still greatly affected by the lower-class problem element. Often the middle-class Negro is separated only by a thin line from the lower class and is too busy maintaining his own precarious adaptation to offer the necessary assistance. Furthermore the Negro, unlike other ethnic groups, has had few values and little culture explicitly his own to guard. He is an American and because he is a product of America his needs are everyone's dilemma.[37]

There is no doubt but that the Negro will continue to win a greater share in American life, and at an ever increasing pace. Yet within and without the South the change in Negro status is confined by social systems with a limited amount of flexibility. Traditional value systems, problems of economic and technological development, lack of political and social maturity still pose barriers and, although the Negro is asking for equality *now* it seems most likely that his aspirations will continue to surpass actual attainment. Nevertheless, the South must realize that changing Negro status and demands are reflections of social change at many levels and cannot be handled without regard for this fact. Just how far the white community is willing to co-operate with the Negro in solving his problems and in realizing first-class citizenship will determine in large measure the future tenor of Negro protest. Certainly the Negro is no longer willing to accept "gradualism" as defined by the South. Without tangible advances there will surely come a point when faith in negotiation and non-violent activity will break down into extensive violence. However, the demagogues and racists, whether white or black, need not gain ascendency, thereby reversing dominant social trends and values within the American social order. The growing maturity of the Negro middle class and the continued development of Negro institutions and organizational life have thus far guided Negro action under the process of change in a responsible and disciplined way. Hopefully, a stable and emotionally healthy leadership and a co-operative followership in both the Negro and white communities will continue to search for ways to bring about a transformation of the color line in as peaceful a manner as possible.

[37] *Ibid.*, pp. 52-53.

XV

Hyman and Sheatsley here document the case for a reasoned approach to ending segregation in the United States. They show trends over time which indicate a gradual change in American attitudes towards Negroes, towards public school desegregation, and towards community integration. Two of their findings are of particular importance: first, the trend in favor of desegregation is virtually unbroken despite incidents that many felt would change these attitudes; and second, attitudes seem to follow action — in those communities which have desegregated schools, more people are in favor of desegregation, a change in attitude occurring after integration. Perhaps the most disconcerting finding, however, is that while the South has come to favor desegregation increasingly, there is considerably less support for this attitude among the younger age group of Southerners tested than among the older. Yet it is also shown that this attitude is not related to bad experiences among this age group with integrated school situations. Education, class, or any other tested variable fail, too, to explain this difference.

HERBERT H. HYMAN AND
PAUL B. SHEATSLEY

Attitudes toward Desegregation

Nearly eight years ago — in December, 1956 — we summarized in these pages the main findings of 14 years of investigation by the National

Opinion Research Center at the University of Chicago on the attitudes of white Americans toward Negro Americans. Those findings showed that a majority of white persons in the North favored racial integration of public schools, believed there should be no racial discrimination in public transportation and said they would have no objection to living near Negroes of their own income and educational status. In the South a majority of whites opposed each of these views.

Another finding, however, was that since 1942, when the studies had begun, white opinion in both the North and the South had moved steadily and in some cases strikingly toward the acceptance of integration. Underlying this long-term trend, it appeared from the surveys, were fundamental changes in old beliefs about the Negro — such as that he is innately inferior to whites — and a continued influx of better-educated and more tolerant young people into the population of white adults.

A retrospective look now makes it seem that at the time of our earlier article the pace of events in the area of race relations was slow, at least compared with the pace of events since 1956. Even then, however, school-integration conflicts in small communities such as Clinton and Oliver Springs in Tennessee, Clay and Sturgis in Kentucky and Mansfield in Texas had led to episodes of violence and drawn national attention. Since then developments have come frequently and dramatically: in 1957 the Little Rock conflict, the first Civil Rights Act to be passed by Congress since the Reconstruction and the first demands for school integration in the North; in 1960 the first "sit-in," which was conducted by Negro college students in Greensboro, N.C., and led to a wave of similar demonstrations in both Southern and Northern cities; in 1962 the riots at Oxford, Miss., and last year the march on Washington. [See Table 1.]

The pace and scope of the Negro protest movement have provoked intensified resistance to integration in some quarters and may even have alienated many whites who are basically sympathetic to the aspirations of Negroes. The surprisingly strong showing of George C. Wallace, the segregationist governor of Alabama, in several Presidential primaries this spring has been interpreted by some analysts as reflecting just such a reaction.

In the light of these developments it is reasonable to ask if the generally optimistic conclusions we drew in our 1956 article are still tenable and if the long-term trend toward the acceptance of integration has been halted or perhaps even reversed. We have a basis for providing some answers to those questions. Last year the National Opinion Research Center, aided by a grant from the Whitney Foundation, was able to make three surveys (in June, November and December) repeating some of the questions asked in the surveys on which the 1956 article was based. The new findings provide a measure of two significant things: the actual shifts in the attitudes of white adults as a result of the eventful developments in race

[TABLE 1.]

Major events in the field of race relations during the past decade are listed chronologically. They indicate the background against which opinions of whites were formed.

Year	Event
1954	Supreme Court decision against school segregation
1955	Court ruling on school integration "with all deliberate speed" Federal order barring segregation in interstate transportation
1956	School integration conflict, Clinton, Tenn.
1957	First Civil Rights Act since Reconstruction; Little Rock conflict
1958	First use of Civil Rights Act in Negro voting case
1959	Closing of public schools in Prince Edward County, Va.
1960	Second Civil Rights Act; Start of "sit-in" movement, Greensboro, N.C.
1961	Freedom rides
1962	James Meredith at University of Mississippi
1963	March on Washington
1964	Congressional debate on third and strongest Civil Rights Act Supreme Court order on reopening Prince Edward County schools

relations since 1956, and the trends of opinion on integration over a span of more than two decades.

Before we discuss these findings we shall briefly describe how the surveys were made. Each survey was designed to include a representative sample of the nation's adult white population and for that purpose involved interviews with 1,200 to 1,500 individuals. The interviewers were white people trained for the task and living in the sample areas. Each interview resulted in a punched card containing the answers and pertinent information about the person interviewed: age, sex, education, place of residence and so on. In this way the National Opinion Research Center was able to compare the opinions of various groups, such as the elderly and the youthful, the highly educated and the poorly educated, and many others.

In discussing the findings we shall use the terms "South" and "North." "South" refers to three regions as defined by the Bureau of the Census: the South Atlantic region (Delaware, Maryland, the District of Columbia, Virginia, West Virginia, North Carolina, South Carolina, Georgia and Florida), the East South Central region (Kentucky, Tennessee, Alabama and Mississippi) and the West South Central region (Arkansas, Louisiana, Oklahoma and Texas). "North" refers to the rest of the country except for Alaska and Hawaii, where no interviews were conducted. [See Figure 1.] Finally, we wish to emphasize that what we have sought to investigate over these 22 years is the trend of white opinion on racial integration. That is why the findings we shall discuss pertain only to the opinions of

[FIGURE 1]

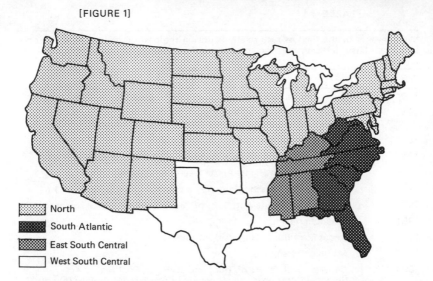

North
South Atlantic
East South Central
West South Central

North and South are differentiated according to the usage in the findings presented in this article. The South consists of three regions as defined by the Bureau of the Census. The North is the rest of the nation except for Alaska and Hawaii.

white adults and do not include the views of the more than 10 million Negro adults in the nation.

The dramatic changes throughout the nation are illustrated by the findings about school segregation, based on the question "Do you think white students and Negro students should go to the same schools or to separate schools?" In 1942 fewer than a third of all whites favored the integration of schools. The attitudes of Southern whites at that time were about as close to unanimity as one ever comes in surveys of the U.S. public: only 2 percent expressed support for integration. Among Northerners in that period integration also represented a minority view, endorsed by only 40 percent of white adults.

By 1956, two years after the Supreme Court decision against racial segregation in public schools, national approval of integrated schools had risen to approximately half of the total white population; in the North it had become the majority view, endorsed by three out of five white adults. Even the South was far from immune to the changing situation. Earlier only one person in 50 had favored school integration; in 1956 the proportion was one in seven. The most recent figures now show not only that the long-term trend has continued but also that in the South it has accelerated. Today a substantial majority of all white Americans endorse school integration. In the North the figure has continued its steady climb and now stands at approximately three out of every four adults. But whereas in the 14 years from 1942 to 1956 the proportion of Southern whites who accepted this principle rose only from 2 percent to 14 percent, the proportion has now risen to 30 percent in just seven years since that time.

That these are real changes rather than accidental results reflecting unreliability of the sampling method is indicated by other findings. In spite of the errors inherent in all sampling procedures, which may run as high as three or four percentage points in samples of the size used in these surveys, the figures for the total white population, in three separate surveys in 1956 and in three other separate surveys last year, did not vary by more than one percentage point. Even the findings for the separate regions, based on smaller numbers and therefore subject to an even larger sampling error, are highly stable.

The surveys repeated in 1956 and 1963 also establish that the changes in national opinion on this question represent long-term trends that are not easily modified by specific — even by highly dramatic — events. The survey last November was conducted within a week after the assassination of President Kennedy, but the national findings remained unchanged in spite of any soul-searching that may have been occurring in the North or the South. In 1956, between the June and September surveys, the attention of the nation had been focused on the first violent crises over school integration in a number of small towns in the border states and in Texas. Again the figures showed no change. The overall picture is thus one of a massive trend, unbroken by the particular news events of the day.

What accounts for the steady and strong rise in support for school integration? One important factor would seem to be the conversion of segregationists. The size of the "Don't know" vote in opinion surveys can be taken as a crude but fair measure of the intensity of the public's views. If large numbers report themselves as undecided, the opinions of the remainder are often lightly held. Conversely, if almost everybody has an opinion on the issue, it is probable that opinions are strong.

It could have been expected that in 1942 — 12 years before the Supreme Court decision and long before the great ferment in civil rights — a considerable number of Americans would have been undecided on the question of school integration. On most issues put to the U.S. public in surveys it is common to find that 10 per cent or more of those interviewed are undecided. Yet in 1942 the "Don't know" group on the question of school integration amounted to no more than 4 per cent of the total.

That group has remained at about 4 per cent since 1942. Therefore the increased support for school integration cannot have come significantly from the ranks of the undecided, leaving the number of staunch segregationists virtually unchanged; nor can it be argued that a number of segregationists have become doubtful of their position and have moved into the ranks of the undecided. The greatly increased support for integration must have come mainly from segregationists who switched to the opposite camp.

There are other indications of the public's strong involvement in the issue of race relations. In last December's survey, prior to any specific questions about integration, respondents were asked: "What, in your opinion, are some of the most important problems facing the United States today?" More people mentioned civil rights and race relations than mentioned any other problem. Similarly, when respondents were asked to rate their degree of interest in a number of public issues, there were more people reporting themselves "very interested" in Negro-white relations than in Cuba or the forthcoming Presidential election.

In sum, the long-term trend toward school integration seems to be moving with considerable force. It has not been reversed even by highly dramatic events. Moreover, integration has been achieving its gains by converting persons with strongly held opposing views.

The problems of Negro-white relations involve many issues other than the integration of schools. For two of these — the integration of neighborhoods and of public transportation — detailed data are available on the trend of public opinion over the 22 years. The question asked concerning neighborhoods was: "If a Negro with the same income and education as you have moved into your block, would it make any difference to you?" The question was asked in this way to eliminate the factor of social class from the discussion and leave the respondent confronted only with the issue of his potential neighbor's color. Since the answer "It would make a difference" could include people who would positively welcome a Negro neighbor, supplementary questions clarified any ambiguity in the matter. The question asked about transportation was: "Generally speaking, do you think there should be separate sections for Negroes on streetcars and buses?"

On these questions the same fundamental trends and underlying processes appear as in opinions on school integration. Opinion has remained highly crystallized, with fewer than 4 per cent unable to decide. And although these questions were asked in only one of the 1956 surveys, so that it was not possible to judge the impact of short-run events at that time, the fact that there was little change between June and December of last year again suggests that attitudes are not greatly modified by such events.

The main findings, which are presented in more detail [in Figure 2], are that support of residential integration rose from 35 per cent in 1942 to 64 per cent at the end of last year among all whites; that for Northern whites the increase was from 42 per cent to 70 per cent and for Southern whites from 12 per cent to 51 per cent, and that during the same period of more than two decades approval of integrated public transportation rose from

[FIGURE 2]

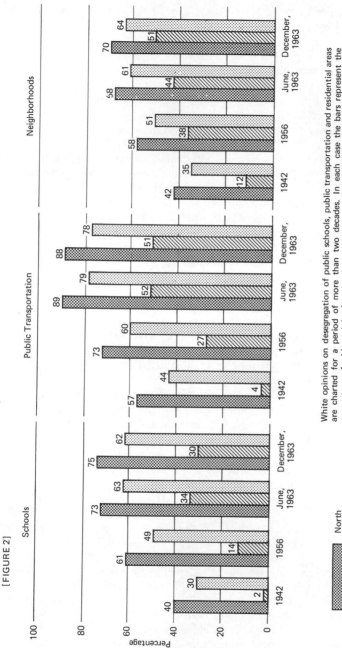

White opinions on desegregation of public schools, public transportation and residential areas are charted for a period of more than two decades. In each case the bars represent the percentage of white adults favoring integration. The spaces above the bars represent the wholly represent persons opposed to integration, for on each issue about 4 percent of the respondents were undecided. Two other surveys in 1956 and one in 1963 produced results consistent with those shown, indicating the reliability of the sampling. The 1963 survey also showed that dramatic events, such as the assassination of President Kennedy, had little effect on the trend of opinion about integration.

44 to 78 per cent among all whites, 57 to 88 per cent among Northern whites and 4 to 51 per cent among Southern whites.

The uniformities in the long-term trends in both the South and the North should not be allowed to obscure certain regional differences in the pattern of opinion on schools, neighborhoods and transportation. For example, the North has been consistently less amenable to residential integration than to integration of public transportation, and the shift in the North over the 22 years has been smallest on the residential issue. Presumably these attitudes reflect the fact that in most of the North whites maintain a social distance from Negroes, although allowing them the legal right to use the same public facilities. This social pattern has contributed to the existence of *de facto* school segregation in the North, even though the great majority of white Northerners are now opposed to school segregation in principle. The pattern is illustrated by the comment of a retired mason in a town in eastern Pennsylvania. After expressing approval of integrated schools and transportation, he said he would object if a Negro of equal education and income moved into his block. He added: "I believe in equality, but not that much."

Having discussed the broad findings of the surveys of the National Opinion Research Center since 1942, we turn to some interpretive remarks and to certain aspects of the findings, particularly as they pertain to views about the integration of schools. We shall first discuss the validity of the responses on which the findings are based. Then we shall examine in some detail opinions about the intelligence of Negroes; the correlation between the support of school integration and the degree of school integration existing in the community; the views of Northerners who have lived in the South and of Southerners who have lived in the North; the correlation between degree of education and support for integration, and the attitudes of different age groups.

It is sometimes argued that in public opinion surveys the respondents do not always reveal their true opinions but instead tend to give the answers they think are expected of them. According to this argument some of the opinion supporting integration is of this character because integration is now fashionable. In our view it is unlikely that such factors inhibited many of the respondents in the surveys we are discussing. The surveys show a substantial number of individuals, even in the North, who express opposition to integration, and the magnitude of the opposition is highest in just those spheres where independent evidence would lead one to expect it: the schools in the South and housing in the North.

On many other questions asked in the most recent surveys white respondents freely expressed opposition to full integration or voiced criticism of Negroes. An example is provided by a question asked last December: "Do you think there should be laws against marriages between

Negroes and whites?" To this 80 per cent of Southern whites and 53 per cent of Northern whites answered affirmatively.

Furthermore, many of the respondents seem to take full account of the moral issues involved and still end up on the segregationist side. For example, a mother in North Carolina gave this response to the question about school integration: "I have mixed emotions. I think they deserve the right, but when I think of my own children going with them, I don't know. . . . Well, I guess I'd say separate schools."

That the demonstrated decline in support of segregation reflects changes in fundamental beliefs is suggested by the long-term trend in white opinion about the inherent intelligence and educability of Negroes. On several occasions since 1942 the National Opinion Research Center has asked the question: "In general, do you think that Negroes are as intelligent as white people — that is, can they learn things just as well if they are given the same education and training?" In the responses to that question there has been a striking change. In 1942 only 50 per cent of Northern whites answered "Yes." Today the figure has risen to 80 per cent. In the South today a substantial majority credits Negroes with equal intelligence, in contrast with only 21 per cent in 1942 [see Figure 3].

This revolutionary change in belief goes far to explain the increased acceptance of school integration over the past two decades. It has undermined one of the most stubborn arguments formerly offered by whites for segregated schools. [Figure 4] shows the relation between belief in the

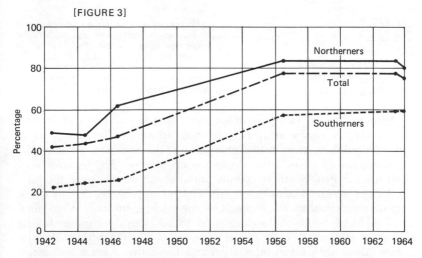

Intelligence of Negroes in the opinion of whites is the subject of this chart. A series of polls in which whites were asked if they believed Negroes to be as intelligent and educable as whites produced the percentages of affirmative responses shown here.

educability of Negroes and the support of integrated schools in the 1956 and 1963 surveys. As one might expect, those who regard the Negro's intelligence as equal to the white's are much more likely to favor integrated schools than those who regard the Negro as inferior in intelligence. There is more than this, however, to be said. Belief in the equal intelligence of Negroes, after rising steadily for 14 years, leveled off in 1956 and has remained stable since then. Support of integrated schools, however, has continued to rise. Plainly there are forces at work in the growing support for the integration of schools other than belief in the educability of Negroes.

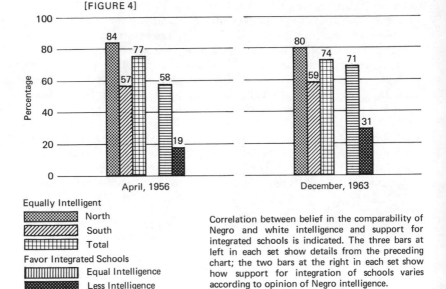

[FIGURE 4]

Equally Intelligent
- North
- South
- Total

Favor Integrated Schools
- Equal Intelligence
- Less Intelligence

Correlation between belief in the comparability of Negro and white intelligence and support for integrated schools is indicated. The three bars at left in each set show details from the preceding chart; the two bars at the right in each set show how support for integration of schools varies according to opinion of Negro intelligence.

Attitudes on school integration vary according to the degree of integration existing in a given area. This becomes apparent when one looks at particular Southern areas instead of regarding "the South" as a homogeneous region, as we have in this discussion up to now. The occurrence of racial crises in some Southern communities but not in others and the varying degrees of official compliance with Federal law suggest that there are large differences within the region. Our surveys bear this out. We divided our sample of Southern localities into three groups according to the amount of integration in the public schools: those with considerable integration, those with token integration and those that remain completely segregated. Since few Southern communities fall into the first classification, respondents living in those areas constitute a tiny fraction of the total, and the sampling error of this particular statistic could be substantial. To give greater strength to the findings we have pooled the results of the surveys in June and December, 1963, and as another check we have compared responses made when the Gallup Poll, at our request, asked Southern whites the question on school integration in June, 1963.

In Southern districts where considerable integration of schools has taken place 54 per cent of white adults favor integration; in districts where token integration has occurred, 38 per cent express favorable attitudes, and in segregated districts 28 per cent favor integration. There is obviously some parallel between public opinion and official action, but which came first? In the desegregated areas did integration come about in response to a more favorable public opinion or did the more favorable public opinion develop only after the official act of desegregation?

Close analysis of the current findings, compared with those of the 1956 surveys, leads us to the conclusion that in those parts of the South where some measure of school integration has taken place official action has *preceded* public sentiment, and public sentiment has then attempted to accommodate itself to the new situation.

In the 1956 surveys of those Southern districts that had already achieved some integration of schools only 31 per cent of white adults expressed approval of the idea. By 1963 the number of such communities had been increased by those districts that only belatedly and reluctantly accepted a measure of integration; in our current sample more than half of the Southern respondents living in communities now classified as integrated to any degree experienced such integration only within the past year, and none of those in areas of considerable integration were exposed to such a level of integration before 1962. One might expect as a result that the proportion approving integration would be even lower than it was seven years ago. Instead approval of integration has risen in such areas from less than a third in 1956 to more than half of their white population today.

Similarly, it was found in 1956 that only 4 per cent of white adults in Southern segregated districts favored the integration of schools. Since then some of these communities have reluctantly adopted a measure of integration, so that the segregated districts that remain might be described as the hard core of segregation. Within this hard core, however, approval of school integration has now risen to 28 per cent of the white public. Thus even in the extreme segregationist areas of the South the tides of opinion are moving toward integration, and in the more progressive areas it seems that official action in itself is contributing to the speed and magnitude of popular change.

In this connection it is relevant to cite the results of the following question, asked repeatedly over the years by the Gallup Poll and included in the

National Opinion Research Center survey of June, 1963: "Do you think the day will ever come in the South when whites and Negroes will be going to the same schools, eating in the same restaurants and generally sharing the same public accommodations?" In South and North alike, whether the community has segregated or integrated schools, more than three-quarters of the white adults believe that integration is bound to come. In contrast, only 53 per cent of the respondents felt that way in 1957. Apparently the pattern is that as official action works to bury what is already regarded as a lost cause, public acceptance of integration increases because opinions are readjusted to the inevitable reality.

Data from the 1963 surveys also enable us to compare opinions in Northern communities that vary in the extent to which Negro and white children attend the same schools. As we have noted, such segregation in the North stems largely from patterns of residential housing rather than from law, but the comparisons with the South are nonetheless of interest. Again we find greater support for integration where integration actually exists and greater support for segregation where there is no integration. In both types of community, however, the overall level of support is much greater in the North than in the South. Among Northern whites living in districts that have segregated schools 65 per cent favor integration; in Northern areas where schools are considerably integrated 83 per cent favor the policy.

A similar pattern of support for integration growing with exposure to integrated situations appears in the findings about people who have moved between North and South. [Figure 5] compares the opinions of four groups: Notherners who have never lived in the South, Northerners who once lived in the South, Southerners who have never lived in the North and Southerners who did at one time live in the North. From the comparison it is apparent that Northerners who once lived in the South differ very little in their views from Northerners who have never been exposed to Southern life. They are only slightly less favorable to integration. In striking contrast, those Southerners who have previously lived in the North differ greatly from those who have always lived in the South. Except on the issue of school integration, the attitudes of Southerners with a history of earlier residence in the North are much closer to those of Northerners than to those of their fellow Southerners. Even on school integration the difference is substantial.

The influence of geographical mobility on Southern opinion may well account for a considerable part of the gross change in Southern attitudes over the recent decades. Although the rate of movement from South to North exceeds the rate from North to South, the Southern migrants represent a relatively small proportion of the Northern population, whereas among Southerners today a considerably larger proportion have

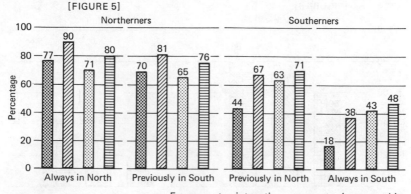

[FIGURE 5]

Exposure to integration appears to increase white support for integration. Northern whites who previously lived in the South show nearly as much support for integration and as much belief in the comparability of Negro and white intelligence as whites who have always lived in the North. Southern whites with previous Northern residence show a markedly higher support for integration and belief in the equality of white and Negro intelligence than Southerners who have never lived outside the South.

had some Northern exposure. Thus the net effect of migration is to strengthen support for integration.

As for the relation between amount of education and support of integration, both the 1956 and the 1963 surveys showed that the better-educated groups, North and South, were more favorable to integration of schools and public transportation than people of less education were. Between the two surveys, however, all subgroups have become more favorable to integration [see Figure 6]. Since the number of cases in the South is small, and since the subgroup estimates are subject to a larger sampling error, we have pooled the two recent surveys.

The most dramatic change of opinion has occurred in the best-educated segment of the Southern white population, where the proportion in favor of integration has increased from only about a fourth to almost half. Lest formal education appear to be a decisive factor, however, note that in 1963 the best-educated white Southerners were not as favorably inclined to integration as the least-educated white Northerners, and that by 1963 those Southerners had not yet reached the level of opinion already exhibited in 1956 by poorly-educated Northerners.

In 1956 it was found that the segment of the white population represented by people 65 and older, in both the North and the South, was least favorable to integration, and the same finding is documented in the recent surveys. One would expect this result on the basis of education

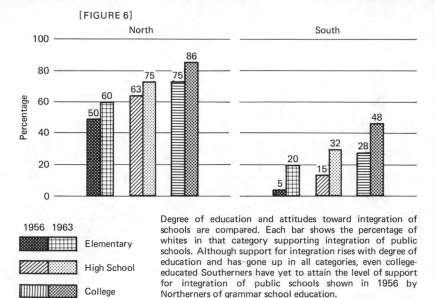

[FIGURE 6]

1956 1963

Elementary

High School

College

Degree of education and attitudes toward integration of schools are compared. Each bar shows the percentage of whites in that category supporting integration of public schools. Although support for integration rises with degree of education and has gone up in all categories, even college-educated Southerners have yet to attain the level of support for integration of public schools shown in 1956 by Northerners of grammar school education.

alone; inasmuch as the expansion of educational opportunity is a development of recent decades, the oldest adults are less likely than the younger ones to have had advanced schooling. Indeed, some of the long-term trends in attitudes toward segregation may simply represent the passing of the oldest generation and its replacement in the population by younger individuals of greater tolerance. The persistence of the difference in attitudes between the oldest group and younger groups would help to account for the further changes in public opinion in more recent years and would augur still more change in the future.

Since the analysis of differences between age groups is so relevant to an understanding of long-term opinion trends, the sample in last December's survey was designed to double the number of interviews with the youngest adults — those from 21 to 24. These extra interviews were not included in the tabulations except for this particular analysis, but by using them here we can place greater confidence in our findings for this age group, which otherwise would account for only a small portion of the national sample. In this way we are able to provide more evidence for a new finding that appeared in the survey of June, 1963, but then could be regarded only as suggestive. The finding, which is reflected [in Figure 7], is that whereas in 1956 the youngest adults were the most favorable to school integration, by 1963 the pattern — at least for the South — seemed to have changed. Although they were never as prosegregationist as the older age groups, the 21-to-24-year-olds appeared in the recent surveys to be less favorable to the integration of schools than the adults aged 25 to 44. The difference is admittedly small and could conceivably be due to sample variation. But the finding appeared in all of last year's surveys; unless it is disproved by subsequent studies one must accept as valid the evidence that the youngest adults are relatively less tolerant than formerly, in spite of the fact that on the average they are more highly educated.

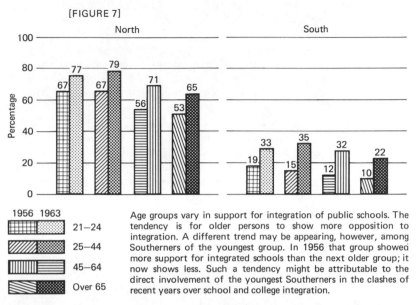

[FIGURE 7]

1956 1963

21—24
25—44
45—64
Over 65

Age groups vary in support for integration of public schools. The tendency is for older persons to show more opposition to integration. A different trend may be appearing, however, among Southerners of the youngest group. In 1956 that group showed more support for integrated schools than the next older group; it now shows less. Such a tendency might be attributable to the direct involvement of the youngest Southerners in the clashes of recent years over school and college integration.

The members of the youngest group in 1956 have, of course, now aged sufficiently to be included in the present 25-to-44 group and have added their earlier quantum of tolerance to that older group's attitudes. Those who are now in the 21-to-24 group were still children in 1956 and so were not included in the surveys of that time. But why, having arrived at the status of young adults, do they not exhibit the larger measure of tolerance characteristic of the equivalent age group in earlier years?

That the phenomenon is clearly evident only in the South suggests an explanation, because this newest group of young Southern adults has lived through experiences quite different from those of the generation of young adults studied in 1956. They have spent their high school and college years in the stormy decade since the Supreme Court decision, and it is they who have been most closely associated with the crises and dislocations that have accompanied the transition to integration in various communities. Actually few of them appear to have suffered directly from these events. They were asked "In what ways have you or any members of your family been affected by integration?" More than four-fifths reported no effects. It is noteworthy, however, that not a single Southerner of this age group spontaneously reported any kind of favorable effect, whereas among Northerners of the same age 5 per cent volunteered an answer describing the personal effects of integration in favorable terms.

Plainly the conflicts of integration have had a great immediacy for the young Southerners. The issue of civil rights is more salient for them than for the older groups in our Southern sample. More of them spontaneously mention race relations as the biggest problem facing the country today. The youngest Southerners are more likely than the next older group to express themselves as believing the Negro protest movement is "violent" rather than "peaceful" and to voice the opinion that demonstrations and protests have "hurt the cause" of Negroes.

Other questions substantiate the likelihood that a change of attitude has occurred among young Southern adults. When asked if their views have remained the same in recent years or have become more favorable or less favorable to integration, it is this youngest group that is more likely than others to report both a change in attitude and a shift away from a favorable opinion. For example, the youngest adults in the South say they have shifted almost two to one against integration in recent years. The older groups report less change of attitude, and when it occurs, the shifts are about equal in both directions.

Apart from this tendency, about the extent or permanence of which we cannot yet be sure, it appears that the attitudes of white Americans of both the North and the South are continuing to shift toward greater acceptance of integration. We cannot be certain that future events will not reverse the course. But the unbroken trend of the past 20 years, and particularly its acceleration in the past decade of intensified controversy, suggest that integration will not be easily halted. In the minds and hearts of the majority of Americans the principle of integration seems already to have been won. The issues that remain are how soon and in what ways the principle is to be implemented.

Bibliography

Grodzins, Morton, "Metropolitan Segregation." *Scientific American*, Vol. 197, No. 4, October, 1957, pp. 33-41.

Hyman, Herbert H., and Sheatsley, Paul B. "Attitudes toward Desegregation." *Scientific American*, Vol. 195, No. 6, December, 1956, pp. 35-39.

Myrdal, Gunnar. *An American Dilemma: The Negro Problem and Modern Democracy*. New York: Harper and Row, Publishers, 1962.

Williams, Robin M., Jr. *Strangers Next Door: Ethnic Relations in American Communities*. New York: Prentice-Hall, Inc., 1964.

XVI

The West Indies present a highly diverse field for the analysis of race relations. They are not one society, but a variety of islands with different traditions and different racial organizations. Although none of the islands has a significant White or Indian population, a variety of skin color groups, the children of past White and Negro alliances, are present. Island societies are stratified by color; light-skinned people are usually urban, better educated, more often employed, and politically more powerful than dark-skinned people. The dark-skinned, rural poor often resort to radical politics and apocalyptic religion to overcome their status. Class, region, religion, and education, summed up in race, fragment West Indian societies.

DAVID LOWENTHAL

Race and Color in the West Indies

MYTHS AND REALITIES

. . . By contrast with the rigidity of race relations in South Africa or the United States, those in the West Indies are indeed free and pleasant.

From *Daedalus*, Vol. 96, No. 2 (Spring, 1967), pp. 581-626. Reprinted by permission of the author and the publisher.

This paper is a by-product of a work being prepared for the Institute of Race Relations (London). I am grateful to Marion Bellamy, W. Haywood Burns, Lambros Comitas, Edward Cumberbatch, Charles Hobson, Max Lowenthal, and Paule Marshall for criticisms and suggestions.

But the rosy image of multiracial harmony has been challenged by a distressed and newly articulate lower class, by West Indian students, and by some popular leaders. "The myth of social and racial integration has been pretty nearly exploded," writes a young Jamaican nationalist. "The accepted passport to preferment seems to be a physical appearance as near to that of the average European as possible."[1] And a Guyanese finds "more race prejudice in the West Indies than anywhere in the world. . . . The Negroes hate the Indians, the dark-skinned people hate the light brown people. . . . They're hopeless."[2]

Local misgivings are confirmed by scholarly inquiries. A survey of race relationships in Martinique and Guadeloupe reports grave antagonisms between white entrepreneurs and colored laborers, local white interdiction against intermarriage, and racial categories that parallel those of class. A study of social stratification in Trinidad depicts a society little resembling the popular misconception of easygoing, egalitarian interracial mingling. The light-colored elite and the black peasantry of Grenada are shown to inhabit worlds not remotely alike.[3] Studies of other islands reveal similar circumstances.

Nowhere in the West Indies does racial discrimination have the sanction of law, and social exclusion based on color, once the rule, is now much moderated. But color distinctions correlate with class differences and govern most personal associations. They are frequently voiced to derogate the darker among the people. . . .

Recent events arouse the concern that in some respects West Indian race relations have actually deteriorated. In British Guiana, the riots and incendiarism of the past decade originated in racial fears and resentments. In Martinique, the immigration of Algerian whites touched off serious race riots. In Jamaica, the distress of slum dwellers explodes now in black nationalism, now in political-party violence, and now in assaults against Chinese shopkeepers who serve as scapegoats. Racial feelings are particularly inflamed where political independence and economic development benefit relatively few while throwing the misery of the many into sharper relief. "If there was justice and equality for us black people," argued a Jamaican, "there wouldn't be so many of us starving while white people in Stony Hill are feeding their dogs with beefsteak. . . . The white peo-

---

[1] "Realism and Race" by A Young Jamaican Nationalist, in "Two Views on the Problem of Race and Colour in Jamaica Today," *West Indian Economist* (Jamaica), Vol. 3, No. 10 (April, 1961), p. 6.

[2] Ivor Leila, "The Changing Attitude to Mixed Marriages," *Flamingo* (London), No. 2 (October, 1961), p. 36.

[3] Michel Leiris, *Contacts de civilisations en Martinique et en Guadeloupe* (Paris, 1955); Lloyd Braithwaite, "Social Stratification in Trinidad: A Preliminary Analysis," *Social and Economic Studies*, Vol. 2, Nos. 2 and 3 (1953), pp. 5-175; M. G. Smith, *Stratification in Grenada* (Berkeley and Los Angeles, 1965).

ple's dogs live better than the black man in this country."[4] A political leader maintains: "The black man eats the least, wears the least, owns the least, prays the most, works the most, suffers the most and dies the most."[5] There is no doubting the truth of these propositions. Jamaica can still be summed up in the familiar lines, "If you white, you all right; if you brown, stick around; if you black, stand back."[6] The differences are less taken for granted than they used to be, but that makes them no easier to endure.

As the more blatant features of prejudice fade away, other aspects come to the fore. "The colour discrimination which still persists in this island is not of any real importance," a Barbadian editorial concludes, "but it is embarrassing."[7] Some Barbadian social clubs still exclude dark people, and the government itself was accused of bias at entertainments where, a black legislator complained, "you see a sprinkling of the population that looks like myself and then you see a whole mass of the [white] minority."[8] In Jamaica "there are still upper class whites who talk and think about damned niggers, and throw their children out of the house for marrying people with a touch of colour."[9] And an editorial contends that "many people in Jamaica still boast that they have never entertained a negroid person in their homes."[10] On the other hand, some insist that they have always been color blind. "Now that racialism is under fire and in retreat," observes a Trinidadian, local whites "profess a lofty scorn for it and are terribly pained when you so much as refer to it."[11] Yet Negroes who try to practice the multiracial integration they preach may be "castigated as 'having a preference for mixing with white people.' "[12] It is not surprising that the former Chief Minister felt it necessary to explain that "Jamaica has a very complex . . . social structure which very few people understand. . . . We're only beginning to unify it."[13]

.   .   .

[4] "Black Shadow Over 'Paradise Isle,' " Newday (Jamaica), Vol. 5, No. 6 (June, 1961), p. 20.

[5] Millard Johnson, cited in S. George Minott, "The P.P.P. and Charges of Race Hatred," Jamaica Times, June 29, 1961, p. 9.

[6] H. Orlando Patterson, The Children of Sisyphus (London, 1964), p. 115.

[7] "Colour Bar Should Be Swept Away," Barbados Advocate, February 13, 1962.

[8] F. L. Walcott, in the House of Assembly, Barbados Advocate, February 14, 1962.

[9] Thomas Wright, "Candidly Yours," Jamaica Daily Gleaner, April 25, 1961, p. 12.

[10] Jamaica Daily Gleaner, May 6, 1964.

[11] C. L. R. James, Beyond a Boundary (London, 1963), p. 65.

[12] Henry Forde, "Barbadians Are Hypocritical about Colour," Barbados Advocate, February 21, 1962.

[13] Norman W. Manley, address at Social Development Conference, quoted in Jamaica Daily Gleaner, July 18, 1961, p. 2.

A great many West Indians, are highly sensitive about matters of color. As one observer put it, to "talk about 'the colour question' or 'race relations' is to pick a way through thorns while walking on eggshells, as even the commonest adjectives of description appear to bear allusive barbs." But to ignore the object is no solution, for "too great a circumspection . . . may also arouse hostility."[14] A visitor found that "the mere mention of colour on the part of a stranger is liable to put the average Guianese on the defensive," while "the effort of avoiding pitfalls can result in a stiltedness that may in itself be considered indirectly insulting."[15]

Some West Indians in fact regard the public airing of color complaints as a sign that they matter less than before. Formerly, writes a Jamaican, "you seldom if ever heard talk and protest about this colour thing, . . . for when something is accepted — accepted so deeply that to drag it up to the surface would be unbearably painful — nobody talks about it. . . . It's only when the pain gets less, when you see an end to it just round the corner, that you dare to drag it into the open and face it. That's why we talk about it endlessly in Jamaica today. For we are, today, nearer to beating it than anywhere else in the world."[16]

HISTORICAL BACKGROUND

Race relations in the West Indies today seem especially benign by contrast with the past. Ethnic distinctions have mattered more and longer there than in any other part of the New World. A local leader terms it "the first area in the world which saw the emergence of this modern problem of race relations and the contact between the so-called 'advanced' and 'backward' peoples."[17] On Caribbean sugar estates, European masters exerted absolute control over the lives of African slaves and Asian indentured laborers. The impact of plantation slavery elsewhere in America, from Brazil to Maryland, was less pervasive. West Indian physical landscapes, social structures, and ways of life are in great measure plantation by-products. . . .

Such conditions, especially Negro slavery, were most marked in the British, French, and Dutch West Indies, and my focus is principally on these non-Iberian realms. Here live twelve million people in fifty separate societies ranging in size from Haiti's five million to tiny islands of a few hundred. They include Jamaica, Trinidad and Tobago, and Barbados, which have gained independence from Britain within the past five

---

[14] A. P. Thornton, "Aspects of West Indian Society," *International Journal*, Vol. 15 (1960), p. 113.

[15] Zahra Freeth, *Run Softly Demerara* (London, 1960), p. 62.

[16] Wright, "Candidly Yours," *Jamaica Daily Gleaner*, April 25, 1961.

[17] Eric Williams, "The Historical Background of Race Relations in the Caribbean," Teachers Economic and Cultural Association, Ltd., *Public Affairs Pamphlets No. 3* (Port-of-Spain, Trinidad, 1955), p. 3.

years; a string of eight semidependent British colonies stretching from the Virgin Islands southward through the Leewards and the Windwards; the French islands of Martinique and Guadeloupe, which in 1948 ceased to be dependencies and became *départements*, integrated in theory but not assimilated in fact with the rest of France; six islands, headed by Curaçao, comprising the semiautonomous Netherlands Antilles; and a miscellaneous remnant — the American Virgin Islands, the Caymans (British), and San Andrés and Providencia (ruled by Colombia but inhabited by folk of Jamaican stock and English speech). Other islands in this Iberian sea are British Honduras in Central America, and in South America the three Guianas: Guyana, which gained independence from Britain in 1966; Surinam, associated with the Netherlands in the same fashion as the Netherlands Antilles; and French Guiana, like Martinique and Guadeloupe, a *département* of France. The Guianas have little contact with neighboring Brazil or Venezuela, but have histories and ethnic compositions similar to those of the Caribbean islands; they are in most ways that matter "West Indian."

Within the non-Iberian Caribbean there is contrast enough. But there are also certain basic similarities among these territories, styles of life that set them apart from Latin America. Spanish and Portuguese ideas and behavior about race, slavery, freedom, and equality differ sharply from those of other Europeans in the New World (though the differences have been exaggerated by apologists on both sides). Their ethnic histories are likewise different. Although Indian bondage was an important feature of colonial Latin America, slavery there seldom played the pervasive role that it did in the British, French, and Dutch islands, where African slaves preponderated. Where slaves were the largest element in the population, racial issues have been most dominant.

These lands have other common features significant for race relations. Because the Indians were early exterminated, the only enduring contacts have been among European, African, and Asian newcomers. Other countries have minority problems, but in the West Indies the "minority" is a numerical majority, and the whole flavor of affairs derives from that fact. Whites are a small and diminishing group, almost everywhere less than 5 per cent of the population; non-whites comprise more than nine tenths of the inhabitants of all but a very few tiny islands. In other parts of the world where Europeans are few — West Africa, India, Southeast Asia — indigenous ways prevail. But in the West Indies there are practically no indigenes; the circumstances of slavery allowed little African culture to survive, and many inhabitants recognize no tradition other than the European. Most of the area has thrown off formal colonial rule but remains linked to London, Paris, and Amsterdam by political, economic, cultural and emotional bonds. . . .

In the West Indies as nowhere else in the New World, Europeans met native Americans only to annihilate them — the Spanish "falling first upon their knees and then upon the Indians," other Europeans not even bothering with the first fall. Columbus and his followers thought of little but gold. Because the islands failed to satisfy this obsession, they abandoned them. Their North European successors outdid the Spanish in treating the islands only as the sources of fortune and the seats of enterprise. Few thought of the West Indies as home or forged any bonds between land and society. The ties between Spanish and Indian in Mexico and Peru, the familial obligations of slaveholders on Latin American haciendas, had no Caribbean counterparts.

The Dutch, French, and English organized the islands as purely commercial enterprises with greater energy and success than had the Spanish. For gold, the North Europeans substituted sugar; for Indian labor they substituted African. As with the Indians, it seemed easier to work Negroes hard and replace them with newly-bought slaves than to look after them and encourage them to reproduce. The Negro was a replaceable machine. . . .

Because the islands were seldom considered fit to live in, most of them failed to develop a true elite. "In British West Indian . . . society," a local historian writes, "a man became a member of the élite only when he qualified as a potential absentee. . . . 'Colonial élite' was a contradiction in terms [to men] . . . whose means permitted them to be élite rather than colonial."[18] No wonder colonial officials complained about the inadequacies of resident West Indian whites. Except for Barbados and, perhaps, Martinique, most men of intelligence and enterprise had gone "home"; those who remained had no qualifications but their white skins. Educated colored men were barred from the elite first by law and later by prejudice. Many West Indian societies were, in effect, truncated structures. Their natural leaders were either in Europe or proscribed by color. They were dominated, instead, by European castoffs and remittance men concerned only to maintain an oligarchy that was their sole compensation for exile. . . .

Whites long considered themselves the only inhabitants of the West Indies. Even those who baptized, punished, or slept with their slaves viewed them as property, not as people. To be sure, the conditions of slavery and the treatment of slaves varied with the nationality and religion of their owners, the nature of the economy, and the numerical balance between slave and free, black and white. Thus the Dutch were reputed crueler slavemasters than the French, the Protestants than the Catholics, sugar planters more demanding than coffee growers, and so on. But these differences were neither substantial nor consistent; the lot of

18 Douglas Hall, "Absentee-Proprietorship in the British West Indies, to about 1850," *Jamaican Historical Review*, Vol. 4 (1964), pp. 27-29.

West Indian slaves was everywhere much alike. In terms of work routine, nourishment, confinement, and punishment they were worse off than any others in the New World. . . .

The West Indian sugar plantation used up slaves at a rapid rate; only continual imports from Africa could meet the planters' needs for labor. In addition to deaths on the Middle Passage, slave mortality in the West Indies probably approached 20 per cent a year. About five million Africans were brought to the British, French, and Dutch Caribbean; yet in the mid-nineteenth century, when slavery ended, the Negro population there was less than two million.[19]

Between the millions of slaves and the dwindling thousands of whites, a third class came to occupy an increasingly prominent position. This was the "free colored" group — manumitted slaves who were often the offspring of white men and slave women, or their descendants. At the end of the eighteenth century the free colored comprised from 5 to 20 per cent of various West Indian populations; by the time of emancipation they outnumbered the whites.

The free colored were distinguished from the slaves not only by freedom but by color. Most of them were free, in fact, because their fathers or grandfathers had been white. They were by and large intermediate in shade — mulatto, quadroon, octroon, and other gradations between white and black. Many free persons were black, and many slaves were colored, but the preponderance of mulattoes among free non-whites and of blacks among slaves shaped a shorthand view that lumped all free persons together as "colored" and all slaves as "black." Most important, whites recognized the free colored as superior to both slaves and to free blacks, and gave them privileges according to their shade. Within the free-colored group itself, rank and privilege largely depended on closeness to white features and ancestors.[20] . . .

[19] See Elsa V. Goveia, "The West Indian Slave Laws of the Eighteenth Century," *Revista de Ciencias Sociales*, Vol. 4 (1960), pp. 75-105; Douglas Hall, "Slaves and Slavery in the British West Indies," *Social and Economic Studies*, Vol. 11 (1962), pp. 305-18; George W. Roberts, "A Life Table for a West Indian Slave Population," *Population Studies*, Vol. 5 (1952), pp. 238-43. Slave conditions are compared in Frank Tannenbaum, *Slave and Citizen* (New York: Vintage Books, 1963); Stanley M. Elkins, *Slavery: A Problem in American Institutional and Intellectual Life* (New York: Universal Library, 1963); Marvin Harris, *Patterns of Race in the Americas* (New York, 1964); and David Brion Davis, *The Problem of Slavery in Western Culture* (Ithaca, N.Y., 1966).

[20] Sheila Duncker, "The Free Coloured and Their Fight for Civil Rights in Jamaica, 1800-1830" (unpublished Master's thesis, University of London, 1959); Winthrop Jordan, "American Chiaroscuro: The Status and Definition of Mulattoes in the British Colonies," *William and Mary Quarterly*, 2d ser., Vol. 19 (1962), pp. 183-200; Elsa V. Goveia, *Slave Society in the British Leeward Islands at the End of the Eighteenth Century* (New Haven, 1965), pp. 258-59, 315-17.

Sexual relationships between white men and colored and black women in the West Indies, especially where white women were few, were openly countenanced; whites customarily had colored mistresses, white fathers regularly placed their colored daughters as concubines, and few colored girls were available for marriage with colored men. White fathers not only recognized their colored children, but often educated them in Europe and left them large properties. . . .

Greater familiarity with colored people led West Indian whites to make fine color distinctions that seemed pointless to Americans, who lumped all folk of African descent together as Negroes. Moreover, being Europeans, white West Indians took a stratified social order for granted and regarded the separate identity of the free colored as a means of consolidating their own control over the hierarchy. . . .

The balance among the three elements of West Indian society was strained, however, as the free-colored group grew in numbers and affluence. In Saint-Domingue, rivalry between the free colored and white immigrants from France was so bitter in the late eighteenth century that both groups ignored warnings of slave revolt and were overwhelmed by it. In the British and Dutch territories, barriers between white and colored remained high; up to the eve of emancipation, law as well as custom discriminated against the free colored. A small racial minority exercised absolute power over social institutions that everywhere discriminated against all non-whites.

Yet within two generations race and color virtually vanished in the eyes of the law. Between the Haitian revolution of 1791 and the emancipation of 1863 in Surinam, all West Indian slaves (outside the Spanish islands) were freed and all legal disabilities against non-whites eliminated. The transition took place in various ways and at various tempos. In Haiti, where slaves and free colored had suffered the most galling restrictions, the revolution reversed the hierarchy; surviving whites were forbidden to own land and mulattoes were penalized by blacks. The British West Indian transition was more orderly, slave-law reforms leading to free-colored civil rights, ex-slave apprenticeship, and final emancipation between 1823 and 1838. Suffrage was limited on the basis of property, not race; juries no longer excluded black and colored men; schools were open, at least in theory, to all. . . .

Nevertheless formal freedom availed most West Indians little in the face of customary discrimination. Indeed, emancipation intensified color prejudice. In the absence of slavery, race assumed paramount importance in social issues. Even the most zealous emancipationists had not expected the freed slaves to gain early equality with their former masters. Failure to create an instant utopia and the supposed decline of the West Indian economy were cited as evidence of Negro inferiority, unfitness for self-rule, and hereditary ineducability. West Indian whites, still in local control, reduced the scope of Negro freedom by means of vagrancy laws, by coercive rental and wage arrangements that tied tenancies to plantation duties, and by state-subsidized indentured immigration that kept estate wages low. . . .

In every West Indian territory, emancipation conferred political equality; in every territory, equality was a legal fiction. Universal suffrage in the French Antilles became meaningless when centralization in Paris deprived local councils of all power. In the British islands there was no thought of a broad suffrage. Whites controlled local legislatures with a handful of "qualified" — that is, rich, educated, and well-connected — men of color; non-whites occupied only a few subordinate governmental niches. The spectre of Haiti and the conviction that Negroes were inferior reinforced white reluctance to yield any power or perquisites. . . . Not until after World War II did the British Indies advance to universal adult suffrage and internal self-rule. . . .

THE PLURAL SOCIETY

Most social systems are held together by general consensus based on a widespread community of interests. But where a dominant minority and a subordinate majority have opposing interests and modes of life, the social structure is validated not by consensus but by force. This kind of society, frequently resulting from the European conquest, enslavement, or introduction of "native" populations, has been termed "plural."

West Indian slave societies were based on force, openly avowed by the slaveowners and governments and more or less resisted by the slaves. After emancipation, a few whites, many of the colored middle class, and some of the former slaves worked to build a society based on consensus and social integration. Such a society nowhere came to pass. The elite minority retained its predominance and, with imperial support, preserved the old distinctions — based now on color rather than on servitude. . . .

West Indian society is still a hierarchy of sections differing profoundly in institutional forms and behavior, culture and values. In some Caribbean lands — Trinidad, Guyana, Surinam — the presence of descendants of East Indian indentured laborers creates a still more complex and divisive situation. But almost every West Indian territory is dominated by a small white or light-colored group whose way of life is both the unattainable envy and the dreadful burden of the predominantly black majority. A growing middle class awkwardly amalgamates traits and institutions from above and below. Middle-class obsession with status based on color emphasizes sectional discontinuities and keeps the whole structure precariously balanced. Brute force and punitive repression figure less as agencies of social cohesion than they did during slavery. But gulfs in living standards and opportunities persist, and some of them are broader than they were. Political independence and declarations of racial unity notwithstanding, pluralism in many West Indian societies shows no sign of disappearing.[21]

In most respects the West Indian social order correlates with color differences, but the pattern of ranking is not everywhere the same. The plural structure has no relevance in a few islands that are racially homogeneous, and color plays little part in considerations of status on French St. Barthélemy (almost entirely white) and on British Carriacou and Barbuda (almost entirely black). . . .

The tripartite association of color with status nevertheless remains a fundamental fact of most West Indian societies. The upper section contains from 2 to 5 per cent of the population, the middle from 5 to 15 per cent, and the lower the remainder. The upper and middle groups — that is, white and colored — have many institutions in common and sometimes unite in opposing the black masses, but their springs of action and self-images differ. The top section practices a somewhat outdated variant of Western European culture and is locally regarded as the authoritative guide to that culture. The black majority's culture amalgamates elements derived from earlier European forms with some African features, filtered through the context of slavery. The middle section combines elements of both the others, usually as uneasy alternatives rather than in a viable integrated form.

Unlike as the sections are in culture and institutions, their evaluations of status and prestige are similar; almost everyone would like to be as European as possible. Basic disparities are apt to be masked by this apparent agreement. Each section professes loyalty to some national or imperial symbol, avoids manual labor, and accepts marriage as an ideal, but this coincidence of values does not show that they share a common way of life; rather, each strives to emulate the elite and discredits its own circumstances and habits. Shared values are an added source of tension because these values are beyond the reach of most West Indians.

. . .

Elite and middle-class West Indians are in daily contact with domestic servants, gardeners, and other employees. But they remain extraordinarily ignorant of the circumstances of lower-class life — which helps to explain why agricultural-extension and social-welfare work is so often ineffectual. Rural cultivators are unlikely to adopt reforms advocated by visitors whose doctrinaire theories, brown skins, and city clothing highlight their lack of local understanding and insight.[22] . . .

21 J. S. Furnivall, Colonial Policy and Practice (London, 1948); Vera Rubin (ed.), "Social and Cultural Pluralism in the Caribbean," Annals, ·New York Academy of Sciences, Vol. 83 (1960), pp. 761-916; M. G. Smith, The Plural Society in the British West Indies (Berkeley and Los Angeles, 1965).

22 Hyman Rodman, "On Understanding Lower-Class Behaviour," Social and

What the sections of society do know about others they usually disapprove of. Each class uses moral dogmas to justify its images. Because these dogmas are mutually incompatible, each group condemns the behavior and attitudes of the others. Thus West Indians tend to "moralize incessantly about one another's actions in order to assert their cultural and social identity."[23] The language is not didactic but censorious; no one really wants other classes to become like one's own.

Legal institutions illustrate how mutual ignorance and moral judgments reinforce West Indian sectional differences. Despite universal suffrage, the chief law-making and law-enforcing agencies reflect elite social views. One is that the lower class is innately criminal. The belief is self-fulfilling for much of the local criminal code and police action is directed against practices that are defined as criminal but are in fact customary — bastardy, praedial larceny, obscenity, obeah, marijuana. The masses see formal law as a class weapon and policemen as their natural enemies; the elite expect preferential police treatment as a matter of course. In the courts, a laborer is gravely disadvantaged by illiteracy and unfamiliarity with the law. Lack of money makes legal aid hard to get, even should he overcome his suspicion of lawyers as representatives of the elite. No wonder many people regard the law as "an alien thing, not felt as applying to their daily life because there are so many basic points at which it runs counter to their habits of thought."[24]

Religious differences further illustrate how sectional hostilities operate. Planters, European officials, and the established churches have tried since the inception of slavery to eradicate voodoo and obeah; they reprobate lower-class revivalist and pentecostal sects as the heathen, African, diabolical superstitions of unlettered savages. The middle class, emphasizing its respectability and its remoteness from African superstition, has led the campaign. Any organized slave activity was potentially seditious; any mass gathering today arouses the fears of the well-off. Response to the Ras Tafari movement in Jamaica is a case in point; wholly ignorant of the aims and creeds of this "back-to-Africa" sect, the elite and the middle

---

Economic Studies, Vol. 8 (1959), pp. 441-50, describes the problems involved. M. G. Smith and G. J. Kruijer, A Sociological Manual for Extension Workers in the Caribbean (Kingston, Jamaica, 1957), warn against neglecting them. James M. Blaut et al., "A Study of Cultural Determinants of Soil Erosion and Conservation in the Blue Mountains of Jamaica," Social and Economic Studies, Vol. 8 (1959), pp. 403-20; and David Edwards, Report on an Economic Study of Small Farming in Jamaica (Kingston, Jamaica, 1961), underline the failure to make contact.

23 Smith, The Plural Society, p. 175.
24 "The Case for Law Reform — 2: The Conditions Affecting Demand," West Indian Economist, Vol. 2, No. 10 (April, 1960), p. 7.

class saw it only as evidence of the depravity and criminal intent of the threatening masses.[25]

Family forms exemplify the complexity of West Indian social structure and attitudes. The three sections share an ideal of married monogamy, but each approaches this ideal by a different route. . . . Although marriage is ultimately desirable, illegitimacy carries little stigma among the folk. But the middle class regards the high rate of illegitimacy as shameful and wicked, proof of promiscuity and immorality. Blaming the lower class for the image of colored West Indians they think Europeans have adopted, middle-class people denounce non-legal unions to show their disapproval of "African" and their loyalty to "European" forms.

The social gradient is steep, and most West Indians find the barriers difficult to cross. The very fact that people do contrast their own lot with that of others, and react bitterly to the discrepancies, evinces a community of discourse. And the minority position of the elite makes it impossible for them entirely to ignore the demands of the majority. Besides this connection, there is a color-class continuum; the social hierarchy is knit together by intermarriage, by acculturation, by assimilation. . . .

At the top, pluralism has positive utility. The successful civil servant adopts elite behavior and then maximizes class distinctions; the successful politician, whatever his origins, identifies himself with the subordinate sector and wins popular favor by stressing the exploitation it has suffered. West Indian societies perpetuate pluralism by encouraging sectional leadership. Struggles for power between popularly-elected rulers and an appointed civil service highlight the absence of consensus.

There is little evidence that the upper classes are anxious to reform this state of affairs or to be less isolated from the masses. Nor are sectional differences becoming less extreme. In 1961 Jamaicans learned that while the economy as a whole was expanding, the gap between the "haves" and the "have-nots" was growing too. Awareness of these discrepancies has also increased. The visibly impoverished are ever more numerous; the Kingston slums held 39,000 in 1958, 60,000 in 1960, perhaps 80,000 in 1964. . . .

THE DIMENSIONS OF COLOR

Race and color do not define West Indian classes. But class grievances are mainly expressed in terms of race and color. The degree of significance varies with class. The elite take their ascription as whites for granted; color is an overt issue among them only in gross transgressions of the

[25] M. G. Smith, Roy Augier, and Rex Nettleford, The Ras Tafari Movement in Kingston, Jamaica (Kingston, Jamaica, 1960); James A. Mau, "The Threatening Masses: Myth or Reality?" in The Caribbean in Transition, Papers on Social, Political, and Economic Development, eds. F. M. Andic and T. G. Mathews (Rio Piedras, P. R., 1965), pp. 258-70.

social code. Nor is color *per se* overwhelmingly important in lower-class communities; the interest in identifying ancestral strains focuses on lines of descent, not degrees of whiteness.[26] But in the middle class color is the crucial determinant of status, and status is the main goal in life. . . . Physiognomy is only one of many ways of perceiving color, which West Indians rank according to appearance, ancestry, and association. Where ancestry is a matter of common knowledge, as it is apt to be in small islands, genotype may be more important than phenotype. . . .

In the final analysis, color is a matter of culture. Whatever their actual appearance, middle-class folk tend to be considered and to view themselves as "colored," while lower-class folk are "black." The adage "every rich Negro is a mulatto, every poor mulatto is a Negro" fits West Indian society today as in the past. Family background, wealth, and education make the distinctions between "colored" and "white" almost as flexible. Many West Indians known to have colored forebears are locally accepted as white. . . .

Physical "color" in the West Indies is not a matter of skin pigmentation alone; it involves a constellation of traits that differentiate European and African. The most important, besides shade, are hair texture and facial structure. These three aspects of physiognomy are almost invariably combined in color attributions. . . .

Yet pigmentation was aesthetically the easiest barrier to hurdle. Blackness was the badge of slavery, but Europeans came to regard it without the abhorrence they professed for kinky hair and thick lips. Planters throughout the islands were attracted by brown or *café-au-lait* skins. West Indian non-whites today hold similar aesthetic values. Antillean exemplars of *négritude* who glorify African beauty single out black skins for praise, but seldom laud other "African" traits.

The ascription of "white," "colored," and "black" varies with metropolitan background and local experience. Mediterraneans of dark complexion are apt to view as "white" folk who might elsewhere be considered "colored." This difference in perception partly explains the much higher proportion of "whites" in the Spanish Caribbean than in the French and British. In Hispaniola, for example, free-colored refugees fleeing the Haitian revolution became "white" when they crossed the border into Spanish Santo Domingo. Subjective change of color, along with Iberian immigration, increased the "white" population of Puerto Rico from 46 per cent in 1777 to 76.5 per cent in 1940.[27]

In the British, French, and Dutch West Indies, identification as

---

[26] G. E. Cumper, "The Jamaican Family: Village and Estate," *Social and Economic Studies*, Vol. 7 (1958), p. 92.

[27] Harry Hoetink, *The Double Image in the Caribbean* (London, in press, 1967).

"white" remains relatively stable, partly because whites are few and their identities well known. But the line between "colored" and "black" fluctuates with the bias of the census-taker and the mood of the populace. The "colored" proportion of Dominica was reported as 30 per cent in 1921, 75 per cent in 1946, and 33 per cent in 1960 — variations explicable only by changes in local evaluations. Jamaica exhibits similar anomalies. Between 1943 and 1960 the "colored" population of Kingston declined from 33 to 14 per cent of the total, while that of one rural parish rose from 11 to 19 per cent. A change in names doubtless played a part; Kingstonians were less chary of being called "African" in 1960 than "black" in 1943.[28] . . .

Perhaps one third of all West Indians are mixtures of white and black — a far smaller proportion than is estimated for the so-called "Negro" population in the United States. West Indians tend to believe that in time the whole population will, through mixing, become increasingly light in color. The reverse is more likely, for both the white and the light-colored populations are declining. In Dominica and Martinique today the population as a whole is visibly light-skinned, but the evolution of most territories is probably in the direction of more blackness rather than less. Until early in the nineteenth century, the increase of colored relative to both white and black resulted almost entirely from unmarried unions between white men and non-white women. Within the past century, stricter white marital standards and a continuing decline of the white population have reduced the numbers and the privileges of their mixed offspring. . . .

Few West Indians, in time, will not have some degree of white genetic inheritance, but for most it will be so small that in West Indian terms they will count as black.[29] The presence of small but influential white and colored remnants, however, will make it hard to forget that color is important. Any change must come from new ways of seeing, which will cease to value color according to the standard that has prevailed for three centuries.

THE BURDENS OF PREJUDICE

. . . Color-awareness is a corrosive and enervating preoccupation that hampers West Indian efforts to cope with other problems. And for all but the very light-skinned, it is also a form of masochism. Those who blame discrimination for every failure believe at heart that their color

---

[28] O. C. Francis, *The Population of Modern Jamaica*, Jamaica, Department of Statistics (Kingston, 1963).

[29] George Cumper, *The Social Structure of the British Caribbean* (*Excluding Jamaica*), Part 2 (Kingston, Jamaica, 1949), pp. 26-27.

makes them inferior. The old white association of blackness with laziness and stupidity is accepted today by many colored and black people themselves. They are schizophrenics who consider the part of them that is "white" good and the part that is "black" bad. . . . Not truly West Indian, they are not anything else, either. Although African nationalism has kindled West Indian pride, Africa and *négritude* are not vivid memories; they are abstractions meaningful mainly to poets and visionaries. Most West Indians still reject Africa for its associations of blackness, barbarism, and slavery. The extent of West Indian identification with an African heritage is inversely proportional to its relevance to daily life. . . .

The difference between African origins and African self-consciousness is clearest in Haiti. Peasant life and faith provide a wealth of African parallels, but interest in African culture is not to be found in the countryside but among French-educated intellectuals. The advocates of *négritude* do not really recall their African heritage; they rediscover it as an adjunct to national and racial pride. The West Indian patriot identifies not with ancient Africa, but with the Africa newly emerged from colonial bondage. . . .

Middle-class West Indians yearn instead to be Europeans. "The Antilles cannot and do not want to be anything other than French," states a Martiniquan. "They are French in spirit, in heart, in blood."[30] This is still the case in Haiti after six generations of independence. French education and manners are dear to the heart of the Haitian elite. . . .

The British West Indies are hardly less British in sympathy and identification. Fealty, not geography, earned Barbados the name "Little England." Jamaicans and Trinidadians also take pride in Commonwealth status, ape English manners, and pursue British honors. . . .

West Indians are, then, unhappy about their color and uneasy about their nationality. A third feature of the local scene is the isolation of white, colored, and black in exclusive social roles. The West Indian white, identified by color with imperialism and oppression, can seldom hope to win an election. No head of government can risk alienating popular support by making many white appointments. Because West Indianization is official policy in all but the French islands, there will soon be few expatriates in local governments. Yet whites, expatriate and local, dominate most economic enterprises, notably those that are subsidiaries of foreign firms. Ten *béké* families own 80 per cent of the cultivable land in Martinique.[31] In St. Vincent whites are only 2.3 per cent of the popula-

[30] Victor Sablé, *La transformation des isles d'Amérique en départements français* (Paris, 1955), p. 176.
[31] Gérard Latortue, "Political Status of the French Caribbean," *Politics and Economics in the Caribbean: A Contemporary Analysis of the Dutch, French and British Caribbean,* Institute of Caribbean Studies, Special Study No. 3 (Rio Piedras, P.R., 1966), p. 162.

tion, but they control the banks, the principal hotels, the newspaper, and practically all the arrowroot estates, St. Vincent's principal industry.[32] Thus the small group that dominates the private sector of the economy and makes most of the important economic decisions participates less and less in public affairs except on an advisory basis.

The colored middle class today controls local government and the civil service. But they have little background in political affairs, little understanding of the life of the people, and no real connection with the mainsprings of economic activity. Like the whites of earlier epochs, they remain attached to old ways of doing things out of fear and ignorance and in order to keep their social privileges. Economic development is regarded as chimerical because those who control the economy mistrust the people, and those who control the people mistrust or are wholly ignorant of economics. . . .

In politics, if nowhere else, the black West Indian now finds every door open; "the 'blacks' feel that they, because of their numbers, have a divine right to rule."[33] But black political leaders are often as remote from the bulk of the people as the white and colored men they have replaced. . . .

This situation endures partly because the bulk of the people are too ill-informed and powerless to secure more responsive leaders, and partly because their resentment is tinged with admiration. A self-made Barbadian is viewed with "a queer blend of pride and prejudice."[34] . . .

CREOLES AND EAST INDIANS

There are other West Indians besides those of European and African descent. Prominent among them are the descendants of more recent immigrants from India, called "East Indians," "Hindustanis," or pejoratively, "Coolies." The rivalry between this group and black, colored, and white, collectively known as "Creoles,"[35] has sparked discord and turbulence in several Caribbean territories, reflecting tensions of a different order than those delineated thus far.

The East Indian community in the West Indies owes its origins to the need West Indian planters felt, after emancipation, for large and steady supplies of labor to work (and keep wages down) on plantations abandoned or neglected by the ex-slaves. . . . Only in Trinidad, British Guiana, and Surinam, where the demand for plantation labor was greatest, did Indians really transform the local scene. In each of these terri-

[32] Andron Wilwright, "Of Colour of Skin and St. Vincent," *Flambeau*, No. 3 (January, 1966), pp. 4-5.

[33] Forde, "Barbadians Are Hypocritical about Colour."

[34] Millicent Payne, "The Chink in His Armour," *Bim* (Barbados), Vol. 10, No. 41 (June-December, 1965), p. 17.

[35] Wally Thompson, "Creoles and Pidgins, East and West," *New World Quarterly*, Vol. 2, No. 4 (Cropover, 1966), p. 11; David Lowenthal, "Population Contrasts in the Guianas," *Geographical Review*, Vol. 50 (1960), p. 51.

tories East Indians now account for nearly half the total population. Early marriages and stable unions give them birth rates that presage their numerical preponderance within a few years.[36] . . .

Despised by blacks as well as whites, East Indians maintained a social cohesiveness that endures to this day, neither intermarrying with Africans nor adopting the ideals of Europeans. Only in this generation have East Indians begun to take much part in West Indian education, business, professional life, and politics, while the Javanese in Surinam have not yet begun to do so. East Indian family patterns, religion, and associations remain separate and different, consciously turned toward "Mother" India and away from the West Indies.

Indian ways of life in the Caribbean now bear little resemblance, however, to those in India. Despite a revival of sentiment since Indian independence in 1947, few of them speak Hindi, wear the *dhoti*, recognize more than a rudimentary vestige of the caste system, or think seriously of returning to India. Clannish, conscious of their "superiority," and uneasy about Creole political domination, they have nevertheless irrevocably cast their lot as West Indians and have assimilated much of West Indian culture and patterns of behavior.[37] . . .

Nevertheless, political parties are racially aligned wherever East Indians are prominent. In Guyana, where East Indian and Creole radicals originally united against the colonial regime, personal and ideological differences split the movement into racial components.

. . .

The racial situation in these three territories is thus strikingly different from that elsewhere in the West Indies. Stresses among diverse ethnic elements, ranked not vertically but horizontally, constitute the principal social problem in Trinidad and the Guianas. Put at the bottom of the social hierarchy by black and colored Creoles, the East Indians rejected this relegation. Instead, they regard themselves as superior to the blacks and even use white and colored stereotypes to validate this evaluation, pointing to their lighter skin, straight hair, and European features. In essence, however, they remain outside the Creole hierarchical structure.[38]

[36] G. W. Roberts and L. Braithwaite, "Mating among East Indian and Non-Indian Women in Trinidad," *Social and Economic Studies*, Vol. 11 (1962), pp. 203-40; Leo Davids, "The East Indian Family Overseas," *Social and Economic Studies*, Vol. 13 (1964), pp. 383-96.

[37] Morton Klass, *East Indians in Trinidad: A Study of Cultural Persistence* (New York, 1961); Arthur and Juanita Niehoff, "East Indians in the West Indies," *Milwaukee Public Museum Publication in Anthropology*, No. 6 (Milwaukee, Wis., 1960); Johan Dirk Speckmann, *Marriage and Kinship among the Indians in Surinam* (Assen, Netherlands, 1965); Annemarie de Waal Malefijt, *The Javanese of Surinam: Segment of a Plural Society* (Assen, Netherlands, 1963).

[38] See Braithwaite, "Social Stratification in Trinidad," pp. 49ff; David Lowenthal, "The Range and Variation of Caribbean Societies," *Annals, New York Academy of Sciences*, Vol. 83 (1960), pp. 789-92. Plural societies else-

Meanwhile their presence in these three countries has to some extent united white, colored, and black in a mutually protective alliance.

. . . West Indian social organization ranges from fragmented Surinam, where ethnic and religious divisions are superimposed on a color hierarchy, to an almost classless Carriacou, where racial and cultural homogeneity prevails. Between these extremes, social pluralism operates to a greater or lesser degree to identify and articulate relationships among classes mainly divided along lines of color. Special circumstances in each West Indian territory serve here to exacerbate, there to attenuate, the nature and stress of class distinctions.

WEST INDIANS AND THE AMERICAN NEGRO

How do these circumstances affect West Indian life, thought, and personality? One approach to such a question is to explore the differences between West Indians and American Negroes. Perhaps the most significant difference is what the names themselves imply. To most white Americans, a Negro is still a Negro first and a man afterwards; the West Indian is a man from the outset in the eyes of the community and, therefore, to himself. The word "Negro," explains a Guyanese poet, is "a label denoting a type of human being who was part of a black minority in a white majority." In America, " 'Negro' meant problem. It had no application to the people living in the Antilles, where they . . . form a black majority."[39] Within the West Indies most designations are geographical. A black or colored man from Jamaica or Martinique is simply a Jamaican or a Martiniquan; it is the white man who must establish his special identity. In the United States the opposite is the case. "Southerner" is invariably taken to mean "white Southerner"; the southern Negro is simply a Negro from the South.[40]

The West Indian may still look to Europe for his elite model, but at home he no longer has to contend with images other than his own; he has inherited the islands and is their majority voice. Despite their extreme dependence on the outside world, many West Indians are conscious, perhaps unrealistically so, of controlling their own national destiny. Their rootlessness and ambivalence notwithstanding, the close association of island identity with culture and even with race gives the West Indian a sense of personal integration rare among American Negroes.

Early recognition of formal freedom and opportunity regardless of race

where resemble the Trinidad-Guiana situation, rather than that of the other West Indies. See Burton Benedict, "Stratification in Plural Societies," *American Anthropologist*, Vol. 64 (1962), p. 1239.

[39] A. J. Seymour, "The Poetical Imagination at Work," *Kaie* (Georgetown, Guyana), No. 2 (May, 1966), pp. 28-30.

[40] Thomas F. Pettigrew, "The Negro American — 2," *Daedalus*, Vol. 95, No. 1 (Winter, 1966), p. 441.

is a source of special pride and satisfaction to West Indians. Until recently, few colored West Indians gained pre-eminent status, and those
who did were seldom dark. But the achievement of top rank by even a
few black men was a safety valve for the ambitious. They could feel that
their depressed status was a matter less of race than of class.

. . .

Those who remain in the islands are apt to conclude that in the United
States all Negroes, however light, are doomed to permanent subordination. Even though successful Negroes in the United States are financially
better off than their counterparts in the West Indies, they are accepted
only to a limited and grudging degree as Negroes in a white world. In the
West Indies, where "Negro" leadership is taken for granted in many
fields, successful black and colored men identify more easily with the
whole society. . . .

But there is another side to the picture. The lot of the great majority
of West Indians does not remotely resemble the ideal. At the bottom of
the social hierarchy the top is too far away to see or to enjoy, except
vicariously. The success of the few who have stormed the portals of the
elite has little meaning to those who struggle every day for a bare living.
The black masses deem it no accident that those who are better off have
lighter skins than they do, and they remember the long history of colored
advance at their expense. The free-colored alliance with whites against
the slaves has endured, socially if not politically, down to the present. . . .

Black dissatisfaction has taken several forms. In Haiti, elimination
of all whites after the revolution left black and colored locked in rivalry
that grew fiercer with the years. It remains potent to this day; in 1966
black government officials laid Haitian unrest at the door of the colored
elite now displaced from power. The cult of *négritude*, the glorification of
Africa and blackness, was born in Haiti and the French Antilles, and the
Martiniquan Aimé Cesaire is one of its principal and most passionate advocates. In the British Caribbean, bitterness between Negro and mulatto
led to black nationalism, exemplified by the Jamaican, Marcus Garvey,
who struck out against white and colored entrenched privilege on behalf
of Negro masses all over the world.

Garvey was said to speak for peasantry whose "natural leaders, both
mulatto and black, have crossed the color line" leaving them "with only
the rudiments of education, . . . grovelling at the bottom" of the
English colonial system.[41] The crux of Garvey's appeal was his assertion of
black unity and virtue. He affirmed pride in being Negro, denounced
colored men who sought assimilation with whites, and taught his followers
to venerate their African connection.

[41] W. E. B. DuBois, "Marcus Garvey," *The Crisis*, Vol. 21, No. 2 (December, 1920), p. 60.

In Jamaica stratification was so intense that Garvey made little head-way against black apathy and self-abasement. But in the United States after 1916, West Indians sparked and for a time practically dominated Garvey's Universal Negro Improvement Association. They enlisted under Garvey's banner as if "they would show these damned American Negroes what British West Indians could do."[42]

. . .

It is easy to exaggerate both the defects and the virtues of the West Indian situation. The problems of poverty and overpopulation, of un-employment at home and closed doors abroad probably perturb West Indians more than inherited prejudices of color. Those who are relatively well off would probably concur in the judgment of a Jamaican resident that these islands "have gone farther toward working out the problems of how people of different colors can live together in harmony and dignity and respect than any other place and any other people I know." In the West Indies he has watched American Negro visitors shed the "protec-tive shield behind which they spend so much of their lives and function simply as human beings in a world of other human beings."[43]

For West Indians who are both poor and black, the outlook — despite self-government and the absence of formal discrimination — is less at-tractive. Scores of recent episodes support a judgment that self-contempt still characterizes the Jamaican masses: the parent who is glad to see her child "marry brown, and forget the roots"; the maid who would never work "for black people"; the black watchman who claims authorities told him not to let "any black people pass"; the black woman who votes for a white candidate "for no black man can help me in this yah country these days."[44]

Both the progress made and the problems remaining in the West Indies are crisply epitomized in a calypsonian's comment on the new order:

> Well, the way how things shapin' up
> All this nigger business go' stop
> I tell you soon in the West Indies
> It's please Mr. Nigger please.[45]

[42] Samuel L. Brooks, "Marcus Garvey, An Analysis," *Interstate Tattler,* quoted in Reid, *The Negro Immigrant,* p. 150.

[43] Peter Abrahams, "We Can Learn to Be Color-Blind," *The New York Times Magazine,* April 11, 1965, p. 38.

[44] Nettleford, "National Identity and Attitudes to Race in Jamaica," pp. 69-70.

[45] The Mighty Sparrow. See James, *Party Politics in the West Indies,* pp. 164-75.

Little, Brown and Company   •   Boston